THE PROMISE AND THE PERFORMANCE

The Leadership of John F. Kennedy

THE PROMISE AND THE PERFORMANCE

The Leadership of John F. Kennedy

By LEWIS J. PAPER

CROWN PUBLISHERS, INC.
NEW YORK

Printed in the United States of America

Published simultaneously in Canada by General Publishing Company Limited

Library of Congress Cataloging in Publication Data

Paper, Lewis J
The promise and the performance.

Includes bibliographical references.
1. United States—Politics and government—1961-1963. 2. Kennedy, John Fitzgerald, Pres. U.S., 1917-1963. I. Title.
E841.P35 1975 973.922'092'4 75-19456
ISBN 0-517-52342-6
Second Printing, March, 1976

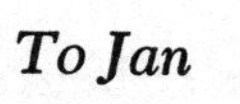
To Jan

I should like to be able to love my country and still love justice. I don't want any greatness for it, particularly a greatness born of blood and falsehood. I want to keep it alive by keeping justice alive.

—Albert Camus
letter to a German friend, 1938

ACKNOWLEDGMENTS

This book reflects several years of research, thinking, and writing. During that time, many people have offered me guidance, research assistance and the benefit of their thoughts on the presidency and John F. Kennedy. To all of them I am of course thankful. Some, however, deserve special recognition because of the important contributions they have made.

Many of the seeds of my thinking were implanted while I was doing research as an undergraduate at the University of Michigan. Three of my teachers, Robert Fischer, Joseph Kallenbach, and Robert Schoenberger, were especially helpful in those early stages.

Over the course of time, some people encouraged me to pursue this project, and they helped to give me the faith that I needed to endure the long hours of hard work. In this respect, I am particularly grateful to Susan Eisenstat, John Greenya, Doris Kearns, Guy Smith, and Oliver Swan.

Many other people who were officials or observers of the Kennedy administration consented to interviews which provided insight into the Kennedy years and the presidency in general. Where appropriate, I have identified them in the book as the source of quotations or information. To them I owe much. I also want to express my appreciation to the staff at the John F. Kennedy Library in Waltham, Massachusetts. Those with whom I dealt, but especially Sylvie J. Turner, the research archivist, were most cooperative and helpful in guiding my research and in providing me with materials from the library. Winthrop Brown, Myer Feldman, and U. Alexis Johnson deserve special thanks for allowing me to use and quote from their interviews on file with the library.

Several other individuals generously gave their time to read parts of the manuscript before publication. Their comments were very helpful to me in reviewing the factual accuracy of the book, sharpening its focus, and strengthening its analyses. Those who assisted me in this way include James MacGregor Burns, Abram Chayes, Myer Feldman, Barry Guryan, Arthur S. Miller, Marcus Raskin, Paula Stern, and Tom Wicker. Any errors and all judgments are, however, my responsibility alone.

I also want to thank Professor Burns for writing a foreword for the book. I am especially flattered by his contribution since his schedule was already full when I invited him to do the foreword.

David Sonenberg provided invaluable service as my attorney, and for that I am very grateful.

Much of the typing was ably done by Edie Geivitz, Ila Gillaspie, and Gail Stewart.

My editor, Philip Winsor, and the entire staff at Crown Publishers have been a joy to work with. Their professional competence as well as their thoughtfulness and warmth have always been in evidence. I am happy to be associated with them.

A special word should be said about my parents. Throughout the course of this project they have demonstrated an unstinting faith in me and my work, and that has always been a great source of encouragement.

But I owe the most to my wife, Jan. She not only typed a good part of the manuscript; she also endured the long hours of work (which occupied many nights and weekends) with that right mixture of encouragement and editorial criticism. She was there to lift my spirits when I felt overburdened by the task, and she was there to bring me down to earth when I sometimes began to feel too smug about my work. In a very real sense, she made it all possible—and worthwhile.

Bethesda, Maryland
April 1975

FOREWORD

There is a popular school of presidential studies that might be called the "Gee Whiz" or "Oh Wow" theory of the presidency. The authors of such works seem to be mesmerized by the presidential mystique and by the ceremony, protocol, and magic that appear to surround the White House. Thus we hear much of the Lonely President, who escapes to the Rose Garden where he wrestles with his soul about some major decision or crisis; of the Absolute-Recall President, who masters bulky memos in minutes and stores them in his encyclopedic mind; of the Decision-making President, who like Napoleon can look over disorderly terrain and come to instant decisions that restore order and put the enemy to rout; of the Omniscient President, whose ganglia stretch to every center of opinion and influence in the nation; of the Dutiful President, who takes a foot-high pile of government documents to bed with him.

The repeated discoveries that the White House is less a place of glamour than of harried, overworked men coping with emergencies and putting out brushfires; that protocol is mainly a bore; that presidents may be petty, erratic, forgetful, ill informed, badly served; that the Chief Executive and his staff spend less time making decisions in a reflective way than in trading, catalyzing, intervening, coping, in short reacting to other persons' decisions—none of this seemed to have a dampening effect on the school of presidential canonization.

The Gee Whiz attitude is a bastard child of a more legitimate and highly controversial concept of history, the Great Man theory. "Universal History, the history of what man has accomplished in this world," proclaimed Carlyle, "is at bottom the History of the Great Men who have worked here." Especially in retrospect of the "strong presidencies," historians and journalists seemed to see national politics and policy as the lengthened shadows of one man. We came casually to talk about the Wilson era, the Roosevelt era, as we will someday—one supposes—the Nixon era. We have yet to see whether Vietnam and Watergate will diminish the uncritical embrace of the presidency over the long run.

The great merit of Lewis Paper's work is to put the Kennedy presidency into both an historical and a political framework. The author deals with Woodrow Wilson and Franklin Roosevelt and other presidents, as well as with John Kennedy, because he sees the presidency as part of a long historical process that fixes the Chief Executive into a set of legacies, precedents, and expectations. He dwells on the presidency as an institution, as well as on Kennedy the man, because he understands the structure of opportunities and closures, of powers and constraints, within which the President operates. The author explores at length key episodes and tendencies of the Kennedy Administration—the painful confrontation of the civil rights issues in the South, the militant anticommunism tinged with skepticism, the fight with Big Steel, the handling of the march on Washington, Kennedy's occasional efforts to "manage" the press, the major international crises—not merely to tell these oft-told stories but to show the kinds of attitudes, myths, understandings, and processes that lay behind the overt actions.

And he returns again and again to a central question—the attitudes and hopes and promises that Kennedy carried into the presidency, compared with the reality that the young President faced. He reminds us that Kennedy had perhaps the most elevated and expansive views of the opportunities and responsibilities of vigorous presidential action of any of the men who had entered the White House. The words are still evocative. "In the decade that lies ahead—in the challenging revolutionary sixties—the American Presidency will demand more than ringing manifestoes issued from the rear of the battle," the candidate of 1960 proclaimed. "It will demand that the President place himself in the very thick of the fight, that he care passionately about the fate of the people he leads, that he be willing to serve them at the risk of incurring their momentary displeasure." And on the eve of the election he said: "We want to be a President and Vice President who have confidence in the people and who take the people into their confidence, who let them know what they are doing and where we are going and who is for his program and who is against . . . who will fight for their legislative programs and not be a casual observer of the legislative process, a President who does not speak from the rear of the battle but places himself in the thick of it, committed to progress and to the great programs and ends. . . ."

How did it all work out? Why was such a good man so often frustrated—why did he so often feel pinioned and shackled by old institutions and current circumstance? What implications does the Kennedy experience have for the future of the presidency? Answers to these questions lie implicitly or explicitly in this work. But a clue to the author's overriding theme can be found in his observation—an observation of compelling importance in the post-Vietnam and post-Watergate eras—that our faith in our leaders must be matched by our confidence in our institutions and procedures.

James MacGregor Burns

May 1975

INTRODUCTION

Between the idea
And the reality,
Between the motion
And the act,
Falls the Shadow.
T. S. Eliot

Why another "Kennedy book"? The question comes to anyone asked to read another work on the presidency of John F. Kennedy, let alone to anyone who would consider writing another such work. The question is legitimate and deserves an answer.

In 1969 and 1970, while I was attending Harvard Law School, I was a teaching fellow at Harvard College and taught in a course on the American Presidency. My students did not fit any single mold or description. Some were very bright and interested in learning; others were not. In both years of teaching, however, I was struck by two things.

First, although most of my students had strong opinions about recent American presidents, the students did not employ any general criteria to help ensure that their judgments about individual presidents were well founded and consistent with each other.

I do not think this phenomenon was unique to my students or to college students in general. Although most people discuss presidential politics at one time or another, and while most people have strong feelings about individual presidents, rarely is any reference made to the criteria employed to render judgments about presidents. More often than not, discussions of presidential politics rely on clichés, emotions, and isolated facts. The principal question asked by most people is not what criteria can help me judge this particular presidential action or policy in terms of some broad social goal, but how does that presidential action or policy comport with my interests and opinions?

To some extent, there is nothing wrong with an individual's invoking his personal interests and opinions in measuring a president's success in providing leadership. After all, a government which does not satisfy the individual needs of the governed cannot be considered very effective. But in assessing a president's leadership, reference should be made to something more than the individual's immediate interests and opinions. For often those immediate interests and opinions are an inadequate gauge of the president's performance.

Thus, a president who proposes military assistance to an ally under attack may be criticized, as Franklin D. Roosevelt was in leasing American destroyers to England in 1940, by those Americans anxious to avoid entanglement in foreign wars—even though such military assistance may, in the long run, be essential to preserving the ally's and, indeed, this nation's security. Or conversely, a president may be praised by many people, as Richard Nixon was, for doing everything within his power to discourage the use of busing to eliminate racially segregated public schools—even though busing may sometimes be the best available means for eliminating such segregation and, in the long run, reducing the racial hatreds which still thread our society. In other words, individual interests and opinions may run counter to the real needs of the society as a whole. Consequently, there should be some general criteria to help the citizen place his individual interests and opinions in proper perspective. Invocation of these criteria, moreover, should help the individual assess the president's ability and willingness to defend constitutional principles, to strengthen the structure of the political system, to balance the citizenry's competing interests in solving problems, and to account for society's long-range needs.

Watergate has not eliminated the need to develop criteria to measure a president's performance. If anything, Watergate highlighted the absence of such criteria and the inability of Congress to fill the vacuum. Throughout the Senate Watergate hearings and the House impeachment hearings, a central issue concerned the standard to be applied to President Nixon. What, in fact, did people have a right to expect from their president? Without first answering that question, it would be difficult to determine whether he should be criticized or, indeed, removed from office.

The House Judiciary Committee's report on impeachment gave a partial and very limited answer to the question. In effect, the report made plain that neither the Constitution nor the Congress would tolerate a president who authorized an illegal use of governmental powers. This, of course, is a bare minimum standard. It states only what we will not accept in a president (an illegal abuse of power). It does not indicate the criteria for assessing the effectiveness of a president who meets that minimum standard. To analogize, no court will permit a lawyer to retain his license to practice if he commits a murder or other felony. But a lawyer who satisfies that minimum standard must do much more to establish his skill as an effective advocate. In short, there should be a more meaningful way of gauging a president's performance than by reference to the criminal code.

There was a second thing which emerged from my teaching experience, and this underscored the absence of any general criteria to measure a president's effectiveness. Almost all of my students had very strong feelings about John Kennedy, and most of these were favorable. Most students, however, were hard pressed to explain their feelings. They could talk about Kennedy's wit and charm, or they could talk about the mythology in which chroniclers of his administration wrapped him, but few students could articulate a really good basis for why they did or did not like Kennedy.

Here, too, I do not think the reaction of my students is unique. More than ten years after his death, most people still have very strong feelings about John Kennedy. The persistence of these strong feelings helps account for the considerable attention Kennedy continues to receive. There have been countless books, articles, speeches, television documentaries, and records about Kennedy's presidency. These materials offer many conclusions about the man and his leadership. But none of these materials makes reference to or outlines general criteria for judgment that ensure that those conclusions reflect reason rather than passion. This observation is particularly applicable to the books about John Kennedy's presidency.

Virtually all of the books about Kennedy's presidency can be categorized in one of two classes: those written by the "mythologists," and those written by the "revisionists." The mythologists, who include William Manchester,[1] Arthur Schlesinger, Jr.,[2] and Theodore Sorensen,[3] among others, made no secret of their admiration for and sometimes love of Kennedy. As a result, these writers, most of whom worked for Kennedy, offered accounts of Kennedy's presidency that greatly inflated his attributes and his achievements. These writers contributed much to the legends that enveloped John Kennedy's memory, although in some cases the contribution may have been made unwittingly. Thus, while claiming that John Kennedy was "almost a legendary figure in life," Theodore C. Sorensen wrote that "it would be an ironic twist of fate if his martyrdom [sic] should now make a myth of the mortal man."[4]

The revisionist Kennedy books had no need to issue a cautionary note like the one made in Sorensen's. These latter works, exemplified first by Victor Lasky's *JFK: The Man and the Myth,* were written by individuals eager to destroy the impression nurtured by the mythologists. There was little serious discussion of where and how John Kennedy had succeeded and failed; the focus of debate instead was whether John Kennedy deserved the legend which had become his. To some extent, the early revisionists' response was much like a discussion of whether or not the Emperor's new clothes fit properly.

In recent years the attempts to strip John Kennedy of his legend have been more scholarly. Two such books, Richard J. Walton's *Cold War and Counterrevolution* and Henry Fairlie's *The Kennedy Promise,* are typical. They do not have Lasky's venom, but they, too, interpret facts and construct theories in an obvious, if not belabored, effort to disabuse readers of the Kennedy myth. Victor Navasky, whose detailed account of Robert Kennedy's stewardship of the Justice Department[5] won critical acclaim, observed, for instance, that Walton's book made presumptions flattering to most, regardless of whether the individual concerned was an Eisenhower or a Khrushchev, but that no such "happy presumptions" were made in Kennedy's favor.[6]

In this setting, it seems clear that there is a need for a dispassionate study of John Kennedy's presidency which relies on some general criteria to measure a president's effectiveness. John Kennedy was a man who generally viewed other individuals with a critical eye. It would be a disservice to the presidency as well as to Kennedy's memory if the analysts of his administration did not view him with that same critical eye, letting the praise or blame fall where it may.

This book is intended to serve that purpose. It is not a descriptive history or an exhaustive analysis of all that occurred during the Kennedy years. Instead, it is an attempt to place the Kennedy presidency in perspective, to present a broad picture of its strengths and weaknesses, its achievements and failures.

A political analysis of this nature often resorts to certain theoretical premises. Where such premises are operative, I have attempted to identify and explain them. At this juncture, it should be noted that three basic premises are evident throughout.

First, presidents are temporary officeholders; the presidency is an established institution in the American political system. The two are neither synonymous nor completely independent of each other. Indeed, the growth of the presidency as an institution and its effect on the incumbent will be influenced significantly by the manner in which the individual president synchronizes his capabilities and values with the powers of the office. In other words, the presidency provides for leadership; it does not guarantee it.

Second, an appraisal of John Kennedy's leadership—or any president's leadership—should account for the context in which the president exercises power and fulfills his responsibilities. Hindsight can and should be used to refine judgments as to the president's ultimate effectiveness. But in assessing the quality of any president's leadership, it should be remembered that presidents do not operate in a world fraught with clearcut moral alternatives of good and evil; rarely is any choice or any event wholly either, but usually a mixture of the two. The content of that mixture, moreover, will not be determined by any objective or absolute standard. It will be colored instead by the perspectives of the president and others as those events occur or as those choices arise. Simply because an error in judgment can be explained afterwards does not mean it was obvious when the judgment was made.

Third, any assessment of a president's performance should include some comparison with the promise the president brings to the White House. The need for this comparison is easy to understand. People should generally be held accountable for the promises they make. This principle is of particular importance with respect to all elected officials but especially the president. Through his campaign statements, as well as through positions and actions he has taken during his political career, a candidate generates many expectations among the public as to what he will or will not do if he is elected. People usually rely on these expectations in casting their votes and have a right to believe that the candidate will be true to his word once he has achieved the office for which he campaigned.

It should be emphasized, however, that a president's performance should not be viewed *solely* in terms of his promise. Occasions may arise when a president is justified in believing that national interests require him to abandon an earlier commitment (a prime example being Nixon's decision to adopt wage and price controls in the summer of 1971 despite his earlier statements that he would never resort to such controls to revive the sagging economy). Likewise, if promise were the sole criterion, a president with minimal promises could be deemed "effective" with a minimal performance. And, if promise were the sole guideline, it would be difficult to judge the effectiveness of a president who assumed the office through the death, resignation, or impeachment of the incumbent.

All these factors suggest why a president should be judged not only in view of his promise but also in light of more general and more fixed norms. Indeed, the extent to which the public can expect their president to be effective will depend greatly on how closely his promises coincide with those norms.

The criteria developed here to evaluate the presidential performance are fourfold:

First, did he have a concept of the presidency as a focus of activity and direction in the nation's public affairs?

Second, did he have methods of decision-making which reflected an ability and will to gather essential information, to understand fully the options available to him, and to choose on the basis of what he thought was in the best interests of the country?

Third, did he use the presidency to educate the public on the issues, to involve them in the solution of pressing problems, and, in general, to lead them in the direction he thought necessary to protect and serve national interests?

Fourth, did he develop and use images of his presidency which inspired support for his policies and confidence in his leadership?

Each criterion will be explained from an historical perspective. This historical development will focus primarily on sketches of presidents in the twentieth century.* Through a brief survey of these presidential experiences, I hope to provide the reader with some understanding of how each of the factors identified in the criteria played a fundamental role in determining a particular president's effectiveness. After each criterion is explained from the historical perspective, it will be applied to the promise and performance of John Kennedy as president. Judgments will then be ventured as to whether or not Kennedy was an effective and wise leader.

One caveat is in order here. By identifying four separate criteria, I do not mean to imply that the distinctions between them are always entirely clear. Quite the contrary. There is a basic interrelationship among the criteria that reflects some overlap. Indeed, the criteria should be thought of as a continuum. A president's concept of the office will affect the way in which he approaches decisions. The effectiveness of those decisions, in turn, will depend greatly on whether or not the president is able to educate his constituencies on the major is-

*The focus here on twentieth-century presidents is not because earlier presidential experiences are irrelevant to the formulation of any criteria for assessing the presidential performance. It simply reflects my belief that there is a closer interrelationship between the experiences of the more recent presidents and the context in which future presidents will exercise the powers of the office.

sues and secure their support for his policy choices. And his constituents' receptivity to his explanations and direction will largely reflect the president's success in establishing images of his presidency which inspire confidence in his abilities and faith that he is fulfilling his responsibilities in a diligent and honest fashion. Given the interconnection between the criteria, it can be understood that a particular action, or series of actions, may provide evidence of the president's concept of the office, the methods by which he makes decisions, his ability to lead the public, and the image he casts among his constituents. In fact, I will often use different elements of the same presidential action to explain or apply different criteria.

In general, the criteria reflect my belief in what can best be described as a "balanced" presidency. The president will almost inevitably be enveloped—at any time and on any issue—by conflicting pressures of enormous political strength. In confronting these pressures, the president may often want to do more than he should; on other occasions, he may want to do less than he should. There is no secret formula for knowing the most appropriate course. But in responding to the dilemmas before him, a president should always try to balance those political pressures against his basic responsibilities.

He is, first and foremost, a democratic leader. Being a leader, he is, by definition, obligated to lead—to play a major role on behalf of the public interests in resolving the important political, economic and social issues of his time. In playing this role, the president is duty-bound to honor the constitutional and legal limitations on the exercise of presidential power. He should also account for public opinions without being tyrannized by them. He should respect the principle of majority rule without forsaking the minority's rights. And he should always weigh the moral implications of any decision he contemplates; for the president should always want to do the right thing.

Regardless of whether or not the reader shares this view of the presidency, one point is clear: any balanced judgment of John F. Kennedy's presidency requires some appreciation of the history of the presidency itself and the men who have occupied the office. For that history formed a large part of the context in which Kennedy was elected to the White House and asked to make the choices that come with the job. And like all presidents, Kennedy was guided by and contributed to the historical trends which make the presidential office what it is today.

There is no illusion here that this book will be the last word on John Kennedy's presidency. Some will take issue with the criteria chosen. Others will dispute the thrust of the evidence presented or make reference to facts not discussed here which might tip the balance of judgment. I make no pretense of enjoying criticism. But if this book helps to stimulate a dispassionate critique of John Kennedy's presidency in particular and of how we judge presidents in general, then the purposes of this book will have been satisfied. It's all a matter of remembering that one good critique deserves another.

CHAPTER 1

John F. Kennedy's Concept of the Presidency

For the American Presidency was a peculiarly personal institution. It remained, of course, an agency of government, subject to unvarying demands and duties no matter who was President. But, more than most agencies of government, it changed shape, intensity and ethos according to the man in charge. Each President's distinctive temperament and character, his values, standards, style, his habits, expectations, idiosyncracies, compulsions, phobias recast the White House and pervaded the entire government beyond.

Arthur Schlesinger, Jr.

The President's Concept of the Office: An Historical Perspective

While the time and circumstances surrounding each of our presidents have varied, for the most part each man assumed the same institutionalized powers with the same basic obligation to interpret and use those powers to ensure the proper functioning of our republican government. The Constitution and laws reveal little about the actual exercise of leadership. Certainly, knowledge of the Constitution and the law in 1960 could not foretell how John Kennedy would respond to issues and execute decisions as president. For an essential difference among our presidents resides in their individual approaches to the office. Thus, analysts in 1960 were more prone to scrutinize Kennedy's personal qualities than the powers he would assume as the nation's chief executive. Their concern was not the potential influence of that office but how he intended to use that influence. In endorsing candidate Kennedy in 1960, for instance, the *New York Times* paid little heed to how his election might affect the institutionalized powers of the presidency; rather, the *Times* was impressed principally by the human qualities

Kennedy would bring to the office and the fact that, if elected, Kennedy did not intend to use his presidential powers to effect drastic changes in the policies of President Eisenhower, his immediate predecessor.[1]

To recognize the personal factors which help define presidential leadership is not to minimize the importance of the external variables which affect American politics. Such variables will play a critical role in determining what the president can and cannot do.

In 1968, for example, candidate Richard Nixon promised that new presidential leadership could restore law and order to the crime-ridden streets of America's cities.[2] There is no reason to doubt that Mr. Nixon was sincere in his desire to achieve this goal; surely its attainment was in his own political self-interest. After almost four years of new leadership, however, President Nixon found that the incidence of all major crimes had increased, in some cases as much as 48 percent.[3] One might argue that a different president who espoused different policies and programs would have been more successful in curbing the incidence of crime. But that argument would not obscure the basic point that there was a limit to what *any* president could do to reduce the incidence of crime. For no president could have removed entirely the social and psychological causes of crime, let alone assumed control of local and state police forces to ensure their efficacy.

The limitations on the president's reach are not all of a social nature. Some limitations simply reflect the dynamics (or lack of dynamics) of presidential politics. An oft-cited example is the governmental bureaucracy. In a classic observation of bureaucratic somnolence, Franklin D. Roosevelt once noted,

> The Treasury [Department] is so large and far-flung and ingrained in its practices that I find it is almost impossible to get the action and results I want—even with Henry [Morgenthau] there. But the Treasury is not to be compared with the State Department. You should go through the experience of trying to get any changes in the thinking, policy and action of the career diplomats and then you'd know what a real problem was. But the Treasury and the State Department put together are nothing compared with the Na-a-vy. The admirals are really something to cope with—and I should know. To change anything in the Na-a-vy is like punching a feather bed. You punch it with your right and you punch it with your left until you are finally exhausted, and then you find the damn bed just as it was before you started punching.[4]

In other words, there are certain inherent limitations on the president's ability to master his environment.

What he does within those limitations is very much a personal matter. To a large degree, he himself must decide the precise nature and scope of his responsibilities; he himself must decide which issues are deserving of his attention and how he should deal with them. And all this is very much dependent on the individual's personality. As James David Barber observed in his study of the presidency, "The degree and quality of a President's emotional involvement in an issue are powerful influences on how he defines the issue itself, how much attention he pays to it, which facts and persons he sees as relevant to its resolution, and finally, what principles and purposes he associates with issues."[5] In short, any assessment of a president's promise or performance should account for the perspective which he brings to the office.

A president's perspective is important not only because it reveals how he views the responsibilities of the office; perspective is also important because it reveals whether the president has the ability and will to use the tools of the office to fulfill those responsibilities. For if he is to succeed in his endeavors, a president will inevitably be required to employ the prestige and resources of his office in order to convince his constituencies and those in government that what he wants of them is in their own interest and in the interest of the country. Harry S Truman touched the heart of this process when he observed of his own presidential experience, "I spend most of my time behind this desk persuading people to do things they ought to do without my asking them."[6] The truth of this observation should surprise no one. For as in all political offices, the decisive ingredient of presidential leadership is power—not necessarily the power to command as prescribed by the Constitution or laws, nor necessarily the power to impose one's will on others, but the power to persuade others in the political arena. Success, then, is often a matter of wanting power and of knowing how to use it. For only those who seek power can find and sustain it; only those who know what it is can properly utilize it to achieve their ends: "influence adheres to those who sense what it is made of."[7] In fact, most effective presidents in our history have demonstrated a certain instinct to exert power—to affect their environment and to lead those around them. Certainly this factor helps explain why some presidents, such as Woodrow Wilson and Franklin D. Roosevelt, achieved more than some other presidents, such as Warren Harding and Herbert Hoover.

In recent years, many political analysts have argued that the centralization of power in the presidency is not a good development. "The colonists rebelled because they felt George III had too much power and erected a Constitution to protect them but it is not certain that it avails anymore," TRB wrote in *The New Republic* during the course of the House Judiciary Committee's impeachment inquiry into Nixon's presidency. ". . . We see that this thing called 'Watergate' was only part of a more systematic aggrandizement of the presidency (a process begun 50 years back) and that it amounted to a kind of mini-'putsch' or power grab."[8] I have no trouble agreeing that excessive concentration of unchecked power in the presidency poses dangerous risks to our form of government and its efficacy in serving the public's interests. But agreement on that point does not necessarily taint the value of presidential power. Presidential power is a neutral force that can be used wisely or foolishly. That some presidents have misused their powers might warrant some institutional changes, but such misuse does not justify a condemnation of any and all attempts by a president to provide strong leadership in the direction he thinks best. By analogy, abuse by some of their right to welfare assistance should not justify a denial of welfare assistance for all.

The upshot of this is that a president should be ever mindful of the constitutional and political constraints on his power; but he should not be afraid to use his office to assume a major responsibility to help resolve the basic social and political issues of the day. Indeed, if he is to be an effective and good leader, a president should accept such a responsibility. Otherwise the resolution of those issues will take shape without his guidance. It is therefore essential that the president have a concept of the office as a focus of activity and direction in the nation's public affairs. That is the first criterion in assessing presidential leadership.

There is, of course, no precise formula to measure the president's concept of the office and how it affects his leadership. But there is no question that it will be evidenced in virtually every decision he makes and every action that he takes. And there is little doubt that that concept will play a major role in determining the extent to which he achieves his goals—or the goals which his constituents have a right to expect of him.

The president's concept of his office very much reflects his upbringing and personal development. Heredity, environment, experience—all cast a giant shadow over the perspective which the president will bring to the office. For the president is a human being like the rest of us—an individual whose basic patterns of character and personality have been molded long before he takes up residence at the White House. While there is no method to isolate the impact of the president's growth on his concept of the office, the evidence leaves little doubt that the seeds of that concept are planted and nurtured by the individual president's lifelong environment and experience. A fuller appreciation of this fact, as well as of the importance of the president's concept of the office, can be gained from a brief survey of some recent presidents.

Theodore Roosevelt, for example, suffered from poor health in his childhood. A consequent desire to compensate for early physical shortcomings motivated him to excel where once he had failed, to be an equal among his peers.[9] His family's ample wealth was instrumental in providing Roosevelt with the training and, to some extent, the opportunity to feed this desire. With little concern for material security, Roosevelt was able to learn the art of boxing, to educate himself with travels, and to develop a taste for daring. This sense of adventure led Roosevelt to enjoy the rough-and-tumble life—whether herding cattle in the West, leading the Rough Riders in the Spanish-American War, or hunting big game in Africa.

However much Roosevelt enjoyed these adventures in themselves, there is no question that he also enjoyed the fact that they invited respect and admiration from his companions and family. A man of robust energy, Roosevelt had an inward need for attention, for the dramatization of events that would place him at the center. As his daughter Alice Roosevelt Longworth commented, "When Theodore attends a wedding, he wants to be the bride, and when he attends a funeral he want to be the corpse."[10] It was only natural that Roosevelt should be drawn to politics. Politics challenged his abilities of thought and speech, and, as revealed in his personal letters, it also offered him the opportunity to be a focal point of events and public affection.[11]

Roosevelt occupied the presidency between 1901 and 1909, a time of growing public demands for progressive reform. The industrial revolution in the United States was entering its adolescence, and with it came a recognition that new measures were needed to ensure that respect for human life and dignity was not sacrificed on the altar of larger profits. Child labor, working conditions in factories, the pervasive power of the large corporations, the rights of labor unions to organize—these were some of the critical issues which began to stir men's and women's thoughts as Roosevelt assumed the reins of presidential power.

Two principal qualities of Roosevelt's character shaped his concept of the role which *his* presidency would play in responding to these issues. First, the principles inculcated in Roosevelt by education and experience underscored the need for fairness and compassion in dealings with people.[12] Second, Roosevelt's intrinsic activism, reinforced in political life by his interpretation of history, led him to believe that the national government, and especially the president, should provide active leadership in resolving the country's pressing problems. In short, Roosevelt loved the power which the White House would afford him and believed it could be used to serve good purposes.[13] In light of his background and his time, then, Roosevelt's concept of the presidency embraced a stewardship theory of executive leadership, and it was a concept that Kennedy would draw upon when he entered the White House. In his memoirs, Roosevelt explained his concept of the presidency:

> My view was that every executive officer, and above all, every executive officer in high position, was a steward of the people bound actively and affirmatively to do all he could for the people, and not to content himself with the negative merit of keeping his talents undamaged in a napkin. I declined to adopt the view that what was imperatively necessary for the nation could not be done unless he could find some specific authorization to do it. My belief was that it was not only his right but his duty to do anything that the needs of the nation demanded unless such action was forbidden by the Constitution or by the laws.[14]

This view of the presidency was not premised entirely on Roosevelt's selfless concern for his country. Roosevelt wanted power because of his need for attention as well as achievement. Not surprisingly, "he wanted dramatic victories, sometimes at the sacrifice of substance. In his judgment, the dramatic act was the best entering wedge for long-term reform."[15] Determined to achieve that reform, Roosevelt used his presidency to take bold initiatives to solve basic problems or to serve basic policies which he believed would serve the public's interests. Examples are plentiful: the Justice Department's initiating an antitrust suit against the powerful Northern Securities Company, a railroad monopoly controlled by J. P. Morgan, James J. Hill, and E. H. Harriman; his mediation of a settlement of the Pennsylvania coal miners' strike in the winter of 1902–3; enactment of legislative proposals to regulate railroads, food processing plants, and meat-packing standards. These were the activities which typified Roosevelt's Administration; and they revealed him as a man anxious to use power to achieve chosen ends and happy to experience the dramatic glory which presidential success can bring. Even after he left office in 1909, Roosevelt never lost this need to be dramatic and controlling.[16] When his successor, William Howard Taft, diverged from Roosevelt's policies, the former President was quick to speak his disapproval and, evidenced by his formation of the Bull Moose Party in 1912, anxious to recapture the presidency.[17]

That Taft—who once enjoyed harmonious relations with Roosevelt—should incur the latter's criticisms stemmed not so much from Taft's desire to be independent of Roosevelt as from the nature of Taft's personality. Although Taft was Roosevelt's handpicked successor, he reflected an obvious difference in political perspective. Taft was a big fellow (when President he weighed in at 332 pounds, a record among presidents) whose natural gifts included a high intelligence and an ability to get along well with people. Although he was generally a very likable person, Taft was also very passive in his personal relations, whether familial, social, or professional. Rarely did he find cause for real anger or aggression, whether when growing up with doting parents in Ohio or when performing the duties of the nation's chief executive.[18]

A judge by profession and conservative by instinct, Taft felt uncomfortable with the uncertainty and personal conflicts of politics. Although he enjoyed the authority of the courtroom, he was not anxious to exert influence over others in the political arena. In his view, politics simply did not have the same dignity as the law. In fact, Taft once wrote his wife, "Politics makes me sick."[19] Taft's passivity also was consistent with his belief that the institutions of government—the legislature, the courts, and the bureaucracy—did not require much direction from the president.[20] It was a faith that would offer Kennedy little hope as he entered the presidency in 1961. Although Kennedy shared Taft's respect for the American political system, as President he became increasingly skeptical of the ability of these institutions of government independently to safeguard the nation's interests; without the continued involvement of the president, Kennedy believed that these institutions would stifle rather than further chosen goals.

Because of his background, then, Taft possessed a concept of the presidency completely contrary to Roosevelt's stewardship theory. Reflecting on his presidential experience in 1915, Taft asserted that

> the true view of the Executive function is, as I conceive it, that the President can exercise no power which cannot be fairly and reasonably traced to some specific grant of power or justly implied and included within such express grant as proper and necessary to its exercise. Such specific grant must be either in the Federal Constitution or in an act of Congress passed in pursuance thereof. There is no undefined residuum of power which he can exercise because it seems to him to be in the public interest.

Taft added that, in his judgment, "the view of . . . Mr. Roosevelt, ascribing an undefined residuum of power to the President, is an unsafe doctrine and that it might lead under emergencies to results of an arbitrary character, doing irremediable injustice to private right."[21] For this reason, Taft felt that a president was limited to those actions which were specifically authorized by the Constitution or by legislation. Watergate as well as recent disclosures regarding presidential misuse of the CIA and the IRS have no doubt sensitized many of us to the concerns expressed by Taft (although it should be remembered that those abuses involved violations of legal prohibitions.) It would be unwise, however, to embrace uncritically Taft's view of the presidency. For his limited perspective also meant that he did not fully share Roosevelt's desire to use the presidency as a "bully pulpit," to exert moral leadership or to inspire concerted governmental action in social and economic sectors. This is not to suggest that Taft was completely unwilling to provide political leadership. In some areas, he proved to be quite effective (his anti-trust program, for example, was more extensive than Roosevelt's). But in most spheres, Taft was quite cautious and quite passive. Thus, when Roosevelt criticized Taft for not pushing many of the reforms initiated during Roosevelt's tenure, Taft responded, "One of the propositions that I adhere to is that it is a very dangerous method of upholding reform to violate the law in so doing; even on the ground of high moral principle, or of saving the public."[22] Of course, a basic (and unanswered) question in Taft's response is whether a president need violate a law when providing moral leadership and urging political reform.

Because he believed the president had a limited role in national affairs, and because he had little inclination or ability to persuade others to support his ideas or policies, Taft's effectiveness as President was often found wanting. Taft's attempt to remove Joe Cannon as Speaker of the House in 1910 is a case in point.

Taft normally showed little interest in providing legislative leadership. Shortly after his election to the presidency, however, Taft decided to initiate a move to unseat Joe Cannon as Speaker of the House of Representatives because Cannon had mocked some of Taft's views in public. Taft took little account of how much support, actual or potential, lay within the House for such an endeavor. Nor did Taft give much attention to how he might convince recalcitrant congressmen that removal of Cannon was in their best interests. Armed with little more than personal pique, Taft's move proved unavailing—in part because he was finally persuaded that unseating Cannon would mean certain defeat of his proposal for downward tariff revision by the Congress. The crowning embarrassment, though, was the fact that the Congress did subsequently reject Taft's proposal for reduced tariffs by adopting the Payne-Aldrich bill, legislation that *raised* tariffs on imports.

Taft's ineptness was not confined to legislative matters. Frequently it was reported that certain officials within his administration were serving private rather than public interests. Here, too, Taft's talents as a leader left something to be desired. The most celebrated case of corruption in Taft's administration was the Pinchot-Ballinger controversy.

Richard A. Ballinger, Taft's secretary of the interior, was accused by a minor government functionary of engaging in corrupt deals which, among other things, allowed selected business interests to acquire public lands for private gain. Because this matter touched the issue of conservation championed by Roosevelt, Gifford Pinchot, chief of the United States Forest Service (which fell under the supervision of the secretary of the interior) and a Roosevelt stalwart, joined the chorus of criticism of Ballinger. While this controversy raged on the front pages of the nation's newspapers, Taft offered no public comment and contemplated no private action. Eventually the controversy dissipated itself when Pinchot resigned, believing that his service was of little value while Ballinger remained his superior. But the episode did little to inspire confidence within the government and among the public that Taft ran a tight ship.

In the end, Taft's concept of a limited presidency and his disinterest in exercising power made it difficult for him to attain desired goals, whether in protecting his administration from corruption or in having Congress adopt his legislative proposals. Consequently, Taft was not only an ineffective President; he was also a very discouraged and unhappy man in the White House. He felt that he did not fit the office.[23]

Unlike Taft, Woodrow Wilson shared Theodore Roosevelt's drive for attention and achievement, a drive which developed, in part, as a response to his childhood environment. Living under the dictates of his father, who was a Southern preacher, Wilson would relate in his later years that his earliest frustration stemmed from an inability to meet his father's demands for perfection. This was particularly so with respect to Wilson's education. Wilson was not enrolled in a public school until he was ten years old. Both before and after that his father was heavily involved in Wilson's education. Whether in debates or in the writing of compositions, Wilson's father would have his son repeat the exercise until Wilson achieved the goals his father had set for him. Regardless of how long it took, the elder Wilson accepted nothing less than the highest performance.[24] Subsequently believing perfection to be attainable and interpreting approbation as achievement, Wilson always made high demands of himself. While there were marked differences between Wilson's and Kennedy's personalities, Joseph P. Kennedy's demands as a father evoked a strikingly similar response from his son—John Kennedy had an uncommon distaste for failure in any endeavor.

Wilson's father inspired more than a drive for perfection in his son. For Wilson also absorbed his father's teaching that each man had his mission in life, that everyone, in the Calvinist tradition, had his "calling." In his masterful study of Wilson, Arthur Link summarized this perspective of Wilson's:

> Mankind, he felt, lived not only by the providence of God but also under his immutable decrees; and nations as well as men transgressed the divine ordinances at their peril. He shared a Calvinistic belief, held in his day mainly by Southern Presbyterians and members of the Reformed churches in Europe, in predestination—the absolute conviction that God had ordered the universe from the beginning, the faith that God used men for His own purposes. From such beliefs came a sure sense of destiny and a feeling of intimate connection with the sources of power.[25]

This perspective had a profound effect upon Wilson's concept of *his* presidency as well as on his ability to persuade others to support his programs and goals. For Wilson's strict adherence to these tenets of Calvinism led him to assume a rigidity in his thinking that resisted suggestions of change or compromise. He sincerely believed that he was destined to be a leader, and, where he had invested his emotions in an issue, that his judgments could not be disputed. Wilson's drive for power, in short, reflected a self-righteousness that rejected the virtues of political bargaining. For example, as president of Princeton University, Wilson became embroiled in a controversy with Andrew West, dean of the graduate school, concerning undergraduate housing facilities. Despite the entreaties of the board of trustees and the faculty, Wilson not only refused to alter his position, even when confronted with a workable solution to the problem; he also felt that West, with whom he had had a close personal relationship, had betrayed their friendship by supporting the compromise. This was not unusual. Almost every cause or position Wilson espoused was a personal crusade which even friends could not attack without Wilson's interpreting it as a criticism of his character.

After a successful term as a reform governor of New Jersey, Wilson was elected President in 1912. At that time, the issues which had first dominated Roosevelt's presidency still preoccupied public thinking and, in fact, had resulted in the formation of strong organizations which demanded effective action from the federal and state governments. The impact of this "progressive movement" was considerable; of the 114 new Democratic congressmen elected in 1912, for example, many could tie their victories directly to their support of progressive governmental action. The setting was ideal for Wilson's beliefs and talents. Maintaining his rigidity, Wilson viewed his presidency as the means of rectifying the political and social abuses which continued to hold the public's attention. Thus "Wilson's dogma was his conviction that the President must be a party man who has the personality and initiative to enforce his views upon the people and upon Congress."[26] Unfortunately, this conviction was buoyed by a considerable dash of self-righteousness.

The fervor of Wilson's self-righteousness was, in his first administration, equally matched by the persuasiveness of his eloquent addresses and by his determination to be a man of accomplishment. He would make a public speech or two, rallying the populace behind his calls to pursue progressive reforms (conveniently embodied in his legislative proposals). Armed with public support, Wilson would frequently convene party caucuses, urging, cajoling, and demanding the congressional support he claimed the people asked for. His ability to lead the congressional members of his party was amply demonstrated by the Congress's enactment of bills which would help correct many abuses and problems which had been a major impetus for the progressive movement. Examples of these bills were the Underwood Tariff Act (which repealed, in part, the Payne-Aldrich Act and reduced tariffs on imports), the Federal Reserve Act (which provided some organization and stability for the country's banking system), the Clayton Antitrust Act (which restricted the anticompetitive activities of business and recognized labor's right to organize and engage in collective bargaining, thereby earning the identification as "labor's Magna Carta"), and the Federal Trade Act (which outlawed certain advertising practices and established the Federal Trade Commission to supervise business practices). The import of Wilson's legislative success is underscored by the fact that there was neither a foreign nor a domestic crisis to stimulate such activity in the early years of his tenure. When compared to Kennedy's legislative accomplishments several decades later, Wilson's effectiveness as a legislative leader appears even more impressive.

Wilson's early success as President confirmed his messianic self-image and solidified his political attitudes even more. In his view, destiny had ordained that compromise was neither necessary nor warranted under his leadership. The acme of Wilson's rigidity was reached in his efforts to secure Senate approval of the League of Nations Covenant, which he had personally negotiated with other national leaders at Versailles, France, in 1919.

This covenant, a product of international negotiations to officially terminate World War I, reflected Wilson's belief that the balance-of-power system was no longer tenable and that only an international organization devoted to peace could ensure international stability. Actually the covenant was mostly Wilson's own doing, and he considered its formulation and approval by the Senate as the climax of his public service. Because of the importance he attached to the covenant and the League of Nations it created, Wilson was not one to underrate the historical significance of its adoption. Seasoned European diplomats—for whom exaggeration was not uncommon—were amazed with Wilson's account of why he believed the League necessary:

> Why has Jesus Christ so far not succeeded in inducing the world to follow his teachings in these matters? It is because He taught the ideal without devising any practical means of attaining it. That is why I am proposing a practical scheme to carry out His aims.[27]

So convinced was he of the righteousness of his views, as well as his ability to represent all peoples, that Wilson issued an appeal to the Italian people when their representative at Versailles, Vittorio Orlando, refused to moderate his position and facilitate agreement on the covenant.[28]

When Wilson returned to the United States from Versailles, he brought with him his view that the newly negotiated covenant served divine purposes. In a speech to the Senate shortly after his return, Wilson tried to make clear that there was no alternative but to accept the covenant *as he proposed it:*

> The stage is set, the destiny disclosed. It has come about by no plan of our conceiving, but by the hand of God who led us into this way. We cannot turn back. We can only go forward, with lifted eyes and freshened spirit, to follow the vision. It was of this that we dreamed at our birth. America shall in truth show the way. The light streams upon the path ahead, and nowhere else.[29]

The Senate was less than convinced. Led by Senator Henry Cabot Lodge, Wilson's presidential nemesis (and grandfather of the man Kennedy would defeat in the 1952 U.S. senatorial election in Massachusetts), the Senate fought to have certain "reservations" appended to the covenant. The substance of each reservation varied, as did the support which each enjoyed within the Senate. In some part, the reservations reflected legitimate concerns about the obligations the treaty would impose on the United States. To a large extent, however, the reservations were a device to check Wilson personally. Along with Lodge, many senators began to resent presidential intrusions on their prerogatives; their memories of Wilson's ever-successful demands on the Congress awakened fears of a de facto dictator and aroused jealousies of individual power, jealousies which so often riddle Washington politics.

In any case, Wilson was advised that the treaty would not win Senate approval unless he accepted many of these reservations. Wilson adamantly refused even to consider them at first and stated that he would not sign the treaty if they were included.* "Better a thousand times to go down fighting," he told his wife, "than to dip your colors to dishonorable compromise."[30] Ultimately Wilson did accept some reservations. But by then the damage had been done. Lines had been drawn, animosities had been created or aggravated, and agreement was all but foreclosed. In March 1920 the Senate refused to advise and consent to the treaty and the United States was barred from joining the League of Nations.

From this brief history, one can realize that Wilson's defeat on the League of Nations proposal in the Senate in large part was due to his own unwillingness to compromise. The significance of Wilson's attitude here was made clear in this assessment by Professor Thomas Bailey, a noted authority on the League fight:

> In the final analysis the treaty was slain in the house of its friends rather than in the house of its enemies. In the final analysis it was not the two-thirds rule [of Senate concurrence], or the "irreconcilables," or Lodge, or the "strong" and "mild reservationists," but Wilson and his docile following who delivered the fatal stab. . . . With his own sickly hands Wilson slew his own brain-child—or the one to which he had contributed so much.[31]

The ironic twist was that Wilson's belief in an assertive executive in the White House proved to be his strength as well as his undoing.

Although Franklin Delano Roosevelt shared neither Wilson's Calvinist philosophy nor his emotional rigidity, he did share Wilson's desire for action and attention. Unlike Wilson, Roosevelt was born into a family with considerable wealth. That wealth and the warm love given by his parents, but especially by his possessive mother, provided Roo-

---

*While much of Wilson's intransigence reflected the self-righteousness he displayed on earlier occasions, it also bespoke the hatred which he had for Henry Cabot Lodge. This latter fact is revealed in the following exchange between Senators Lodge and James Watson in the spring of 1919:

Senator Watson: "Senator [Lodge], suppose that the President accepts the treaty with your reservations. Then we are in the League, and once in, our reservations become purely fiction."

Senator Lodge: "But, my dear James, you do not take into consideration the hatred that Woodrow Wilson has for me personally. Never under any set of circumstances in this world could he be induced to accept a treaty with Lodge reservations appended to it."

Senator Watson: "But that seems to me to be a rather slender thread on which to hang so great a cause."

Senator Lodge: "A slender thread! Why it is as strong as any cable with its strands wired and twisted together."

Watson, *As I Knew Them* 200–201 (1936).

sevelt with a security and geniality which he carried throughout life. The ease with which Roosevelt's needs were met in early life led him to demand much from his environment. But after attending preparatory school at Groton, he attended Harvard College, where life was not as simple as on his father's Hyde Park estate. Nonetheless, Roosevelt very much rose to the occasion, attaining a wide popularity among his fellow students and becoming editor of *The Crimson,* the school newspaper. At this point Roosevelt showed signs of activity that were to serve him well in his political life. As one biographer states of Roosevelt's editorship of *The Crimson,* "The pleasure gained from the sport of maneuvering and manipulation, and the status that came with political prize, held strongest appeal for him. Unwittingly, in these pursuits he took the first stride toward becoming an effective politician."[32]

Soon after leaving Harvard and graduating from Columbia Law School, Roosevelt decided to enter politics as a full-time profession. His rise was meteoric. In 1910 he became a New York State senator and led a successful fight against the corrupt leadership of Tammany Hall; in 1913 President Wilson appointed him as assistant secretary of the navy; and in 1920, at the age of thirty-eight, he was nominated by the Democratic party for the vice presidency of the United States. And all throughout Roosevelt enjoyed the political life because it enabled him to achieve very real goals: ". . . though I had studied these problems [of government] in the theoretical form, I found them even more absorbingly interesting because of their concreteness and their human application."[33]

In 1921, Roosevelt was stricken with polio, and from then on he never regained use of his legs (a fact not often appreciated today). Roosevelt's bout with polio and its aftermath had a very real influence on his attitudes and political skills. Not only did he develop a greater compassion for those struck by misfortune; he also became imbued with an even greater determination to be liked as well as respected by others and, ultimately, to achieve the political success he had dreamed of before polio cut him down. The effect that polio had on Roosevelt's relations with people was summarized well by Arthur Schlesinger, Jr.:

> They were his vital links with life, and his extroverted Rooseveltian sociability was compounded by his invalid's compulsion to charm anyone who came to his bedside. He sought more intensely than ever to know people, to understand them, to win them to him. Sometimes he even blurred his own feelings in an excess of amiability. . . .[34]

Roosevelt's experience with polio, in other words, did not dampen his buoyant spirit or his enthusiasm for politics. In 1928, he captured the governorship of New York and proceeded to set a pace of activity and action, particularly in the provision of governmental services during the Great Depression, which quickly brought him to national attention again. Determined to achieve larger goals and ever sure of himself, Roosevelt reached for and was elected to the presidency in 1932.

Roosevelt's need for action and popular favor—which had increased while he was governor of New York—were the underpinnings of his belief that the fulcrum of American government was the presidency. Those needs, in turn, were complemented by the sense of security and determination which Roosevelt developed in his youth and nurtured in his early political life. As chief executive, then, Roosevelt was able to broaden the powers of the presidency not only because he thrived on personal power and immensely enjoyed the game of politics; he also had a unique self-confidence in his ability to control the reins of government. As Schlesinger commented, in 1933 "Roosevelt had moved into the White House as if he were repossessing a family estate. He now spoke for and to the nation with dignity and ease and evident enjoyment."[35]

Unlike Wilson, though, Roosevelt did not philosophize in depth on the nature of governments or debate the need for a consistent, well-thought-out approach to programs and politics. When asked to describe his political philosophy, Roosevelt replied that he was "a Christian and a Democrat—that's all."[36] This glib response probably was, in part at least, theatrics on Roosevelt's part; but no doubt it also was shorthand for indicating his willingness to shift gears to meet changing circumstances. There was, in short, no refined creed which would structure Roosevelt's thoughts or thread all of his actions.

Roosevelt's first New Deal, for instance, did not reflect a grandiose program approved by the public in the 1932 presidential election. In fact, Roosevelt not only failed to develop a real program in the 1932 campaign; he was also frequently at pains to distinguish his policy positions from those of Herbert Hoover, the Republican presidential nominee. Although Roosevelt did promise the country a "new deal" when he accepted the Democratic party's presidential nomination, the ensuing campaign did not result in the issuance of statements or speeches which specified exactly what that "new deal" was. Most of Roosevelt's speeches articulated vague generalities and broad policies (such as a pledge to balance the budget—a pledge quickly forgotten after he was inaugurated) with which few could disagree. Elmer Davis, a reporter who followed Roosevelt in that 1932 campaign, observed, for example, that "you could not quarrel with a single one of his generalities; you seldom can. But what they mean (if anything) is known only to Franklin D. Roosevelt and his God."[37]

Excepting the atmosphere created by the depression, the contest between Roosevelt and Hoover was vaguely similar to the debate concerning the differences between Kennedy and Nixon in 1960. For like the candidates in 1960, the distinction between Roosevelt and Hoover was more along personal lines than along policy lines. In contrast to Hoover, Roosevelt viewed the nation's desperate plight as an invitation for executive leadership to achieve the country's recovery. Interpreting the traditional laissez-faire attitude of the federal government as an impediment to needed change, Roosevelt reminded his public that "eternal truths will be neither true nor eternal unless they have fresh meaning for every new social situation."[38] The public was thus assured that, whatever the nature of the specific programs adopted, a Roosevelt Administration would do *something* to ease the country's pervasive ills. Roosevelt, in short, usually had the opportunity as well as the will to exert leadership in an immobilized nation. Conversely, the absence of any similar crisis in 1960 not only limited the opportunities for Kennedy to exercise leadership; it also dampened his will to be as forceful as Roosevelt.

The incredibly swift response of the Congress to Roosevelt's initiatives in those first 100 days of his new administration mistakenly led Roosevelt to regard himself as an undisputed leader of the people. Unquestionably, much of Roosevelt's success with Congress reflected his own abilities of persuasion. In describing Roosevelt's congressional relations, James MacGregor Burns paid tribute to the skillful manner in which Roosevelt dealt with congressional committee chairmen who were, by and large, a rather independent lot:

> Since committee chiefs had power, he would deal with committee chiefs. And he did so with such charm, such tact, such flexibility, such brilliant timing, such sensitivity to the leaders' own political problems that the President's personal generalship often meant the difference between passage and defeat of key bills. Time and time again he won the support of men like [Senators] Glass and Harrison and Tydings and Sumners and Doughton not because they liked the New Deal in general or the measure in particular but because they liked and were willing to defer to the man who was President. Roosevelt's leadership talents lay in his ability to shift quickly and gracefully from persuasion to cajolery to flattery to intrigue to diplomacy to promises to horse-trading—or to concoct just that formula which his superb instincts for personal relations told him would bring around the most reluctant congressman.[39]

Notwithstanding these considerable skills of persuasion, Roosevelt's success with Congress was not entirely a matter of his own doing. In large part, Roosevelt had merely capitalized on a Congress that was amenable to support almost any program that promised some resistance to the depression which enveloped the country, a depression which had shaken the confidence and security of the people. Thus, as Roosevelt fostered a self-image of invincibility, he became somewhat divorced from the political realities and found subsequent defeat awaiting many bills introduced after the initial "honeymoon" period.

In any case, Roosevelt's overwhelming reelection to the presidency in 1936—capturing 523 electoral votes and 60 percent of the popular vote—confirmed his self-image of invincibility in much the same way that Wilson's early successes confirmed his messianic self-image. And like Wilson, Roosevelt's self-image fueled his faith in an activist presidency, a faith which remained intact despite subsequent setbacks. Congress's defeat of Roosevelt's 1937 court-packing bill aptly illustrates the point.

This bill was firmly rooted in Roosevelt's disgust with the Supreme Court. During his first term, the Court voided several New Deal measures because, according to the Court, they were unconstitutional. These judicial decisions infuriated Roosevelt, who felt that the Court was unnecessarily blocking his attempts to bring economic recovery to the nation. Accordingly, he and his attorney general, Homer S. Cummings, devised a plan to increase the number of New Deal-oriented justices on the Supreme Court. Essentially, the plan proposed that for every justice over seventy years of age (six filled that description in 1936) who did not voluntarily retire, the President could appoint another justice, the limit for the Court being fifteen. The plan was framed in a legislative proposal seeking judicial reform on all levels of the judiciary. Members of Congress, but especially those on the Democratic side of the aisle, reacted bitterly to this attempt to tamper with the judiciary and defeated the bill. Roosevelt's excessive self-confidence was largely undisturbed, however, and it allowed him to believe erroneously that he could purge the Democratic party in 1938 of elements opposed to his leadership. In these and other situations, Roosevelt was shown—as all presidents should be—that there are constitutional and political limits on the reach of a president's influence. But these defeats did not check Roosevelt's urge for power or success; instead, they were an incentive for him to retreat, solidify his political strength, and prepare for election to an unprecedented third term as president.

A man of a long, disciplined army career, Dwight David Eisenhower stood in direct contrast to Franklin Roosevelt. To understand this distinction, it is first necessary to recognize something of Eisenhower's background. He was born to soft-spoken parents who had a somewhat fatalistic view of life and did not inspire in their son a desire to master his environment. As James David Barber noted in his study of presidential character, "Eisenhower emerged from his history a believer in peace, in harmony, in cooperative endeavor. Neither of his parents pushed him toward extraordinary achievement, any more than Coolidge's had him. He was not fired up to change the world; he wanted to play baseball. His family had taught him to bear reverses stoically, to turn away from anger, and to let be what had to be."[40] Given this outlook, it is not surprising that Eisenhower found himself well-suited to a career in the army. Through his West Point education and through his years of association with top-ranking officers, such as Douglas MacArthur, Eisenhower fashioned an ability to execute plans formulated by others. The result was that Eisenhower was not so much a military strategist as he was a military organizer. And even when presented the opportunity for exercising power—as when he directed the Allied Command during World War II, until that time the most powerful army in the world's history—he rarely showed much interest in exploiting the opportunity. In 1945, for instance, he denied himself greater power and his country a more significant victory over Germany, waiting in Frankfurt while the Russians pushed their battered army across Eastern Europe toward Berlin (and thereby ensuring that the Soviet Union would maintain control over that part of Europe).

Elected President in 1952, Eisenhower had the concept of himself trying to reconcile a nation divided over the Korean War and rampant inflation. But his style was not power politics. Because of his background, particularly his military experience, he preferred organized responsibilities to the art of personal persuasion. Efficiency and proper etiquette, he felt, were the primary hallmarks of a successful president. In effect, Eisenhower's instincts—however commendable—did not reflect a firm grasp of political realities and responsibilities. Eisenhower, in fact, once admitted at a presidential press conference in 1955 that he quite frankly did not like politics.[41] Not wont to seek power, Eisenhower naturally never attained the political influence and effectiveness achieved by some of his predecessors.

While he did not pursue political power, Eisenhower did not entirely fail in achieving promised and chosen goals. He promised the electorate in 1952 to end the Korean War, and in 1953 he did preside over the negotiated settlement of the Korean conflict; he promised also to restore public respect for the presidency, and he did, over the course of his tenure, acquire a public stature matched by few, if any, presidents before or since. But these achievements should not obscure the shortcomings of Eisenhower's presidency—shortcomings whose impact, in some cases, were not fully felt until after he left office.

Thus, the moral quality with which Eisenhower imbued his presidency did not spread to the rest of government. Much of this reflected Eisenhower's disinterest in trying to persuade others to adopt his views.* As an example, turning red in the face, Eisenhower would frequently complain of Senator Joseph McCarthy's intimidating investigations in the early years of his first administration; but Eisenhower felt that he had neither the power nor the responsibility to interfere, publicly or otherwise. Despite the national climate which abetted these investigations, and despite their adverse effect on the lives of thousands of Americans, many of whom served in Eisenhower's executive bureaucracy, Eisenhower viewed the McCarthy investigations as strictly an internal affair of the Senate. In a like manner, Eisenhower had little interest in controlling the affairs of his own executive branch. When Secretary of Defense Charles E. Wilson prevailed upon Eisenhower to provide guidance in the administration of defense policy, Eisenhower was irate: "Look here, Charlie, I want *you* to run Defense. We *both* can't run it, and I *won't* run it. I was elected to worry about a lot of things other than the day-to-day operations of a department."[42]

The result of this disinterest in control was the formulation of government policy which often showed little concern for how it squared with Eisenhower's views or goals. Budgets were proposed and Eisenhower invited congressional cutbacks; international commitments were made by the State Department and Eisenhower ignored them in making other international commitments;** a civil rights bill drafted by the Justice Department was introduced in Congress and Eisenhower said that he did not understand it. For these and other blunders, Eisenhower often conveyed the impression to critical observers that his leadership was less than surefooted.†

---

*Sherman Adams, Eisenhower's top aide for six years, disclosed that Eisenhower "once told the Cabinet that if he was able to do nothing as President except balance the budget he would feel that his time in the White House had been well spent." Quoted in Barber, *The Presidential Character: Predicting Performance in the White House* 161 (1972).

**A prime example of this occurred after the 1956 Suez War between Israel and Egypt. The United States successfully pressured Israel to withdraw from Arab territories which it had captured in that short conflict. The Arab nations were concerned lest Israel's withdrawal signify any American commitment to Israel. Secretary of State Dulles assured the Arabs that it did not. At the same time, however, Eisenhower was dispatching a letter to Israeli Prime Minister David Ben-Gurion confirming an American commitment to protect Israel's access to international waterways, including the Straits of Tiran. See Draper, *Israel and World Politics* 22 (1968); Eisenhower's letter to Ben-Gurion is reprinted in *ibid.* at 140.

†In 1957, liberal columnist Doris Fleeson captured Eisenhower's unsureness with a parody of the Gettysburg Address as Eisenhower might have given it.

> I haven't checked these figures, but 87 years ago, I think it was, a number of individuals organized a governmental setup here in this country. I believe it covered certain Eastern areas, with this idea they were following up based on a sort of na-

In the last analysis, Eisenhower was a likable man who was more concerned with commanding popularity than influence; but he often failed to realize that favorable public opinion polls could not guarantee respect for his policies. As Emmet John Hughes observed, Eisenhower's principal distinction was not so much in his preference for an institutionalized presidency as in his indifference toward personal power in the White House. A strong-willed person with firm ideas of leadership, he sought to be a nonpolitical president. His passive attitude toward acquiring the presidency—and later toward using its resources—was perhaps captured best in Eisenhower's remark to an aide when a sudden surge of popularity for the Democratic party's candidate, Adlai Stevenson, seemed to threaten Eisenhower's election to the White House in 1952. "That's okay. If they [the public] don't want me, that doesn't matter very much to me," he said. "I've got a hell of a lot of fishing I'll be happy to do."[43] Such a casual attitude toward attaining the presidency would never be attributed to Kennedy.

John F. Kennedy: The Influence of the Early Years

Those frustrated with Eisenhower's leadership could draw hope from the fact that on January 20, 1961, a new President of the United States would be inaugurated. Under his aegis, the vitality of the presidency would once again be tested as the nation groped its way through a new age, an era marked by nuclear weaponry, technological advances, and soaring human aspirations. The successes and failures of the new administration would depend on innumerable factors, some obvious and some obscure. But one factor would be of undisputed importance in chartering the voyage of this new administration: the new President's perspective and abilities. Notwithstanding the independence of contributing forces and events, the new President's thoughts and activities would be widely scrutinized and appraised, approved and criticized—everyone assuming that his judgments would be central to the state of the Union.

At the time of his inauguration in 1961, John Kennedy was a man untried by executive leadership. While he had spent fourteen years in Congress, he had never known the quandaries or demands that inevitably arise in any high executive office in our political system. Nor had he experienced the pressure of ultimate responsibility for the plight of his countrymen or for the futures of their children. But such inexperi-

---

tional independence arrangement and the program that every individual is just as good as every other individual.

Quoted in Johnson, *1600 Pennsylvania Avenue* 319 (1960).

ence would not diminish the impact that his ideas and ideals would have on his effectiveness as a national leader. Indeed, without this experience in executive leadership, he would naturally have to rely on his ideas and ideals more than some previous presidents who could depend, to a certain extent at least, on their reactions to past executive problems as guidelines for meeting presidential dilemmas.

Kennedy's lack of executive experience did not necessarily mean that he would have an initial handicap in fulfilling the promises of his New Frontier. Our history is replete with presidents whose capacity for leadership was in no way impaired by a lack of previous executive experience. The governmental experiences of Abraham Lincoln, one of the strongest presidents in American history, were limited to one term as a congressman before he became President. Similarly, because his experience in executive leadership was minimal, Harry S Truman was awed by the dimensions of the presidency upon assuming office in 1945.* Yet he, too, proved to be an able leader in many demanding situations. On the other hand, few men were as well seasoned for the presidency as Herbert Hoover. With three decades of executive experience, including eight years as secretary of commerce, his leadership capabilities seemed unquestionable. But those capabilities proved to be of little value to Hoover as he tried to manage the nation's most serious economic crisis after he became President. In other words, regardless of the roads which carried them to the White House, all presidents ultimately had to rely greatly on judgments made in the moment of decision, judgments whose soundness could not be determined by the nature of their previous experiences.

Like those presidents who served before him, then, John Kennedy would find that his political values, as a product of his character and development, would be crucial in determining the extent to which his presidency would adequately solve problems and protect the democratic principles of government upon which our political system is based. In every situation he faced, in every decision he made, in any law he executed, his values would strengthen or weaken his resolve. In a similar manner, his attitudes would feed upon his thoughts, encouraging a particular response to the questions of his advocates or the challenges of his adversaries.

An underpinning of Kennedy's leadership, consequently, would not only be his view of the problems confronting the nation, but also his

*Learning of his ascendancy to the presidency upon Franklin Roosevelt's death on April 12, 1945, Vice President Truman implored the reporters with him, "Boys, if you ever pray, pray for me now."

understanding of the responsibilities the presidency required him to meet as well as the powers it afforded him to fulfill those responsibilities. John Kennedy's concept of his presidency, as a reflection of his attitudes and personality, would therefore help determine his success in meeting the needs and in protecting the interests of the country. To appreciate the contours of that personality and the attitudes it inspired, it is first necessary to trace Kennedy's development from childhood to inauguration as President of the United States.

John Fitzgerald Kennedy was born in Brookline, Massachusetts, on May 29, 1917, the second son born to Rose and Joseph Kennedy. Rose Kennedy, the daughter of a former mayor of Boston, is a devout Catholic who had led a privileged life as a young girl. She was educated at the finest Catholic schools, traveled widely, and was exposed to an assortment of dignitaries who regularly visited with her father. When I met her briefly at Hyannis Port in the summer of 1970, she conveyed the same qualities of discipline and warmth which were her mainstays in rearing her brood of nine children. Joseph Kennedy, on the other hand, was a man driven unceasingly by the need to succeed. At the birth of his second son, Joseph Kennedy was earning $20,000 as an assistant manager of a Boston shipping yard—a considerable sum in those days. The drive for success was to propel him to greater achievements, and within the next two decades he was to become a producer of Hollywood films, a powerful broker in the nation's stock exchanges, and a confidant of President Franklin D. Roosevelt who enjoyed the pleasure of high-level appointments (chairman of the newly created Securities and Exchange Commission in 1934, chairman of the Maritime Commission in 1937, and ambassador to England in 1938).

The impact of John Kennedy's parents, as well as his brothers and sisters, on his early development was considerable. There seems little question but that his family's imprint would help shape patterns of thought and activity which were to remain with Kennedy throughout life. There is always a risk of distortion or oversimplification in any analyst's attempt to structure Kennedy's, or any individual's, early development. Nonetheless, it does seem that three general themes pervaded Kennedy's youth, themes that would be evident in Kennedy's character and attitudes when he assumed the reins of presidential power.

First of all, the dynamics of the Kennedy family stressed a loyalty which, coupled with Joseph Kennedy's financial successes, created a sure sense of security. The emphasis on security was not accidental. Rose Kennedy recalled, for instance, that she tried to imbue all of her children with

> . . . a sense of responsibility and a sense of security. They knew exactly what they were expected to do and tried to do it for the most part, and the confidence, I think, of stability, which some children do not have and which older people do not always have, and I always told them that if they were given faith when they were young, they should try to nurture it and guard it because it's really a gift that older people valued so much when sorrow came or difficulty came.[44]

The effect of these admonitions on John Kennedy, as well as on his brothers and sisters, was telling. Despite the competition among the siblings—which has become embossed in legend by many chroniclers of the Kennedy presidency—the Kennedy children seemed to reflect a warmth and loyalty toward one another that was a shield against adversity.* In part, the sense of security was protected by the family's ample wealth (in 1930, while millions of Americans learned the despair of poverty, thirteen-year-old Kennedy wrote his mother from Canterbury, a private school in Connecticut, "Please send me the Litary [sic] Digest, because I did not know about the Market Slump until a long time after, or a paper."[45]). But the sense of security greatly depended on a feeling that other people really cared about you and that that concern

---

*In his detailed account of Robert Kennedy's stewardship of the Justice Department between 1961 and 1964, Victor Navasky observed the imprint of the family code of loyalty and the sense of security it induced:

> What distinguished the Kennedy family from other first families was that, contrary to contemporary cliché, they were not merely a tightly knit group, a closed circle, a clan, a clique for the privileged few. They were more like an extended family, an informal organization, a network. Membership was relatively open. There was, of course, the hard-core blood Kennedy family. But there were Kennedys by marriage like Sargent Shriver and Stephen Smith and Ethel Kennedy; there were Kennedys by political alliance ("before [the 1960] Wisconsin [primary]") like Byron White and Joe Dolan; Kennedys by having dated one of the Kennedy girls, like White's deputy, Bill Geoghegan, who had dated Jean; Kennedys by having served on the Rackets Committee, like Walter Sheridan and James J. P. McShane and Carmine Bellino; Kennedys by having gone to school with Bobby, like Dean Markham and David Hackett; Kennedys by ordeal, like Burke Marshall and Nicholas Katzenbach, who passed the test of early Justice Department crises. The list is long, which made the Kennedy family phenomenon that much more pervasive. For in addition to enjoying the special rights and privileges that went with membership, they were all on notice, like members of that other family which Luigi Barzini wrote about in *The Italians*—the Mafia—that being a Kennedy was a state of mind, a philosophy of life, a conception of society, a moral code, a particular susceptibility prevailing among all members of the family. They are taught in the cradle or are born already knowing that they must aid each other, side with their friends and fight common enemies even when the friends are wrong and the enemies right. Navasky, *Kennedy Justice* 330 (1971).

would survive individual hardships or failure. After entering the White House, John Kennedy reminisced with Arthur Schlesinger, Jr., one night about this mutual affection:

> My father wasn't around as much as some fathers when I was young, but, whether he was there or not, he made his children feel that they were the most important things in the world to him. He was so terribly interested in everything we were doing. He held up standards for us, and he was very tough when we failed to meet those standards. The toughness was important. If it hadn't been for that, Teddy might be just a playboy today. But my father cracked down on him at a crucial time in his life, and this brought out in Teddy the discipline and seriousness which will make him an important political figure.[46]

The significance of the sense of security imbued in Kennedy should not be underestimated. It meant that Kennedy's self-confidence—a major product of security—was not tied primarily to his individual achievements. Whatever importance Kennedy attached to his endeavors, he did not—in contrast to Lyndon Johnson, Richard Nixon, and some other presidents—generally view them as tests of character. For Kennedy's character and self-confidence were rooted in a family love and security that transcended individual experiences. While he would always retain a certain sensitivity to criticism, Kennedy did not seem to feel that such criticism could rock the foundations of his character, his self-confidence, or his sense of purpose.

Kennedy's sense of security ultimately became a foundation from which to pursue individual achievement because of a second theme which threads his early development: gradual absorption of his father's urgings to succeed in whatever endeavor he undertook, a burning drive to be the best. Kennedy's father, much more than his mother, believed that one's level of achievement was very dependent on an individual's determination, that success rarely was a result of chance. Joseph Kennedy therefore encouraged his children, but especially his sons, to thrive on competition. When Kennedy and his older brother, Joe, Jr., participated in sports contests, for example, their father would take a special interest in the effort they expended to be first. Rose Kennedy remembered a typical exchange after the elder Kennedy had watched his sons in a sailing race: "He didn't know anything about sailing, and he'd say, 'Why was your sail not as large as the other one? Why was it flapping when the other one was straight, and the other one won the race and you didn't?' And then the boys would say, 'Well, we bought our sails three years ago.' And their father would say, 'Well, why don't you tend to those things and find out what's going on? If you're in a race, do it right. Come in a winner; second place is no good.' "[47] The ambition Joseph Kennedy tried to instill in his sons was epitomized by his remark to *New York Times* columnist Arthur Krock: "For the Kennedys, it's the [outhouse] or the castle—nothing in between."* In a word, Joseph Kennedy conveyed an aura of ambition and high-mindedness in his family, an aura not without effect on all the children and particularly on the sons.

To recognize the influence of Joseph Kennedy on his son John does not mean one must assume a Freudian approach to politics. Nevertheless, there is no doubt that John Kennedy's drive for perfection, his desire to succeed in any endeavor, in great part grew from his father's teachings and Kennedy's concomitant desire to please his father. As with Theodore Roosevelt and Woodrow Wilson, because this ambition was instilled early, it became an integral part of Kennedy's personality. Buoyed by his father's confidence in him, familiarized with politics by his father's activities, the ease with which John Kennedy later applied his ambitions to politics was hardly unexpected. This was particularly so since Joseph Kennedy believed that politics was a noble profession for the man of material wealth.

Shortly before Kennedy's 1960 presidential campaign, his father told a journalist, "I certainly have encouraged the boys' interest in public service because I honestly feel—and this is no baloney—that we owe a great debt to our government. But I don't think I really pushed my sons in any particular direction."[48] This encouragement acquired greater weight when Kennedy's older brother, Joe, Jr., was killed in a crash of an experimental navy plane in Europe in 1944. Until then, the family—including Kennedy—had generally assumed that Joe, Jr., would be the Kennedy son to enter politics. Young Joe's death changed all that, and afterward Kennedy seemed to feel a special obligation to undertake the political career that was to have been his brother's.** But Kennedy always seemed to remember his parents' belief that those privileged by material wealth owed something to those less fortunate. Kennedy's recognition of this latter belief was evidenced in his statement to the Massachusetts State Legislature one week before his 1961 presidential

---

*Krock, *Memoirs: Sixty Years on the Firing Line* 338 (1968). Joseph Kennedy made this remark after John Kennedy had made an unsuccessful bid for the vice-presidential nomination at the 1956 Democratic Convention. In Joe Kennedy's eyes, it was better to wait for the presidential nomination than to accept second spot on the ticket.

**When President, Kennedy told his special counsel, Theodore Sorensen, "I never would have run for office if Joe had lived." Sorensen, *Kennedy* 15 (1965). Apparently, that was more an indication of Kennedy's desire not to compete with his older brother *outside the family sphere* (remember loyalty) than an indication that Kennedy was not interested in politics as a profession.

inauguration that "of those to whom much is given, much is required."*

The extent to which Kennedy could give something other than material wealth would depend greatly on the talents he developed. In this light, a third theme of Kennedy's early life became significant: a determined, albeit somewhat sporadic, pursuit of education, buoyed by a quick wit. The genesis of this theme lay principally with Kennedy's father. Joseph Kennedy had a high regard for education, and he devoted considerable attention to deciding which schools his children should attend. "Their father followed their careers very closely even when they were young,"[49] Rose Kennedy once said. "It was not a question of putting them in one school and letting them go along. He used to talk to the people in Boston who were interested in education to find the proper schools for them."[50]

Rose Kennedy herself reinforced the importance of education. "We talked to [the children] a lot during mealtimes, and we would talk about things that were interesting from the point of view of history—current events," she recalled. "You would never see Jack without a book in his hand."[51] No doubt this latter observation was only a mother's way of saying that her son had a healthy appetite for self-education, a proposition confirmed by the fact that Kennedy was one of very few students at Choate, a private school in Connecticut, who subscribed to and read the *New York Times.*

Despite this interest in education—which was geared principally toward an understanding of history—Kennedy's intellectual development was slow at first. Perhaps part of the explanation lies in the fact that, in his early life, Kennedy had few personal crises—often the anvil upon which meaningful values are forged. Neither sharing the economic crises of most Americans nor their concern for material well-being, he apparently felt little need to take life seriously. Nor did he suffer the anguish of anti-Irish bigotry, for Joseph Kennedy had moved his clan from the class-divided sections of Boston to Riverdale, New York, when his second son was only nine years old.

Kennedy's carefree attitude was best reflected in the quick wit which he showed both in and out of school. George St. John, Kennedy's tutor at Choate, once wrote Joseph Kennedy in 1933 about this wit and its place in his son's life:

> Jack has a clever, individualistic mind. It is a harder mind to put in harness than Joe's—harder for Jack himself to put in harness.

---

*Gardner (ed.). *To Turn the Tide: The Presidential Speeches of John F. Kennedy* 5 (1962). This is an adaptation of an aphorism which Rose Kennedy would often quote to her children from the Bible: "To whom much has been given, much will be required." Rose Kennedy, *Times to Remember* 118 (1974).

> When he learns the right place for humor and learns to use his individual way of looking at things as an asset instead of a handicap, his natural gift of an individual outlook and witty expression are going to help him. A more conventional mind and a more plodding and mature point of view would help him a lot more right now; but we have to allow, my dear Mr. Kennedy, with boys like Jack, for a period of adjustment. All that natural cleverness Jack has to learn how to use in his life and work, and even how to cover it up at times, how to subordinate it and all the rest.[51]

George St. John found the elder Kennedy's response to these and other comments to be sympathetic. No one had to impress Joseph Kennedy with the need for self-discipline in taking full advantage of educational opportunities and in being successful generally. So when young Jack informed his father that he would attend to his educational responsibilities at Choate with greater diligence, Joseph Kennedy's reaction was more than encouraging:

> Now, Jack, I don't want to give the impression that I am a nagger, for goodness knows I think that is the worst thing any parent can be. After long experience in sizing up people, I definitely know you have the goods and you can go a long way. Now aren't you foolish not to get all there is out of what God has given you. . . . After all, I would be lacking even as a friend if I did not urge you to take advantage of the qualities you have. It is very difficult to make up fundamentals that you have neglected when you were very young and that is why I am always urging you to do the best you can. I am not expecting too much and I will not be disappointed if you don't turn out to be a real genius, but I think you can be a really worthwhile citizen with good judgment and good understanding.[52]

The advice seemed to pay off, and by graduation from Choate, Kennedy had pulled himself up to stand sixty-fourth in a class of 112.

From Choate, Kennedy first matriculated at Princeton University in 1935, mainly to be with many of his friends who also entered Princeton. But a bout with jaundice forced Kennedy to remain out of school for almost the entire academic year. Princeton lost much of its appeal for Kennedy when he was a year behind his friends, and so he decided in the fall of 1936 to go to Harvard College, from which his father had graduated in 1912. At Harvard, Kennedy was not a serious student until his junior and senior years. Torbert Macdonald, Kennedy's Harvard roommate, remembered that Kennedy "was not particularly what then was called a 'grind,' somebody who just worked for work's sake and tried to get great grades just to impress people" (although Kennedy did graduate cum laude from Harvard in 1940 with a magna cum laude on his senior thesis).[53] Kennedy likewise generally avoided involvement in the student activism inspired by contemporary controversies (although he did participate in school athletics). Perhaps, as with many students, this lack of involvement reflected a desire to retain the carefree life of his childhood. Even Kennedy's first encounter with the suffering and brutality of war in a 1937 trip to Europe provoked more curiosity and wonder than involvement. Writing to his father from a turbulent Spain, Kennedy acknowledged that "95% of the people in the U.S. are so ignorant of what's happening here. While I, too, felt it would be good for Franco to win . . . I can see that it would be the worst thing."[54] Yet there remained the aloof attitude of one who observes but is not absorbed by his experience. Not that Kennedy was completely blind to the horrors of war; like many youths of similar background, he simply could not identify easily with the people who suffered those horrors.

Kennedy's emotional detachment toward war gave way when the Germans sank the British liner *Athenia* in 1939. His father, then the American ambassador to the Court of St. James's in London, dispatched his twenty-two-year-old son (on a semester's leave from Harvard) to Glasgow to interview the survivors of the tragedy and to determine what assistance the embassy could lend to the American travelers. Seeing the tears and the anxieties of fellow Americans, listening to their accounts of lost companions, Kennedy began to sense his proximity to the pains and suffering of nations in armed conflict. It was here, then, that John Kennedy first shared the tragedy of war. Understandably, it was here that his thoughts first spiraled toward what would be his senior thesis at Harvard and his first book—*Why England Slept.*

Why England Slept

Returning to Harvard in the fall of 1939 after a semester abroad, Kennedy began work on his senior thesis. The thesis was to be a seventy-page analysis of the British reaction to Germany's rearmament and Hitler's aggressive policies in the late 1930s. When Kennedy completed the thesis in May 1940, it was 150 pages and, as he wrote to his father, "represents more work than I've ever done in my life."[55] Kennedy showed the thesis to Arthur Krock, a family friend, and Krock suggested that Kennedy think of publishing an expanded version. After consulting with his father about the idea, Kennedy agreed and, with the assistance of Krock and some of his college professors, had the book ready for publication in the fall of 1940.* Kennedy accepted Krock's

*It is of some interest that Kennedy's book was one of the first published by Wilfred

other suggestion to title the book *Why England Slept*, as Kennedy explained it to his father, to provide "a sort of contrast to Churchill's *While England Slept*" (a book which recounts the history of Germany's rearmament in the 1930s, a rearmament which violated the terms of the Versailles Peace Treaty and which threatened another European conflict).[56]

Why England Slept is of considerable significance in explaining Kennedy's ideas of government and politics. For it divulges a developing attitude toward the role of governments and their leaders which was similar to the attitudes Kennedy brought to the White House twenty years later. That this book should reflect seeds of Kennedy's later thoughts was in part dictated by the nature of the book's subject. In this small work, Kennedy examines the reluctance of England to prepare, militarily and psychologically, for the threat of war posed by Hitler's jingoistic policies. Kennedy probed the effects of England's history on her populace and on her leaders. He tried to penetrate the illusion of security and the fear of involvement which immobilized the nation despite the hostile portents of Hitler's policies. As Kennedy tells it, there were two basic explanations for England's failure to respond to those policies in a realistic manner.

First, the British public was slow to believe that Hitler's belligerent rhetoric and aggressive actions represented much more than the impotent postures of a frustrated leader. There was little to make the British public realize their views of European politics might require some adjustment, that Hitler's rhetoric and Germany's rearmament were indicative of the pervasive destruction and death that were soon to grip Europe. In part, Kennedy argued, the British people's complacency revealed a general resistance to accepting changes in perceptions of the world: "Because of the inertia of human thought, nations, like individuals, change their ideas slowly."[57] Given this inertia, British criticism of Hitler was initially directed more at the methods he used than at the things he actually did. But inertia was only part of the story. In Kennedy's eyes, the British complacency toward Hitler represented a certain smugness, an arrogance premised on extreme self-confidence:

> No discussion of Britain's psychology would be complete unless some mention were made of the national feeling of confidence, even of superiority, that every Englishman feels and to which many Americans object. This feeling, while it is an invaluable asset in bearing up under disaster, has had a great effect on the need Britain felt for rearming. The idea that Britain loses every

---

Funk, Inc., a company which was the beneficiary of some Joseph Kennedy generosity. The book did well, selling about 80,000 copies. Kennedy made about $40,000 from royalties. He bought a Buick and donated the English royalties to the bomb-devastated town of Plymouth, England.

> battle except the last has proved correct so many times in the past that the average Englishman is unwilling to make personal sacrifice until the danger is overwhelming.[58]

In this setting, one can appreciate the public pressure which induced British Prime Minister Neville Chamberlain to negotiate an agreement with Hitler when the two met at Munich in 1938. The English wanted to believe, even at the price of ignoring reality, that peace would remain undisturbed. Chamberlain fed that self-defeating wish by concluding an agreement with Hitler which the prime minister proclaimed would ensure "peace in our time." Had the public not held so tenaciously to its illusions, Kennedy indicates, Chamberlain might have been more willing to realize that the peace secured by that agreement was no more real than the Emperor's new clothes. Thus did Kennedy pin on the British public much of the responsibility for allowing Hitler's aggressive policies to unfold in the late 1930s without much resistance.

England's slowness to respond to Hitler could not be explained entirely by reference to public attitudes. A second explanation concerned England's political leadership. In Kennedy's eyes, "much of the cause of England's failure may be attributed to the leaders."* Part of that failure was the inability of the leaders to recognize the threat which Hitler's policies posed to England's security, indeed, to her very existence. So when Hitler did finally strike, England's defense capabilities were found seriously wanting. But the gravest error of England's leadership, Kennedy contended, was the failure to educate the public, to address their thoughts to the realities of Hitler's army instead of to vain hopes for "peace in our time." For most governmental policies—but especially those defense policies which demand public sacrifice—require considerable public support to be effective. Having failed to educate the public about Hitler, England's leaders had no political base to support a new program of defense preparedness until Hitler's surprise attacks on England quickly changed public opinion. In the

---

*In a prepublication draft of the book, Kennedy had paid little attention to the failures of British leadership. After reading this draft, Joseph Kennedy wrote his son that he should not be so lenient with England's leaders, because they are "supposed to look after the national welfare, and to attempt to educate the people." Kennedy accepted his father's advice, and replied, "Will stop white-washing [British prime minister] Baldwin." Kennedy made some revisions throughout the text and added the following paragraph to the conclusion:

> At times it may appear that I have tried unjustifiably to clear the leaders of responsibility. That is not my view. But I believe, as I have stated frequently, that leaders are responsible for their failures only in the governing sector and cannot be held responsible for the failure of a nation as a whole. Kennedy, *Why England Slept* 175 (Dolphin ed. 1961).

end, it was very much a case of the leaders following the public rather than vice versa.

Kennedy concluded that England's experience should be an invaluable lesson to the United States. For that experience demonstrated that the wish for peace is no substitute for the arms required to defend peace:

> We must always keep our armaments equal to our commitments. Munich should teach us that; we must realize that any bluff will be called. We cannot tell anyone to keep out of our hemisphere unless our armaments *and the people behind those armaments* are prepared to back up the command, even to the ultimate point of going to war. There must be no doubt in anyone's mind, the decision must be automatic: if we debate, if we hesitate, if we question, it will be too late.[59]

But Kennedy's concern was not only that the United States acquire and be willing to use armaments to protect against foreign aggression at some indeterminate time in the future. More specifically, he also seemed concerned lest Americans not recognize that Hitler's war in Europe posed a considerable danger to the security of the United States, that the American public could not divorce itself from what was then happening thousands of miles across the Atlantic Ocean:

> We withdrew from Europe in 1920 and refused to do anything to preserve the democracy we had helped to save. We thought it made no difference to us what happened in Europe. We are beginning to realize that it does. . . .
>
> I say therefore that we cannot afford to let England's experience pass unnoticed. Now that the world is ablaze, America has awakened to the problems facing it. But in the past, we have repeatedly refused to appropriate money for defense. We can't escape the fact that democracy in America, like democracy in England, has been asleep at the switch. If we had not been surrounded by oceans three and five thousand miles wide, we ourselves might be caving in at some Munich of the Western World.
>
> To say that democracy has been awakened by the events of the last few weeks [the Nazi *Blitzkrieg* and the British retreat from Dunkirk] is not enough. Any person will awaken when the house is burning down. What we need is an armed guard that will wake up when the fire first starts or, better yet, one that will not permit a fire to start at all.[60]

These were words that, as time was to show, America would have done well to heed earlier than it did. (In fact, Franklin D. Roosevelt, campaigning for his third term as President when Kennedy's book was published, assured the American public that American boys would not be sent to fight overseas even though he privately understood the imminence of America's involvement in the European conflict.)

I have quoted at length from *Why England Slept* because I believe that this book does much to illuminate the basic views Kennedy would bring to the presidency as well as the concept he would have of his presidential responsibilities. As I will try to show, throughout his congressional years, his 1960 campaign, and until late in his presidency, Kennedy was greatly concerned that America might again fall asleep at the switch, that the lessons of England's pre-World War II experience would be forgotten, that America might have its own Munich—with all the false hopes for peace and the subsequent devastation when the illusion of peace was shattered. This concern reached an acme in the 1962 Cuban missile crisis when the United States and the Soviet Union seemed poised for war because of the Soviet installation of offensive missiles in Cuba. In these critical moments, President Kennedy would remember the lessons of why England slept and reject suggestions that he give the Soviet Union whatever would be necessary to remove the threat of an American-Soviet nuclear confrontation. Indeed, shortly after the missile crisis was resolved, Stewart Alsop and Charles Bartlett—close friends of Kennedy—published in the *Saturday Evening Post* what most insiders considered to be a semiofficial account of the events of the crisis. The account quotes one high government official as saying that UN Ambassador Adlai Stevenson—who had argued that there was little sense in going to war over the missiles—had wanted a Munich. Years later, after the *Saturday Evening Post* collapsed, a former editor disclosed that the quoted official was Kennedy himself and that he had insisted that those words be published.*

But now I am getting ahead of my analysis. The basic point is that *Why England Slept* is a well-documented account of an experience Kennedy would never forget. The book is described by Henry Luce in the foreword as a dispassionate work, and to a large extent this description is accurate. Until the conclusion, the book offers little evidence to show Kennedy's emotions on issues which were then literally and figuratively consuming Europe. But the book's conclusion does show some compassion for the suffering then being borne by England. The conclusion also seems to be an emotional cry to the American reader to realize that England's fate will be his or hers unless America builds up

*Kenneth O'Donnell, Kennedy's appointments secretary at the time, says that Kennedy was really dismayed by this characterization of Stevenson. O'Donnell and Powers, *Johnny We Hardly Knew Ye* 366 (1972). But JFK never publicly disavowed the characterization.

her arms and accepts the risk that they may have to be used against Germany. And underlying this argument is the assumption that England's preservation may be essential to America's. Kennedy thus sharply took issue with the isolationism which dominated much of the American public's thinking, and the fact that he argued in emotional terms in support of one side of a raging public controversy—whether America should be concerned about the European conflict—belies any suggestion that *Why England Slept* is entirely dispassionate.*

After graduating from Harvard in 1940, Kennedy entered Stanford Business School. He found the academic life boring and decided to enter the armed forces. He was initially rejected by the army because of a back injury he had sustained from playing football. In typical Kennedy fashion (remember the drive to succeed), he followed a strict regimen of strengthening exercises for five months and was finally able to pass the navy medical exam. Once in the navy, Kennedy was assigned a desk job. After the Japanese strike at Pearl Harbor, he applied for sea duty—perhaps a display of obligation, or perhaps just a display of that sense of adventure which he had nurtured since childhood. Through use of his father's contacts, he finally did land a sea duty assignment. As almost everyone knows, Kennedy was later given command of a PT boat, the PT-109. Kennedy's experience in the navy, especially his courage in saving his crew after a Japanese destroyer split his PT boat in two, is well known and need not be elaborated upon here.[61] Of perhaps equal significance is that Kennedy's navy experience did not dilute his wit** or his sense of competition. This sense of competition was so strong that Kennedy would even race his PT-109 with other PT boats—until one race in the Russell Islands when his reverse gear failed and the PT-109 ploughed into a gas dock, much to the consternation of the squadron commander.

His tour of duty over, Kennedy returned to the United States in 1944

---

*At no point did Kennedy explicitly take a position as to whether or not the United States should provide military assistance to England. The basic premise of the book, however, is that America's fate may be tied to England's fate. Therefore, the book seems to suggest that military assistance to England may be a necessary action for the United States in preparing America's defenses.

**Kennedy writing to his younger brother, Robert, from the Solomon Islands in 1944, shortly after Robert had enlisted in the navy:

> The folks sent me a clipping of you taking the oath. The sight of you up there was really moving, particularly as a close examination showed that you had my check London coat on. I'd like to know what the hell I'm doing out here while you go stroking around in my drape coat, but I suppose that's what we are out here for—so that our sisters and younger brothers will be safe and secure—frankly, I don't see it quite that way. At least, if you're going to be safe and secure, that's fine with me, but not in my coat, brother, not in my coat. Lieberson (ed.), *John Fitzgerald Kennedy: As We Remember Him* 44 (1965).

and helped prepare a book, *As We Remember Joe,* in memory of his fallen older brother (a book which Joseph Kennedy could never bring himself to read).* And he also had to consider what career he should undertake. He toyed briefly with a job as a reporter for the Hearst newspapers, but boredom with that job and his interest in politics led him back to Boston, a race for a congressional seat, and the start of a political career that was to lead him to the White House.

The Congressional Years and Political Maturity

On April 11, 1946, John Kennedy filed papers to run in the primary for the Democratic congressional nomination from Massachusetts' eleventh district—an area covering parts of Boston and Cambridge. It was, in a way, a somewhat brash act. With the exception of his years at Harvard, Kennedy had not lived in the Boston area since he was nine years old. He had no real residence in the area and, in fact, had fulfilled the candidate's residency requirement by renting an apartment at 122 Bowdoin Street in Boston only a short time before filing his nomination papers. He had no experience in Boston politics (or any politics for that matter), was not supported by any regular party organization, and while Joseph Kennedy's name was well known in some circles, Kennedy's face, to say the least, was not a very familiar one on the streets of the eleventh district. But Kennedy had decided that he wanted to run for elective office, and you had to start somewhere.

He relied to some extent on his family's wealth and contacts, but the operation was really all Kennedy's. He recruited old friends and made new ones to help him in this effort. College cronies like Torbert Macdonald, navy pals like Red Fay, and new acquaintances like Dave Powers—all were asked to accomplish what then seemed like a long shot: get a Kennedy elected to public office.

The crux of the campaign was Kennedy himself. He generally arose at 6:00 or 6:30 A.M. so that he could shake hands with the workers at the Charlestown Navy Yard and the factories. From morning until late

---

*In this book, Kennedy recalled the qualities which he found so admirable in Joe:

> Things did not come easy to him. I think his accomplishments were due chiefly to the amazing intensity with which he applied himself to the job at hand. I do not think I can ever remember seeing him sit back in a chair and relax. Even when he was still, there was always a sense of motion forcibly restrained about him. And yet his continuous motion did not have its roots in restlessness or nervousness but rather it came from his intense enthusiasm for everything he did and from his exceptional stamina. Quoted in McCarthy, *The Remarkable Kennedys* 104 (1960).

Looking back from November 22, 1963, an admirer of John Kennedy could use these same words to describe the fallen President.

at night he knocked on doors, climbed the tenement steps, and attended innumerable parties, speaking to anyone who would listen, turning on the boyish charm that came so easily, joking and relating his thoughts on the economic problems of the district and the political uncertainties of the newly won world peace. It was no small task for Kennedy. Throughout his youth he had been rather shy with strangers, and even Joseph Kennedy would show surprise that this son of his could approach strangers now and introduce himself as a contender for their congressional nomination. No doubt this was one of the last times that Joseph Kennedy would underestimate his second son's drive to succeed, to catch the brass ring. For in this primary Kennedy gave it his all, ignoring the football and navy injuries which still plagued him, pushing himself to the point where his campaign workers became very concerned for his health. But he persevered and enjoyed an easy victory over his nine primary opponents. The Democratic nomination was virtually tantamount to election, and in November 1946, twenty-nine-year-old John Kennedy became the eleventh district's representative in Congress.

It is a curious phenomenon to think back to the time when John Kennedy was a freshman congressman with virtually no national recognition. Here, in 1946, was a man who had literally thrust himself on the national political scene and, within the relatively short span of fourteen years, would dominate that political scene. When he campaigned for the presidency in 1960, Kennedy tried to cast himself as the hope of the liberals (in part to win the support of those who still saw Adlai Stevenson as the liberals' standard-bearer). But it was not always so. In 1946, Kennedy was describing himself as a "fighting conservative," although that probably reflected his instinct as to what he should be more than it represented any commitment to some articulated philosophy. And there may be some basis for believing that that instinct was sound, at least from an electoral perspective. For Kennedy was to be reelected to Congress in 1948 and 1950, and in the 1952 election he was to stage a major upset victory by capturing a United States Senate seat from the Republican incumbent, Henry Cabot Lodge, Jr., a well-respected man with sixteen years of Senate service (and a grandson of Woodrow Wilson's political nemesis).

However interesting and impressive these electoral victories, they did little to define how Kennedy would respond to his political obligations. Electoral victories alone are not the stuff of which responsible representation or effective leadership is made. In other words, the quality of Kennedy's performance in Congress and later in the presidency would depend more on his character and intellect, nourished by political experiences, than on his ability to please the crowds on election day.

The congressional years were formative ones for Kennedy. In many ways, he was writing on a clean slate. For a variety of reasons—some of which I will explore—Kennedy's opinions and perceptions as a congressman and then as a senator would change and, in some cases, even be reversed completely. Despite these changes and shifts, three basic traits seem to thread Kennedy's congressional years, traits which would greatly shape his concept of his presidency: first, a certain independence of thought and action which, in part, reflected an unstructured approach to government and politics; second, a belief that the federal government has a broad responsibility to help those trapped by misfortune of almost any kind; and third, a belief that the federal government should undertake whatever steps were necessary to protect against communism both at home and abroad. To some extent, of course, these three traits reflected Kennedy's views on the substance of issues and the priority they should receive from the federal government. But to a large degree, these traits also revealed Kennedy's view of the president's responsibilities and how he should fulfill them. And that view, in turn, would link Kennedy's personality with the office he assumed on January 20, 1961.

The independence of thought and action which Kennedy showed during his congressional years, for instance, no doubt reflected a mix of factors, some of which will escape the probes of historians. But the roots of this independence are not entirely obscure. To begin with, Kennedy's youth lacked the emotional experiences that often lead other men and women to commit themselves to specific causes or philosophies. Nor did he feel the need to build his security on an association with a particular group or political movement. His self-confidence rested more on his estimate of his own abilities than on his identification with any philosophy or his participation in any activity. He was comfortable being himself, had few anxieties as to whether he should be satisfied with his personality, and rarely felt the urge to join any particular group or movement. This attitude was perhaps epitomized best during the 1960 campaign when Kennedy was asked if he was exhausted. Kennedy replied that he was not, although he felt sorry for Nixon because he was convinced that Nixon was very tired. Asked to explain this answer, Kennedy responded, "Because I know who I am and I don't have to worry about adapting and changing. All I have to do at each stop is be myself. But Nixon doesn't know who he is, and so each time he makes a speech he has to decide which Nixon he is, and that will be very exhausting."[62]

Kennedy's satisfaction with himself probably contributed to the unstructured manner in which he approached political problems. In Kennedy's eyes, philosophy was no match for reason and pure intelligence. One dissected and analyzed a political problem; there was little virtue in grinding out a solution from a preconceived creed or ideology. Rationality was the key. As Kennedy would later say glowingly of McGeorge Bundy, his national security adviser in the White House, "You can't beat brains."[63] And during his presidency, Kennedy's White House staff liked to describe the Kennedy team as a group of pragmatic realists rather than as adherents to a particular philosophy of government, liberal or otherwise. In fact, Kennedy once remarked that he felt ill at ease with the doctrinaire liberals of the Americans for Democratic Action.

Later many people, but especially critics of Kennedy's decisions to expand American involvement in Vietnam, would question whether Kennedy and his staff really were pragmatic or realistic. But to the extent those terms indicated an unstructured approach to governmental problems, they contained a good deal of truth. For Kennedy did believe that success in American politics required one to avoid dogmatic attitudes. Like Franklin Roosevelt, Kennedy regarded the essential mainstay of our political system as its flexibility, its capacity to meet arising needs and balance conflicting interests within established institutions, in a word, its nonideological cast. To Kennedy, then, there was little necessity or benefit in viewing issues or policies through an ideological lens. Indeed, to commit oneself to an ideology, any ideology, was counterproductive. Such commitments, Kennedy thought, shackled one with emotional chains, imposed predetermined responses to problems, and reduced the flexibility required if reasonable men were to resolve their differences. It was basically a matter of being able and willing to compromise your views for the sake of achievement. George St. John, Kennedy's tutor at Choate, recalled a visit Kennedy made to his alma mater's History Club shortly after he was elected to the House of Representatives. St. John vividly remembered that there Kennedy

> spoke of the necessity of compromise in politics. He made the point very strongly that one had to understand the needs of other states and other people and side with them in order to get help for programs that one deeply believed in. He said that one might say one would have nothing to do with anything except one's own ideals, but in that case, (a) no legislation that one believed in would get passed; and (b) one would not be reelected to Congress. To serve usefully and realistically, one had to live realistically in political life.[64]

Compromise—it was a key to how Kennedy viewed the game of politics, whether when representing Massachusetts' eleventh district or when representing the entire nation from the Oval Office in the White House. And the need to compromise would be a much-invoked explanation as to why Kennedy would often hesitate to exercise his congressional or presidential powers to propose or effect changes he thought necessary or justified. No one would ever mistake John Kennedy for a radical who would always stand firm on principle.

Kennedy's caution and flexibility in politics did not mirror an insensitivity to the need for ideals in politics. Instead, it seemed to reflect his understanding of our democratic institutions. This seems particularly evident from the admiration Kennedy had for John Buchan's book *Pilgrim's Way.*

This work, a series of autobiographical essays by England's Lord Tweedsmuir, greatly influenced Kennedy's attitudes toward democratic government and its participants. Reading and rereading it, Kennedy found Buchan's thoughts sensitive to the dilemmas of democratic government and appropriate to an understanding of American culture. Notwithstanding the diversity of subjects covered by the book's essays, several themes persist throughout the writing. Citing the role of history and tradition in the development of America's government, for example, Buchan states that democracy is "primarily a spiritual testament, from which certain political and economic orders naturally follow. But the essence is the testament; the orders may change while the testament stands."[65] Kennedy generally agreed with Buchan that the spirit of democracy was the lasting structure upon which ever-changing policies and programs could be laid. He also agreed with Buchan that the need for decisive leadership in a democracy could never obscure the necessity for the people's support of and involvement with the government's programs. Without such involved participation, both men realized that leadership would be seriously handicapped and the system of government extremely vulnerable to external pressures. In short, a leader could not be effective—or reelected—if he moved at a quicker pace than his constituency.

No doubt this reasoning applied when, as President, Kennedy told his staff that he could not undertake too many controversial actions until after his reelection to the presidency in 1964, a time when he would have no future elections to worry about. Thus, when advisers like Chester Bowles and Adlai Stevenson urged Kennedy to recognize Communist China, a move which was not well supported by public opinion, Kennedy informed them that it would have to wait until after the 1964 election. When asked to correct the injustices done to J. Robert Oppenheimer, John Paton Davies, and Charlie Chaplin—men cursed in the public's eye in the 1950s because of their alleged communist sympathies—Kennedy replied that he could help one but not all three, at least not until after the 1964 election. And when Senator Mike Mansfield urged Kennedy in 1962 to withdraw American forces from Vietnam, Kennedy told him he would—but only after the 1964 election. Kennedy's "pragmatic" view of politics was further borne out in a conversation I had with James Reston, the *New York Times* columnist, in the summer of 1967. I asked Reston what one experience typified his memory of Kennedy. Reston thought for a moment and then remembered,

> One time I asked him what he wanted to achieve as President. He gave me this puzzled look. I felt it was a good question, so I rephrased it. He still remained puzzled. I rephrased it a third time and got the same reaction. I then mentioned something about bringing about greater unity in the Atlantic Community and he immediately started giving points and rolling off statistics. It had to be something specific. He was not interested in philosophical concepts, only the practical.

Reston's comment also underscored the fact that Kennedy was not, contrary to a popularized image, an intellectual. He enjoyed having intellectuals around him, but he could not join in their abstract inquiries. He was quick to grasp the ideas they proffered, but reluctant to formulate them himself. Committed to neither a liberal nor a conservative faction, he could exploit whatever ideas suited his needs at the time. In this vein, James MacGregor Burns was probably right in saying that Kennedy thought he was offering Adlai Stevenson the ultimate tribute when he described the former Illinois governor as "beholden to no group or section, belonging to neither a left wing nor a right wing."[66]

Kennedy was not only free of ideological chains, liberal or otherwise; he also felt free to act independently of other political leaders. During most of his congressional years, he was a political maverick, a man who was not part of the congressional "establishment" and who felt little desire to accede to the dictates of that establishment. "I think that would be the one characteristic I remember about him then—that he voted the way he damn well pleased," Congressman Richard Bolling later said of Kennedy, with whom he served in the House. "Even in those days," said Bolling, "I think it was clear that he more than most politicians was his own man."

Whatever the explanation for this independence, it was a fact of life, and it helped explain how Kennedy could sometimes deflect the pressures of his colleagues. Thus, despite pressure from House Minority Leader John McCormack, Kennedy refused to sign a letter from Massachusetts congressmen in 1947 petitioning the governor to release James M. Curley from prison.* Even though his refusal angered the

---

*James M. Curley had been a patriarch of Boston politics. Between 1910 and 1946 he had served as a United States congressman, mayor of Boston, and governor of Massachusetts. A practitioner of machine politics, Curley was imprisoned in 1945 (while still serving as a congressman) for embezzlement. His popularity and political leadership were a

powerful McCormack, Kennedy disagreed with the principle of the petition and remained tenacious in his position. McCormack was not the only leader to feel the sting of Kennedy's independence. Representative Kennedy also criticized fellow Democrat President Truman and his State Department for being responsible for the communist takeover of China in 1949.[67] And when the American Legion, a rock of the "establishment," opposed his veterans' housing bill in 1949, Kennedy responded that "the leadership of the American Legion has not had a constructive thought for the benefit of this country since 1918."[68]

Senator Joe McCarthy's investigations of communist infiltration in the federal bureaucracy—in which McCarthy showed utter contempt for fellow human beings—provide another apt illustration of Kennedy's independence. McCarthy initiated these investigations on the pretext that Congress had a duty to expose those in the bureaucracy who had communist sympathies. As the investigations progressed from 1950 to 1954, many senators, sensing the ugliness of McCarthy's tactics and feeling that the investigations would damage the Senate's integrity, began to press for termination of the hearings as well as condemnation of McCarthy.

Entering the Senate in January 1953, Kennedy at first resisted pressures to join this chorus of criticism. His father had personal ties with McCarthy, and his brother Robert was working on McCarthy's staff (although Robert Kennedy shortly resigned in protest and then helped write the Senate report censuring McCarthy). Moreover, Kennedy was not convinced that investigating communist infiltration in the government was a bad thing. (At a seminar at Harvard College in November 1950, Kennedy mentioned that not enough was being done to get rid of the communists in the government, that he "knew Joe [McCarthy] pretty well and he may have something. . . ."[69]) Kennedy also believed that the Senate had tacitly approved of McCarthy's investigations by providing him with the necessary funds. In a sense, Kennedy's position reflected little more than political expediency; he wanted to say something without really saying anything. Theodore C. Sorensen, Kennedy's legislative aide, explained it in a much more delicate manner. Sorensen said that Kennedy viewed the controversy more as a legal one than as a philosophical one and thus "answered constituent mail on the question with caution, candidly stating his views on specific issues but avoiding a commitment on the man."[70]

When the question of McCarthy's censure finally came up for debate

---

rock of granite, however, and this was confirmed when the people of Boston elected him mayor while he was still serving his prison sentence. It was reported that Curley was the model for Frank Skeffington in Edwin O'Connor's 1956 novel, *The Last Hurrah.*

Ironically, it was Curley's former seat in Massachusetts' eleventh congressional district that Kennedy had captured in the 1946 election.

on the Senate floor in 1954, Kennedy decided that he would support censure—not so much because McCarthy's investigations threatened the civil liberties protected by the Bill of Rights as because McCarthy's tactics threatened the integrity and prestige of the Senate as a public body. Kennedy's reaction to McCarthy revealed a great insensitivity to civil liberties and common decency. Kennedy himself later regretted his cautious approach. But he had decided for independent reasons to remain aloof from the controversy, and the pressures of his colleagues could not divert him from that course. As he campaigned for the presidency in 1960, Kennedy was quite sensitive about the matter and often turned cold when people brought it up; but he refused to alter the public record—even when his position drew fire from the liberals whose support he needed so much.*

Kennedy's independence was not confined to confrontations with political leaders. He also could be independent of public opinion, whether domestic or international, when convinced that adherence to certain principles or positions deserved priority. This independence was exemplified during the Senate debates on American participation in the Saint Lawrence Seaway Project in 1953 and 1954. As originally conceived in the early 1930s, the project was to be a joint American-Canadian effort to improve the navigability of the Saint Lawrence River. The purpose of the project was to make this river usable as an international waterway for commercial and military purposes. Public opinion in New England had always opposed the Saint Lawrence project because it posed economic risks for that area (mainly because it would probably mean a decrease in the trade coming in and going out of Boston's port). Accordingly, most of New England's congressional delegations had always opposed the measure. In fact, no senator or congressman from Massachusetts had ever voted for the measure on the six occasions it had come up for a vote in twenty years.

---

*Kennedy never did vote on McCarthy's censure when it finally came to a vote in 1954 because he was in Florida recuperating from a serious back operation. At the 1960 Democratic Convention in Los Angeles, Eleanor Roosevelt, widow of Franklin D. Roosevelt, said that she would switch her support from Adlai Stevenson to Kennedy if Kennedy would publicly state his views on the McCarthy censure. Although Kennedy had decided to support the censure, he declined Mrs. Roosevelt's request—he felt that such a statement would be a *post facto* declaration and hence meaningless (a feeling not shared by those who were concerned in 1960 about Kennedy's commitment to protect civil rights and liberties).

Shortly after his election to the presidency, Kennedy visited Eleanor Roosevelt at her Hyde Park estate. Kennedy was somewhat concerned about reports that Mrs. Roosevelt did not trust him (reports which had credibility with him because of their confrontation at the Democratic Convention). After sitting down with Mrs. Roosevelt, Kennedy bluntly asked if it was true that she did not really trust him. No, I don't, she replied. Although the meeting ultimately proved to be a congenial one, Kennedy left feeling that Eleanor Roosevelt was tough and deserving of much respect.

In two major speeches, Kennedy discussed his decision to break with this tradition. First of all, he was not persuaded that completion of the project would greatly harm New England's economy. But whatever the adverse economic effects of the Saint Lawrence Seaway, Kennedy believed that national economic and security interests required its adoption. In announcing his support for the project, Kennedy stressed his

> opposition to the idea that New England's interest is best served by opposing Federal programs which contribute to the well-being of the country, particularly when those programs increase the purchasing power of New England's customers. Where Federal action is necessary and appropriate, it is my firm belief that New England must fight for those national policies.
>
> ****
>
> To those in my State and elsewhere who oppose our participation in the construction of this project for national security merely because the economic benefits go elsewhere, I would say that it has been this arbitrary refusal of many New Englanders to recognize the legitimate needs and aspirations of other sections which has contributed to the neglect of, and even opposition to, the needs of our own region by the representatives of other areas. We cannot continue so narrow and destructive a position.[71]

Kennedy was breathing life into the lecture he had delivered to Choate's history class seven years earlier.* In fairness to New England's other senators, it should be noted that Kennedy's decision to vote for the project was in part motivated by the realization that Canada would build the Seaway even if the United States did not participate. But this fact in no way made Kennedy's vote any more comprehensible to the Massachusetts voters, people whose eagerness to protect their economic interests generally outweighed any desire for international cooperation.

This same independence of thought emerged again when the French faltered in their struggle to maintain a colonial hold on Vietnam. When

---

*After Kennedy finished this speech, Senator Herbert Lehman of New York rose on the Senate floor and said, "I was very glad indeed to hear the Senator from Massachusetts say that we had passed the stage where we could consider these matters in a provincial or parochial manner and that, as Senators and as Representatives of the people of the United States, we were bound by the responsibility imposed upon us to consider these matters from a national standpoint." 100 *Congressional Record* 241 (1954). Later, Senator George Aiken of Vermont commented that Kennedy's vote for the Saint Lawrence Seaway project "was the first time I realized that he had a great deal of courage, because he was voting against the desires of influential people in his own community and his own state." Interview with George Aiken, Oral History Project, John F. Kennedy Library, pp. 4–5.

World War II ended, the French returned to occupy what was then called Indochina (and which included Vietnam). The ostensible understanding of the Allied leaders was that French occupation would be only temporary and that French efforts would be geared toward preparing Indochina for independence. In furtherance of this end, the French made several promises of independence to Ho Chi Minh, the acknowledged leader of the Vietnamese nationalist forces. Within a short time, these promises of independence were shown to be illusory. Ho then initiated a wide network of guerrilla activities to rid Vietnam of the French colonials. The French knew little about defending against guerrilla warfare in Asia, and it showed. Within a few years, the French found their defenses crumbling and their control of the countryside growing progressively weaker. French public support for the Indochina war was also crumbling, and the French realized that their hold on Indochina would disintegrate completely without outside help. In 1954, the French pressed the United States for military assistance to aid them in their battle with the Vietnamese guerrillas, and spokesmen for the Eisenhower Administration indicated that an affirmative response might be forthcoming.

The eagerness of many administration officials to provide the French with military assistance in Indochina is not surprising. American opinion greatly feared these nationalist movements because they were viewed as part of a monolithic international communist conspiracy to destroy democracy. Moreover, there seemed to be external evidence to justify these public fears. After all, hadn't McCarthy shown on television (his investigations having been televised) that the fingers of this communist conspiracy had already reached into American government? The fears of the public were largely shared by John Foster Dulles, Eisenhower's secretary of state and the principal architect of Eisenhower's foreign policy. He urged Eisenhower to let the United States support the French not only with money and equipment but with American troops as well (ultimately Eisenhower vetoed the use of American troops in Indochina, although he did permit the dispatch of a few hundred American "advisers" to Indochina).

John Kennedy was not one to dismiss casually fears of communism. Indeed, as I will show, it was a major preoccupation of his during his congressional years. Nonetheless, Kennedy seriously questioned the wisdom of providing American assistance to the French in their struggle with the Vietnamese guerrillas. He had made two trips to Indochina, one as a congressman in 1951 and one as a senator in 1953. While there, he had sought out reporters, like the *New York Herald Tribune*'s Homer Bigart, and indigenous leaders to learn the bitter facts that the French briefing officers might wish to conceal from a visiting American congressman. Kennedy came away convinced that the

French effort was doomed to failure, principally because the guerrillas commanded wide support among the people, whereas the French-installed government enjoyed little popular support. So when it seemed that the Eisenhower Administration, with broad support from the American people, might grant the French request for assistance, Kennedy felt obliged to speak against it.

"The time has come for the American people to be told the truth about Indochina," he declared in a speech on the Senate floor on April 6, 1954. The fact was, Kennedy said, that the French had virtually no support among the Vietnamese people and that, in these circumstances, any prognosis of a quick victory—even with American assistance—rested on false expectations.* "I am frankly of the belief," Kennedy continued, "that no amount of American military assistance in Indochina can conquer an enemy which is everywhere and at the same time nowhere, 'an enemy of the people' which has the sympathy and covert support of the people."[72] Notwithstanding these observations, Kennedy was not suggesting that either France or the United States abandon the war against communism. Quite the contrary. Kennedy concluded that the critical struggle against communism could be won only when the West renounced once and for all the colonial designs of past years and enlisted the efforts of the *independent* peoples of Indochina. Kennedy's independence of thought here, therefore, was evidenced not only by his opposition to the French colonials in Indochina, but also by his rejection of the conventional wisdom that the cherished victory over communism could be brought closer if the United States granted France's request for military assistance. (Prior to this speech, Kennedy told Edmund A. Gullion, a young foreign service officer whom he had met in Indochina, that this position "is going to cost me some votes with my French Catholic constituents, but it seems like the right thing to do."[73])

Kennedy's independence of thought on the Indochina question inspired him in 1957 to scrutinize the French colonial policies in Algeria. This North African colony was home for one million French people and for nine million Moslems. In 1954, violence erupted there as the National Liberation Front, a nationalist group, initiated a campaign to win independence for Algeria. As in Indochina, the result was

*In June 1952, Secretary of State Dean Acheson offered this optimistic commentary on the French efforts to defeat the Vietnamese guerrillas: "The military situation appears to be developing favorably. . . . Aggression has been checked and recent indications warrant the view that the tide is now moving in our favor. . . . We can anticipate continued favorable developments." Quoted in 100 *Congressional Record* 4672 (1954). If the name is changed to Rusk and the date to any time between 1965 and 1968, this sounded very much like the predictions of quick victory for America in the Vietnam War.

an intricate network of guerrilla activities which the French army found difficult to suppress. A steady stream of French soldiers flowed into the colony until the numbers approached a half million. The fighting was brutal, and reports of torture as well as destruction were widespread. As the fighting dragged on, the French public became very disgruntled with the policies of their government, the Fourth Republic. With their government tottering on the brink of collapse, most French officials were, to say the least, extremely sensitive to any foreign discussion of or involvement in the quandary. Nevertheless, feeling that the French were trying to bury a problem which was beginning to have international repercussions, Kennedy decided to raise the issue in a speech on the Senate floor on July 2, 1957.

Kennedy initially observed that the French policy in Algeria was bankrupt: it was depleting France's resources without bringing stability or independence to Algeria. Nor could the United States, he believed, stand idly by while the French used American weapons to perpetuate this bankrupt policy and, at the same time, jeopardize the goodwill of France as well as of the United States in Africa and in other continents where colonized peoples struggled to gain their independence. Moreover, said Kennedy, this goodwill would not be restored by conceiving new economic and social reforms for Algeria. "We must accept the lesson of all nationalist movements," Kennedy stated, "that economic and social reform, even if honestly sponsored and efficiently administered, do not solve or satisfy the quest for freedom."[74] He then offered a resolution which urged the Eisenhower Administration to assist the parties in resolving the bitter conflict, concluding with an eloquent appeal to the ideal of freedom for all peoples.

The speech quickly drew fire from all quarters. Eisenhower publicly criticized it, as did Secretary of State John Foster Dulles. Dean Acheson, the Democratic stalwart of the foreign policy establishment, also castigated Kennedy for trying to impose his views on American foreign policy. Even the liberal press was critical. In a sharp rebuttal to Kennedy's view, the *New York Times* editorialized,

> Senator Kennedy has probably added fuel to a raging fire with his speech and resolution yesterday suggesting that the United States use its good offices to solve the Algerian problem. It took courage—perhaps rashness—to present a case so critical of French policies. As a Democrat and a Senator he is certainly entitled to criticize our own Administration's policies on this issue, but considering the sensitivity, jealousy and distrust the French have shown of our motives, an intervention of this type is at the very least risky.[75]

Despite this criticism, Kennedy held fast and affirmed his position in another speech on the Senate floor on July 8, 1957. One may disagree with the merits of Kennedy's view—although I, for one, believe that his position was not only morally sound but also the position best able to serve American and French interests.* Whatever one's view of Kennedy's position, however, there is no denying the fact that the speech was a clear (and much publicized) example of the independence Kennedy had shown earlier and would show again in the Congress and later in the presidency.

While much of Kennedy's independence had its psychological roots in his family relationships and other experiences, this independence also seemed to reflect Kennedy's attitude toward the role of the individual in history. While he realized that even the most determined individuals could not be effective leaders without a degree of favor from their followers and events, he deeply respected the ability of single individuals to control their own fortunes and, indeed, to alter history. Sensitive to the inevitable need for change in society, Kennedy recognized that meaningful innovation depended very much on the depth of a leader's insight, on the steadfastness of his purpose. This historical perspective probably found its seed in the days of his childhood when Kennedy's mother would constantly encourage him to read about the great men in history. Jacqueline Kennedy once said of her husband, "You must think of him as this little boy, sick so much of the time, reading in bed, reading history, reading the Knights of the Round Table, reading Marlborough. For Jack, history was full of heroes. . . . Jack had this hero idea of history, the idealistic approach."[76] No doubt this was more the reverie of a wife than the analysis of an historian, but it contained a kernel of truth. For Kennedy very much appreciated the impact which individual leaders could have on their futures as well as on their environments.

If John Kennedy respected the role of leaders in history, then he primarily admired their virtue of courage. Ever mindful of his father's singular and successful efforts to achieve the fortune and power denied to many other descendants of Irish immigrants, Kennedy was attracted to the man who demonstrated an ability to buck the tide for the chance of attaining high goals (turning the tide of history would be one of the themes of Kennedy's first State of the Union Message). Thus, in *Why England Slept*, he praised the courageous stance of Winston Churchill in urging his country to rearm; and he studied political mettle in his second book, *Profiles in Courage.*

---

*In fact, the French Fourth Republic did collapse, and Charles de Gaulle was elected President of France in 1958. Shortly after his election, de Gaulle adopted a policy of conciliation designed to resolve the Algerian issue. In 1962, Algerians were offered a chance to determine their own destiny and chose independence.

This book, written in 1954 while Kennedy was recuperating from a back operation, describes the courage illustrated by ten senators whose positions had few, if any, political supporters. Kennedy studied these men because he was impressed by their toughness, and he believed much could be learned by recounting their experiences. That all of these senators suffered in unpopular positions is not to depict courage merely as tenacity in the face of defeat. Rather, Kennedy tried to show that, for politicians, maintaining commitments despite the disfavor of their public or of their colleagues is a most difficult task. Asserting the national interest before their regional ties revealed the depth of these senators' convictions, the quality of their characters. To Kennedy, this kind of courageous leadership was ultimately a foundation of responsible government.

But if Kennedy appreciated courage in political leaders, it was not an absolute ideal removed from reality. He understood the diverse and conflicting pressures of American politics which often militate against displays of courage. Indeed, Kennedy saw politics as "the fine art of conciliating, balancing, and interpreting the forces and factions of public opinion, an art essential to keeping our nation united and enabling our Government to function."[77] The need for compromise, however, did not entail a complete abandonment of principles. For *Profiles in Courage* concludes with a moral exhortation: "a man does what he must—in spite of personal consequences, in spite of obstacles and dangers and pressures—and that is the basis of all human morality."[78] These were words Kennedy would sometimes remember and, especially with respect to civil rights and Vietnam, would sometimes forget when he exercised presidential powers. But above all else, these were the words of a man who saw independence as a proper hallmark of a public official's approach in fulfilling his obligations.

This same concern for independent thinking was evident during the 1960 presidential campaign. Kennedy's remarks with respect to economic matters provide perhaps the most appropriate examples. As Eisenhower's tenure was drawing to a close, the country was enduring another recession—its third in eight years. Economic growth had slowed down to less than 3 percent—a growth rate lower than those of Western European nations and the Soviet Union—and unemployment was approaching 7 percent of the labor force. It was not a happy time for many people, but it certainly did provide a ripe issue for the Democratic presidential nominee. And Kennedy exploited it to the hilt.

He continually spoke of the major responsibility the federal government should assume in combating the nation's economic problems. At one point he identified that task as "the central domestic responsibility of the next administration . . . "[79] And later at the University of Wisconsin's fieldhouse in Madison, he said he would consider economic stagnation "to be the No. 1 domestic problem which the next President of the United States will have to meet. He will have to use monetary and fiscal tools far more effectively, far more vigorously, than the present administration has been willing to do."[80] And in Kennedy's eyes, this included a willingness to experiment with new ideas and new programs; he repeatedly emphasized that the government should not be afraid to act independently of the past in trying to solve the problems of the present. This was, in fact, one of the bases upon which Kennedy tried to distinguish himself from the Republican nominee, who he claimed was tied to the tired rhetoric and effete programs of the Eisenhower Administration. Indeed, Kennedy told a business group in New York City that it should prefer his candidacy since a Democratic administration "would maintain greater flexibility" in using fiscal and monetary policies to deal with economic issues.[81]

All this was not said in a vacuum. In stressing the high priority to be given to economic matters, Kennedy made it clear that the government's efforts should be designed ultimately to alleviate the desperate economic plight of millions of Americans. "The United States in the 1960's will be meeting its great times of challenge, and also its great time of opportunity," Kennedy declared in Ohio as the campaign was nearing an end. ". . . We are going to have to build a better life for our people. As long as there are 15 million American homes which are substandard, as long as there are millions of Americans who are not even paid a dollar an hour, as long as there are hundreds of thousands of Americans out of work, living on an average unemployment compensation check of $31 a week—what do they do when they go out of a job? Where do they go to work? How do they keep their families? How do they pay their rent? These are the problems that disturb America."[82] Kennedy's preoccupation with economic problems, in short, revealed not only his faith in independent thinking; that preoccupation also reflected a second theme which dominated his actions and statements as a member of Congress: a belief that the federal government has a broad responsibility to help those trapped in almost any kind of misfortune. Not that Kennedy was a soft touch for anyone with a social cause or a bad break. There were many kinds of misfortune to which he was largely insensitive. He felt no need, for example, to press the case of those men and women whose careers were destroyed ruthlessly by McCarthy's Senate investigations. And although the economic viability of many farms, particularly small ones, was threatened by the industrialization and high productivity of the land in the postwar years, Kennedy did not support parity price supports in his early congressional years (a position he would reverse in his Senate years when he remembered that farmers also vote in presidential elections). Many would later claim that Kennedy's failure to appreciate the misfortune in these and other cases showed how detached he was from the anxieties and miseries experienced daily by so many people. There is some truth to that. There were simply many kinds of despair and misfortune with which he could not identify easily. In a 1959 speech in South Dakota, for instance, he admitted quite candidly that he really knew little about the problems of the country's farmers.

But if Kennedy sometimes seemed detached from the suffering around him, it was not because he lacked any compassion. To begin with, he always felt the tug of his parents' teaching that public service of some kind was an obligation of those privileged by good fortune, that it was necessary to remember how desperate life was for so many. In addition to this teaching, Kennedy's ability to identify with those who suffered was broadened by the hardships and tragedies which he experienced. His older brother died in the war, and his sister Kathleen died in a plane crash in France shortly afterward. Another sister was mentally retarded and had been committed to a mental institution. He had moreover witnessed the horrors of war, in Europe as a student and in the Pacific Theatre as a lieutenant in the navy. And throughout his adult life Kennedy suffered health deficiencies and injuries. In 1954 and 1955 he underwent serious back operations to correct the college football injuries that had been aggravated by his navy experience. In fact, his condition was so serious after the operation in 1955 that he was given the last rites of the Catholic Church. These events no doubt had a tremendous effect on Kennedy. Claude Pepper, who served in Congress under Roosevelt and Kennedy, once related to me his belief that "much in the same way that polio mellowed Franklin Roosevelt, Kennedy's physical pain deepened his compassion."* But however deep this compassion, Kennedy was not one generally to show it by speaking or acting in emotional terms. Sorensen said that this was because Kennedy felt so deeply about certain things. Perhaps. Whatever the explanation, there seems no question but that Kennedy was uncomfortable with overt displays of emotion.

Kennedy's reluctance to show his own emotions did not prevent him from sensing the obligation of a government to help those of its citizens who were victimized by circumstances or their fellowmen. One of the principal preoccupations of Kennedy's first years as a congressman, for instance, was federal subsidies for housing. Kennedy's concern here was understandable. Between 1946 and 1950, there was a marked shortage of adequate housing. In part, this shortage reflected the fact

---

*Pepper also recalled a trip Kennedy made to Florida in November 1963 when Kennedy told Pepper the terrible revulsion he had felt after shooting a deer on Lyndon Johnson's Texas ranch and how he could never do that again. I'm not sure this is indicative of Kennedy's compassion for his fellowman, but it must be indicative of something.

that during the early 1940's much of the nation's industrial resources had been invested in the war effort. As millions of veterans returned from overseas in 1946, the shortage approached crisis proportions. In response to this situation, Congress established a scheme of rent controls to be enforced by local governments. While the rent controls harnessed some of the greed of the landlord, they did little to build needed housing. In this setting, Kennedy believed the federal government was obligated to fill the void. In numerous floor speeches, laden with statistics and references to studies (a trademark of major Kennedy speeches), he urged his colleagues to do more than permit locally supervised rent controls, particularly since local governments did not always enforce the controls fairly. What was needed, Kennedy stated, was a national housing program that would afford veterans and others the opportunity to have decent homes. [83]

Kennedy's concern that Americans have access to the daily necessities of life also helped explain the considerable attention he gave throughout his congressional career to labor practices. In general, this attention seemed to flow from a belief that people should have an opportunity to earn a good wage, free from exploitation or discrimination, whether by the government, the employer, or even the unions. Thus, Kennedy spoke against the 1947 Taft-Hartley Act (vehemently opposed by organized labor because it limited a union's right to strike) because he thought it made "the Government a vital, inept and prejudicial participant in labor-management relations throughout the country."[84] But Kennedy's concern with labor practices was not confined to the federal government's involvement. In 1951 and again in 1957 he introduced (but did not really push) bills to eliminate discrimination against women in employment, and in 1953 he introduced (and again did not really push) a bill to prohibit racial discrimination in employment.[85] In 1953, he made a major floor speech urging an increase in the minimum wage for the nation's workers.[86] And in 1957 he accepted a position on Senator McClellan's Labor Rackets Committee, a committee which was to investigate abusive labor union practices.* From his extended service on this committee, Kennedy fashioned a bill to help correct many of the union abuses and frauds exposed during the committee's hearings and investigations. Surprisingly enough, organized labor's opposition to the bill was not that great. For this rea-

*A couple of Democratic senators with presidential ambitions refused to serve on this committee for fear that it would alienate the union leadership, a treasured friend in any Democrat's presidential campaign. At first, these fears may have seemed well based. Kennedy's participation on the committee soon led AFL-CIO President George Meany to exclaim of Kennedy, "God save us from our friends." In the end, however, labor enjoyed Kennedy's support on most matters.

son, the bill passed easily in the Senate in 1958 and was praised by the *New York Times* as a "triumph of moderation and a powerful blend of principle and political savvy." The bill died in the House, however, and Kennedy introduced it again in the next Congress. It again passed the Senate easily and again found resistance in the House. Kennedy chaired a joint Senate-House conference to iron out the differences, and while the conferees ultimately agreed on a bill (lavishly praised again by the *Times*), Kennedy did not want his name attached to the bill because many of the House-sponsored amendments antagonized the labor unions too much.

Many, if not most, of Kennedy's sympathies in domestic issues, of course, were based on political considerations. At least it seems more than coincidental that many of the issues which concerned Kennedy in his congressional years—housing, employment, fisheries, and water pollution—were issues of primary concern to his Massachusetts constituency.[87] Similarly, while he supported civil rights legislation, that support was often given in a *pro forma* fashion (especially in his early congressional years)—in part because the civil rights movement did not capture the public's sympathy until the late 1950s, and Kennedy had little knowledge or experience to help him understand the bitter plight of the nation's blacks. These domestic political considerations cannot so easily explain many of the international issues which concerned Kennedy.

There were, for example, few Latin Americans in Massachusetts' eleventh congressional district. Yet Kennedy seemed to show a real concern for the plight of America's neighbors to the south. In the late 1940s it was thought that every country needed a large defense arsenal to protect against the contagion of communism, and Latin-American countries were no exception. In the immediate postwar years, Congress appropriated considerable sums to augment the sagging defenses of Latin-American countries. No one could say that Kennedy was soft on communism, even in those early congressional years. But he saw little value in gouging Latin America with such defense programs. When a defense appropriations bill for South America came up for a vote when he was in the House, Kennedy often offered amendments to cut the appropriations drastically. "It does not seem to me that there is any use spending as large an amount of money on this military equipment to South American countries," Kennedy told his House colleagues when a $51 million military aid bill was debated in the spring of 1952. South American countries were not threatened by the Soviet Union, he said, and he believed that the money could be better spent by giving the South American countries technical assistance to help their starving populations.[88]

This concern for oppressed people in foreign lands was evidenced in other areas as well. Shortly after he reached the Senate, Kennedy voted for a resolution strongly condemning the Soviet Union's persecution of Jews, Greek Orthodox, and other minorities in that country.[89] He also cosponsored a Senate resolution condemning a revival of anti-Semitism in the Soviet Union and urging the United States to take action to alleviate concern for the future of Soviet Jews.[90] His concern for oppressed people also showed when he spoke of lands exploited by outside powers. His speeches on Indochina exemplify this concern. After his first trip to Indochina in 1951, for instance, Kennedy often spoke of the implicit racism in the Western powers' policies. "We are a white race," he once remarked to a Massachusetts group, "and it is against the white race that all of these peoples have had to make their fights for independence."[91] A few years later he commented that it would be difficult for the United States to assist the people of Indochina because of their hatred for "the white man who bled them, beat them, exploited them, and ruled them."[92] Whatever else one may say of these observations, they suggested a sensitivity to people less fortunate than most Americans.

A like concern was evident when Kennedy spoke of the people in Eastern Europe, people whose countries were, for all practical purposes, ruled by the Soviet Union, people living behind what Winston Churchill once described as "the iron curtain." In the 1950s Kennedy supported the Eisenhower Administration's "Liberation Policy"—a calculated response to the political suppression in Eastern Europe. Its commitment to the principle of self-determination made the policy particularly consistent with Kennedy's earlier statements on colonialism. In 1956, however, the "Liberation Policy" proved impotent as Soviet tanks snuffed out the Hungarian revolution against the Soviet-controlled regime. There were, to be sure, many political considerations to rationalize the Administration's frozen reaction; but by the same token, as Kennedy mused, "one needs little imagination to appreciate the feeling of frustration which overcame the people of Eastern Europe to hear that the United States had never meant the obvious implications of its 'Liberation Policy.'"[93]

As Kennedy approached his 1960 presidential campaign, he devoted more and more attention to the neglect of the oppressed in the United States and throughout the world. Not that he wallowed in emotional tales of human misery. He was not one to get maudlin or sentimental about these things. But he did express his belief that a country as rich as the United States owed something to the less fortunate. As he campaigned across the country in 1960, he criticized the electorate's lack of sensitivity to the problems of their fellow citizens, their willingness to turn a blind eye where the civil rights of their fellow citizens or the hunger of other peoples was concerned. He exhorted people to join in an effort to solve these problems of their fellowman (most Democratic presidential nominees talk about "joining an effort" to do something), and he found that this theme struck a responsive chord in the large crowds which thronged to see him. The theme probably reached its acme when Kennedy gave a nationally broadcast address from Philadelphia in the closing days of the 1960 campaign. Uppermost in his mind on this day was a recent statement by Eisenhower that the electorate should reject those (meaning Kennedy) who downgraded America and said that its government had ignored the needs of the people. The real enemy, said Eisenhower, was the Soviet Union with its lack of compassion for the millions of people imprisoned behind the Iron Curtain.

This criticism incensed Kennedy, and he responded that Americans could not fight for freedom abroad if they were insensitive to the plight of those at home:

> If we lack compassion for those who are sick and poor or aged here at home, we cannot convincingly show such compassion abroad. We cannot identify ourselves with the hundreds of millions of people to the south of us who fight not only Communism but also misery, ignorance, starvation, disease.
>
> If human rights and human dignity are not shared by every American, regardless of his race or his color, then those in other lands of other creeds and colors, and they are in the majority, will treat our claims of a great democracy with suspicion and indifference.
>
> If we demonstrate no vitality here in the United States, no leadership in our own country, no imagination in meeting our problems here at home, if great quantities of our food, for example, rot while the world goes hungry, if our people are complacent and self-satisfied, content with things as they soon will be, then our prestige and our influence and our contribution to the cause of freedom will surely continue to decline.[94]

Much of this, of course, was the hyperbole that all campaigns produce. Nor was there much indication as to how Kennedy expected the ordinary citizen to show his compassion for those at home and abroad—except, perhaps, by voting for him for president. But to some extent these words did reflect a genuine concern which Kennedy had for those touched by misfortune.

Kennedy's compassion for the less fortunate did not entirely dominate his political concerns during his congressional years. It was not even first on his priority list. That honor belonged to another political interest, one which involved the third basic theme of Kennedy's actions and statements as a member of Congress: a belief that the federal government should undertake whatever steps were necessary to protect against communism in the United States and abroad.

In *Why England Slept*, Kennedy had examined the passivity of the world's two largest democracies in responding to the growing dangers of Hitler's Third Reich. When Kennedy entered Congress in 1946, the threat of Nazism had been removed only to be replaced by a fear which many American and British leaders had of the Soviet Union. From the very beginning of his congressional career, Kennedy was among those who saw dangers in Soviet intentions. In his eyes, there was little difference between the expansionistic totalitarianism of Hitler and Stalin. So, from his first days as a Massachusetts representative, Kennedy offered ardent support to almost any program or policy which was designed to educate the public about or protect the public from what he saw as a monolithic, international communist conspiracy to destroy democracy, and with it the United States. He voted to give the House Un-American Activities Committee the funds it wished to investigate the existence of communist members and sympathizers in the United States.[95] He supported legislation that would prevent an employer or employee from seeking relief at the National Labor Relations Board unless he first signed an anticommunist affidavit (otherwise a federal agency might be in the "awkward" position of assisting a communist worker or group).[96] And after the communist takeover of China in 1949, he offered a bill to prohibit American assistance to any country that exported strategic war materials to China.[97]

Kennedy's concern with communism continued unabated after he entered the Senate in 1953 and even after the Senate's censure of Joe McCarthy in 1954. Everywhere he looked, he continued to see the dangers of communism. For this reason, Kennedy cosponsored a Senate resolution, adopted shortly after McCarthy's censure, which reaffirmed the need for a vigorous and diligent investigation of communist subversion. Kennedy likewise thought the United States should take affirmative action in the international arena to shield against the advance of communism. He therefore believed the United States' role should be greater than that of a "volunteer fire department," rushing in to douse the fires of communist aggression wherever they broke out. (Remember that, in *Why England Slept*, Kennedy spoke of the need for democracies to have a guard who would not fall asleep at the switch, who would do more than wake everyone up when the house was burning down.) In a speech before the Conference of the American Friends of Vietnam in June 1956, Kennedy pursued this comparison of the United States with a volunteer fire department. In that speech, he argued that the effectiveness of American foreign policy was weakened by

> the overemphasis upon our role as "volunteer fire department" for the world. Whenever and wherever fire breaks out—in Indochina, in the Middle East, in Guatemala, in Cyprus, in the Formosan Straits—our firemen rush in, wheeling up all their heavy equipment, and resorting to every known method of containing and extinguishing the blaze. The crowd gathers—the usually successful efforts of our able volunteers are heartily applauded—and then the firemen rush off to the next conflagration, leaving the grateful but still stunned inhabitants to clean up the rubble, pick up the pieces, and rebuild their homes with whatever resources are available.
>
> The role, to be sure, is a necessary one; but it is not the only role to be played, and the others cannot be ignored. A volunteer fire department halts, but rarely prevents, fires. It repels but rarely rebuilds; it meets the problems of the present but not of the future.[98]

However deeply Kennedy believed in preventive medicine as the best response to the communist conspiracy he saw, his faith in the American "volunteer fire department" remained intact. He seemed to feel that communist aggression almost anywhere in the world could have a direct bearing on the security of the United States. For he believed that communist successes would feed upon themselves until, convinced that democratic forces were unwilling or unprepared to offer an adequate defense, the communists would engage the United States directly in mortal combat. This was, in effect, the domino theory first articulated by Eisenhower when trying to explain the need for the numerous defense pacts Dulles negotiated with countries throughout the world.

Kennedy's view of the communist menace had a direct bearing on how he interpreted presidential powers and on the concept he would have of his own presidency. The juncture of Kennedy's views on communism and the American presidency was made clear in an exchange he had with Senator Wayne Morse on the Senate floor on March 1, 1957. Congress was then considering a resolution, sponsored by the Eisenhower Administration, that would authorize the President to undertake whatever steps he thought necessary—including the dispatch of American troops—to defend against communist aggression in the Middle East. Although he was very "dissatisfied" with the ambiguous wording of the resolution, Kennedy informed his colleagues that he would vote for it anyway. As Kennedy explained it, he thought his dissatisfaction with the resolution was far outweighed by the need to impress the communists, especially the Soviet Union, with America's willingness to fight for democracy. Moreover, said Kennedy, the resolution did not in any way expand the existing powers of the President, and this, too, justified his decision to vote for it.

A dialogue then ensued between Kennedy and Morse. This dialogue is particularly illuminating—not only in exposing Kennedy's views on presidential powers, but also in showing that Morse was far more sensitive to the dynamics of presidential politics than Kennedy. For the concerns echoed by Morse here are the same prophetic concerns he would raise when another President exhorted the Congress to adopt the Gulf of Tonkin Resolution in 1964, a measure which gave the President similar authorization to combat communist aggression in Southeast Asia. Because the dialogue between Kennedy and Morse is so revealing, I believe large portions of it deserve to be quoted in full:

> MR. KENNEDY: The President of the United States, if he felt the national interest were at stake, could take the United States into war without consent of the Congress, although he would subsequently be obliged to come to the Congress for approval. But there is nothing that lessens the authority of the President to use United States forces if he thinks the best interests of the United States are at stake.
>
> MR. MORSE: I think the Senator is as dead wrong as he can be, because what will happen under the resolution will be that we will give the President predated authority, when what we ought to say to him is, "You will have to tell us what the facts are which, in your opinion, justify the sending of American boys into the Middle East. Then, under Article I, section 8 of the Constitution, Congress will decide whether you shall send them there. If you have already done so, because you thought there was a great emergency that could not await a report to Congress then Congress will decide whether you should bring those boys back."
>
> But I am not going to vote to give the President any power to make war in the Middle East by a predated declaration of war.
>
> MR. KENNEDY: How does the power granted in the resolution hinder the President's power to declare war or, as Commander in Chief, to protect the security of the Nation?
>
> MR. MORSE: I think the Senator from Massachusetts knows very well that after Congress gives the President the power, it is not likely to take it away from him. The Senate cannot escape the fact that once this predated approval is given to any President no Congress is likely to renege on it. What we ought to do is to prevent Congress from getting into such a position that it can be said, "after all, Congress gave the President advance authority and now it is not fair after a President has relied upon it to attempt to take it

away." I am against giving the President any advance authority to send boys into war in the Middle East prior to a declaration of war by Congress.

MR. KENNEDY: Where in the resolution as it is presently drawn is there any provision for advance authority? Where in the resolution is there a provision for a predated declaration of war? Will the Senator read the language?

MR. MORSE: Yes. . . . The language used in the [resolution] does not in any way change the fact that Congress will be authorizing the President of the United States, by a predated grant of authority, to commit an act of war. We will be giving tacit approval to the President in advance to send American boys in the Middle East. I do not propose to vote for any resolution which contains any language that could be subject to such an interpretation by any President. If the Senator will just read the resolution as modified by the committee he will see that the language still permits the President to commit an act of war with the tacit advance approval of Congress.*

On its face, this dialogue seems to expose Kennedy as a man determined to use any means to squelch the threat of communism. In part, of course, that was true. During the presidential campaign, he left no doubt that the president possessed broad powers to deal with communism and other international matters. In one of his first press conferences after announcing his candidacy for president, Kennedy stated plainly that the American chief executive has the power "to place us in war . . . without the consent of Congress."[99]

Kennedy's view of the matter was not entirely autocratic. He understood that public support—or at least public acquiescence— was critical to the sustenance of any American foreign policy. In his later Senate years, he therefore devoted considerable attention to communicating information to the public about the dangers of communism. In August 1957, for example, he introduced a bill which would authorize the compilation and distribution of "educational materials" concerning communism. And in numerous speeches he voiced concern about the American public's complacency in responding to communist aggression. This concern was perhaps exemplified by a Senate speech Ken-

*103 *Congressional Record* 2877–81. (1957). The resolution was finally adopted by Congress on March 5, 1957. In 1958, Eisenhower invoked the resolution as authority to dispatch American troops to help suppress an insurrection in Lebanon. This move was so widely criticized in domestic and international circles that Eisenhower withdrew the troops after a short time and never again invoked the resolution to send American troops anywhere.

nedy gave in 1958 in which he lectured his colleagues about the need for military preparedness (he would later develop this theme in his presidential campaign, arguing that the United States had fallen behind in a "missile gap" with the Soviet Union, a possibility which disturbed many Americans). In this speech, Kennedy referred repeatedly to England's experience in the 1930s, arguing that the United States should accelerate its defense programs lest the United States experience a fate similar to England's. Immediately after the speech, the following exchange occurred on the Senate floor:

> MR. SYMINGTON: Would my able friend from Massachusetts agree that the situation which the United States faces in the late 1950's may have considerable comparability with the situation faced by the British in the late 1930's?
>
> MR. KENNEDY: The Senator is completely correct. . . . During an 8-year period in a 10-year period we have found the balance of power shifting against us.
>
> I think the image is too close for our own security. We do not have a strong neighbor across the Atlantic, as the British did in their moment of peril. We are the backbone, and the buck cannot be passed any further than us. That is why I feel that inasmuch as the United States is the great hope of the Free World, we should not permit the balance of power to shift against us, which would not only have the effect of tempting the Soviet Union to initiate an all-out attack, but would also affect the position of our diplomacy, the security of our bases, and other things.*

Tempting the Soviet Union with weakness. Another Munich—but this time for America. America's lack of toughness in Berlin, in Latin America, or Vietnam. These were fears that were to dominate Kennedy's views on foreign policy until a few months before his death. Firmness above all else. Toughness with your adversary—it was a belief, maybe an obsession, that would lead Kennedy, as President, to risk nuclear confrontation with the Soviet Union in Cuba, to sacrifice American lives in support of a corrupt government in Vietnam, and to build a conventional defense arsenal that no successor President would dare dismantle.

As Kennedy campaigned for the presidency in 1960, there was much to support his view of the principal challenge to which American for-

---

*See 104 *Congressional Record* 17569–75 (1958). In a speech at the University of Rochester in 1959, Kennedy echoed this same theme. Believing that the American public had developed a "Maginot Line" mentality with respect to the dangers of communism, Kennedy urged his audience to discard their complacency.

eign policy would have to respond. Numerous public officials and periodicals were continually warning about the dangers of the international communist conspiracy spearheaded by the Soviet Union.[100] The cards were stacked against anyone who counseled moderation, who tried to show that the Soviet Union's aggressive rhetoric indicated that they were apprehensive about American intentions much in the same way that we were apprehensive about Soviet intentions and that our toughness only reinforced the basis for Soviet toughness. It was a constantly turning Ferris wheel that stopped spinning—or at least slowed down—only after the nuclear confrontation actually seemed imminent in Cuba in 1962.

But that's anticipating the analysis of later chapters. The point here is that John Kennedy soared toward the presidency on the wings of anticommunism, believing that his presidency would have a unique responsibility to do anything necessary—even wage war by executive fiat—to defeat the communist foe. With another president in the early 1960s, such a concept of the presidency might have had consequences far more disastrous than those which actually resulted. But Kennedy had a saving grace—if saving grace it be: his personal qualities and his other political concerns. For even when presidential responsibilities were thrust upon him, Kennedy remained willing—within certain limits—to approach problems in an unstructured manner, not always concerned with how his responses might square with any ideology or any previous position he had taken in Congress or in the 1960 campaign. He was, in a word, far less prone to take himself or his causes seriously than were the public or those who worked with him. This trait, coupled with his belief that he had an obligation to help oppressed peoples in other lands, would lead him eventually to ask tough questions and demand hard answers about this anticommunist crusade and the destruction wrought in its wake.

But through it all, he never doubted his power or his responsibility as President to do what he thought necessary for the country's interests. In his first major address after announcing his presidential candidacy, Kennedy laid bare his concept of the presidency. It was one which placed him in direct contrast with Eisenhower, Hoover, and Taft. "Whatever the political affiliation of our next President," Kennedy told the National Press Club, ". . . he must above all be a Chief Executive in every sense of the word. He must be prepared to exercise the fullest powers of his office—all that are specified and some that are not." To meet this responsibility, Kennedy added, the president could not be a passive broker trying to preserve the status quo. "We will need instead," he said, "what the Constitution envisioned: a Chief Executive who is the vital center of action in our whole scheme of government." Moreover, Kennedy argued, "the White House is not only the center of political leadership. It must be the center of moral leadership—a 'bully pulpit,' as Theodore Roosevelt described it. For only the President represents the national interest. And upon him alone converge all the needs and aspirations of all parts of the country, all departments of the Government, all nations of the world."[101]

Kennedy did not deviate from these principles as he ran around the country seeking electoral support. Everywhere he went he stressed the vital role which the President should play in public affairs. "I run for the Presidency," he intoned in the New York Coliseum two days before the November election, "because the Presidency is the center of action in a free society and because it is up to the President to set before the American people the unfinished business of our society."[102] It was, in a word, the promise of daring leadership. In time, Kennedy would wonder, as would many of his supporters, if he had not promised too much.

The Concept in Action

Kennedy's ideals of presidential leadership thus offered the promise that broad responsibility would be the guideline for action, that confidence in his abilities and faith in the office would be a continuing source of innovation and progress. It was enough to stir the heart of any optimist, and indeed many people were excited as the day of Kennedy's inauguration approached. The expectant mood in Washington was aptly captured by Arthur Krock in the *New York Times* a week before the inaugural ceremonies. "The air of excitement over the coming Presidential succession that already pervades this capital city," Krock wrote, "has a quality which brings reminders of 1933. . . . Not since the same day drew near in 1933 has this community, inured to change, throbbed with the same sense of lively anticipation of things to come."[103] Things were going to get moving again, problems were going to be solved, the tide of communism turned back. It was all part of that "can-do" spirit which exuded from Kennedy's presidential campaign.

Kennedy's political career and presidential campaigning assured the public that much of this presidential dynamism would be concentrated in two basic areas: having the federal government try to help those trapped by misfortune, and having the federal government undertake whatever measures he deemed necessary to protect against communism at home and abroad. And in whatever sphere he acted, there was the promise that President Kennedy's concept of the office would not embrace a commitment to any structured philosophy or creed of government; his view of the office suggested instead that he would try to approach specific problems in the most rational manner, almost without regard to how that approach would square with conventional wisdoms and party labels.

To a large extent, Kennedy did maintain in the presidency a certain independence of thought and action. Logic, intelligence, cost-benefit analyses—these were the proper means to solve political problems. In the Kennedy White House one did not debate concepts or waste time trying to categorize a suggested solution as "liberal" or "conservative," whatever those labels meant. The people Kennedy chose as his closest advisers reflected this perspective. McGeorge Bundy, for example, a scion of an established Boston family and the dean of Harvard College, was a Republican, but he was bright, very bright. His capacity to analyze and solve problems was, within certain circles, legendary. Intellectual theories and political philosophies did not cloud his vision of the world's problems. Understandably, then, Kennedy felt confident in choosing Bundy as his adviser for national security affairs, a choice Kennedy never regretted.

The same was true of Robert S. McNamara, Kennedy's choice for secretary of defense. McNamara's great forte was statistics and cost-benefit analyses. As president of Ford Motor Company, he was largely responsible for Ford's outselling Chevrolet in 1957 and 1958—a truly remarkable feat in the auto industry—basically because he knew how to dissect a problem and solve it. Ford politics, to the extent it had politics, were Republican. No matter. McNamara was a problem-solver with confidence, determination, and sheer intelligence. In Kennedy's eyes it was an unbeatable combination, and within a short time McNamara's efficiency made him a Kennedy favorite. And so it went with almost all of the major appointments in Kennedy's Administration. Political debts—especially campaign debts—had to be paid, but to the extent he felt free to choose, Kennedy generally chose men who saw problems as challenges to be met in the best way possible, not as opportunities to serve a particular political philosophy.

The Kennedy penchant for solving problems as problems and not as pieces in a philosophical jigsaw puzzle did not ensure success in every area—a point which will become clear when I examine in the next chapter Kennedy's manner of making decisions. Nonetheless, Kennedy's independence of thought and action was evident in numerous dilemmas he wrestled with in the White House. The civil war in Laos provided an early and apt illustration.

On January 19, 1961, the President-elect met with the incumbent President in the White House. In that meeting, Eisenhower reviewed some of the critical problems Kennedy would inherit with the presidency. Eisenhower dwelt at length on the situation in Laos. A civil war was in full swing in that small Southeast Asian country. The communist guerrillas, the Pathet Lao, had showed considerable strength, and the pro-American forces, led by General Phoumi Nosavan, were offering little resistance. The situation had been complicated further by American intervention. The Eisenhower Administration saw Laos as another pawn in the Cold War struggle with the Soviet Union. Vast amounts of American money, equipment, and even some advisers had been poured into Laos in an effort to control the course of the war. And when Souvanna Phouma, the Laotian premier, showed signs in 1959 of discarding his pro-American posture for a policy of neutrality, the CIA conspired (successfully) to depose him and replace him with a leader more amenable to American views. But it was largely an exercise in futility. The situation was deteriorating fast, Eisenhower informed Kennedy, and something had to be done. Laos could not fall to the communists, because if it did, all of Southeast Asia would fall with it. "You might have to go in there and fight it out," Eisenhower was reported to have told Kennedy.[104] It was a somber meeting, and Kennedy quickly realized that being President was no joyride.

Kennedy, of course, was not one to disregard the communist menace in Laos or anywhere else. He had proven that in Congress and in the 1960 campaign. But he saw little value—and a great cost—in fighting a land war with communism in the jungles and plains of Laos. However, he was deeply concerned that an American withdrawal might not be well received by the American public or other nations. Eisenhower had already committed American resources and prestige to the Laotian struggle, and Kennedy felt he could not alter that commitment without some explanation other than the blunt truth—that it wasn't worth it. As he told Arthur Schlesinger, Jr., "We cannot and will not accept any visible humiliation over Laos."[105]

Nonetheless, in his first presidential press conference on January 25, 1961, Kennedy made it clear that he had no intention of using the United States as a "volunteer fire department" to douse the Laotian fires unless it was absolutely necessary:

> The United States is anxious that there be established in Laos a peaceful country—an independent country not dominated by either side but concerned with the life of the people within the country.
>
> . . . And the United States is using its influence to see if that independent country, peaceful country, uncommitted country, can be established under the present very difficult circumstances.[106]

An independent, uncommitted country—it seemed as though the anticommunist warrior was abandoning the crusade. Kennedy's posture is all the more interesting since Soviet Premier Khrushchev had announced in a speech on January 6, 1961—a speech carefully read by Kennedy—that the Soviet Union would encourage wars of national liberation like the one then raging in Laos. To Kennedy, the speech confirmed his fear that the deadly competition between democracy and communism would continue unabated after his inauguration, and he was not one to recoil from competition (although Kennedy later learned from his ambassador to Moscow, Llewellyn Thompson, that Khrushchev had no intention of involving the Soviet Union directly in the Laotian struggle. "Why take the risk?" Khrushchev asked Thompson. "It will fall into our lap like a rotten apple."[107]). As the weeks passed, the pro-American Laotian forces continued to falter, and Kennedy became even more convinced that a political settlement was the only rational solution to this problem. In his press conference of March 15, 1961, he reaffirmed his support for a "genuinely independent and neutral Laos."[108]

Meanwhile, the Laotian civil war was a hotly debated topic in the administration's inner circles. Advisers and cabinet heads considered whether ground would be lost in the Cold War struggle if the United States did not escalate the American military presence in Laos. The debate was complicated by the army's reluctance to get involved in Laos, although the army chiefs demanded that 250,000 troops be sent in if the United States should decide to jump in feet first. As the hostilities in Laos escalated, the debates likewise intensified, and Kennedy felt that he was being pushed toward an option he did not want to choose: full-fledged military participation by the United States. The pressure showed in his press conference of March 23, 1961, when Kennedy talked of having SEATO send in forces to halt continued communist aggression in Laos. Shades of the anticommunist crusade were returning, but not for long. Rationality was the key, and full-fledged American participation in the Laotian struggle, Kennedy was still convinced, was not rational.

In April 1961, he dispatched Averell Harriman to negotiate a political settlement in Geneva at a meeting of the International Control Commission, the multinational group which arranged a settlement of the French-Indochina War in 1954. Largely through Harriman's efforts, a cease-fire was negotiated in May 1961. Although the Laotian struggle would emerge every few months thereafter as a mini-crisis, Kennedy never wavered from his determination to resolve that conflict at the negotiating table instead of on the battlefield. "We must never face the President," Harriman told Winthrop Brown, the American ambassador to Laos, "with the choice of abandoning Laos or sending in troops. This is our job, to keep him from having to make that choice."[109] Eventually, an agreement—however untidy—was concluded in Geneva in July 1962 establishing a neutral government in Laos and removing that country from the American public's mind until Nixon escalated American military involvement in the renewed struggle in 1970.

Kennedy's response to the Laotian struggle is significant for two basic reasons. First, it showed that his responses to problems did not flow from any structured view of the world. Here was a man who believed in the Cold War, who saw the threat of communism in every war of national liberation, who had promised the electorate in 1960 that he would stand firm to the communists—and yet a man who, to a large extent, could temper those beliefs and promises when they were at odds with the rational answer to a problem.

Second, Kennedy's response to the Laotian war showed that, as when he served in Congress, he could be independent of public opinion where he believed national interests required it. From the beginning, the public was persuaded that the struggle in Laos was symptomatic of the communist conspiracy to destroy democracy. Yet here was their President, an avowed anticommunist fighter, informing them that the United States really had no battle to fight in Laos, or at least that the United States wanted no part of any fight in Laos. Such an attitude smacked of naïveté or weakness in the public's eye, and newspaper editorials and commentators did not hesitate to voice those conclusions. Even newspaper columnist Joseph Alsop, Kennedy's personal friend, minced no words in observing that Kennedy's attempt to negotiate a settlement in Laos was nothing less than defeatism. Kennedy no doubt had a hard time accepting such criticism from his friends, not to mention others. But American military involvement in the Laotian struggle had no reasonable basis, and nothing the pundits said convinced him otherwise.

Kennedy's independence did not always require him to buck the tide of public opinion. In some cases, his independence reflected his belief that the President had an affirmative obligation to serve certain interests which the public supported. Kennedy's involvement in the steel price controversy in 1962 is a case in point.

During the presidential campaign, Kennedy had made it clear that he thought the President should play a major role in trying to achieve price stability in the country even though he was under no constitutional or statutory obligation to do so. In October 1960, for example, he told a business group,

> . . . I believe that the next administration must work sympathetically and closely with labor and management to develop wage and price policies that are consistent with stability. We can no longer afford the large erratic movements in prices that jeopardize domestic price stability and our balance of payments abroad. Nor is there

a place for the kind of ad hoc last-minute intervention which settled the [1959] steel strike.

Without resorting to the compulsion of wage or price controls, the President of the United States must actively use the powers of leadership in pursuit of well-defined goals of price stability. For those powers—of reason, moral suasion, and informed public opinion, influencing public opinion—have by no means been exhausted to date.

True to his promise, Kennedy did try to exercise leadership to achieve price stability. One area in which he concentrated his efforts was the steel industry. After several months of meetings, hard work, and close supervision, the White House, with the able assistance of Labor secretary Arthur Goldberg, helped negotiate an informal wage-price settlement in early 1962 between the steel industry and the steelworkers. In essence, the agreement provided that the steel companies would not raise prices and the steelworkers would ask for only minimum wage increases in negotiating their next contracts (which were signed by the beginning of April). Since steel prices affected so much of America's industries, this agreement to hold the line on steel prices promised to check the inflationary movement of the economy. The settlement was a milestone for collective bargaining in the steel industry because all of the steel companies, including United States Steel (the largest), accepted the agreement without the incentive of international crisis or statutory price regulation (thus distinguishing the agreement from those made in the late 1940s and early 1950s).

On April 10, 1962, Roger Blough, chairman of the board of U.S. Steel, made an appointment to see Kennedy late in the afternoon. When he entered the Oval Office, Blough almost casually handed Kennedy a press release which announced that U.S. Steel, in direct contravention of the wage-price agreement, was planning to increase the price of its steel by $6 a ton—the increase to take effect that night. Kennedy was, to say the least, startled. Blough's action represented a negation of the steel industry's good faith in the wage-price negotiations. It was difficult to resist the conclusion that in those negotiations Blough had been, in a word, deceitful. Kennedy was in no mood to condone or accept Blough's action. Indeed, after Blough left, Kennedy exploded with anger. "My father once told me that all steel men were sons of bitches," he told his special counsel, Theodore C. Sorensen, "and I did not realize until now how right he was."[110] Reminiscing before a group of Harvard law students several years later, Goldberg recalled that Kennedy was angered not only because Blough had insulted him personally, but especially because the steel chairman's surprise move was a direct and gratuitous affront to the Office of the Presidency. If

Blough's action were not challenged, Kennedy believed it would erode the trust which the steelworkers had placed in the President and would also make it difficult to secure the trust of other labor organizations. As other steel companies followed U.S. Steel's action in raising prices, Kennedy's irritation heightened. "Are we supposed to sit there and take a cold, deliberate fucking?" he rhetorically asked *Newsweek*'s Benjamin Bradlee. "Is this the way the private enterprise system is really supposed to work? When U.S. Steel says 'Go,' the boys go? How could they all raise their prices almost to a penny within six hours of each other?"[111] At a press conference on April 11, Kennedy made it clear publicly how he felt:

> At a time when restraint and sacrifice are being asked of every citizen, the American people will find it hard, as I do, to accept a situation in which a tiny handful of steel executives, whose pursuit of private power and profit exceeds their sense of public responsibility, can show such utter contempt for the interests of 185 million Americans. . . . Some time ago I asked each American to consider what he would do for his country, and I asked the steel companies. In the last twenty-four hours we had their answer.[112]

Thus began what administration officials privately referred to as "the battle of Blough's run." Kennedy aides quickly prepared an agenda for action by administration officials. The measures proposed included a letter to a grand jury (presumably urging investigation of possible violations of price-fixing statutes), urging the FTC to conduct its own inquiry, delaying the issuance of a tax ruling allowing for greater depreciation by the steel companies, encouragement of congressional investigations and consideration of permanent legislation, and "encouragement of a proxy fight for new directors" (of the steel companies, presumably).[113] As reported by the press, Kennedy followed up on virtually all of these suggestions. (He personally telephoned Senator Estes Kefauver, chairman of the Senate Judiciary Subcommittee on Anti-Trust and Monopoly, at home at night and secured a commitment from Kefauver that his committee would initiate its own investigation of the matter.) McNamara also held a press conference at which he made clear that steel companies raising their prices would not get government contracts. The pressure exerted by the administration was considerable; the steel companies were beginning to feel the pinch, and it hurt. Eventually, Inland Steel, one of the major companies, promised Kennedy that it would not raise its prices. With that promise, the logjam was broken and the other companies began to have second thoughts about their precipitous action. Within seventy-two hours of Blough's announcement, all the steel companies rescinded the price increase, thereby keeping the wage-price settlement intact and allowing Kennedy to retain the trust which his office had originally secured in negotiating the settlement (although a year later Kennedy remained silent when U.S. Steel raised its prices on 75 percent of its products—he obviously did not want to appear to be *too* antisteel).

Kennedy's success here was achieved at some cost. Many rightly questioned the administration's tactics in pressuring the steel companies to rescind the price increases. Not that Kennedy did anything illegal or tried to serve goals unrelated to the public interest. It was simply that many of his actions did not reflect a neutral enforcement of the laws; those actions represented instead a selective use of the levers of government to achieve ends which the President alone had decided were in the public interest. "The very immensity of government power demands . . . that it be used in a disinterested manner, and only for the exact purposes intended," Yale law professor Charles Reich wrote in *The New Republic* a couple of weeks later. "Any other use gives a President the ability to force people to do things which under the law he has no right to require. It means that people offend the President at their peril. . . . It was dangerously wrong for an angry president to loose his terrible arsenal of power for the purposes of intimidating and coercing private companies and citizens."[114]

Kennedy was aware of these criticisms. At a private party two months later he acknowledged them—with a touch of humor—in making a toast to the attorney general. Kennedy said he had been talking to Thomas F. Patton, president of Republic Steel, and that he had been telling Patton "what a sonofabitch he was." Continuing, Kennedy said that Patton had asked why the tax records of all the steel executives were being reviewed and why all their telephones were being wiretapped. "And I told him," Kennedy said, "that I thought he was being wholly unfair to the Attorney General and that I was sure that wasn't true." Kennedy said he then called the attorney general, who told him that it "was wholly untrue." Kennedy paused and then commented, "But, of course, Patton was right."

Robert Kennedy then interrupted from the floor, saying, "They were mean to my brother. They can't do that to my brother."[115] Much of this was said in jest. But in some respects it contained a kernel of truth. The strong fidelity among the brothers did make them overly protective of each other—even, sometimes, if it entailed a disregard of the ethical restraints on the government's power.

In any event, Kennedy believed he had a broad responsibility to deal with other aspects of the nation's economic problems as well. And he approached many of these other economic problems with the same independence of mind. This was particularly true of his efforts to use budget deficits to revive the sagging economy.

In 1958 and again in 1960, the country had experienced recessions which had slowed economic growth and increased unemployment. In fact, when Kennedy assumed the presidency in 1961, the unemployment stood at 6.9 percent of the labor force. Not surprisingly, he believed that one of his priorities as President would be the need to stimulate economic growth and reduce unemployment. Kennedy soon realized that the stopgap measures of the past would not be entirely adequate, that a new response was needed, a response not tied to past resolutions or to prevalent myths. Kennedy stressed this belief when he spoke before the White House Conference on National Economic Issues in May 1962. Most of us, Kennedy observed, have been conditioned to view problems, economic or otherwise, in terms of political labels. Such thinking, however, would be of little benefit in solving the nation's economic problems. "The fact of the matter is," Kennedy continued, "that most of the problems, or at least many of them, that we now face are technical problems, are administrative problems. They are very sophisticated judgments which do not lend themselves to the great sort of 'passionate movements' which have stirred in this country so often in the past. . . . So how can we look at things as they are, not through party labels, or through position labels, but as they are and figure out how we can maintain this economy so that it moves ahead."[116]

Kennedy picked this theme up again when he gave the Yale commencement address on June 11, 1962 (during which he observed, after receiving an honorary degree, that he had the best of both worlds, a Harvard education and a Yale degree). The central domestic issues of our time, Kennedy said, "relate not to basic clashes of philosophy or ideology but to ways and means of reaching common goals." The past could be instructive, but it could not resolve the problems of the present. Kennedy believed that his generation, like every generation before it, had to "move on from the reassuring repetition of stale phrases to new, difficult, but essential confrontation with reality."[117] Kennedy then proceeded to examine the myths that continued to mold perceptions of the country's economic problems.

Among the myths Kennedy considered was the belief that stability in the nation's economy required a balanced budget. This choice was not accidental. After continuous consultations with his advisers, outside economists, and European leaders, Kennedy was more and more persuaded that increased spending by all sectors of the economy—consumer, business, and government—could provide the stimulus needed to increase growth and reduce unemployment. The difficulty with this response, at least from the American public's perspective, was the prevailing myth that economy in government—like economy in an individual family's finances—required a balanced budget. To most people, it did not seem like sound policy for the government to spend more than it "earned" in any one year from taxes. (In fact, one Gallup poll showed that 72 percent of the public opposed a tax cut while there was a budget deficit.) But if the government had to balance its budget, Kennedy argued, then it could not increase its expenditures or reduce taxes at will, even though such measures might increase the flow of money in the economy and eventually reduce unemployment.

Kennedy's view of the matter was not widely shared in business or public circles, and his speech at Yale did little to destroy the myth about the balanced budget. Having sensed this lack of support, Kennedy retrenched and announced on August 13, 1962, that he would not seek a reduction in taxes for the present. But his rationality and independence prevailed, and in his 1963 State of the Union Message Kennedy told a joint session of Congress that he would introduce a bill to reduce taxes by $13.5 billion over a three-year period and that he regarded enactment of this bill as the most important domestic issue facing Congress. The bill was introduced on January 24, 1963, and was finally enacted in December 1964—one year after Kennedy's untimely death.

However much Kennedy appreciated independence of thought and action, and however great his respect for rationality in solving problems, he still remained an adherent of political compromise, and in many areas he proceeded with considerable caution, even sacrificing rationality along the way. Sometimes the compromises were made quietly within the confines of the executive branch. Kennedy, for example, was reluctant to authorize the military's use of napalm in South Vietnam—he had seen the horrifying pictures of what it could do to the human body. But the military pressed for usage of some kind and Kennedy, fearful that a total prohibition might weaken his support among the military, authorized limited use of napalm in areas where there were no concentrations of civilian population. This compromise disappointed many in the administration. But no compromises were as disappointing as the ones Kennedy made in the area of civil rights.

When the civil rights movement caught fire in the 1950s, Kennedy was not among its leading advocates. He of course understood and accepted the need for equal treatment of the races. But none of his friends or close associates was black; he had had little exposure to the violent racial hatred in the South or the more subtle but equally bitter bigotry in the North; and, while he had sponsored some remedial legislation in Congress, he was unsure exactly how far the federal government should go in trying to combat the problem. As the presidential campaign began, he recognized that he would need the electoral support of the black communities. He therefore asked some of his campaign aides, but especially Harris Wofford, to set up meetings with the black civil rights leaders. From these meetings, as well as from long discussions with Wofford and other members of his staff, he sensed that he would have to speak out more vigorously on civil rights matters.

Almost by accident, the Democratic platform at the 1960 convention included a pledge for strong federal action in the civil rights area.* Kennedy picked up this standard and repeatedly spoke of his deep commitment to federal action to protect civil rights. On September 1, 1960, for example, twenty-three senators joined him in a statement which expressed support for "effective civil rights legislation" and pledged "action to obtain consideration of a civil rights bill by the Senate early next session that will implement the pledges of the Democratic platform."[118] In Los Angeles on September 9, Kennedy again promised strong civil rights action if he should become President. "First, as a legislative leader, the President must give us the legal weapons necessary to carry on and enforce the constitutional rights of every American," Kennedy declared to the applause of his audience. He then moved on to the President's other responsibilities in civil rights.

> Second, as Chief Executive, the next President must be prepared to put an end to racial and religious discrimination in every field of Federal activity [applause] by issuing the long-delayed Executive order putting an end to racial discrimination in federally subsidized and supported housing. . . .

> Third, as a moral leader, the next President must play his role in interpreting the great moral issues which are involved in our crusade for human rights. He must exert the great moral and educational force of his office to help bring about equal access to public facilities—from churches to lunch counters—and to support the right of every American to stand up for his rights—even if that means sitting down for them. For only the President, the representative of all interests and sections, can create the understanding and the tolerance which is necessary if we are to make an orderly transition to a completely free society. If the President does not himself wage the struggle for equal rights—if he stands above the battle—then the battle will inevitably be lost.[119]

One month later, Kennedy appeared in New York City at a constitutional rights conference sponsored by his campaign and attended by

*During the discussions on the civil rights plan, Chester Bowles, chairman of the Platform Committee and a Kennedy adviser, became concerned that his moderate draft might be diluted by the southern contingent. To improve his bargaining position, Bowles and the other civil rights supporters strengthened their draft far beyond anything to which Kennedy had then committed himself. Robert Kennedy, unaware of the change in the Bowles draft, urged the Kennedy supporters to vote for it. Only after it was adopted—to the great surprise of everyone—did the Kennedys find out what it included.

almost every principal civil rights leader in the country. In accepting the conference's recommendations for strong federal action, Kennedy spoke forcefully of his commitment to act. "The Democratic platform pointed the way on the great issue of constitutional rights and on other issues," he said. "The task of the new Democratic administration will be to turn it into a reality, to translate it into action, into legislative and executive action."[120] Statements such as these—not to mention Kennedy's call of sympathy to Mrs. Martin Luther King, Jr., when her husband was imprisoned in a Georgia jail on a trumped-up charge in the fall of 1960—inspired hope among the civil rights activists that a Kennedy victory in 1960 would add a new and powerful voice to their cause, a voice that would increase the chance of success on a number of fronts.

It was not long after Kennedy's election that these hopes proved to be somewhat empty. Kennedy was still committed to the ideal of equality for America's blacks, and he did not hesitate to use the full panoply of his presidential powers to protect that ideal when Governor Ross Barnett of Mississippi and Governor George Wallace of Alabama defied the law in refusing to integrate state universities. And, accepting the suggestion of White House aide Fred Dutton, he authorized the establishment of a subcabinet committee to discuss ways of improving federal services in the civil rights areas.[121] But Kennedy was not eager to expend needed political capital to further a cause which was not fully accepted by the public or, more importantly, by the powerful southern congressmen and senators who dominated Congress's committees. In Kennedy's eyes, politics was largely the art of compromise, and too much presidential activity in the civil rights field was just not good politics.

At times, this eagerness to compromise produced some comic confusion among administration officials. The subcabinet group, for instance, worked for a long time in trying to desegregate the restaurant and motel services along interstate highway 40 in Maryland, a road commonly used by motorists traveling between Washington, D.C., and New York City. On one occasion, newspapers reported that an African diplomat was refused service on Route 40. Kennedy called Angier Biddle Duke, the State Department's protocol officer and a member of the subcabinet group, and mentioned the article. Biddle replied, in an almost apologetic way, that the group was really working hard to prevent this sort of thing. "Well, that's not what I'm calling you about," Kennedy said. "I'm calling to tell you to tell these African ambassadors to fly. You tell them I wouldn't think of driving from New York to Washington. It's a hell of a road, Route 40. I used to drive that years ago. Why the hell would anyone want to drive down on Route 40 when you can fly today? Tell them to wake up to the world and fly." A little perplexed at the President's response, Biddle called Wofford, who was also working with the subcabinet group, and asked, "Are you sure the President is fully behind our efforts?"[122]

So, much to the consternation of the civil rights activists, Kennedy was, as a standing Washington joke had it, long on profile and short on courage when it came to fighting for civil rights. In making judicial appointments in the South, for instance, he often deferred to the wishes of southern senators, appointing men like Harold Cox (a college roommate of Senator Eastland of Mississippi who, while sitting as a judge, once referred to blacks as "chimpanzees") and E. Gordon West (who called the Supreme Court's *Brown* decision outlawing racial segregation in public schools "one of the truly regretable decisions of all times"). At the same time, Kennedy refrained from appointing any blacks to judgeships in the South because the southern men on the Hill would not have it (although Kennedy did appoint ten blacks to judgeships in other parts of the country). These actions were particularly ironic since Kennedy had come to believe that litigation rather than legislation was the most appropriate and most effective way to attack the inequalities endured by blacks.*

Even as he contemplated strengthening executive committees to combat employment discrimination in the federal government and with government contractors, Kennedy was anxious to avoid public fights on the civil rights issue. Privately, he told his aides several times during the first couple of weeks in office "that he want[ed] his appointees to get working on elimination of discrimination in the agencies. . . ."[123] But he was equally concerned about taking public actions which would rock the boat too much; he thought the political waters were already too rough. After meeting with John Hannah, chairman of the Civil Rights Commission, in early February 1961, Kennedy sent a memo to Sorensen. "Dr. Hannah recommends that I put out a report that in ninety days I will analyze what can be done to improve the employment of Negroes by the federal government," Kennedy said. "He feels that it would indicate my interest and put the matter on ice for a

---

*Careful research has suggested that Kennedy's judicial appointments were no worse than Eisenhower's and, from the civil rights perspective, somewhat better. Dr. Mary Curzan, for example, studied selections for the federal bench in the fifth circuit (which includes most of the Deep South and border states) and drew the following conclusion: Kennedy appointed five segregationist judges, three moderates, and eight integrationists, while Eisenhower appointed five segregationists, eight moderates, and two integrationists. Although Kennedy's appointments collectively offered more hope for protection of civil rights than Eisenhower's appointments, the statistics omit one glaring distinction: both publicly and privately Kennedy had committed his administration to the protection of civil rights; Eisenhower had made no such commitment. Thus, although Kennedy had a better record than Eisenhower in judicial appointments, people had a right to expect much more from him. See Victor Navasky, *Kennedy Justice* 269 (1971).

while. Would you think about this and perhaps talk to him."[124] For a leader who promised to act decisively and dramatically in civil rights matters, it was certainly inconsistent for Kennedy even to consider putting any part of the issue on ice. In any event, Hannah's advice apparently had some effect. In announcing one month later the creation of the new Committee on Equal Employment Opportunity, Kennedy emphasized that he was "directing a complete study of current government employment practices—an examination of the status of members of minority groups in every department, agency and office of the Federal government."[125]

All things considered, however, the creation of this Committee on Equal Employment Opportunity was movement in the right direction. The committee constituted a consolidation of two existing executive committees and added considerably to their personnel as well as to their power to ensure compliance with their presidential mandate. (Despite the added enforcement powers, no government contracts were ever canceled during Kennedy's Administration as a result of job discrimination, although the committee did improve minority employment opportunities in many areas.) This was not the only major effort made by the administration in its first couple of years to deal with civil rights issues. The Justice Department, for example, also instituted or supported dozens of civil rights lawsuits, most of them in the South. These and other measures represented a step forward. But they were not nearly enough to solve the problem or alleviate the frustrations of the civil rights leaders. They wanted Kennedy to introduce the comprehensive legislation he had repeatedly spoken of in the 1960 campaign. But for a variety of reasons, Kennedy continued to believe the introduction of such legislation to be fraught with political risks he did not want to take. Only in the face of national crisis was he willing to forsake compromise and propose the kind of legislation which many had expected from him in 1961. The crisis involved here was Alabama's Governor George Wallace's refusal in the spring of 1963 to allow the admission of blacks to the University of Alabama. There were speeches and protest marches and demonstrations. But above all, there was Bull Connor, Birmingham's sheriff, enforcing justice on the city streets with dogs and billy sticks and fire hoses—a spectacle which swept the television screens and front pages of America's newspapers. Even then, most of Kennedy's close advisers argued against the introduction of civil rights legislation. But Kennedy believed otherwise, in great part because of his brother Robert. "When President Kennedy sent up that bill every single person who spoke about it in the White House—every one of them—was against President Kennedy sending up that bill," Assistant Attorney General Burke Marshall later recalled. "The conclusive voice within the government at that time, there's no question about it at all, that Robert Kennedy was the one. He argued it, he felt it, he understood it. And he prevailed."[126]

Kennedy's positive response to his brother's urgings here in part reflected the President's sensitivity to his responsibility to help end human suffering. From the beginning of his presidency, he was mindful of the despair, poverty, and disease which was prevalent (and largely unnoticed) in large pockets of the United States as well as in other parts of the world. He also knew that all this misfortune could not be eliminated by the wave of a presidential wand. In response to a reporter's question about protest demonstrations by armed forces reservists, Kennedy candidly acknowledged life's inequities and the inability of any President or any government to remove all of them:

> There is always inequity in life. Some men are killed in a war and some men are wounded, and some men never leave the country, and some men are stationed in the Antarctic and some men are stationed in San Francisco. It's very hard in military or in personal life to assure complete equality. Life is unfair.[127]

While he saw no hope of correcting all of life's inequities, Kennedy was eager and willing to alleviate certain ones, especially those not shrouded in political controversy. Most of Kennedy's first actions as President, for example, were directed at helping those caught by misfortune. Thus, in his first week as President, Kennedy issued a memorandum ordering a review of the Food-for-Peace program (directed by George McGovern), wrote a letter to Congress urging enactment of the Distressed Area Redevelopment bill (legislation designed to relieve hardship resulting from chronic unemployment in certain areas), increased the American food supplies being shipped to starving families in the Congo (where a major civil war was in progress), and asked Abraham Ribicoff, the newly appointed secretary of health, education and welfare, to undertake arrangements to care for Cuban refugees in the United States.

Throughout his presidency, Kennedy continued to show concern for those overcome by circumstances or unfairly exploited by their fellowman. Virtually all of his domestic legislative priorities, for example, were directed toward easing the hardships of life—redevelopment, minimum wage, housing, social security, public welfare, and mental illness. Kennedy's compassion for his fellowman was not confined to legislative affairs. Where the circumstances allowed it, and where the need was especially great, he showed his concern by ignoring political constraints and even bureaucratic hurdles. The ransom arranged for the 1,113 Bay of Pigs prisoners exemplified this trait.

The prisoners' fate evolved from a plan developed by some Cuban refugees and the Central Intelligence Agency in 1959. Essentially, the plan's object was the overthrow of Fidel Castro, the Cuban revolutionary who had assumed power on January 1, 1959. The goal was to be achieved by an air attack and then an invasion by the refugees on Cuban shores. The refugees had great expectations for their plan. Reportedly, Castro's support among the army and the Cuban people was deteriorating; the refugees consequently (and erroneously) assumed that the army would not offer much resistance and that the people would rally to the invaders' side. Eisenhower was sympathetic to the plan, and the reasons are easy to understand. A self-professed Marxist, Castro's initial flirtation with communism soon blossomed into a love affair with the Soviet Union. Within a short time, Soviet advisers, technicians, and matériel were flowing into Cuba. This development greatly concerned the American administration, whose foreign policy was deeply rooted in the Cold War psychology. And this concern led Eisenhower to believe that the United States had a moral obligation (and much to gain strategically) by assisting Cuban exiles who wished to free Cuba from the grip of communism. The plan was therefore approved by Eisenhower in 1960, and CIA agents subsequently trained the refugees in the hot jungles of Guatemala.

Although the plan had been developed and approved by the Eisenhower administration, it was executed after Kennedy was inaugurated president. On a foggy morning in April 1961, the invaders tried to establish a beachhead at the Bay of Pigs in Cuba. Their hopes for success were short-lived. Within a couple of days, Castro's superior forces squelched the invasion. Many men were killed, and more than a thousand were taken prisoners.

Kennedy felt largely responsible for the fate of these prisoners. After all, the Bay of Pigs invasion had been planned and carried out under American auspices, and Kennedy himself had supervised the general strategy of the invasion—although he refused to allow direct participation by American combat forces. In May 1961, Kennedy learned that Castro would consider releasing the prisoners for a considerable amount of farm equipment, food staples, and medical supplies. Kennedy unofficially sponsored the creation of a citizens committee to explore the possibilities of arranging the swap. The legal, financial, and political difficulties proved considerable, and more than a year passed without agreement. But after the missile crisis, the Kennedy brothers resolved that the deal should be completed by Christmas. In the ensuing month, Robert Kennedy solicited pledges from private companies to donate $44 million worth of goods and arranged for the Department of Agriculture to donate another $9 millon worth of food staples.

In the meantime, political commentators were lambasting the ransom operation, contending that legal procedures were being ignored (Kennedy had secured a ruling from the Internal Revenue Service to permit the donating companies to deduct the cost of their pledges from their tax returns) and that the selfish whimsy of the Cuban dictator was being honored. All this criticism was to no avail. Kennedy had gotten the men into Castro's prisons, and he would get them out. And so the arrangements proceeded as scheduled. The ransom was delivered and the prisoners released by Christmas Day, 1962. On December 29, 1962, Kennedy met with the brigade of Cuban prisoners in Miami. When the former prisoners presented him with their bullet-torn brigade flag, the one they had carried in the invasion, Kennedy—unaccustomed to showing his emotions in public—was brought to tears.

This same compassion—minus the tears—was evident in other areas when Kennedy's attention focused on the senseless suffering of other human beings, whether in the United States or abroad. Myer (Mike) Feldman, who served as deputy special counsel in the White House, told me, for instance, that Kennedy "was sympathetic to my suggestions that informal influence be exerted by the U.S. to open the gates of the Soviet Union to Jews who wished to emigrate."[128] In October 1963, in fact, Kennedy personally asked Soviet Foreign Minister Andrei Gromyko (despite objections from the State Department) to ease the emigration restrictions on Soviet Jews. (Gromyko insisted that Jews were treated no differently from others who wished to emigrate.) This was only part of Kennedy's efforts to work with his staff and his administration to explore avenues by which the Soviet Union could be persuaded to prevent persecution of Jews.

Kennedy was particularly intent, however, upon bettering the plight of exploited and disadvantaged peoples in the underdeveloped countries. He seemed to have a real feel for their anxieties, their frustrations, and their hopes. The thrust of Kennedy's perspective toward these underdeveloped countries was symbolically and dramatically cast when, in one of his first votes in the United Nations, Adlai Stevenson, Kennedy's representative at the UN, voted for a resolution supporting independence for the Portuguese colony of Angola in Africa. This vote was well received in the underdeveloped countries, but it raised quite a few eyebrows in the European colonial powers (just as Kennedy's Senate speech on Algeria had) and even in Congress, where colonialism was still viewed by many as the white man's burden to "civilize" the peoples of Africa and Asia.* And when political commentators and

---

*Kennedy's association with the freedom movements in Portugal's African colonies was roundly criticized in a report of a Senate subcommittee chaired by Senator Allen Ellender of Louisiana. The United States should aid, not condemn, Portuguese efforts to bring "progress" to its African provinces, Ellender said. After all, Ellender continued, the Governor General of Angola was correct in observing that the "natives" were "shiftless" and "incapable of self-government." *A Report on United States Foreign Operations in Africa,* Doc. 8, 88th Cong., 1st Sess., pp. 20, 115 (1963).

congressmen criticized the statement of G. Mennen Williams, Kennedy's chief adviser on African affairs, that Africa should be for the Africans (implying that the European colonials should get out), Kennedy responded, "I do not know who else Africa should be for."[129] Sentiments such as these were echoed by Kennedy in other forums, and in a very real way they seemed to touch the lives of the peoples in the underdeveloped countries. Thus, in the course of his presidency, Kennedy endorsed a peaceful revolution in Latin America "to satisfy the basic needs of the American people for homes, work, and land, health and schools"; in his first months in the White House he proposed a broad foreign assistance program so that the United States might meet its "obligations to the sick, the poor, and the hungry, wherever they may live"; and in his 1963 State of the Union Message he pledged American financial assistance to developing and nonaligned nations so that they might "strengthen their independence and cure the social chaos in which communism always has thrived."[130] The programs supporting these noble commitments rarely had the magic quality of the rhetoric. But for peoples struggling to be recognized in their quest for status and independence, the commitment and the rhetoric were often a significant step forward.

In the White House, as when he served in Congress, Kennedy's compassion for his fellowman was often subordinated to the drive to defend against the encroachment of communism. As veteran White House reporter William Shannon observed approvingly early in the Kennedy presidency, "The whole purpose and rationale of the Kennedy Administration is organized intellectually around this concept of unified national strength, mobilized and deployed for the single overriding purpose of defeating the Russian-Chinese combine."[131] This observation may have overstated the case, but the truth was that Kennedy was very concerned about communist forces—not only because he thought they posed a real threat to the United States but also, and perhaps more importantly, because he expected the Soviet leaders to test his strength and firmness in the crucible of a real confrontation.

If Kennedy had any doubts on this score, they were removed when he met Soviet Premier Khrushchev in Vienna in June 1961. After the meeting, Kennedy was visibly shaken. He had studied the Russians, he knew their history, he knew Khrushchev, he was intellectually prepared for the meeting. In his eyes, it was basically a matter of matching arguments—Marx and Lenin against Jefferson and de Tocqueville—but reason would win the day. Kennedy was wrong, and it was rather disconcerting. During the talks Khrushchev harangued Kennedy, bullied him, and threatened him with actions the Soviet Union was contemplating in Berlin and elsewhere to increase the pressures on the United States. Kennedy was not prepared for this. Averell Harriman and French President Charles de Gaulle, who knew the Russians and Khrushchev well, had warned Kennedy that Khrushchev would initiate the discussions with a harangue; ignore it, they advised, and in time he will settle down; Kennedy listened to this advice, but in the heat of debate it sometimes receded to the background and Kennedy tried, in vain, to debate—but reason was not supreme here. "If Khrushchev wants to rub my nose in the dirt," Kennedy later told James Wechsler of the *New York Post,* "it's all over."

According to Arthur Schlesinger, Jr., Kennedy was worried that "Khrushchev might interpret his reluctance to wage nuclear war as a symptom of an American loss of nerve. Some day, he said, the time might come when he would have to run the supreme risk to convince Khrushchev that conciliation did not mean humiliation. . . . But how to convince Khrushchev short of a showdown? 'That son of a bitch won't pay attention to words,' the President said bitterly on another occasion. 'He has to see you move.' "[132]

Kennedy's resolve to meet the threat of communism was indeed tested early in his administration—even before he met Khrushchev at Vienna. This first test came in deciding whether or not to give the go-ahead to the Bay of Pigs invasion plan initially approved by Eisenhower.

Kennedy did not learn of the plan until after his election. His first reaction was mixed. He felt that he could not justify complete military intervention by the United States in this endeavor; politically and militarily, it was simply too risky. He nevertheless believed that his limited support was crucial if the promises of his campaign speeches (pledging American assistance to those Cuban exiles who wanted to free Cuba from the grip of communism) and his inaugural address (supporting the survival of freedom everywhere) were to be meaningful—especially since Castro's close association with communist powers inspired public fear that America's security was in danger. The situation moreover brought reminders of 1956, when Kennedy had witnessed the adverse psychological effects of Eisenhower's inaction in Hungary. Kennedy felt his bluff was being called and, in these situations, one had to be tough. His closest advisers supported the plan unanimously (although some outside the inner circles did not). He gave his approval (although, with the exception of air cover, he directed that there be no American involvement in the actual combat). Only after the invasion was launched on a bleak morning in April 1961 did Kennedy realize that he had miscalculated, that his anxieties about communism had smothered his reasoning powers. He canceled supporting air strikes and readied himself for the fiasco the invasion proved to be.

Kennedy accepted full responsibility in public for the failure (observing that success has a hundred fathers while defeat is an orphan). But he did not renounce his crusade against communism. (Indeed, lest his indecision in the Bay of Pigs invasion be interpreted by the Soviet Union as weakness, he ordered the American military advisers in Laos to shed their civilian disguises and don their uniforms in the open.) A few days after the Cuban invasion, Kennedy addressed the American Society of Newspaper Editors in Washington, D.C. Although the Cuban fiasco was fresh on everyone's mind, Kennedy was not contrite. Quite the contrary. He declared in clear, firm language that the crusade against communism was alive and well in the Kennedy White House, that, in fact, the crusade would be intensified. During the Bay of Pigs invasion, Khrushchev had wired Kennedy that he should show restraint and not interfere in the internal affairs of other countries. To this Kennedy replied in his speech,

> Let the record show that our restraint is not inexhaustible. Should it ever appear that the inter-American doctrine of non-interference merely conceals or excuses a policy of nonaction—if the nations of this Hemisphere should fail to meet their commitments against outside Communist penetration—then I want it clearly understood that this Government will not hesitate in meeting its primary obligations which are to the security of our Nation!
>
> Should that time come, we do not intend to be lectured on "intervention" by those whose character was stamped for all time on the bloody streets of Budapest![133]

Kennedy did not stop there. He proceeded to outline for the editors the larger lessons of the Cuban fiasco. Communism was trying to place its stranglehold on the free nations, and the peril to freedom could be removed only if the self-discipline of the free could match the iron discipline of the mailed fist. Then, in a ringing passage, Kennedy invoked the specter of a tireless struggle with communism from which he would not shrink. The passage is so revealing of Kennedy's attitude that it merits quotation in full:

> Finally, it is clearer than ever that we face a relentless struggle in every corner of the globe that goes far beyond the clash of armies or even nuclear armaments. The armies are there, and in large number. The nuclear armaments are there. But they serve primarily as the shield behind which subversion, infiltration, and a host of other tactics steadily advance, picking off vulnerable areas one by one in situations which do not permit our own armed intervention.
>
> Power is the hallmark of this offensive—power and discipline and

> deceit. The legitimate discontent of yearning people is exploited. . . .
>
> We dare not fail to see the invidious nature of this new and deeper struggle. We dare not fail to grasp the new concepts, the new tools, the new sense of urgency we will need to combat it—whether in Cuba or in South Vietnam. And we dare not fail to realize that this struggle is taking place every day, without fanfare, in thousands of villages and markets—day and night—and in classrooms all over the globe.
>
> The message of Cuba, of Laos, of the rising din of Communist voices in Asia and Latin America—these messages are all the same. The complacent, the self-indulgent, the soft societies are about to be swept away with the debris of history. Only the strong, only the industrious, only the determined, only the courageous, only the visionary who determine the real nature of our struggle can possibly survive.
>
> No greater task faces this country or this administration. No other challenge is more deserving of our every effort and energy.[134]

Reading this speech—which was probably the most eloquent exposition of Kennedy's deep-seated drive to thwart the communist menace—one can easily see that the lessons of why England slept still dominated his thoughts. Nor was there any reason to believe that Kennedy was out of step with the thinking of the country. On May 5, 1961, George Gallup's opinion poll showed that 61 percent of the public approved Kennedy's handling of the Bay of Pigs invasion (only 15 percent disapproved) and that 83 percent approved of his performance as President (only 5 percent disapproved). Newspapers throughout the country were also rallying to Kennedy's call to fight the communist menace. (On the day of his speech to the newspaper editors, a *New York Times* editorial declared that "the United States is engaged in an all-out struggle to save the Western Hemisphere for democracy and freedom.")[135]

In this context, it is no wonder that Kennedy was susceptible to pressure to escalate the American military commitment to Vietnam. He had already resolved to accept a political settlement in Laos. He could not accept a similar political settlement in Vietnam without bringing into question his self-proclaimed determination to stand firm in the face of the communist onslaught. And that was something he did not want to do.

As for the risks of full-scale American military intervention in Vietnam, Kennedy felt he could control them. When Undersecretary of

State George Ball told him that the introduction into Vietnam of even 8,000 American troops would soon lead to a commitment of 300,000, Kennedy reportedly laughed and said, "George, you're crazier than hell."[136] And when Congressman Frank Thompson, Jr., tried to warn Kennedy about those same risks of a growing military involvement, the President replied forcefully, "I know about those risks, but they're never going to materialize *because I'm going to stop it!*"[137] Since in his view the risks were manageable, Kennedy did not want to foreclose all American military support for Vietnam. He was publicly committed to the domino theory. And he did not want to close his eyes to the communist activity in Vietnam. Before the year was out, he had sent 3,200 American military "advisers" there. (Kennedy rejected out-of-hand the Joint Chiefs' suggestion that he dispatch 205,000 American troops to Vietnam.)

No less in Berlin than in Vietnam could Kennedy shrink from the communist threat. Even before his election to the presidency, he had believed that Berlin could well be the ultimate test of American determination to resist communist advances. He had said as much in speeches on the Senate floor, campaign addresses, and in published interviews. In his third televised debate with Nixon on October 13, 1960, for example, Kennedy spoke of his resolve, if elected President, to defend Berlin:

> I have stated on many occasions that the United States must meet its commitment on Berlin. It is a commitment that we have to meet if we're going to protect the security of Western Europe. And, therefore, on this question, I don't think that there is any doubt in the mind of any American. I hope there is not any doubt in the mind of any member of the community of West Berlin. I am sure there isn't any doubt in the mind of the Russians. We will meet our commitments to maintain the freedom and independence of West Berlin.[138]

The basis of Kennedy's concern was readily apparent. Berlin, located 110 miles inside the boundaries of East Germany, is a divided city, with the western part governed by West Germany and protected by the allied powers (England, France, and the United States) and the eastern part governed by the communist dictatorship of East Germany (and legally protected by the Soviet Union). The official status of the city in 1961—as well as of the two Germanys—was in a state of limbo. For there was no official document which recognized the divided status of the two Berlins or even the two Germanys. The Soviet Union had long threatened to sign a separate peace treaty with East Germany and to establish all Berlin as a "free" city which would not enjoy the protective power of the allied countries.* This threat had caused anxiety among many in the United States, for if the Soviet threat materialized, East Germany would have a legal right to close the roads of access from West Germany to West Berlin (the Soviet Union had tried that tack in 1948). West Berlin thus seemed to symbolize the determination of the West, and especially of the United States, to resist advances by the communist powers to isolate and then swallow democratic nations. Indeed, opinion polls at the time showed that 71 percent of the American public would rather fight a war with the Soviet Union than accept a blockade of Berlin.

Khrushchev renewed the threat of a Soviet treaty with East Germany when he met Kennedy in Vienna. Two days after that meeting, the Kremlin issued an aide-mémoire which formally proposed that the Soviet Union conclude a separate peace treaty with East Germany and that both the Soviet Union and the allied powers terminate their responsibility for (and rights in) Berlin.

Kennedy saw this aide-mémoire as the prelude to another test of wills with communism. Kennedy's interpretation was reinforced by the advice of former Secretary of State Dean Acheson, to whom Kennedy listened closely. It's not really Berlin, Acheson told Kennedy. It's Europe, Asia, Africa—in short, Berlin was the wall holding back the flood and Kennedy could not pull his thumb out from the dike without drowning in the communist deluge that would surely follow. The Soviet Union was throwing down the gauntlet, and surrender now would have disastrous consequences far beyond the perimeters of Berlin. Although he did not agree with all of Acheson's views on the issue, Kennedy concurred on this point. In a press conference on June 28, 1961, Kennedy made it clear that he attached a great deal of importance to the status of Berlin and to the American response to the Soviet proposal:

> It is of the greatest importance that the American people understand the basic issues involved and the threats to the peace and security of Europe and of ourselves posed by the Soviet announcement that they intend to change unilaterally the existing arrangements for Berlin.[139]

Many—including Adlai Stevenson, Senators Mansfield and Fulbright, even Prime Minister Macmillan of Great Britian—counseled

*Because Germany was divided into two independent sectors immediately after World War II, neither the allied powers nor the Soviet Union ever signed a peace treaty with Germany. The hope—especially among the Germans—was that their country would soon be reunited. A peace treaty could not be signed on behalf of East or West Germany without acknowledgment that the two sectors were independent countries. Therefore, if the Soviet Union signed a peace treaty with East Germany, it would signify that East Germany was an independent country.

moderation, but their counsel fell, for the most part, on deaf ears. Kennedy had promised that he would stand firm to the communist menace, and he was not about to weaken in an actual confrontation. The situation grew worse. On July 25, 1961, Kennedy gave a nationally televised speech on the Berlin "crisis." The Soviet Union is threatening to strip us of our rights and people of their freedom in Berlin, Kennedy said. The United States would not let this happen—not only because the United States was committed to defend Berlin but also, said Kennedy, because Berlin "has now become—as never before—the great testing place of Western courage and will, a focal point where our solemn commitments stretching back over the years since 1945 and Soviet ambitions now meet in basic confrontation."[140] Kennedy then outlined the steps he intended to take to prepare for the imminent confrontation: more troops, more ships, more planes, and a steel will.

Kennedy's address was greeted with pride and agreement in most quarters. "In a speech at once solemn, determined and conciliatory," the *New York Times* editorialized the next day, "President Kennedy last night reasserted American leadership of the free world and outlined some of the measures and the sacrifices that are necessary to safeguard our survival and our heritage in the face of the Soviet challenge. We are confident that the American people and free men everywhere will support him."[141] And indeed they did. Polls showed that more than three of every four people in the country with an opinion approved of Kennedy's response. Some people of course did not share Kennedy's view of the matter (Richard Rovere had written in *The New Yorker* immediately prior to Kennedy's televised speech that the administration appeared to be contriving a "crisis"). But the vast majority of the people were prepared to accept Kennedy's good faith in announcing that the Soviet Union was forcing a test of wills in Berlin.

The confrontation never materialized. The communists built a wall around East Berlin (thus preventing East Berliners from escaping to freedom in West Berlin), while Kennedy and the United States watched helplessly. But then negotiations between the two adversaries began in earnest, and it was agreed not to agree on how to resolve Germany's, and with it Berlin's, fate.

It was all an instructive experience for Kennedy. In public he had sounded tough, hard as nails, but in the quiet of his Oval Office, talking it over with his brother Robert, he sensed how close he had brought the country to war, and that being so close, a small miscalculation, a misunderstanding, a mistake in judgment, and it would all be over. It was indeed a sobering thought. But it was not enough—at least not yet—to make Kennedy take a hard look at this anticommunist banner he held so high.

So when rumors spread in the late summer of 1962 that the Soviet

Union was installing offensive missiles in Cuba, Kennedy directed that the rumors be verified. He would not jump the gun as he had in Berlin—he had learned that much from his experience. Even when numerous congressmen and senators (mostly from the Republican side of the aisle—it was an election year) called on Kennedy to take action, he remained resolute in his position—he would not undertake action unless he was convinced that the missiles were indeed of an offensive nature (for then the missiles could reach cities deep inside the United States). He even resisted (unsuccessfully) a congressional resolution that would express concern about the situation and the need to protect against the Soviet threat in Cuba. But soon it was confirmed that the missiles were in fact offensive, and then Kennedy felt constrained to take action (even though McNamara observed that "[a] missile is a missile. It makes no great difference whether you are killed by a missile fired from the Soviet Union or from Cuba."[142]). Within a week's time, Kennedy decided to and did impose a quarantine on strategic matériel being shipped to Cuba.

The process by which Kennedy decided upon the quarantine, as well as the significance that process has for the American political system, are critical matters which I will return to in later chapters. For present purposes, the point is that once the offensive nature of the missiles was confirmed, Kennedy felt he had to deal with it in *public* rather than in *private* through diplomatic channels. Both Congress and the public were clamoring for some assurance that Kennedy's promise to stand firm to communism was still good, that the pressure of ultimate responsibility had not softened him. Those demands could not go unheeded, Kennedy believed, without a great political sacrifice. Indeed, when Robert Kennedy later suggested to the President that he had no choice in the matter, that he would have been impeached if he had not reacted forcefully in some way, the President considered it for a moment and replied, "That's what I think—I would have been impeached." [143] (In fact, in a special opinion poll released on October 24, 1962, George Gallup found that 84 percent of the public approved Kennedy's imposition of a quarantine on Cuba—only 4 percent disapproved—and that many of those who approved voiced the qualification, "but it should have been done sooner.")

Many political commentators—but especially those who were directly involved in the decision-making process—later pointed to the Cuban missile crisis as President Kennedy's finest hour. It was the moment when his tenacity, his "machismo," was exposed for all to see and to respect. The Cuban missile crisis was indeed a success for Kennedy—but not because of his determination to stare down Khrushchev and his compatriots in the Kremlin. Quite the opposite. It was a success precisely because Kennedy's "toughness" did not entirely govern his decision in the confrontation with our Cold War adversary. Compassion, sensibility, and moderation ultimately prevailed.* In his memoir of the missile crisis, Robert Kennedy recalled a discussion the President had with him, Sorensen, and appointments secretary Kenneth O'Donnell in the midst of the crisis. In this discussion, Kennedy indicated that he was concerned not so much with saving face as with saving lives:

> "The great danger and risk in all of this," [President Kennedy] said, "is a miscalculation—a mistake in judgment." . . . That was what he wanted to avoid. He did not want anyone to be able to say that the U.S. had not done all it could to preserve the peace. We were not going to misjudge, or miscalculate, or challenge the other side needlessly, or precipitously push our adversary into a course of action that was not intended or anticipated.[144]

And so Kennedy wanted to give Khrushchev ample room to remove the missiles without public humiliation. Kennedy therefore kept postponing any decision to initiate a decisive military action—even after an unarmed American U-2 reconnaissance plane was shot down over Cuba at the height of the crisis and the pilot killed. Kennedy's procrastination paid off, and within a week of the quarantine's imposition, Khrushchev agreed to dismantle the offensive missile sites. Even columnist Walter Lippmann, who felt Kennedy should have resorted to normal diplomatic channnels rather than a quarantine, was impressed with the President's actions. "In October 1962, he showed that he has not only the courage of a warrior, which is to take the risks that are necessary," Lippmann wrote of Kennedy in 1963, "but also the wisdom of the statesman, which is to use power with restraint."[145]

With the missile crisis resolved, Kennedy realized even more clearly the need to make an accommodation with the Soviet Union, to free the world of these Cold War crises. As Kennedy observed in a speech at American University on June 10, 1963, a speech which signaled clearly Kennedy's shift of emphasis from confrontation to conciliation, "Above all, while defending our own vital interests, nuclear powers

---

*It is of some significance that Dean Acheson, whose advice had been a major influence in pushing Kennedy toward crisis confrontation in Berlin, was also present in the first meetings to consider how the United States should respond to the Soviet missiles. But Acheson's recommendation for decisive military action—an air strike over Cuba—was rejected by Kennedy, and before the crisis was resolved, Acheson left Washington and returned to his Maryland farm. Later, Acheson claimed that Kennedy's success in the Cuban missile crisis was due to "dumb luck."

must avert those confrontations which bring an adversary to a choice of either a humiliating retreat or a nuclear war. To adopt that kind of course in the nuclear age would be evidence only of the bankruptcy of our policy—or of a collective death-wish for the world."[146] Freed to some extent of the chains first forged when writing *Why England Slept,* Kennedy devoted greater attention and energy to the negotiation of a treaty with the Soviet Union limiting nuclear testing. Kennedy had always regarded agreement on such a treaty as a priority item (he claimed that the greatest disappointment of his first year in the presidency was the failure to conclude a nuclear test ban treaty). For agreement on such a treaty would not only remove the fallout dangers of continued testing, but would also be a symbolic step toward the reduction of tensions between the United States and the Soviet Union. But after the Cuban missile crisis, and particularly after his American University speech, Kennedy's outlook and the political climate were more conducive to the successful negotiation of the coveted treaty. The treaty was finally agreed upon by the United States and the Soviet Union in July 1963, and signed in October 1963. Thus did Kennedy's new sensitivity to human suffering overcome, for a time at least, his inclination to be a Cold War warrior.

The shifts in Kennedy's policies during his presidency, however, did not indicate a corresponding shift or alteration in his concept of the presidency. Throughout his tenure, he saw the presidency as a focus of activity and direction in the nation. He saw the presidency as the pinnacle of opportunity in public service. "I suppose anybody in politics would like to be President—that is the center of action, the mainspring, the wellspring of the American system," Kennedy remarked in response to a reporter's query in 1961. ". . . At least you have an opportunity to do something about all the problems which . . . I would be concerned about anyway as a father or as a citizen. . . . And if what you do is useful and successful, then . . . that is a great satisfaction."[147]

Opportunity—that was a theoretical keynote of Kennedy's presidency. Unlike Woodrow Wilson or the two Roosevelts, he had little drive to extract approval or concessions from others unless that support was useful in solving problems. Likewise, because he was more oriented toward solving problems than toward serving a particular philosophy of government, he was usually interested in knowing only whether his policies and programs would work and whether they would be supported by those who had to implement them as well as those who had to live with them.

Kennedy's critical and practical view of himself in the presidency was a two-edged sword in terms of his effectiveness as a leader. On the one hand, he could cast a cold eye toward a problem and consider alternative solutions without regard to how they might square with political or philosophical labels. His response to the situation in Laos is exemplary in this regard. On the other hand, he often lacked the fervor or determination to achieve particular ends which motivates others who seek power or who pursue a particular philosophy. Especially when he did not feel the push of public support—his civil rights posture in 1961 and 1962 is a prime example—Kennedy showed an undue amount of political caution. While he saw the presidency as a focal point of political events, he had a considerable respect, maybe too much respect, for the role of the public in political affairs. (Was he still tied to the view of *Why England Slept,* in which he assigned to the public the major responsibility for England's lack of preparedness?) Once he had the impetus of public support, Kennedy was more apt to gather his own momentum. Without that impetus, he usually wavered or held back, and the independence of thought and action which he had showed in Congress became compromised.

Evaluating Kennedy's effectiveness as a leader, or any president's effectiveness, is not simply a matter of understanding how his concept of the office influenced his decisions, however. Such an evaluation also requires some understanding of how Kennedy acquired and used information in weighing alternative options to solve problems and, in general, to meet his responsibilities. Exploring Kennedy's methods in making decisions thus becomes the next area for consideration.

CHAPTER 2

John F. Kennedy's Methods of Decision-Making

The political art deals with matters peculiar to politics, with a complex of material circumstances, of historic deposit, of human passion, for which the problems of business or engineering do not provide an analogy.

Walter Lippmann

The President's Methods of Decision-Making: An Historical Perspective

Presidents are continually making decisions—even, sometimes, if the decision is not to decide. Rarely do these decisions involve the drama popularly associated with "great" moments in history—Woodrow Wilson's decision to ask Congress to declare war on Germany in 1917, Franklin D. Roosevelt's decision to declare a "bank holiday" in 1933, or Harry S Truman's decision to drop the atomic bomb on Japan in 1945. The far greater number of presidential decisions represent an unheralded continuum in the development, promulgation, and implementation of policies. Some decisions are more important than others. But almost every decision has some effect on policy, if only to help set the stage for the next decision.

From this perspective, it is clear that any president's effectiveness in exercising leadership depends in great part on the decisions he makes. His understanding of the issues, the people he listens to, and the choices he makes—all these factors are crucial in determining whether his concept of the presidency can find expression in governmental programs and policies.

Making the "right" decision is of course no easy matter. Unless the president chooses to rely on chance—and some have—the president must secure information concerning the dimensions of problems and, indeed, whether there are problems. He must understand the options available to him and the probable consequences of each one. He must then weigh these options not only in terms of his established goals but also in terms of what is practical and what is politically palatable to his various constituencies.

There are rarely any simple choices between good and evil forces. Usually it is a question of balancing competing alternatives which have both benefits and disadvantages. Any thoughtful person who has considered, for example, the problems in achieving a full employment economy without inflation can appreciate the difficulty of these presidential choices. But the president cannot escape these decisions, especially in our modern society. Responsibility for the state of the nation will be laid at his doorstep—regardless of what he decides to do (or decides not to do). His action or inaction, in other words, will not only guide governmental programs and policies; it will also shape the attitudes of people whose cooperation and support are essential to his success.

The manner in which the president formulates and executes his decisions thus delineates another component of presidential leadership. It is not enough for him to promise leadership. It is not enough for him to assert goals toward which he will work. He must obtain the information and make the choices that will breathe life into these promises and goals. This, then, is the second criterion in judging the effectiveness of presidential leadership: the ability and will of the president to gather essential information about the problems which confront him, to understand fully the probable consequences of available options, and to choose on the basis of what he believes is in the best interests of the country.

In one sense, application of this criterion simply requires using common sense: people should know what they're doing before they do it. They should have a good grasp of the problem and the alternatives for dealing with the problem. And if other people will play a role in implementing a decision, then it makes sense to consult with those people before the decision is made. If, for example, a contemplated policy will require legislation for its implementation, then it is usually prudent for the president to confer with appropriate congressional leaders. Not that a president should completely bend his will to accommodate members of Congress or anyone else. But he should understand what, if any, cooperation he can expect from them and whether alteration of his plans is necessary or appropriate.

A president, of course, does not have unlimited time, energy, and resources. He rarely has the opportunity to study a matter or consult with people until he is completely satisfied that he understands it fully. The press of events and other demands on his time may force him to make a decision before he wants to. Some decisions, moreover, will be more important than others and will necessitate more attention. In this context, it is clear that a president must establish his own priorities. To some extent, he will have a free hand in choosing his priorities; but to a large extent, his priorities will be influenced by events and circumstances beyond his control.

I have no shorthand formula for how a president establishes his priorities or the procedures he should follow in acquiring information and considering alternatives. There is no shopping list of "priority" problems; nor is there any checklist of people who should be consulted on any particular matter. But there is no question that, as a general principle, a president should try to consider as much information from as many divergent sources as time and circumstance permit, especially when the matter at hand is a controversial and important one. Otherwise, he faces increased risks that his decision will be changed by those (especially in Congress) who disagree with it, resisted by those who must implement it, and criticized by those who must live with it. An apt illustration of those risks is provided by President Ford's decisions in September 1974 to pardon Richard Nixon and give him control over the Nixon presidential tape recordings and papers.

Before making those decisions, Ford did not consult with anyone in Congress—not even the Republican leadership. That was, for Ford, a strategic mistake. For members of Congress might have advised him that Congress would protest loudly presidential actions which would, in effect, thwart a full accounting of the Watergate scandals. The agreement on the tapes and papers was particularly ill-advised in this respect. For that agreement allowed Nixon to limit access to all the tapes and papers, even for use in judicial proceedings; and it gave him the power to destroy eventually all the materials.* In short, the agreement raised the prospect that the courts, the Congress and the public would be deprived of vital evidence concerning the Watergate abuses.

---

* The agreement provided that all the Nixon materials would be temporarily stored by the federal government, with Nixon agreeing to donate some of the materials at a later date. Starting in 1979, Nixon was authorized to order the destruction of any tapes he chose; the agreement also stated that "such tapes shall be destroyed at the time of [Nixon's] death or on September 1, 1984, whichever event shall first occur." In other

A few days after the Ford decisions were announced, I spoke with Senator Gaylord Nelson about the possibility of introducing legislation to reverse the tapes and papers agreement. Nelson decided to propose legislation to have the federal government take permanent control of the Nixon presidential materials and make them available for use in judicial proceedings (subject of course to any constitutional or legal rights Nixon or anyone else might assert). Nelson then telephoned Senator Sam Ervin, who had chaired the Senate Watergate Committee (and who, I had been told, was "boiling mad" over the agreement). Ervin, then chairman of the Senate Government Operations Committee, told Nelson he would cosponsor the legislative bill and push it through his committee quickly. The congressional response was indeed quick. Nelson introduced the bill on September 18, the Government Operations Committee unanimously reported it out on September 26, and the Senate approved it overwhelmingly on October 4; after a month-long recess for the midterm elections, the House passed the measure by voice vote and it was sent to Ford for signature on December 9. Throughout these proceedings, the bill (which was amended in certain respects) commanded virtually unanimous support in Congress—even the Republican leadership accepted it. As the bill was moving toward enactment, Nelson told me that "it was foolish of Ford to think he could get that agreement by Congress. At a time when everyone was demanding the full truth about Watergate, how could we acquiesce in a presidential decision to bury the truth?"

The Ford decisions on the Nixon pardon and the tapes and papers agreement also underscore the fact that the president's responsibility for decision entails more than just absorbing information and considering alternatives for action. He should also have the good sense—and, when necessary, the courage—to do what he thinks will best serve the interests of the country. Again, there is no easy formula for knowing what is best. A president may sometimes undercut his own purposes if he blindly follows his own judgment without taking into account what the country will accept; on the other hand, a president must be willing to act independently of special interests—including his own political interests—if he concludes that the national interests require it.

Having said all this, I nonetheless recognize the inherent difficulties

---

words, the tapes would have to be destroyed upon Nixon's death—no matter when that occurred. The agreement provided further that Nixon could begin withdrawing the papers from storage beginning in 1977; implied in that provision was the right of Nixon to destroy the material (there was no requirement for him to return the withdrawn materials). Nixon-Sampson Agreement Relating to Presidential Materials, Sept. 6, 1974, reprinted in Senate Rpt. #93–1181, Comm. on Gov't. Operations, U.S. Senate, 93rd Cong., 2d Sess. 7–10 (1974).

in trying to assess a president's methods of decision-making. Presidential decisions—like most human choices—involve personal matters of heart and mind that do not easily admit to outside scrutiny. John Kennedy ultimately appreciated the complexity of the presidential decision-making process. A few months before his death, he wrote in a foreword for a book by his chief speechwriter, Theodore Sorensen, that

> the American Presidency is a formidable, exposed, and somewhat mysterious institution. It is formidable because it represents the point of ultimate decision in the American political system. It is exposed because decision cannot take place in a vacuum: the Presidency is the center of the play of pressure, interest, and idea in the nation; and the presidential office is the vortex into which all the elements of national decision are irresistibly drawn. And it is mysterious because the essence of ultimate decision remains impenetrable to the observer—often, indeed, to the decider himself.[1]

In other words, presidential decision-making is an art rather than a science. It requires judgment rather than quantitative calculation. Since judgment is, in the final result, a personal matter never allowing complete scrutiny by the outside observer, one may not be able to account for all of the factors which shape any presidential decision. But even within these limitations an analysis of a president's methods of absorbing information and executing decisions can develop conclusions about his ability to provide direction in the maze of modern government.

To probe decision-making in the White House is not to search for a definite structure or a stabilized procedure of presidential leadership. The methods of presidential decision-making fluctuate not only with the personalities of the incumbents, but also with the topics for discussion. The aides he depends on at the moment, the events which happen to occupy his thoughts, the references he respects, such as a particular item by a news columnist—all may interact with his attitudes to converge in a particular decision or a specific instruction to his subordinates. But this interaction is neither ordained in heaven nor predetermined in government.

Thus, the continuity of policy between presidents is largely a matter for each president to decide for himself. Examples abound. Franklin Roosevelt's decision to develop the atomic bomb did not free his successor from agonizing over whether the bomb should be dropped on Hiroshima. Similarly, the fact that Eisenhower initiated the Bay of Pigs invasion plan had a certain degree of influence on Kennedy's eventual support; but Eisenhower knew that his formulation of the plan in 1960 could not assure its execution in 1961 under a different president. Perhaps the most telling example of the malleability of a presidential decision is found in the Vietnam conflict. Each president since Eisenhower has felt a certain moral obligation to reaffirm his support for this small Asian country; although such pressure stemmed, in part, from each president's sense of continuity, the commitments of his predecessors did not completely limit his options or dictate his decisions. Each president retained the freedom to decide—and rationalize—the level of military support the United States should furnish Vietnam. In short, in examining the methods by which presidents make decisions, it should always be remembered that we are talking about one human being who is not bound by the past and who, for better or worse, shares all the frailties and limitations of each one of us. This point was aptly summarized by George Reedy in his extremely thoughtful book, *The Twilight of the Presidency:*

> It is assumed that there is something called a "decision-making process" which can be charted in much the same fashion as the table of organization for a business corporation. The fondest dream of the academic political scientist is to trace this flow chart in such a way that it will be available for study, comment, criticism, and possibly improvement. . . .
>
> The fact is that a president makes his decisions as he wishes to make them, under conditions which he himself has established, and at times of his own determination. He decides what he wants to decide and any student of the White House who believes that he is making a contribution to political thought when he analyzes the process is sadly mistaken. At best—at the very best—he can only contribute to human knowledge some insights into the decision-making process of one man.[2]

As a matter of history, Reedy is correct. There is no one single "proper" method of presidential decision-making. Each president has a different style, a different method of operation, which is adapted to his peculiar needs and personality. And whatever that style, it is not likely to reflect the rigid structure of an Erector set or the complete rationality of a mathematical theorem.

This is not to suggest, however, that there is nothing to be learned from a study of a president's methods of making decisions. Quite the contrary. Any president who wants to avoid the mistakes of the past would do well to study the records and styles of his predecessors. In the first days of his administration, for example, Kennedy received several memos from Fred Dutton, a White House aide, quoting historical works on the decision-making styles of Franklin Roosevelt, Eisenhower, and other presidents.[3] As a student of history, Kennedy thought there might be some benefit in at least understanding what earlier presidents did to help ensure that they made the right choices. This thought is sound. A study of modern presidents does demonstrate that the method of decision-making—the ability to secure information and understand available options—was often crucial to the president's effectiveness in exercising leadership.

Consider the presidency of Theodore Roosevelt at the turn of the century. A man of enormous energies, he sought action and drama at every stage of his life. This passion for activity followed Roosevelt to the White House. He treasured the opportunity to wield the reins of power. As he wrote to a friend, "I love the White House; I greatly enjoy the exercise of power."[4]

Given this love of action and drama, it was only natural that Roosevelt should view the president as a "steward" of the people who was obligated to use the office to remedy the injustices of society. And there was plenty of injustice when he succeeded to the presidency in 1901. The almost monopolistic growth of large industries had been achieved at the expense of the public. The industrial giants exploited laborers of every age and sex, who worked in poor conditions and for little pay; there were few laws to protect the consuming public from the substandard quality of the goods produced by these industrial giants; and there was little effort to enforce the antitrust laws to protect the small businessmen from the large corporations' cutthroat tactics.

The need for reform, then, was obvious. But Roosevelt did not act impulsively. He understood that success required planning, and planning required information. He had to know whether the country at large would support reform legislation. He had to know whether the conservative leaders of Congress would accept such legislation. And he had to know whether the government would enforce it if such a legislation was enacted. All these interests had to be considered, because to him, "the task of politics was to reconcile opposing elements in a fragile equilibrium through compromise."[5]

These information needs coincided with Roosevelt's personality and habits. He was by nature a gregarious man who had a driving curiosity, a need for close personal relationships, and a desire to be liked. He was always a prolific letter writer (approximately 100,000 of his letters are still available). He continued this letter writing in the White House. Leaders in labor, business, and politics throughout the country received an almost endless stream of letters from 1600 Pennsylvania Avenue. More often than not, the letter solicited information: What is the mood of your community? What are the pressing problems there? What should be done? Is the federal government doing its job?

These frequent contacts with the people complemented Roosevelt's efforts with their representatives in Congress. He ingratiated himself with the conservative leadership (who, not surprisingly, were to play important roles in deciding whether Roosevelt would be nominated by the Republican Party in 1904 for a second term). He tried to gauge the prejudices, the weaknesses, and the strengths of these legislators—all with an eye toward deciding the limits of what he could achieve in Congress. Typical here were Roosevelt's frequent meetings with Joe Cannon. As Speaker of the House of Representatives, Cannon exercised almost dictatorial power in deciding the fate of any legislation. If he opposed a bill, he could invoke any one of numerous procedural devices to ensure that it never reached the House floor for a vote. In this light, it was not difficult to understand why Roosevelt so often sought Cannon's company. Years later, Cannon reflected on these meetings:

> After I became Speaker of the House, my conferences with President Roosevelt were frequent, two or three times a week when Congress was in session, and sometimes daily. The President would write a note . . . "Come up some evening for a long talk, Tuesday or Wednesday or Thursday evening about 9:30, if you can, so that we shall be free from interruption." . . . We found it more convenient to meet in the evening . . . and it was then, sitting about the fire or later in his study, we talked things over until midnight.[6]

From these and other meetings with congressional leaders, as well as in meetings with other political leaders, Roosevelt sensed in his first years that the prospects were not good—politically or legislatively—for reform as strong as he liked. Amidst his long conversations with congressional leaders, compromises were struck which did result in legislation but which did not completely satisfy the leaders of the progressive movement. (Roosevelt, in a fit of pique, once referred to ardent social reformers in a derogatory manner as "muckrakers" who keep their eyes on the ground as they incessantly rake "the straws, the small sticks, and the dust off the floor"[7]—statements such as these, needless to say, did not upset the congressional conservatives whose support Roosevelt solicited.)

A sense of compromise—a recognition of what he thought was politically acceptable—also guided Roosevelt's heralded antitrust policies. Because it represented the first real attempt to control the mushrooming power of industrial monopolies, Roosevelt's selected antitrust activities received wide attention and brought fame to his motto that "a man should speak softly and carry a big stick." In fact, however, Roosevelt's antitrust activities were quite modest in scope, especially when compared to the activities of William Howard Taft and later Franklin D. Roosevelt. (Thurman Arnold, the assistant attorney general who directed the most expansive antitrust program under the second

Roosevelt, once referred to Theodore Roosevelt's antitrust policies as "the big stick that never hit anybody."[8]) From his information sources, however, Theodore Roosevelt simply believed that he did not have sufficient support in Congress or the country to execute a stronger antitrust program.

This all began to change after Roosevelt's election to the White House in 1904. Not only did he have the added stature of being elected in his own right (until then he was simply filling out the unexpired term of the assassinated William McKinley); Roosevelt also enjoyed the momentum of a progressive movement that was growing stronger throughout the country and even in Congress. Sensing opportunities for bolder actions, Roosevelt—while not abandoning entirely his willingness to compromise—pushed for more effective reform measures, such as a bill for federal meat inspection and a bill to provide the first federal regulation of drugs. Roosevelt also sensed the power of decision in foreign affairs. He built up the navy, sent it around the world and dared the Congress to challenge his authority; he continued his policy of dispatching American troops to Caribbean countries whenever he thought important American interests were being threatened (which, however beneficial to those American interests, often violated accepted precepts of international law); and he almost unilaterally directed the building of the Panama Canal when Congress and other nations balked at carrying out the project. And toward the end, Roosevelt appreciated—as Kennedy would—not only the President's obligation to make the difficult choices; he also recognized the importance of understanding the limitations within which those choices would have to be made. Roosevelt's sensitivity to the burdens and limits of presidential choices is reflected in a letter he wrote to his son Kermit in 1907 concerning some problems in completing the Panama Canal:

> New difficulties have come up in connection with Panama. The truth is that I have a great number of tasks to do, and that except in a very few of them, either the best men I can get have weak streaks in them, or the conditions under which I work are so faulty that to accomplish even a moderate amount of good is exceedingly difficult. In other words the great majority of the instruments with which I work have each some big flaw. I have to endeavor to bear down as lightly as possible on the flaw and get the best results I can in spite of it; and when the instrument finally breaks, grin and pick up another one, probably no better, and work as long as I can with it in its turn.[9]

Woodrow Wilson did not fully share Roosevelt's understanding of the need for information and the limits of the president's choices. This, in turn, reflected differences in character and personality. Criticism of any kind was viewed by Wilson as a personal affront, and many friends and associates were abandoned at the slightest suggestion that they disagreed with an opinion or action of his. Argument, debate, compromise, and, most of all, admission of error—these were all alien to Wilson's view of life.

Wilson's insecurity was balanced by an almost blind faith in himself. With rare gifts of oratory and high intelligence, he possessed a drive for power which enabled him to rise quickly from an obscure lawyer to a noted constitutional scholar, then governor of New Jersey, and ultimately in the 1912 election to the presidency. These grand achievements did little to inspire humility. "Remember," he told an aide shortly after his accession to the White House, "that God ordained that I should be the next President of the United States."[10] In a word, Wilson felt that he was destined to achieve greatness—and to be appreciated for it without qualification.

This spirit accounted for two basic and almost paradoxical elements of Wilson's methods of decision-making.

On the one hand, he displayed a confident aggressiveness in involving others in the making of presidential decisions. Before deciding upon a major policy or action, he sought facts and opinions from members of Congress, his administrators, and other political leaders. Once having made his choice, he labored tirelessly to engage Congress and his administrators in the implementation of those decisions. He worked closely with the Democratic party caucus in reviewing the administration's legislative priorities, for example. He also organized frequent meetings between cabinet officers and congressional leaders to map strategy for the enactment of the reform legislation he intended to or had already proposed. After one of these meetings one congressman said that Wilson had impressed everyone "that we are all—President, Congress, and people—in the presence of an irresistible situation."[11]

Whatever doubts other congressmen may have had about the situation, there was no doubt about the irresistible force of Wilson himself. He understood that he had both the responsibility and the power of decision to help correct the injustices of American society. And there was much evidence of Wilson's success in drawing upon the resources of Congress and the administration to meet that responsibility, especially in his first term. The Federal Reserve Board Act, the Clayton Anti-Trust Act, the Federal Trade Act—these and other reform measures represented significant steps toward the solution of basic social and economic problems.

There was a second major trait which characterized Wilson's method of making presidential decisions: a stubborn refusal on most occasions to seek or accept the counsel of his cabinet, the Congress or other political leaders after his choice had been made. Wilson's secretary of state, for example, observed that "arguments, however soundly reasoned, did not appeal to him if they were opposed to his feeling of what was the right thing to do. Even the established facts were ignored if they did not fit in with his intuitive sense, this semidivine power to select the right."[12] Early in Wilson's presidency, Colonel House—who was virtually the only adviser in whom Wilson placed any real confidence and trust—also recognized that Wilson often revealed a closed-minded attitude. Visitors to the White House—whether from Congress, the cabinet, or elsewhere—were not often asked their views on the merits of a chosen course; they were usually asked only to support it. People who volunteered advice (especially if it was critical) were rarely invited back to the White House. Wilson's distaste for advice—and his concomitant fear of rejection—were almost always in evidence. Indeed, House confided to his diary in April 1914 that he almost laughed when Wilson remarked to him that he always sought the advice of others. On another occasion two years later, House lamented that Wilson's isolation from advisers undermined his ability to make sound decisions:

> No one can see him to explain matters or get his advice. Therefore they come to me and I have to do it at long-range which is difficult and unsatisfactory. The President lacks executive ability and does not get the best results from his cabinet or those around him.[13]

This problem was equally apparent when Wilson met with foreign leaders to negotiate the Versailles Treaty. He relied almost exclusively on his own intuition and knowledge. Others on the American delegation were not consulted; they were not even informed of what Wilson's position was. As a result, offers of cooperation and compromise made to other members of the American delegation were never exploited; there was simply no way to communicate those offers to Wilson or to advise him on their merits.

Wilson similarly secluded himself from the senators whose support of the treaty was of obvious importance. Not one senator was appointed to the American delegation; and Wilson refused to keep them informed of developments in the negotiation of the treaty. Upon returning to the United States during a break in the negotiations, Wilson did confer with members of the Senate Foreign Relations Committee—but only after he made public statements delineating the position he would demand that the Senate support. Only at the end did Wilson make any effort to bargain with the Senate leaders over the treaty; but even then he was not really interested in accommodating their views. That close-minded attitude no doubt contributed to the Senate's rejection of the

Versailles Treaty and American participation in the League of Nations. The lesson was not lost upon Kennedy, and in negotiating the test ban treaty in 1963 he made a concerted effort to consult with and keep the Senate informed of developments.

In many ways Franklin D. Roosevelt represented the antithesis of Wilson in making presidential decisions. Although Roosevelt shared Wilson's concept of the presidency as a center of activity and direction in the nation's affairs, Roosevelt's character and temperament were quite different. And this helped to account for significant differences in the way he approached and executed decisions in the White House.

Roosevelt was a gregarious person; he relished his relationships with people and in these relationships he displayed a warmth which Wilson rarely revealed. As an assistant secretary of the navy in Wilson's Administration, Roosevelt began to develop the techniques of acquiring information and making decisions which he would bring to the White House. He eagerly sought out people of all stations to learn the facts and opinions which he should account for in making any decision. It was not only a matter of understanding the parameters of the choices to be made; it was also a tool for self-education. Wilson's secretary of war, Newton Baker, worked closely with Roosevelt and took note of his ceaseless efforts to be in touch with people:

> Young Roosevelt is very promising, but I should think he'd wear himself out in the promiscuous and extended contacts he maintains with people. But as I have observed him, he seems to clarify his ideas and teach himself as he goes along by that very conversational method.[14]

In cementing his relationship with people, Roosevelt often showed an easy grace, a quick wit, and a charm which made him quite an appealing figure. People simply liked to talk with him; he created the impression that he really listened and, most important, that he really cared. This facility for touching people was enhanced after Roosevelt's bout with polio in the early 1920s. The disease left his legs paralyzed and created doubts that he could continue his promising political career. From this experience Roosevelt's compassion for others was enlarged. More than ever, he understood the despair of someone afflicted by disease he could not cure or made helpless by circumstances he could not control. More than ever, he wanted to please people and be liked by them. As Arthur Schlesinger, Jr., observed, this trait had both advantages and disadvantages:

> Roosevelt found it hard . . . to refuse people, to send them away, to hurt their feelings. But the desire to be liked also opened him up to their needs and fears. It explained in great part the genius for as-

> similation which was developing within him and which was giving him so extraordinary a receptivity. Invisible antennae stretched out, picking up with faultless precision the intangibles of human emotion. The individual case was for him the center of the learning experience; from it, he extrapolated with bold confidence to the nation and the world.[15]

The experience with polio also enabled Roosevelt to make decisions, even difficult ones, with much greater equanimity. ("If you had spent two years in bed trying to wiggle your big toe," he commented in later years, "after that anything else would seem easy."[16])

Buoyed by his own self-confidence and encouraged by his wife, Eleanor, Roosevelt was determined to resume his political career. It proved to be a wise decision. In 1928 he was elected to the first of two terms as governor of New York, and in 1932 he was elected President of the United States.

Roosevelt assumed the reins of national leadership at the height of the Great Depression—between twelve and fifteen million people were unemployed, more than forty-six hundred banks had been closed, approximately one family in seven was on relief, mortgages on thousands of farms were being foreclosed, and, to say the least, the prospects for the future did not seem bright. In this atmosphere the importance of presidential leadership could not be understated. The public's high expectations of quick action from Roosevelt were captured by Will Rogers, who said, "The whole country is with him just so he does something. If he burned down the Capitol we would cheer and say, 'Well, we at least got a fire started anyhow.' "[17]

Roosevelt understood the need for immediate action—not only to provide some benefits to people but also to restore their faith in government and in themselves. In his inaugural on March 4, 1933, Roosevelt declared that "This nation asks for action, and action now. . . . We must act, and act quickly."[18] Sensing both the need and responsibility for decision, Roosevelt did move quickly. He asked Congress for new emergency powers. (Within 100 days of Roosevelt's inauguration the Congress enacted fifteen major administration proposals establishing new agencies and new relief programs.) He also directed those in his administration to make the benefits of the welfare laws available as soon as possible. And there was an immediate response to this presidential mandate. Typical was the reaction of Harry Hopkins, whom Roosevelt appointed as administrator of the Federal Emergency Relief Administration. Within two hours after he entered office, Hopkins spent $5 million in relief ("Hunger is not debatable," he said); and within a year his newly created Civil Works Administration had four million people employed in public service jobs. ("Well," he told FDR, "they're all at work, but for God's sake don't ask me what they're doing."[19])

The frenetic pace and accomplishment of Roosevelt's first months in office were of course not sustained throughout his twelve years' tenure. Before too long Roosevelt began to appreciate the difficulties in removing the nation from the womb of depression. Indeed, the marks of depression—high unemployment, low productivity, and limited growth—continued to mar the face of the nation until the shadows of World War II led to rapid increases in government economic planning and spending. But throughout his presidency, Roosevelt continued to refine the methods of decision-making which he began to develop before he entered the White House.

To begin with, he actively sought the companionship and advice of people with creative minds and sharp intellects. During the 1932 campaign he relied heavily on the thoughts and proposals of a group of college professors, most of whom were from Columbia University and who achieved national fame as Roosevelt's "brain trust." Once in the White House, Roosevelt maintained his faith in personal contacts as the optimum source of information, new ideas, and assurances that his decisions were being implemented. He continued to surround himself with men and women who could pepper him with facts, opinions, and proposals for action. After the report of the Brownlow Committee* in 1937, he also increased the size of his White House personal staff to ensure the ready availability of valued assistants. In addition to his personal staff, Roosevelt maintained close personal contact with those in government who were responsibile for implementing his decisions. He was constantly on the telephone or holding meetings, picking an administrator's brain about a program's effectiveness, about suggestions for improvement, and about public reactions. Everyone was asked to strain for the limit. The reaction of one governmental agency chief was illustrative. "After spending an hour with the President," he said, "I could eat nails for lunch."[20]

But Roosevelt did not rely exclusively on those in Washington for his information. Quite the contrary. He was most interested in the

---

*The reference here is to the *Report of the President's Committee on Administrative Management,* Washington: Government Printing Office, 1937. The committee was chaired by Louis Brownlow and was therefore commonly referred to as the Brownlow Committee. The study was initiated because many, including Roosevelt, felt that the administrative burdens on the President required that he have his own executive staff to help him fulfill his responsibilities. In 1939, Congress authorized the President, upon the recommendations of this report, to appoint a certain number of assistants.

For background on the Brownlow Committee's report, see the second volume of reminiscences by Louis Brownlow, *A Passion for Anonymity,* University of Chicago Press, Chicago, 1958, chapters 28, 30, 31, and 33.

views of those who lived with the federal government's programs and policies across the vast expanse of the country. He often relied on the information his wife, Eleanor, would bring him from her frequent trips throughout the country. He also urged his assistants and subordinates to travel widely to assess the impact of the government's work. "Pay no attention to what people are saying in Washington," he instructed one aide. "They are the last persons in the country to listen to."[21] Roosevelt, in short, understood that government programs could be effective and supported by the public only if they were formulated on the basis of information from broad and divergent sources. This dependence was aptly summarized by Arthur Schlesinger, Jr.:

> The first task of an executive, as he evidently saw it, was to guarantee himself an effective flow of information and ideas. And Roosevelt's first insight—or, at least, his profound conviction—was that, for this purpose, the ordained channels, no matter how simply or how intricately designed, could never be enough. An executive relying on a single information system became inevitably the prisoner of that system. Roosevelt's persistent effort therefore was to check and balance information acquired through official channels by information acquired through a myriad of private, informal, and unorthodox channels and espionage networks. At times he seemed almost to pit his personal sources against his public sources. From the viewpoint of subordinates, this method was distracting when not positively demoralizing. But Roosevelt, with his voracity for facts and for ideas, required this approach to cross-check to the official system and keep it alert as well as to assure himself the balanced and various product without which he could not comfortably reach decisions.[22]

Drawing upon this information, Roosevelt would build the public consensus, congressional support, and administrative receptivity for the decisions he thought necessary. But Roosevelt was generally hesitant to make his choices until a decision was in fact necessary. He much preferred to let the issue crystallize, the public understanding take root, and the congressional consideration be thorough. Once having made his choice, Roosevelt monitored the situation to determine whether changes in circumstance or opinion necessitated shifts in policy. In this sense, he envisioned himself as the quarterback of a large football team. "If the play makes ten yards," he told a press conference in April 1933, "the succeeding play will be different from what it would have been if they had been thrown for a loss. I think that is the easiest way to explain it."[23] In short, Roosevelt rarely made a final commitment on anything. This flexibility inevitably gave him vast opportunities to meet and adapt to new situations. As examples, he inaugurated his administration with a protectionist economic policy (removal of the gold standard in 1933) and then shifted to an internationalist trade policy (the Reciprocal Trade Agreements Act of 1934); he reversed his initial policy of cooperation with business (the National Industrial Recovery Act in 1933) to regulation of it (Security and Exchange Act in 1934). The inconsistency in these shifts was more apparent than real; for Roosevelt was responding to changing events and circumstances, to the need for attracting and sustaining a broad base of support.[24]

Even under the threat of world war Roosevelt was hesitant to act without some assurance that an important presidential decision would enjoy the necessary support in Congress and among the public. The exemplary case concerns the famous destroyer deal with England in 1940. Besieged by Nazi planes and surrounded by Nazi boats, England was in desperate need of American military supplies, especially destroyers. Winston Churchill, then Prime Minister of England, explained this need in urgent personal pleas to Roosevelt.

Because of the strong isolationist sentiment within the country, Roosevelt was reluctant to act without explicit congressional authorization. His staff advised him that the President had the constitutional authority to exchange American destroyers for a lease on British ports as American bases; but Roosevelt felt that a constitutional justification would not suffice if the public and the Congress rebelled against his decision—as he expected they would. After broad consultations with public leaders and members of Congress, Roosevelt was advised that the congressional leadership could not, given the country's isolationist mood, explicitly endorse such an exchange; but, because the matter was so crucial to England's survival, they would not publicly protest a unilateral executive agreement consummating the deal. Roosevelt then made the destroyer agreement with full confidence that his decision would not alienate his public or congressional supporters.

It was rare when Roosevelt deviated from this general method of decision-making. Indeed, one of the few exceptions—his proposal to "pack" the Supreme Court in 1937[25]—made clear to all that laying a foundation is of obvious importance to ensuring the success and effectiveness of a presidential decision. In this particular instance Roosevelt relied on the advice of only one assistant, Attorney General Homer Cummings. Despite the fact that the proposal required congresssional approval, Roosevelt did not consult any of his supporters in Congress—not even Senate Majority Leader Joe Robinson, the individual who would be asked to push the bill through the legislative process. Nor did Roosevelt follow his normal practice to seek the advice of political leaders who could give him an assessment of public opinion. The results were instructive. The same public which only months earlier had voted overwhelmingly to reelect Roosevelt viewed the court-packing proposal as an attempt to usurp the constitutional power of the courts. His Democratic supporters in Congress were equally outraged and led the fight to defeat the proposal (even the Vice-President, John Nance Garner, ignored Roosevelt's personal plea for him to return from his home in Texas to help rally congressional suport for the proposal). And, in the end, the proposal suffered a quiet death, leaving behind a President with his confidence and power momentarily shaken.

For my purposes here, the important point is this: Roosevelt's court-packing plan was doomed not only because of its merits but also because of the methods Roosevelt used to draft and present it. In his zeal to alter the complexion of the Supreme Court, Roosevelt ignored the basic tenets of decision-making which he had applied so successfully in the past. As James MacGregor Burns commented in his thorough study of Roosevelt,

> The fatal weakness of Roosevelt's plan lay partly in its content and partly in the way it was proposed. The plan itself seemed an evasive, disingenuous way of meeting a clear-cut problem. It talked about judicial efficiency rather than ideology; it was aimed at immediate personalities in the Court rather than the long-run problems posed by the Court. The manner of presentation—the surprise, Roosevelt's failure to pose the issue more concretely in the election, his obvious relish in the job, his unwillingness to ask his cabinet and his congressional leaders for advice—alienated some potential supporters. More important, this method of presentation prevented Roosevelt from building a broad coalition behind the bill and ironing out multifarious tactical details before springing the attack—behind-the-scenes activities in which Roosevelt was highly adept.[26]

This of course was not the first time a president got "burned" because he failed to consult those whose advice and support were critical to the success of his decisions; nor was it the last. But the basic point was not lost upon Kennedy. He paid close attention to congressional views when the implementation of a policy or decision required congressional action.

Few people, however, admired FDR more than Lyndon B. Johnson. A young schoolteacher from rural Texas, Johnson came to Washington, D.C., in 1931 to work as a staff secretary for a Texas congressman. After serving for a brief time, Johnson returned to Texas to win a special election as congressman in 1937. From the moment he arrived in his new position, Johnson developed a great affection for FDR. He saw in Roosevelt a real leader, an individual who understood the burdens of the common man and who was willing to use the vast powers of government to ease those burdens. FDR, in turn, took Johnson under his wing, confided in him and tutored him in the ways of government. It is hardly surprising, therefore, that Johnson would constantly invoke Roosevelt's presidency as the measure of his own success as President. The irony—and tragedy—is that Johnson often could not or would not emulate the ways of his famous tutor in making decisions. And this difference does much to explain why Johnson's policies failed so miserably in particular areas but especially in the Vietnam War.

Alexander Hamilton wrote that "energy in the Executive is a leading character in the definition of good government."[27] It is not clear whether Johnson relied on Hamilton's advice, but it is clear that Johnson brought to the White House a boundless energy which made his presidency one of the most active in legislative and political affairs. "Lyndon acts as if there is never going to be a tomorrow," his wife once said, and this is part of his code: "When you have something to do, don't just sit there. Do it, and do it fast."[28] From early morning to late at night he was constantly on the telephone (a large one with many buttons), or in meetings with his aides, the bureaucrats, members of Congress, other politicians, and world leaders. Like Roosevelt, he derived much of his information from these personal contacts with people. And like Roosevelt, he believed that personal contact was the best means for ensuring that the government was responding to the President's directions and executing his decisions as *he* wanted them executed.

The flavor of this style is perhaps captured best in a conversation Johnson had with some close friends in a New York City restaurant shortly before his death in January 1973. He had just paid a visit to President Nixon in the Oval Office, and the visit inspired him to reminisce about his days in the White House. He displayed a particular fondness for his large telephones with the many buttons. "If I needed to get hold of somebody," he recalled, "all I had to do was mash a button. And I mean anybody," he continued. "Even some little fella tucked away in one of those agencies. If I thought he should have the answer to something, I'd just get him on the horn." This, he maintained, was the only way to ensure that the sprawling maze of government remained responsive to the President's leadership. Otherwise, he said, "the day will come when you wake up and discover that the damn thing is running *you.*" He then paused to reflect upon his visit with Nixon earlier that day. He could hardly believe the fact that Nixon had just one telephone: "Just *one* dinky little phone to keep in touch with his people." And there were only three buttons on that phone. "That's all," LBJ intoned. Then—with reference to the ethnic backgrounds of

Nixon's top three advisers (H. R. Haldeman, John Ehrlichman, and Henry Kissinger)—Johnson exclaimed, "Just three buttons, and *they* all go to Germans!"[29]

Johnson's appreciation for the art of leadership here was nurtured in more than twenty years on Capitol Hill, six of them as Senate Majority Leader. There he had maneuvered much legislation through Congress, cajoling, pleading, bargaining with men and women whose habits, tastes, prejudices, and opinions he had come to know intimately. It was, in fact, this intimate acquaintance with the procedures and people of Congress which helped him to secure enactment of most of his major legislative proposals (of 200 major bills proposed by Johnson in 1965 and 1966, 181 were enacted into law).

But Johnson's Senate years also revealed the weaknesses which would make life so difficult for him in the White House. Despite his impressive skills as a lobbyist and negotiator, Johnson was not very tolerant of criticism or people who refused to follow his lead. Having chosen a course of action, he was insistent that there be no dissent—expecially from those upon whose support he relied. A Senate colleague recalled this Johnson trademark shortly after he assumed the presidential office on 1963:

> . . . he will not change course even when he knows he is wrong, because he has a preposterous idea he is bound to lose face if he does. The only advisers he will listen to are those who will tell him what he wants to hear, for he is not a man who tolerates listening to both sides of a problem.[30]

The fear of rejection, of failure, and the concern that people would be disloyal—these were the qualities which often shaped the decisions of Johnson's presidency. And underlying these concerns was a more basic anxiety—a fear that he might not have the requisite talents to be a good president. "I know I've got a heart big enough to be President," he once mused. "I know I've got guts enough to be President. But I wonder whether I've got intelligence and ability enough to be President—I wonder if any man does?"[31]

Once having made a decision, therefore, Johnson was not prone to seek or accept advice which might draw into question the soundness of that decision and, by implication (in Johnson's eyes at least), his ability to exercise presidential leadership. The most dramatic and tragic illustrations of this trait were of course found in the decisions Johnson made with respect to American involvement in the Vietnam War.

Throughout his congressional years Johnson was a staunch defender of the anticommunist crusade initiated by President Harry Truman and pursued under the presidency of Dwight Eisenhower. He believed that America must be constantly on the watch, able to police the world, and to douse the revolutionary fires sparked, he believed, by a monolithic communist conspiracy. As Vice-President under John Kennedy, Johnson's faith in this anticommunist crusade remained undiminished. He continued to subscribe to the "domino theory" articulated by Eisenhower and endorsed by Kennedy—a belief that if one Asian country succumbed to communism the other countries would soon fall like dominoes into the lap of communism. This view colored Johnson's perception of people, places, and policies in Asia. (After a visit to Vietnam as Vice-President, Johnson hailed Vietnamese President Diem as Asia's Winston Churchill—despite the dictatorial and ruthless policies enforced by Diem against his fellow countrymen.)

Upon assuming the presidency, Johnson made clear that the American commitment to Vietnam (which Kennedy himself was beginning to question) would not be abandoned or qualified. The reasons were, to a large extent, very personal for Johnson: "I am not going to lose Vietnam. I am not going to be the President who saw Southeast Asia go the way China went."[32] Having settled upon this policy, Johnson all but foreclosed any reconsideration which might have spared the country—and his presidency—the agonies which were soon to follow.

On December 5, 1963, Johnson convened a meeting of the National Security Council to review major international problems and the principles which would guide his administration's foreign policies. At that meeting Johnson implored those in attendance to consider "the other fellow's point of view" in resolving the issues of international affairs. But, at least as far as Vietnam was concerned, the exhortation was really mere window dressing. This became very clear at subsequent NSC meetings. The very format of those meetings made robust debate and open disagreement very difficult. The difficulty here can be understood from Chester Cooper's firsthand account of a typical NSC meeting on Vietnam:

> The NSC meetings I attended had a fairly standard format: the Secretary of State first presented a short summary of the issues, the Secretary of Defense added his comments, and there was some fairly bland and desultory discussion by the others present. Because many around the table had not participated in, nor indeed been told of the detailed advance discussions, "gut" issues were seldom raised and searching questions were seldom asked.
>
> The President, in due course, would announce his decision and then poll everyone in the room—Council members, their assistants, and members of the White House and NSC Staffs. "Mr. Secretary, do you agree with the decision?" "Yes, Mr. President." "Mr. X, do you agree?" "I agree, Mr. President." During the proc-

ess I would frequently fall into a Walter Mitty-like fantasy: When my turn came I would rise to my feet slowly, look around the room and then directly at the President, and say very quietly and emphatically, "Mr. President, gentlemen, I most definitely do *not* agree." But I was removed from my trance when I heard the President's voice saying, "Mr. Cooper, do you agree?" And out would come a "Yes Mr. President, I agree."[33]

Within a short time Johnson dispensed with most NSC meetings; he did not even care to create the impression of debate and agreement. Most decisions were made in the quiet of the Oval Office when only Johnson and a few advisers were present. This method of decision-making enabled Johnson and his advisers to avoid the hard questions which were being raised by their own intelligence briefings and by accounts published in America's newspapers—questions which not only raised doubts about the effectiveness of American policy in Vietnam but also about the purposes those policies were designed to serve. Thus did Johnson make the most critical decisions concerning the Vietnam War—to bomb North Vietnam and to increase the level of American troops stationed in South Vietnam—without the searching inquiries which so often characterized Franklin D. Roosevelt's method of making decisions.

Indeed, it became a widely known secret in the higher levels of government that the only person who could dissent from the Vietnam decisions was George Ball, a soft-spoken, highly articulate lawyer who served as undersecretary of state. Ball's persistent and discursive dissents (he once wrote a 100-page memorandum for Johnson on Vietnam policy) were tolerated in part because Ball's manner of presentation was not abrasive and in part because he soothed consciences troubled by the lack of debate. This point was made forcefully by George Reedy, who served as Johnson's press secretary:

Strangely enough, an official devil's advocate is more likely to solidify the thinking of the President . . . than it is to make the President pause. During President Johnson's administration I watched George Ball play the role. . . . The cabinet would meet and there would be an overwhelming report from [Secretary of Defense] Robert McNamara, another overwhelming report from [Secretary of State] Dean Rusk, another overwhelming report from [White House adviser] McGeorge Bundy. Then five minutes would be set aside for George Ball to deliver his dissent. The others . . . because they expected him to dissent . . . automatically discounted whatever he said. This strengthened them in their own convictions because the cabinet members could quite honestly say, "we've heard both sides of this issue discussed." . . . They heard it with wax in their ears.[34]

Johnson's distaste for criticism and dissent was so well established that close advisers were dissuaded from bringing to him the facts and opinions which might make Johnson feel uncomfortable. For example, when Arthur Goldberg, Johnson's United Nations ambassador, considered raising his opposition to the Vietnam policies at an NSC meeting, a colleague advised him against it. Recalling their days in Kennedy's cabinet, the colleague reminded Goldberg that "Kennedy didn't mind disagreement. It didn't bother him. But disagreement really bothers this President. He is going to do what you dislike anyway; so let's not upset him by having an argument in front of him."*

In the end, then, Johnson's policies in Vietnam—whatever else may be said about them—did not reflect a thorough consideration of all the relevant information. To a very large degree he isolated himself from the facts and opinions that might have exposed the weaknesses of existing policy or underscored the strengths of alternative policies. Sadly, but not unexpectedly, Johnson's Vietnam policies failed to achieve peace for the Asian people and led many Americans to wonder whether their great sacrifices had been made for legitimate purposes.

Richard Nixon was among those who recognized the havoc Johnson's policies had brought to the country and, far more important to his political fortunes, the Democratic Party as well. Campaigning for the presidency in 1968, Nixon would not attack the merits of Johnson's Vietnam policies (principally because, as time would show, he basically agreed with them); but Nixon did sense the need to assure the electorate that his presidency would not repeat the closed atmosphere of Johnson's tenure, the secrecy which alienated so many Americans and made them feel that their interests and opinions were not considered in the councils of government.

Anxious to contrast his style with that of Johnson, Nixon promised the electorate that he would conduct an "open" presidency in which all ideas and interests could be heard. The most forceful and eloquent expression of this promise was contained in an address Nixon made on national radio on September 19, 1968. In this address, he first made clear that his concept of the presidency was an activist one in the spirit of Theodore Roosevelt:

> The days of a passive Presidency belong to the simpler past. Let me be very clear about this: The next President must take an activ-

---

*Quoted in Arthur Schlesinger, Jr., *The Imperial Presidency* 185 (1973). The pressures for conformity were so great in Johnson's Presidency that government officials were reluctant to express their true feelings to one another. Townsend Hoopes, an assistant secretary in the Defense Department, wrote that "in the Pentagon the Tet offensive [of January 1968] performed the curious service of fully revealing the doubters and dissenters to each other, in a lightning flash." Hoopes, *The Limits of Intervention* 145 (1969).

> ist view of his office. He must articulate the nation's values, define its goals and marshal its will. Under a Nixon Administration, the presidency will be deeply involved in the entire sweep of America's public concerns.

In responding to these concerns, Nixon stated, the president would have to accept his "duty to decide." But in making these decisions, the president could not closet himself away in the solitude of his office. With a not-so-subtle swipe at Johnson, Nixon continued:

> It's time we once again had an open administration—open to ideas *from* the people, and open in its communications *with* the people—an administration of open doors, open eyes, and open minds.

To achieve this goal, it was important (at least so he said) to listen to the dissenters and even to encourage criticism and comment from his own advisers:

> We should bring dissenters into policy discussions, not freeze them out; we should invite constructive criticism, not only because the critics have a right to be heard, but also because they often have something worth hearing.
>
> And this brings me to another related point: The President cannot isolate himself from the great intellectual ferments of his time. On the contrary he must consciously and deliberately place himself at their center. . . .
>
> This is one reason why I don't want a government of yes-men. It's why I do want a government drawn from the broadest possible base—an administration made up of Republicans, Democrats and independents, and drawn from politics, from career government service, from universities, from business, from the professions—one including not only executives and administrators, but scholars and thinkers.
>
> While the President is a leader of thought, he is also a user of thought, and he must be a catalyst of thought. . . .
>
> Officials of a new Administration will not have to check their consciences at the door, or leave their powers of independent judgment at home. . . .[35]

A catalyst of thought. A man who sought criticism, who invited independent judgment. A man who appreciated the importance of different perspectives. This is the way a president should approach decisions. Alas, for Nixon (and the country), this was also political hyperbole.

However genuine Nixon's belief in these statements as abstract principles, they ran contrary to the realities of his character. He was—by temperament, personality, and history—a loner, a man who saw himself constantly engaged in battle (he always referred to the "warfare of politics"). And being in battle, he was prone to view criticism as the parry of an adversary.

In many ways, in short, Nixon is a deeply suspicious and insecure man; there are few people in whom he could place any trust. (When White House counsel John Dean referred to one man as "a friend of ours," Nixon responded quickly, "Nobody is a friend of ours! Let's face it."[36]) In the beginning of his administration, Nixon did make an attempt to be accessible to new men and new ideas. He sensed that his reelection would depend on the creativity of his staff—especially if, as expected, the Democratic nominee were Senator Edward Kennedy. It was during this period that Nixon accepted the advice of Harvard professor Daniel Moynihan to propose an innovative welfare program (later identified as the Family Assistance Plan). The period of "openness" was short-lived, however. Cabinet officers and other political leaders outside the inner circle made Nixon feel uncomfortable. They pressured him to endorse programs—like the Model Cities Program and the supersonic transport plane—which he really did not like. He leaned toward his natural inclination to isolate himself from almost everyone, even those whose ideas, cooperation, and support were crucial to his administration's success.

This drift toward isolation proved to be Nixon's undoing. For the people he chose to rely on the most—H. R. Haldeman, John Ehrlichman, John Mitchell, and Charles Colson—had little government experience and little regard for principled conduct. In their judgment, there was only one question to be asked: What does the President want or need? Colson aptly summarized this attitude when he was sentenced to jail in the spring of 1974 for his illegal White House activities. "During the time I served in the White House," Colson said, "I rarely questioned a Presidential order. Infrequently did I question the President's judgment. I had one rule—to get done that which the President wanted done."[37]

Nixon's drift toward isolation accelerated after Senator Kennedy's unfortunate experience at Chappaquiddick Island in the summer of 1969. Although White House aides publicly sympathized for the young woman who died and her family, privately they were gloating. They were confident that this mishap eliminated any chance that Kennedy would face Nixon in his 1972 reelection effort. With this new confidence in Nixon's reelection came a willingness to throw caution to the wind. There was no need now to invite independent thought.

(When White House aide Jeb Magruder wrote a memo proposing some new idea for presidential action, Haldeman returned it with the curt note: "Your job is to do, not to think."[38]) There was no need now to tolerate the musings and suggestions of cabinet members (Interior Secretary Walter Hickel was forced to write—and release to the press—a letter to Nixon criticizing his decision to invade Cambodia because Hickel's repeated requests for a meeting with Nixon were just as repeatedly rebuffed).

But the impact of the new mood was not confined to the internal workings of the administration. There was no need now to placate Congress either. Nor was there any need now to demonstrate to the public Nixon's support for innovative welfare programs or other liberal measures. There was no need, in short, to appease anyone about anything. In their book *The Palace Guard,* Dan Rather and Paul Gates capture the essence of this new mood in a passage that merits full quotation:

> Thus a new course was set. What had started out as a euphoric reaction to Chappaquiddick soon crystallized into a hard and bitter determination to poison the atmosphere with the politics of spite and vendetta—to wage unceasing war on Congress, the press, and . . . even members of their own cabinet who dared question the wisdom of the new strategy. This resulted from the concentration of power in the hands of men who, because they had no background experience themselves in the world of Washington—or in government on any level—chose to transform the White House into an embattled fortress, sealing it off from what they regarded as an alien city around them, a city infested with hostile groups seeking to bring harm to them and their President. Yet, because so much of the poison was bottled up within those walls, it was inevitable that it should spread inward, and that they themselves should become its ultimate victims.[39]

This mood—and arrogance—made possible the break-in at the Democratic National Committee's headquarters in the Watergate office building. But the Watergate break-in was not an isolated incident. It represented only one in a series of unlawful activities and abusive practices organized by the Nixon White House. The abuses took many forms—wiretaps on newsmen and government officials who had not violated the law; an illegal break-in of Daniel Ellsberg's psychiatrist's office; a willingness to use public offices to protect and secure favors from political allies; an improper dissemination of confidential tax returns of thousands of individuals (prompting Senator Lowell Weicker to compare the IRS to a "public lending library"); Nixon's creation of an extralegal intelligence unit to do the spying which the FBI would not do; and Nixon's approval of a security plan which his staff advised him was "clearly illegal" because it involved burglaries and uncontrolled wiretapping.

Regardless of the particular form, each of these and other abuses reflected a dangerous attitude whose roots can be traced back to the presidencies of Kennedy, Johnson, and others. Each of these presidents placed a high premium on personal loyalty to him and a willingness to serve his established goals. But, with few exceptions, each president also accepted the constitutional and legal constraints in securing that loyalty or in achieving those goals. Under Nixon the constraints evaporated. Personal loyalty to the "boss" was equated as patriotism, and criticism was viewed as treason. Free speech, the right of privacy, the rule of law—these and other fundamental principles could be waived if the "boss" wanted something done.

Having no respect for the institutions of constitutional government, it was quite natural that the Nixon White House should reflect contempt for the constitutional and legal constraints which make ours a government of laws and not of men. Their abusive and unlawful efforts, though pervasive and of far-reaching effect, were generally well camouflaged. Few, if anyone, in Congress or the press or the public at large really knew the extent to which America was slowly being transformed into a police state of one-man rule.

Nixon's isolation was so great that even he did not fully appreciate the significance of the misdeeds perpetrated by his administration. By the late spring of 1973 virtually all of his office time was spent with his new chief of staff, Alexander Haig, and his press secretary, Ronald Ziegler—two men whose faith in Nixon enabled them to cooperate with the charade of the administration's clean record.* The depth of the illusion (or charade) was revealed in a May 1974 interview which Nixon gave to Rabbi Baruch M. Korff, director of a supportive citizens' group. At this late juncture more than thirty White House aides and

---

*On June 4, 1973, Nixon, Haig, and Ziegler reviewed transcripts of the White House tapes (the existence of which had not yet been publicly disclosed). The subject at hand was whether the tapes—which provided considerable evidence of Nixon's own criminal liability—demonstrated Nixon's involvement in the Watergate scandals. The following exchanges then occurred:

Nixon: Really, the God damn record is not bad, is it?
Ziegler: Makes me feel very good.

* * * *

Nixon: As you know, we're up against ruthless people.
Haig: Well, we're going to be in great shape now, 'cause we're going to prepare.

Hersh, "Tape Reveals New Kind of White House," *New York Times*, July 21, 1974, p. 38.

Nixon campaign associates had been indicted or convicted of Watergate crimes; the House impeachment proceedings were moving inexorably forward. Nixon could nevertheless tell Korff that Watergate would be regarded by future historians as "the broadest and thinnest scandal in American history, because what was it about?" In his view, it was simply the folly (albeit illegal) of a group of overzealous men. Was there no substance to the charges documented daily in the press, he was asked. No, Nixon replied, "as far as the people in the media are concerned, it is an ideological thing. As I said, if I were a liberal, Watergate would be a blip."[40] The enemy was there; their guns were being fired; he would not flinch. As in his other crises, he had made a decision to tough this one out—alone if necessary. But this battle he was destined to lose. For having failed to honor his campaign promise to conduct an open presidency, Nixon could not see that the real enemy lay inside—not outside—the White House gates.

John F. Kennedy: The Promise and the Willingness to Be Open-Minded

The presidential office that John Kennedy entered in 1961 was very similar to the office that Richard Nixon abandoned thirteen years later. In fact, there has been a remarkable continuity in the institutions and customs of the federal government in the twentieth century—especially since the tenure of Franklin D. Roosevelt when the responsibilities and size of government were broadened to cope with the Great Depression. But those institutions and customs did not guarantee Kennedy any information he might need to understand the issues; nor did those institutions and customs determine what choices he would face or what decisions he would make. Thus, to examine Kennedy's ability to gather information and to execute decisions is to understand how—and indeed whether—Kennedy implemented his ideas and ideals of presidential leadership. To praise the achievements of his leadership or to pinpoint its failures one must penetrate the extent to which his decisions were responsible for those results.

As with presidents before and since, Kennedy's decisions would be shaped by a multiplicity of factors personal to him: his ideals, his understanding of the facts, his judgment of what would work, his assessment of what was politically acceptable. The usefulness of information he received would depend on his ability to relate it to his political, social, and economic environment. A president must fathom the circumstances and problems which confront his several constituencies. He must touch the thoughts of others, have some sense of decisions they may be contemplating, and understand how his subsequent actions are likely to affect those thoughts and decisions. Otherwise the success of his efforts becomes extremely dependent on chance, ensuring that the probability of error will be very high. Like other presidents, in short, Kennedy's personality, his intelligence, his attitudes, his sensitivity to others—all these factors would play a basic role in molding his decisions.

In order to define the nature of Kennedy's promise in making decisions, it is necessary to review some dominant themes in his personal and political development. The home of Kennedy's youth was a busy place. There were, to begin with, the numerous brothers and sisters. Visits from friends were frequent wherever "home" happened to be—in Hyannis Port, in Bronxville, or in Palm Beach. Often the friends were Joe Kennedy's associates in politics and business. But in any case, lively discussions were commonplace. And all of the children were encouraged to draw upon their travels, their experiences, or their reading, to speak their piece, to contribute an idea or an opinion.

Through all this, learning was the key. Joe and Rose Kennedy wanted their children to have a broad exposure to the world, an understanding of what it was like and the diverse experiences which it offered. And, above all, they wanted their children to be a part of that world, to have the training and self-confidence to pursue their interests wherever they might lead. As Rose Kennedy recalled recently,

> On the whole I think my conviction that my children should have many "learning experiences" and should use their minds to the fullest capacity, discovering the world for themselves through personal encounters with the world outside, worked out well and perhaps had something to do with their curiosity, their enthusiasm for new adventures, their confidence in knowing that life was exciting.[41]

The family's considerable wealth of course made it easier to provide these "learning experiences." There is no question, however, that his parents' guidance had much to do with John Kennedy's attitudes and habits.

Kennedy's education was not pointed in a particular direction: Joe Kennedy wanted his children to understand another individual's perspective and beliefs; despite his own conservatism, he did not want his children's thinking blindly chained to the strictures of conservatism or any other philosophy. This attitude led him to arrange for his two eldest sons, Joe, Jr., and Jack, to be tutored by one of the foremost socialist philosophers of the day, Professor Harold Laski of the London School of Economics. To Rose Kennedy this seemed strange; but to Joe it made perfect sense. "These boys are going to have a little money when they get older," he explained, "and they should know what the 'have nots' are thinking and planning." To be sure, Joe Kennedy did not agree with Laski's writings. "But I never taught the boys to disapprove of someone," he said, "just because I didn't accept his ideas. They heard enough from me, and I decided they should be exposed to someone of intelligence and vitality on the other side."[42]

There is no reason to believe that John Kennedy's brief experience with Laski converted him into a Marxist.* But there is much reason to believe that his parents' attitude—coupled with Kennedy's own instincts, reading habits, and travels—nurtured an active interest in the world around him. He was almost always open to new ideas, new people, and new experiences. His sense of adventure and his thirst for knowledge kept him moving. He was constantly traveling. As a congressman from Massachusetts (who was not on the Foreign Affairs Committee) he made numerous trips abroad—to Europe, Asia, South America. Once there, he was not content to rely exclusively on briefings from government officials. He understood that their statements were too often tailored to square with official policies, that consistency too often received priority over accuracy.

In discussing Kennedy's 1951 trip to Indochina, for example, I explained how he sought out embassy officials and newspaper reporters in the area who would speak freely about French colonial rule and the popular strength of the guerrillas. Upon his return to Boston, Kennedy gave a report over the radio, and his remarks reflect the same sentiments he would voice three years later when he opposed American military assistance to the French in Indochina.

> In Indochina we have allied ourselves to the desperate effort of a French regime to hang on to the remnants of empire. There is no broad, general support of the native Vietnam Government among the people of the area. To check the southern drive of communism makes sense but not only through reliance on the force of arms. The task is rather to build strong native non-communist sentiment within these areas and rely on that as a spearhead of defense rather than upon the legions of [French] General de Tassigny. To do this apart from and in defiance of innately nationalistic aims spells foredoomed failure.[43]

These trips to Indochina and elsewhere throughout the world made Kennedy sensitive to the problems of daily living which beset the world's underdeveloped nations. Because he was willing to search beyond the official representations of governments, he could see that the cold war between the United States and the Soviet Union was largely an abstraction for many of these nations. As he told the Ameri-

*Within a month after he arrived in London in the summer of 1935, Kennedy developed jaundice and had to return home.

can Society of African Culture in 1959, the peoples of the underdeveloped countries ". . . are more interested in achieving a decent standard of living than following the standards of either East or West."[44] He recognized that the competition with the Soviet Union for influence in the underdeveloped world would not be ruled by ideology; leaders of emerging governments would be swayed more by appeals to the physical well-being of their countrymen than by appeals to individual philosophies.

These experiences are important not only for what they reveal of Kennedy's view of the world; they are equally important for what they reveal of Kennedy's personality and how he made decisions. In all his travels and reading, he was often anxious to learn, to approach a situation or a problem with an open mind. This, in turn, introduced a definite strain of flexibility in his thinking. Although he often committed himself publicly to a particular position, he was sometimes capable of changing his position if new facts or new advice convinced him otherwise. Thus, in 1949 he publicly criticized President Truman and the State Department as being responsible for the ascendancy of communist rule in China; in 1957 he wrote that it was a myth to suggest "that China was lost because of the action of a few diplomats . . . rather than because of underlying revolutionary forces."[45]

A change in position was also evident in Kennedy's attitude toward American economic aid as a means of fighting communism. In 1951 he stated in an address to the Boston Chamber of Commerce that "Uncle Sugar is as dangerous a role for us to play as Uncle Shylock. . . . We cannot reform the world. There is just not enough money in the world to relieve the poverty of all the millions of this world who may be threatened by communism. *We should not attempt to buy their freedom from this threat.*"[46] Within a few years, however, Kennedy was writing and speaking of American economic aid as a means of liberating India, Poland, and other nations from the communist menace.[47]

Politics no doubt played a great part in explaining some of these changes in position. Kennedy did not want to appear irresponsible or unresponsive to public opinions.* Even when finally convinced that

---

*It is very possible, for instance, that political motivations underlay Kennedy's 1949 remark that Truman was responsible for the loss of China. In *Why England Slept*, one of his basic themes was that it was myopic to base the failures of public policy (there, British Prime Minister Chamberlain's appeasement policy) exclusively on the shoulders of a nation's leaders and that, especially in a democracy, one had to account for public attitudes and other larger political forces. By trying to make Truman a scapegoat for the "loss" of China in 1949, Kennedy was of course ignoring his own counsel. But in 1949 most of the public were looking for scapegoats to explain communism's victory there. And, as the age of McCarthyism approached, Kennedy certainly did not want to appear "soft" on communism by talking about the forces of history.

he was right, he was therefore sensitive to criticism that he had been wrong. One example involves his 1957 Senate speech attacking French colonial policy in Algeria. When the speech evoked widespread criticism from newspapers, diplomats, and political analysts, Kennedy called his father and suggested that perhaps it had been a mistake to lambaste French policy. "You lucky mush," his father responded. "You don't know it and neither does anyone else, but within a few months everyone is going to know just how right you were on Algeria."[48] Kennedy did not recant his position, and within a year President Charles de Gaulle moved to grant Algeria independence.

In campaigning for the presidency, Kennedy made clear his promise to be a President who would in fact be open to diverse ideas and broad sources of information. Less than a month before he formally announced his candidacy, he conducted a far-ranging interview with John Fischer of *Harper's* magazine (published in *Strategy for Peace,* a campaign book consisting of selected Kennedy speeches). In a discussion of the federal bureaucracy, Kennedy expressed his belief that under Eisenhower

> . . . every head of a department is overburdened. My judgment would be that they delegate and rely on subordinates, so that instead of really getting the best minds in the country to study a problem without prior commitment to an agency, you're really getting a staff operation, which gives the President a pre-compromised final solution without revealing to him the alternatives that might have been open. That appears to be the way President Eisenhower prefers to work. I'm hopeful it isn't the way a future President will work because I'm convinced that discussion and differences and new points of view should be brought to bear on the President.[49]

Less than two weeks after he announced his candidacy, Kennedy again emphasized his view that a president "must master complex problems as well as review one page memoranda. He must originate action as well as study groups. He must re-open the channels of communication between the world of thought and the world of power."[50] Kennedy repeated this theme throughout the campaign—but always reminding his audiences that, in the end, he would never shirk from the responsibility of ultimate decision. In making this point, he would constantly refer to the cabinet meeting which Lincoln conducted right before he issued the Emancipation Proclamation in 1863. "'I have gathered you together,'" Kennedy would quote Lincoln, "'to hear what I have written down. I do not wish your advice about the main matter. That I have determined for myself.'"[51]

Much as Kennedy had promised, flexibility did follow him to the

White House. Although he was very sensitive about the appearance of switching positions, he was generally able to listen to advice that a policy should be changed or a program modified. Myer Feldman, who served as Kennedy's legislative assistant in the Senate and then as his deputy special counsel in the White House, commented on this quality:

> John F. Kennedy, I think, grew continually. It seems to me that when he would make his mind up about a program or idea, it was never inflexible; it was always subject to modification if he could be convinced that his original reaction no longer held true.[52]

Certainly this quality was evident in Kennedy's response to poverty in America. In many ways, Kennedy's travels abroad were more extensive than his travels within the United States. In many respects, he had a better feel for the problems confronting the people of foreign nations than those confronting the people of his own country. As a congressman and senator he had of course seen poverty in the United States. But he had never lived with it. And he had only a limited understanding of its causes and of how it affected the hearts and minds of people who saw no escape from it. Campaigning for the presidency in West Virginia in 1960, Kennedy witnessed poverty of extraordinary dimensions. Miners with no jobs. Children with dirty faces and no shoes. Homes that were little more than shacks. All this made a deep impression on him, and after he entered the White House he was determined to do something about it.

One proposal, embodied within a bill introduced by Senator Hubert Humphrey, called for the creation of a Youth Conservation Corps which would supply badly needed jobs for America's unskilled youth and at the same time help to conserve America's natural resources. At first Kennedy was definitely opposed to the idea. In his mind it was merely a resurrection of the Civilian Conservation Corps established under Franklin Roosevelt. Kennedy did not want to provide a boondoggle of public service employment; and being unfamiliar with the problems of conservation, he did not really appreciate the importance of this kind of conservation program. But he invited discussion on the matter, read reports, and listened to his aides' explanations. In time, he reversed his position and, in a speech at a 1963 conference in Minnesota, publicly endorsed the Humphrey proposal as a major means of combating unemployment and in advancing the conservation ethic.

The Youth Conservation Corps was not an item of major public controversy; for this reason, it would be idle to offer it as the real test of Kennedy's flexibility in the White House. It is always easier for a president to reverse his position when the political costs are minimal. A more telling example of Kennedy's flexibility is provided by the Vietnam War.

Kennedy assumed the presidential office committed to the defense of the Vietnam state which had won its independence from France in 1954. In his mind, American support was politically and economically necessary. In a speech before the American Friends of Vietnam Society in 1956, Kennedy declared that

> Vietnam represents the cornerstone of the Free World in Southeast Asia, the keystone to the arch, the finger in the dike. Burma, Thailand, India, Japan, the Philippines and, obviously, Laos and Cambodia are among those whose security would be threatened if the red tide of Communism overflowed into Vietnam. . . . Moreover, the independence of Free Vietnam is crucial to the free world in fields other than the military. Her economy is essential to the economy of all Southeast Asia; and her political liberty is an inspiration to those seeking to obtain or maintain their liberty in all parts of Asia—and indeed the world. The fundamental tenets of this nation's foreign policy, in short, depend in considerable measure upon a strong and free Vietnamese nation. [53]

Thus did Kennedy fully and warmly embrace the "domino theory" first articulated in Eisenhower's administration. Kennedy repeated these views frequently during his Senate years, and there was no reason to believe he entered the White House in a different frame of mind. (In his inaugural address, after all, he did speak of bearing "any" burden to assure the survival of liberty.)

The Vietnam War did not occupy many headlines in the nation's newspapers when Kennedy assumed the reins of presidential power. But some critical decisions awaited him. The communist National Liberation Front had stepped up its terrorist attacks in 1959 and 1960, and Kennedy was advised that South Vietnam needed increased American military and economic assistance if it were to survive these attacks. Kennedy anticipated that he would provide this increased aid and that eventually it might even be necessary to dispatch American troops to assure the survival of Vietnam. In part, this anticipation was based on his belief that the NLF was being aided by North Vietnam and that the guerrilla war really represented aggression by one country (North Vietnam) upon another (South Vietnam).

Never one to turn aside a challenge (especially when it seemed to test his "toughness" in facing decisions), Kennedy prepared to throw the force of American power into the fray. He established a school for counterinsurgency at the army's training camp in Fort Bragg, North Carolina. He dispatched Vice-President Johnson and then two White House aides, General Maxwell Taylor and Walt Rostow, to Vietnam to assess the situation there and make recommendations as to the kind of assistance the United States should provide Vietnam. Their reports helped persuade him to pledge American military support for Vietnam and, by the end of 1961, to send 3,200 military advisers there* (although he knew that the introduction of American military personnel into South Vietnam violated the Geneva Accords of 1954, an international agreement which the United States had promised to honor). Meanwhile, there was a fierce debate within the inner circles of the administration about the desirability of sending many thousands of American combat troops to South Vietnam. The very fact that Kennedy entertained this option suggests the depth of his personal commitment to provide American military support for Vietnam.**

Slowly, however, Kennedy began to question the wisdom of that commitment. Senate Majority Leader Mike Mansfield returned from a visit to Vietnam in 1962 and advised Kennedy that President Diem's government did not command the support of the people, that Diem's rule was in fact autocratic, that the situation was deteriorating, and that Kennedy should rethink his policies on Vietnam. At first Kennedy was angered by Mansfield's negative report. He was also annoyed by frequent newspaper reports from Vietnam which seemed to confirm the soundness of Mansfield's conclusions. But soon doubts began to surface among Michael Forrestal, Paul Kattenberg, and other administration officials who visited Vietnam. Their doubts were reinforced by numerous intelligence estimates. By 1963, for example, the CIA had already discounted the validity of the domino theory:

> With the possible exception of Cambodia, it is likely that no nation in the area would quickly succumb to Communism as a result of the fall of Laos and South Vietnam. Furthermore, a continuation of the spread of Communism in the area would not be inexorable.[54]

This conclusion complemented information that the Vietnam conflict was a civil war and not a case of aggression from the North. Numerous reports made clear that Diem's ruthless leadership was a continuing source of unrest—and terrorism—in South Vietnam. Lack of popular support for Diem's regime naturally made it easier for the NLF to recruit soldiers from and win the allegiance of the local popu-

---

*By November 1963 there were 16,000 American military "advisers" in South Vietnam.

**Even then, however, there were limits on Kennedy's commitment. At a White House meeting in 1961, Governor Nelson Rockefeller of New York suggested that Kennedy use tactical nuclear weapons to end the fighting in Southeast Asia. Kennedy politely rejected the suggestion.

lation. This, in turn, undercut the notion that the NLF's expanded manpower depended upon the infiltration of North Vietnamese soldiers. Indeed, on April 5, 1963, Kennedy's Special Group for Counter-Insurgency concluded that "we are unable to document and develop any hard evidence of infiltration [by North Vietnam into South Vietnam] after October 1, 1962."[55] In short, the philosophical and factual bases of Kennedy's Vietnam policies were beginning to soften (although there were still plenty of advisers—especially in the Department of Defense—who continued to reaffirm the wisdom of Kennedy's initial policies and, in fact, continued to urge increased American military intervention). In time, the prospects of American troops becoming bogged down in a land war in Asia began to haunt Kennedy—such visions invoked reminders of the misguided French policies which he had criticized as a congressman and as a senator. By the late spring of 1963, Kennedy had more or less concluded that the United States could not continue to support the dictatorial rule of Diem, and, more importantly, that it just might be wise to remove the United States entirely from the military tangle in Vietnam. After a White House meeting with the congressional leadership (during which Mansfield again criticized American policies in Vietnam), Kennedy privately assured Mansfield that he would withdraw American military advisers from Vietnam after the 1964 election (when Kennedy would presumably be reelected). Later Kennedy explained his reasoning to his appointments secretary, Kenneth O'Donnell. "In 1965, I'll become one of the most unpopular Presidents in history. I'll be damned everywhere as a Communist appeaser. But," he continued, "I don't care. If I tried to pull out completely now from Vietnam, we would have another Joe McCarthy red scare on our hands, but I can do it after I'm reelected. So we had better make damned sure that I am reelected." O'Donnell asked Kennedy how he would accomplish the withdrawal. "Easy," said Kennedy. "Put a government in there that will ask us to leave."[56]

It would be naïve to make too much of these statements to Mansfield and O'Donnell. Kennedy probably saw merit in Mansfield's position and was probably anxious to assuage Mansfield's concerns. It is doubtful, though, that Kennedy was making these same assurances to Senator Richard Russell, chairman of the Senate Armed Services Committee, or the Joint Chiefs of Staff. Nonetheless, actions were taken which suggest that Kennedy was seriously rethinking his Vietnam policies. By September 1963 he suspended American aid to Diem until needed political reforms were implemented. Throughout the late summer and early fall of 1963, the Kennedy administration implicitly encouraged a plot to depose Diem, a plot which achieved success on November 1, 1963. And in the late fall a statement was issued from the White House indicating that 1,000 American military advisers would be withdrawn from Vietnam in early 1964.

People can—and do—speculate about whether Kennedy would have carried out his private assurances to extricate the United States from Vietnam. I cannot answer that question. But the point here is that Kennedy possessed an open attitude toward problems. In making decisions, he often demonstrated a flexibility which allowed him to switch positions if the facts warranted it. And in the case of Vietnam, it is entirely possible that he really did intend to modify his earlier position and withdraw American military personnel.

Kennedy's flexibility was complemented by and in part reflected an almost insatiable curiosity. Robert Lovett, who served in high government positions in the Roosevelt and Truman administrations, was often called upon by Kennedy as an unofficial adviser.* Reminiscing about these frequent contacts with Kennedy, Lovett felt that

> . . . he possessed an extremely intelligent mind whose quickness seemed to be sharpened by an intuitive quality. He had a real thirst for knowledge which was wide ranging and engaging in its keenness.[57]

This view was shared by most others in government. Having served every Democratic President since Franklin Roosevelt, Charles Bohlen, Kennedy's and Johnson's Ambassador to France, said of Kennedy that he had ". . . never heard of a President who wanted to know so much."[58]

Those who knew Kennedy socially were equally impressed by his inquiring mind. I remember discussing Kennedy with Benjamin Bradlee in 1967. Bradlee, then managing editor of the *Washington Post,* was a close friend of Kennedy's (they had been neighbors in Georgetown when Kennedy was a senator and saw each other frequently after Kennedy moved to the White House). I was doing research for my undergraduate thesis at the University of Michigan and was naturally anxious to talk about Kennedy's personal characteristics as President. He was damn curious about almost everything, said Bradlee. Always asking questions, trying to find out about something that was new to him. A typical example, Bradlee explained, was Kennedy's persistence in knowing all the details of Philip Graham's purchase of *Newsweek* magazine in 1961—an arrangement which Bradlee helped engineer. Bradlee recalled that Kennedy ". . . had to know all the facts, what

---

*In fact, Kennedy had offered Lovett his choice of three cabinet posts—Treasury, Defense, or State. Lovett declined, however, because of poor health.

lawyers I had spoken to, which bankers and newspapermen, and all the financial aspects."[59]

This curiosity of course was most acute in political matters. Kennedy had a driving urge to know about political people and events. He read the works of Chinese communist leader Mao Tse-tung and Cuban revolutionary Che Guevara because, like his father, he believed it important to know how the other person thinks. And when it became clear by 1963 that he would probably oppose Senator Barry Goldwater in the 1964 presidential campaign, Kennedy instinctively wanted to learn about the extreme right-wing groups who looked to Goldwater as their national spokesman. Kennedy asked his aides to supply him with magazines, reports, and statistics about these right-wing groups. What sort of person belonged to them? What did they really believe? How strong were they? Once he was told of a radio address by a right-wing spokesman which bitterly attacked him as a communist. People don't really believe that crap, do they? the President inquired. On the contrary, replied the aide, many people accept speeches such as this as the gospel truth. This response only heightened Kennedy's curiosity about these right-wing people (and increased his desire to defeat Goldwater in 1964 and, he hoped, to stifle the fires of political extremism in America).*

It would, of course, be misleading to convey the impression that Kennedy was intensely curious about all political subjects. Like all of

---

*In the summer of 1963, Myer Feldman sent a five-page, single-spaced typed memorandum to Kennedy concerning the operation, financing, and political strength of the country's right-wing groups. The memo is fascinating not only for what it reveals of right-wing groups but also for what it says about Kennedy's keen interest in them.

The memo pointed out, among other things, that right-wing groups annually spend between $15 and $25 million, that they have programs on 1,000 radio stations across the country, that 74 percent of the 150 1962 congressional candidates endorsed by the right-wing group, Americans for Constitutional Action, were elected, that the John Birch Society had an income of $737,000 in 1962, that the right-wing preacher Rev. Carl McIntire recently acquired a resort hotel for $300,000, that Life Line Foundation, the tax-exempt creation of conservative Texas billionaire H. L. Hunt, had an income of $447,000 in 1962 from its radio broadcasts and newsletters, and that the Hunt Food Company had made contributions to the Life Line Foundation and then deducted them as a business expense even though "that company may sell no food whatsoever within 1,000 miles of the place of broadcast."

On the basis of his research, Feldman concluded

—"that many foundations are using tax exempt funds for political purposes, that business corporations receive deductions, except that the deduction is described as an expense rather than a contribution, and that many people are being misled by false claims."

—that the "Federal Communications Act is being violated where there is not a fair presentation of both sides of a question."

—that the "Post Office Department subsidizes the distribution of much of the material

us, some subject areas appealed to him more than others. And some subjects—such as agriculture—bored him. But on the whole, he had an inordinate amount of curiosity, and this opened him up to information he might otherwise not have acquired. Being aware of this curiosity, many aides—but especially Arthur Schlesinger, Jr.—poured a stream of articles, reports, and letters into his office, alerting him to new developments on a particular issue or perhaps apprising him of a political commentator's analysis of a particular bill.

Kennedy did not rely entirely on the initiative of his aides in obtaining information on important issues. When concerned about a particular matter, he would often ask his aides to give him articles and reports that summarized the contrasting arguments. If he thought a presidential decision was necessary, he would direct pointed inquiries at his staff, either personally or by a short memo. One indicative case concerns an embargo on imports from Cuba. Within a month after entering the White House, Florida senator George Smathers suggested that Kennedy move to prohibit the importation of tobacco, vegetables, fruits, and other goods from Cuba. Kennedy immediately directed a memo to McGeorge Bundy, his adviser for national security affairs. After outlining Smathers's suggestion, Kennedy raised a series of questions:

> What is [Undersecretary of State] George Ball's judgment of this? Would it save us valuable dollars in gold reserves? Would it make things more difficult for Castro? Would it be in the public interest?[60]

This same quest for information was often evident in meetings Kennedy conducted. He was almost always pushing for information, ideas, and opinions. One experienced visitor to the White House noted, in this vein, that "Kennedy conducts a restless meeting when he is in quest of information he does not have. He pokes at his men with questions, rushes mentally off, sometimes before they finish, when he catches the gist of what they are saying before they get it out."[61]

In obtaining information, Kennedy rarely relied exclusively on those in government. He understood that a vast reservoir of talent and experience lay outside the government circle, and he meant to take advantage of it. University professors especially often received inquiries from the White House. So did those who had had considerable experience in

---

> circulated by the radical right. For instance, *Human Events,* with an average circulation of 80,000 copies a week, is subsidized by the Post Office in the amount of approximately $65,000 a year."

In closing, Feldman noted that "the radical right-wing constitutes a formidable force in American life today." Memorandum from Myer Feldman to President Kennedy, August 15, 1963, President's Office Files, John F. Kennedy Library.

government, such as Dean Acheson or Robert Lovett. In soliciting their advice and ideas, Kennedy almost always encouraged candor and listened intently. Lovett's impressions are again instructive on this point:

> . . . President Kennedy had a quality which I have rarely seen in any holder of the Chief Executive office; that is, the willingness to have the person whose advice he sought answer with complete frankness and, if necessary, bluntness without leaving any apparent scars where a course of action he was considering taking was opposed or where something that he had done was queried as being perhaps unwise or maladroit.[62]

Roy Wilkins, director of the National Association for the Advancement of Colored People, also saw Kennedy frequently and had a similar reaction: Kennedy "had, while not excessive warmth as you measure it with other warm people, he had a grace and a charm and above all an intelligence on this [civil rights] thing that immediately invited you in to commune with him on it, so to speak."[63]

Again, it would be misleading to paint Kennedy as a completely open man who never winced at or discouraged criticism. Most of the people outside government whose advice Kennedy solicited were influential "Establishment" figures; for the most part, these were people who had climbed up the institutional ladder (whether by marriage or hard work), people who moved in circles acceptable to any highbrow society. Lovett, for instance, was a senior partner in the New York investment firm of Brown Brothers Harriman and Company; Acheson was a senior partner in one of Washington, D.C.'s most prestigious law firms, Covington and Burling. Those who did not move in these circles—civil rights leader Martin Luther King, Jr., representatives of the American Civil Liberties Union, independent newspaper columnists, such as I. F. Stone, to name a few—were infrequently, if ever, invited to the White House to give the President their advice.

There were also many matters about which Kennedy was very sensitive, areas in which criticism or frank advice was not welcomed with open arms. Perhaps the best and worst of Kennedy's willingness to seek candid opinions were displayed in a meeting he had in February 1961 with two representatives of the Americans for Democratic Action, economist Robert Nathan and civil rights advocate Joe Rauh. Nathan initiated the meeting by proposing massive increases in government spending to cure the nation's ills and, most important, to eradicate the 7 percent unemployment rate. Kennedy resisted the proposal; the problem, he explained, was that 93 percent of the people were employed and the other 7 percent did not have enough political clout to overcome the frugal-minded people who dominated Congress. "But," he said to Nathan, "I want you to keep this up. It's very helpful now for you to keep pushing me this way."[64] Taking this cue, Rauh spoke up on behalf of civil rights matters. During the campaign Kennedy had repeatedly promised action to overcome the neglect of the past. But, in Rauh's judgment, the action taken within Kennedy's first month of office was far from satisfactory. As with Nathan, Rauh said he hoped Kennedy would also accept his constant pushing on civil rights matters. Rauh remembered that he had ". . . never seen a man's expression turn faster. He said, 'Absolutely not. It's a totally different thing. Your criticism on civil rights is quite wrong. . . .' Kennedy turned on me with great force."* Kennedy's sensitivity here was partly explained by his concern that he could not fulfill his campaign promises, that diverse political pressures prevented him from moving as quickly as he wanted to in civil rights. However real this concern, it should not have been an excuse to shut off debate on the matter. Extended debate might have exposed possible fallacies in the initial decision not to move more quickly in civil rights matters.

Kennedy's reaction to Rauh was not unique. Kennedy was capable of turning aside others who offered criticism on sensitive issues. But for the most part, Kennedy did appreciate the importance of seeking information—even critical information—from diverse sources. Information alone, however, cannot adequately enable a president to realize the full scope of the issues which press themselves upon him. A president must be able to retain the knowledge that he derives from his curiosity and pointed questions. In this regard, Kennedy was somewhat unusual. Those in and out of government would continually marvel at his ability to read quickly through a report and then discuss it in detail. After a press conference in 1962, columnist James Reston reported, "How Kennedy knew the precise drop in milk consumption in 1960, the percentage rise in textile imports from 1957 to 1960, and the number of speeches cleared by the Defense Department last year—1,200—is not quite clear, but anyway he did."[65] White House military aide Chester Clifton similarly observed that "it was always surprising how thoroughly Kennedy read, although rapidly, and how well he remembered."[66] This quality was of particular benefit to Kennedy with his personal staff. Sorensen recalled, for instance, that before advising the President, an aide would usually study all the ramifications of an issue, checking and rechecking his sources. Never sure when Kennedy

---

*Interview with Joseph Rauh, Jr., Oral History Project, John F. Kennedy Library, pp. 101–2. Although Rauh would occasionally meet with White House aides to discuss civil rights matters, this was the last time Rauh visited Kennedy to advise him personally. When Kennedy finally decided to push for substantive legislation in June 1963, however, Rauh was invited back to the White House for a large meeting Kennedy had with civil rights leaders. At that time Kennedy singled Rauh out and told him that it was going to be "a long, tough fight, but we have to do it." *Ibid.* at 104.

would have already familiarized himself with the problem—or, like Franklin Roosevelt, have another adviser working on the same project—the aide was not only concerned with enlightening the President but also with avoiding the great embarrassment if Kennedy should illuminate an inadequacy in the aide's report.

Kennedy's retentive mind was not merely a tool to control the White House staff. Primarily interested in solving problems, Kennedy was eager to seek the information and ideas which would facilitate the development of optimum solutions. Kennedy's quick recall frequently enabled him to ask the right questions. In fact, it was an open secret among Kennedy's staff that the first question was usually the toughest; Kennedy had a tendency to initiate conversations by focusing immediately on the essence of the problem. Therefore, if you could get by that first question, you would probably survive the rest of the discussion. In any event, these pointed inquiries often helped Kennedy to appraise the political feasibility of any course of action. Walter Heller, Chairman of Kennedy's Council of Economic Advisers, remembered how quickly the President was able to grasp the subtleties of economic policies in the national and international sectors. (This was no small achievement; Kennedy continually reminded Heller that he had received a "C" in economics at Harvard and that he would need a lot of tutoring.) Kennedy's personal involvement in the preparations for the GATT conferences—an international meeting to pursue means of reducing tariffs—was partly a result of his instinctive responses to Professor Heller's lectures and lengthy memos. Kennedy's ability to learn economics quickly was also evident in his 1962 address at Yale University, during which he proposed a tax cut on personal income despite an impending $11.9 billion government deficit. Heller had previously discussed with Kennedy the multiplier effect—a Keynesian concept which hypothesized that the more money an individual consumer possessed, the more he would spend and that this, in turn, would actually produce an increase in the nation's Gross National Product with an expanded tax base from which the government could collect revenue.[67] It was not Heller, but Kennedy who made the final decision to propose the tax cut; and while he received memos and draft speeches from Bundy, Schlesinger, and Sorensen, it was Kennedy who wrote most of the Yale speech explaining the rationale of this proposal.

There were occasions when Kennedy preferred to ignore the information he received. Usually this occurred when he felt "blindness" to be politically expedient. The case of the famous "missile gap" is a prime illustration. During the presidential campaign, Kennedy vigorously and repeatedly criticized the Eisenhower Administration for allowing the Soviet Union to overcome the United States in the development of armed missiles; and he promised that, if elected, he would act quickly to close this gap. Shortly after becoming President, Kennedy instructed Defense Secretary Robert McNamara to study the matter. McNamara found that the United States still commanded a great lead in missiles and announced this fact at a press conference. Almost immediately a statement was issued by the White House claiming that McNamara was mistaken. The White House statement was not based on any information superior to McNamara's. The White House statement was based simply on a conviction that the administration should not admit the absence of a "missile gap."

There were probably two principal reasons for this White House disclaimer in early 1961. First, a public statement acknowledging the absence of a "missile gap" would have undermined Kennedy's credibility in the public's eyes; after all, if there really was no "missile gap," then it must have been a figment of Kennedy's campaign strategy, a deceptive ploy to have the public believe that a Republican president's laxness had endangered our security and that a new Democratic president could correct the mistake. There was probably a second reason for recanting McNamara's findings: the absence of a "missile gap" would remove a major justification for Kennedy's expanding defense program. Despite McNamara's findings, Kennedy still believed that the country's defense needs warranted massive increases in the military arsenal. Without the "missile gap" it would be more difficult for the administration to explain those increases to the public.* In any event, the "missile gap" question remained a sensitive one in Kennedy's eyes. He was always anxious to establish the accuracy of his campaign statements. As late as May 1963, Kennedy wrote to Bundy, "I want to be able to demonstrate that there was a military and intelligence lag in the previous administration that started the missile gap."[68]

This, to say the least, was not presidential leadership at its best. But this episode does underscore one basic point: the value of any information depends on whether it is actually used and, if so, for what purpose. Kennedy clearly understood this. He knew that an abundant flow of information was of little value without an assertive executive in the White House. He knew that only a president willing and able to make decisions could employ the immense information at his disposal. And he recognized, to some extent at least, that the president's responsibility for decision was more easily explained than executed. Indeed,

*Although Kennedy would not publicly admit the absence of any missile gap, and while he did push for increased spending in the development of missiles, he did establish some limits on defense spending. Thus, he refused to fulfill the Eisenhower administration's commitment to develop the experimental—and costly—skybolt missile; and he also refused to spend the money which the Congress twice appropriated for the construction of the expensive B-70 bomber plane.

Eisenhower had admonished him on this point when they met the day before Kennedy's inauguration. "There are no easy matters that will ever come to you as President," Eisenhower said. "If they are easy, they will be settled at a lower level."[69]

It was not long before Kennedy learned the truth of this assertion. Early in 1961, biracial groups of people began "freedom rides" into the Deep South. Anxious to dramatize the far-reaching racial discrimination which pervaded almost all aspects of life in the South, these people traveled by bus from city to city and state to state, trying to sit at the segregated restaurants and use the segregated rest rooms at the various bus terminals. Violence erupted almost immediately. Buses were burned, the freedom riders subjected to harassment and even arrest by local law enforcement officials whose sympathy for segregation outweighed their concern for the equal protection of the laws. Because the roads traveled were interstate routes under the jurisdiction of the federal government, and since Kennedy had publicly committed his presidency to the protection of civil rights, his obligation to act was clear.

Early one morning, therefore, Attorney General Robert Kennedy and Burke Marshall, the assistant attorney general for civil rights, went to the White House to explain their recommendations for decision: a presidential call to John Paterson, governor of Alabama (where the most recent riots and bus burnings had occurred), and the filing of a legal complaint. They met with Kennedy in his upstairs bedroom for breakfast (Kennedy was in fact still wearing his pajamas). The meeting lasted only about a half hour. But in that time Kennedy absorbed the necessary information and accepted his responsibility for decision. As Marshall remembered,

> He didn't talk much, he listened. He listened with a good deal of intensity. As I say, he accepted it. I just have the feeling that within the course of . . . fifteen or twenty minutes he understood the whole thing, all its implications; that he was prepared to take the necessary action; that he realized that there was going to be all sorts of consequences in the future; and that he saw all of this and accepted it and digested it and that was it. He didn't make a speech about it or anything. The questions that I remember were in terms of timing and in terms of how should he make these efforts with Governor Paterson. . . .*

---

*Interview with Burke Marshall, Oral History Project, John F. Kennedy Library, pp. 8–9. The legal complaint was filed but Paterson never accepted Kennedy's telephone calls. Paterson, reflecting the views of the white majority in his state, thought the freedom rides were part of a sinister conspiracy to create chaos and embarrass the government. "But, you see, these were not really bona fide travelers," he later said of the freedom riders. "There were young white girls traveling with Negro boys. The whole thing was set

This same willingness to act was apparent when James Meredith tried to become the first black to register as a student at the Univeristy of Mississippi in September 1962. Meredith applied for admission in 1961. The university naturally opposed the admission. Expecting that, Meredith filed a legal suit and ultimately secured an order from the United States Supreme Court directing his admission to the university. Needless to say, this did not go down well with most of the Mississippi white population. To them, it was heresy to suggest that a black man could enter a white school—especially when it was *their* white school. Their sentiments were reflected in their governor's response to the court decision: "We will not surrender to the evil and illegal forces of tyranny."[70] As the day of registration approached, thousands of whites gathered at the university to protest Meredith's admission. Violence bubbled near the surface.

Again, the federal government's obligation to act was clear—not only because of Kennedy's public commitment to civil rights but also because Meredith's admission rested squarely on the order of a federal court. The matter was fraught with complications, however. Law and order is basically a responsibility of the states, and Kennedy was not anxious to overstep his jurisdiction. On the other hand, Mississippi Governor Ross Barnett made no secret of his sympathies, and they did not give Kennedy peace of mind. When the university trustees refused to honor Meredith's court order, the controversy reached a fever pitch. A federal court of appeals temporarily relieved the trustees of their power and ordered Governor Barnett to register Meredith. The possibility of mob violence seemed imminent, and the White House and Justice Department were, to say the least, rather concerned.

Attorney General Robert Kennedy spoke with Barnett on the telephone several times. While Barnett continually expressed his desire to avoid violence, he was reluctant to assure the attorney general that he could maintain law and order as long as Meredith insisted on entering the university. And he also made clear that he would not—could not,

---

up to influence the local populace. They'd get off the bus and head for the nearest restaurant and places that were traditionally used by white people and go in and sit down. And if they couldn't start any trouble any other way, they'd rub against the fellow on the stool next to them." From this perspective, there were great political risks for Paterson in accepting the President's telephone call—a call, he knew, which would seek his cooperation in making it possible for these freedom rides to continue. "Now, I always figured that when it came right down to where it's either going to be a riot or not, or troops or not, that I'd get that call from the White House," Paterson said, "and the way that it would be put to you would be in such a way that you could not give an answer without absolutely ruining yourself politically at home. . . . And they said the President was calling me, and I didn't take the call because I knew what that call was. This was the final appeal. This was the thing that would make or break me. And I didn't take that call, and that was one of the worst mistakes I ever made. That's right." Interview with John Paterson, Oral History Project, John F. Kennedy Library, pp. 37, 41.

he said—obey the federal court's order to register Meredith. In fact, the governor informed the attorney general that he himself would physically block the entrance of the university building where Meredith was to be registered. "Our courts have acted too and our legislature have [sic] acted too," Barnett told Robert Kennedy in the early afternoon of Tuesday, September 25th. "I am going to obey the laws of Mississippi." Kennedy tried to remind Barnett that, as governor, he was also obligated to defend the United States Constitution and the laws of the United States, which superseded any conflicting state laws. The governor remained intransigent. "This institution is supported by the taxpayers of this state," he exclaimed, "and controlled solely by the trustees." "Governor, you are a part of the United States," Robert Kennedy retorted. "We have been a part of the United States but I don't know whether we are or not," Barnett replied. "Are you getting out of the Union?" the attorney general sarcastically asked.[71]

All this argument was to no avail. That same day Barnett physically stopped Meredith, accompanied by U.S. marshals, when he tried to register. In a telephone conversation later that evening, Barnett explained to the attorney general how he had read another proclamation defending the state's prerogatives. Exasperated but not intimidated, Kennedy said that Meredith would attend classes anyway. Barnett urged the attorney general to reconsider his decision; Meredith's attendance would inevitably result in physical harm to him and others, he warned. "It's best for him not to go to Ole Miss," Barnett told the attorney general. "It's so much better for him." "But he likes Ole Miss," Kennedy quietly replied.[72]

Over the next few days the issue was not resolved. The likelihood of violence seemed greater. President Kennedy decided to speak with Barnett himself. On the afternoon of Saturday, September 29, Kennedy placed a call to the governor and initiated the first of several telephone conversations. In this initial conversation, Kennedy emphasized that, while it was an unpleasant situation for all concerned, he would not shrink from his constitutional responsibility to execute the laws:

President: . . . I am concerned about this situation down there as I know you must be.

Governor: Yes, I am concerned about it, Mr. President. It's a horrible situation.

President: Well now here's my problem, Governor. I don't know Mr. Meredith and I didn't put him in the University, but on the other hand under the Constitution I have to carry out the orders of the Court. Now I have to carry that order out. I don't want to do it in any way that causes difficulty to you or anyone else, but I've got to do it. Now I would like to get your help in doing it.

* * * *

President: . . . The difficulty is we got two or three problems. In the first place, what can we do—in the first place is the Court's order to you, which I guess you are given until Tuesday. What is your feeling on that? What is your position?

Governor: Well, Mr. President it is a serious matter and I want to think it over, until Tuesday anyway.

President: Now let me say this.

Governor: You know what I'm up against, Mr. President. I took an oath you know to abide by the laws of this State and our Constitution here and the Constitution of the United States. I'm on the spot here, you know, I've taken an oath to do that and you know what our laws are in reference to this.

President: Yes, I understand that, but now we got . . .

Governor: We have a statute which was enacted a couple of weeks ago stating positively that no one who had been convicted of a crime or whether the criminal pending against [sic], would not be eligible to the institutions of higher learning and that's our law and it seems like the Court of Appeals didn't pay any attention to that.*

President: Right, well of course the problem is, Governor, that I've got my responsibility just like you have yours. . . . [73]

The conversation ended with Kennedy promising to call again, and Barnett thanking the President for his support on a poultry program. Within an hour, Kennedy telephoned Barnett again to see whether he had decided upon a course of action, and, most especially, whether the Mississippi governor was prepared to maintain order:

President: Now as I understand it, Governor, you will do everything you can to maintain law and order.

Governor: I'll do everything in my power to maintain order.

President Right.

Governor: We don't want any shooting.

President: I understand. Now, Governor, what about—can you maintain this order?

---

*On September 20, 1962, the Mississippi State Legislature passed a law making anyone under criminal indictment ineligible for admission to the university. The state had filed trumped-up criminal charges against Meredith.

Governor: Well, I don't know. That's what I am worried about. I don't know whether I can or not. I couldn't have the other afternoon—there was such a mob there it would have been impossible. There were men in there with trucks and shot guns and all such as that—not a lot of them, but some, we saw, and . . . certain people just . . . they were just enraged. You just don't understand the situation down here.

President: Now the only thing is I've got my responsibility—not my order I just have to carry it out, so I want to get together and try to do it with you in the way that is most satisfactory and causes the least chances of damage to people in Mississippi—that is my interest.

Governor: Will you be willing to wait awhile and let the people cool off on the whole thing?

President: How long?

Governor: Would you make a statement to the effect, Mr. President, that under the circumstances existing in Mississippi that there will be bloodshed—you want to protect the life of James Meredith and all other people and under the circumstances at this [time] it just wouldn't be fair to him and others to try to register him.

President: At what time would it be fair?

Governor: I don't know—we could wait—it might be in two or three weeks—it might cool off a little.

President: Would you undertake to register him in two weeks?

Governor: Well, you know I can't undertake to register him myself.

President: I see.

Governor: You all might make some progress that way.

President: Well, we would be facing—unless we have your assurance—your support . . .[74]

Kennedy closed the conversation by asking Barnett to call back after he had discussed the matter with his aides and decided what he would do. Later that evening, Barnett called and renewed an earlier offer to have Meredith registered at the university campus at Jackson, thus avoiding the mobs which had gathered at the main university campus at Oxford. Seeing no other course, Kennedy reluctantly agreed. Within a few hours, however, Barnett withdrew this offer, and it became even clearer that the governor could not maintain law and order. Kennedy accordingly nationalized the Mississippi national guard and ordered army units located in Tennessee to proceed to support the security actions being taken at Mississippi. On Sunday, September 30, Kennedy addressed the nation on television to explain his actions, and on the following Monday Meredith was registered.

Many wished Kennedy accepted his responsibility for decision in the legislative areas of civil rights with the same determination he evinced in resolving the Meredith and freedom rides controversies. Certainly there was enough information available to justify the adoption of corrective legislation. But, unlike the buses and the university, Congress was not in danger of being burned down, and Kennedy could rationalize his procrastination in introducing substantive legislation by reference to public apathy and congressional resistance. This procrastination justifiably disappointed most of those in the civil rights movement; and it reinforced the notion that Kennedy would act in this controversial matter only when pressured by external forces.

To some extent, Kennedy's contradictory responses to the civil rights issues underscored the limitations on his ability to make sound decisions. Even before he entered the White House, Kennedy recognized these limitations. But the presidential experience soon taught him that the human, political, and institutional limitations in making decisions were even greater than he had anticipated. Interviewed on national television on the eve of his second anniversary in the White House, Kennedy commented that

> . . . the problems are more difficult than I had imagined them to be. The responsibilities placed on the United States are greater than I imagined them to be, and there are greater limitations upon our ability to bring about a favorable result than I had imagined them to be. And I think that is probably true of anyone who becomes President because there is such a difference between those who advise or speak or legislate, and between the man who must select from the various alternatives proposed and say that this shall be the policy of the United States. It is much easier to make the speeches than it is to finally make the judgments, because unfortunately your advisers are frequently divided. If you take the wrong course, and on occasion I have, the President bears the burden of the responsibility quite rightly. The advisers may move on to new advice.[75]

In short, the impediments to action—psychologically, politically, and institutionally—were substantial.

But these limitations could not be an excuse for inaction. Kennedy had campaigned on the understanding that his presidency would embrace the principle articulated by Franklin Roosevelt: "Better the occasional faults of a Government that lives in a spirit of charity than the consistent omissions of a Government frozen in the ice of its own indifference."[76] This, of course, was not the end of the matter. Kennedy wanted his administration to represent more than a spirit of charity. He wanted a government that was both responsible and effective. And on numerous matters he did live up to this ideal; on many other matters he did not.

In either case the result was often affected by his relationships with those who provided him with information and were asked to implement his decisions. Therefore, a full appreciation of Kennedy's talents in making decisions requires close scrutiny of those relationships.

The White House Staff

In his famous advice to Prince Lorenzo de Medici in the sixteenth century, Machiavelli emphasized the value of the prince's personal staff:

> The choosing of ministers is a matter of no little importance for a prince; and their worth depends on the sagacity of the prince himself. The first opinion that is formed of a ruler's intelligence is based on the quality of the men he has around him. When they are competent and loyal he can always be considered wise, because he has been able to recognize their competence and to keep them loyal. But when they are otherwise, the prince is always open to adverse criticism; because his first mistake has been in the choice of his ministers.[77]

However old this advice, it is not dated. Time and again throughout the course of history, leaders have often found that their successes, their failures, and sometimes even their lives depended on the competence and loyalty of their personal staffs.

This is no less true of American presidents, especially since Franklin D. Roosevelt's tenure. Prior to FDR's presidency, the American chief executive's personal staff was quite small, sometimes including no more than a couple of secretaries. Pressures for change began to grow under FDR. The vast increase in governmental programs, coupled with America's expanded role in international affairs, naturally gave the President a lot more to do. In response to these pressures, the Brownlow commission was established to study the matter, and the essence of its findings were summarized in one sentence: "The President needs help." And so Congress in 1939 authorized the President to hire additional assistants who would help him administer his responsibilities but who would have no independent authority of their own.

Today, there is no question that the president continues to need the assistance of a personal White House staff (although Louis Brownlow would no doubt have been surprised to find that his report resulted in a White House staff under Nixon which numbered almost six hundred and exercised considerable power). Because of the massive responsibilities confronting each president, it is difficult for him to absorb all the information required for meaningful decisions. It is also impossible for the president to communicate personally with all those whose cooperation is crucial if his decisions are to be executed properly. Every president must therefore rely to a larger extent on the executive staff that shares offices with him in the White House.

But the White House staff—if it is to serve the president's and the nation's best interests—should be more than extra eyes to do his reading or extra mouths to communicate his decisions. Because of their proximity to the president, and because he often depends on them for advice, they are frequently in a unique position to influence his decisions. They are, to begin with, the ones who can and should alert the president to developments he may not foresee, to criticism he may wish to ignore, to ideas he may not have considered. Having done this, they can pierce a president's isolation, remind him of his fallibility when he would prefer to believe otherwise, and urge him to act when he would prefer to do nothing.

All this, of course, is easier said than done. Presidents, it should be remembered, are human. There is a natural tendency among presidents to dispense with personal aides who make life uncomfortable by giving the president information which makes him feel unappreciated or by pressuring him for decisions he does not want to make. Reflecting on his experience as Lyndon Johnson's press secretary, for example, George Reedy commented that a strong president "has a propensity to create an environment to his liking and to weed out ruthlessly those assistants who might persist in presenting him with irritating thoughts."[78]

Reedy is only partially correct, Almost every president—regardless of how "strong" or "weak" he might be—shapes his staff and directs their functions to suit his own personality and his own ideas of leadership. This was certainly true of Kennedy. His White House staff was a direct reflection of his values, attitudes, and goals. The size, nature, and functions of the staff were dependent not so much on history as on Kennedy's own views. Thus, almost all of Kennedy's principal White House aides shared Kennedy's conception of the presidency as a political office which provided many opportunities to solve specific problems. Although most of his staff were first-rate intellects, very few were ideologues interested in advancing a particular philosophy or a particular theory of government. In this respect, it is noteworthy that the most ideological, and perhaps most liberal, of Kennedy's aides—Arthur Schlesinger, Jr.—commanded little influence except in matters relating to Latin America and the United Nations (where Schlesinger had a special responsibility).

In examining the dynamics of Kennedy's White House staff, it would be easy to consider it as a monolithic force which moved frictionlessly to serve his interests in making decisions. But such a characterization would be wrong. There was some tension between certain members of the White House staff. Over the years of many campaigns and many legislative battles, friction had been sparked between people who had worked on Kennedy's Senate staff (Sorensen, Feldman, Goodwin) and those who had worked principally in organizing his campaigns (the famous, or as the case may be, infamous "Irish Mafia" consisting of, among others, O'Brien, O'Donnell, and Powers). Kennedy himself acknowledged this friction; indeed, Fred Dutton, a former aide to California governor Pat Brown who was not aligned to either group, was placed on the White House Staff with the understanding that one of his responsibilities would be to act as a buffer between the two groups. Although the interoffice tensions never reached crisis proportions, they no doubt played a part in the ability of the staff members to cooperate with one another. With this caveat in mind, it can be said that three principal traits characterized Kennedy's White House staff, traits which reflected the roles that staff played in making the decisions of his presidency.

First of all, Kennedy's White House staff did not operate under institutionalized rules and procedures. Kennedy had little faith in hierarchies and organizational charts.This attitude was a real contrast with that of Kennedy's immediate predecessor, Dwight Eisenhower. Because of his long career in the army, Eisenhower placed great emphasis on the orderly flow of information and decisions through a sieve of established committees and set procedures. For the most part, he authorized his staff, under the direction of Sherman Adams (who retained the title of "The" Assistant to the President), to sift through the paraphernalia of the bureaucracy and present him, in most cases, only with the final choices.

Kennedy believed that Eisenhower's staff operation impeded his effectiveness in making sound decisions. Reliance on formal structures, Kennedy believed, could hamper rather than facilitate a discussion of substantive issues. The paper lineage of responsibilities could perhaps ensure efficiency but it could not guarantee effectiveness. In Kennedy's eyes, too much organization stifled debate; it denied him access to a broad scope of information and ideas; and, perhaps most importantly, it undercut his ability to understand the real merits of available options. Kennedy consequently had little desire to rely on institutionalized committees and approved a staff recommendation to eliminate the Planning and Operation Boards of the National Security Council as well as sixteen other executive office agencies that Eisenhower had created.

In fact, Kennedy was even prone to ignore the National Security Council, his statutory advisory board on national security affairs. Kennedy, for his part, resorted to his faith in those he knew. Thus, when Kennedy wanted someone to visit Vietnam and apprise him of the situation there, he did not turn to the council; he instead dispatched White House aides McGeorge Bundy, Michael Forrestal, Maxwell Taylor, Walt Rostow, and others whose intellect and judgment he respected. He likewise trusted Arthur Schlesinger and Pierre Salinger, both White House aides, to appraise the problems in Latin America and the Soviet Union, respectively, in their sojourns to those areas.

Kennedy's attitude toward staff structures is perhaps best reflected in the fact that there were no meetings with the whole staff in his presence. If Kennedy wanted information or an opinion from an aide, he would dictate a short memo or, more frequently, simply ask to see the aide. On the other hand, Kennedy was very accessible if a member of his staff wanted to see him. There were two entrances to Kennedy's Oval Office: through the office of his appointments secretary, Kenneth O'Donnell, or through the office of his personal secretary, Evelyn Lincoln. During the day, O'Donnell tended to be very protective of Kennedy's time; Mrs. Lincoln was far more tolerant of staff intrusions. Although an aide normally checked with O'Donnell, it was very common for the aide to avoid a possible rebuff from O'Donnell by passing through Mrs. Lincoln's office. Toward evening it was even easier to see Kennedy. His assistants frequently entered the Oval Office around six or seven o'clock at night to discuss the day's events or a particular matter which warranted the President's consideration.

This frequent contact with his staff helped ensure that Kennedy kept abreast of the problems and issues with which they dealt. The relaxed and personal atmosphere also affected the way Kennedy used his White House staff. While each of his assistants was assigned to cover certain specific areas, Kennedy never hesitated to ignore those jurisdictional lines. Since his White House staff was relatively small—it rarely included more than twenty aides at any one time—staff versatility became a virtual necessity for Kennedy's informal method of operation. Myer Feldman recalled, for example, that Kennedy would often ask him to perform chores—such as talking to a senator about a particular matter—which fell outside his normal responsibilities.[79] Feldman's experience was not unique; in fact, Kennedy often asked assistants—sometimes on a regular basis—to draft memos or fulfill other responsibilities which were unrelated to their regular duties. Thus,Ted Sorensen was initially Kennedy's principal speech writer and an adviser on domestic policies; but he frequently received assignments that involved relations with congressmen and research into problems of foreign affairs. Similarly, although McGeorge Bundy was Kennedy's adviser on national security affairs, he helped draft the Yale address on the tax cut and was asked for his opinions in other areas outside national security as well.

Kennedy's unstructured, personalized approach to his assistants complemented a second dominant trait of his White House staff: an overriding desire among the staff members to serve Kennedy's personal political interests and goals. There is, of course, nothing unique about this trait; almost every president before and since Kennedy has demanded a considerable amount of personal loyalty. And not without good reason: no executive wants assistants who cannot be trusted or who will work at cross-purposes with the executive's interests and goals.* Under Kennedy the emphasis on personal loyalty was pronounced. "Our loyalty to Kennedy transcended everything. There wasn't anything we wouldn't do for him," Myer Feldman candidly told me. "Presidential assistants are of course always loyal to their bosses," he added. "But our feelings were so unique it made those other staff people look like a bunch of Judases." This kind of deep loyalty may have been unique; but it also often undermined Kennedy's desire to secure the information and make the decisions effective leadership requires.

In order to understand the drawbacks of this excessive demand for loyalty, one must first appreciate its advantages. Loyalty to the President generally meant feeding Kennedy with ideas, information, and comments which he could use to meet stated goals or improve established programs. Sometimes the ideas were accepted (one being press secretary Pierre Salinger's suggestion that Kennedy conduct press conferences which would be televised live). Sometimes the staff proposals were ignored or rejected (one being Harris Wofford's proposal in May 1961 that Kennedy issue a strong public statement about the moral importance of protecting people's civil rights—a statement which would make good on Kennedy's campaign promise to provide the moral leadership he claimed Eisenhower had not provided on the civil rights

---

*Franklin Roosevelt provided perhaps the classic explanation of why most Presidents place such a high premium on personal loyalty. Wendell Willkie once asked Roosevelt why he continued to rely so much on Harry Hopkins, a frail man who was disliked and distrusted by many in and out of government. Roosevelt replied,

> I can understand that you wonder why I need that half-man around me. But—some day you may well be sitting here where I am now as President of the United States. And when you are, you'll be looking at that door over there and knowing that practically everybody who walks through it wants something out of you. You'll learn what a lonely job this is, and you'll discover the need for somebody like Harry Hopkins, who asks for nothing except to serve you.
> Robert Sherwood, *Roosevelt and Hopkins*, pp. 2–3 (1948)

issue). But in either event, these staff initiatives enabled Kennedy to consider ideas and actions which might otherwise have escaped his attention. Loyalty to Kennedy also meant that his aides would try to protect him from his own slips. At numerous times Kennedy would explode about a criticism someone made or an action that was ill advised. On some of these occasions, he would dictate an angry letter which his aides felt would be better destroyed than mailed since it would achieve nothing except to alienate the intended recipient; and at those times it was not unusual for Sorensen, Feldman, or some other aide to take the letter from Mrs. Lincoln's desk and show it to Kennedy a few days later when his anger—as well as his impulse to send the letter—had faded.

The problem was that personal loyalty to Kennedy often became a substitute for good government. When Kennedy made his wishes clear about a particular matter, it was common for a staff member to accept the President's decision without questioning. Newspaper "leaks" are a prime example.

As in his youth, Kennedy was a voracious reader in the White House. Each day he reviewed many newspapers and magazines not only to obtain new information, but also to see how the actions of his presidency were being reported. Sometimes, as in other presidencies, an administration official would leak information to a newspaper or magazine describing a governmental action being contemplated or a governmental action which the president did not want publicized. On many of these occasions, Kennedy would get quite angry. He would then dictate a memo or call in an aide and demand that the culprit—the person who leaked the information—be found. One example was this memo from Kennedy to Bundy in the summer of 1961:

> Can you find out where the newspaper stories came from this weekend on the Vietnam military intervention into Southern Laos. Those stories were harmful to us. Probably exaggerated. Makes it very difficult for us now to attack the Vietminh [a communist guerrilla group] for its intervention in Laos.[80]

Sometimes the results had a comical touch, as the occasion when Kennedy told Salinger in 1961 to spare no effort in finding out who leaked a newspaper story about an imminent embargo by the United States on imports from Cuba. Salinger devoted two days to meeting the request before he struck pay dirt. He reported back to Kennedy immediately that he had found the culprit:

JFK (eagerly): Who was it?

Salinger (gleefully): You.

JFK (crestfallen): What do you mean?

Salinger: Didn't you tell [Senator George] Smathers? Well, George told some friend of his on the Tampa Tribune.[81]

In any event, these inquiries were usually carried out by the staff without any question as to whether it was really that important to find the source of a leak, whether any real harm had been caused to the public interest by the leak, or, indeed, whether the publication of such information did not really serve a basic tenet of democratic society: the notion that the public should have broad access to information concerning all stages of the governmental process. Kennedy's sensitivity to press criticism, in other words, often discouraged questions from aides too loyal to see that such sensitivity was often unwarranted and almost always at odds with a belief in a free press. Indeed, this same loyalty frequently led the staff to be more sensitive about press criticism than Kennedy himself. It was not uncommon for reporters and political commentators to receive telephone calls from the White House staff complaining about articles that they felt were unduly critical. This was hardly the attitude of a White House which wanted information and opinions from diverse and antagonistic sources.

Personal loyalty to the President also affected matters of governmental policy. In many matters—but especially controversial ones—the staff was prone to confuse Kennedy's political fortunes with the principles of good leadership. Owing in great part to Kennedy's narrow victory over Nixon, many on the White House staff (like Kennedy himself) were often anxious to avoid any action or policy which might offend an important electoral group (the 1964 presidential election was always in sight). Civil rights provides an appropriate illustration. Many of the staff argued against strong presidential action in that area (particularly the introduction of legislation) not because they thought it to be bad policy but because they thought it to be bad politics: except for a limited number of liberal sympathizers, these staff members believed that such strong action would not attract the political support of anyone except the Negro community and that, in fact, such strong action would alienate many influential leaders as well as key electoral groups.

Business policy was another area in which personal loyalty was sometimes given priority over good government. Kennedy, like most Democratic presidents, was concerned about reports and political gossip which labeled his administration as one unsympathetic to business interests. This concern was particularly acute after Kennedy successfully pressured U.S. Steel and other steel companies in April 1962 to rescind a price increase which violated an agreement negotiated by the White House between the steelworkers and the steel companies.[82] Many (again including Kennedy himself) feared that the administration's actions in resolving that controversy would not, to say the least, boost its image among business groups. In public, Kennedy tried to make light of the situation. At a New York Democratic rally on his birthday, May 29, 1962, he joked that he had received a telegram from U.S. Steel Board chairman Roger Blough which read, "In honor of your birthday, I believe that you should get a raise in pay. . . . P.S. My birthday's next month."[83] Despite this and other humor, Kennedy regarded the situation as quite serious. Indeed, there was genuine apprehension within the administration that there was now no hope of corralling the support or cooperation of the business interests in any governmental activity (or in the 1964 presidential election).

This apprehension was heightened by a slump in the stock market one month later. Numerous business leaders and business publications sharply attacked the administration and Kennedy personally for being antibusiness and for causing the stock market slump. Few stopped there. Many added that Kennedy's policies would impede economic growth in the country and cause another recession. These attacks did not reflect the opinions of all businessmen; but they did command considerable support among business leaders on Wall Street and elsewhere. (The criticism also gave rise to jokes that, while the stock market fell when Eisenhower had a heart attack in 1955, the market would soar if Kennedy had a heart attack in 1962.)

In June 1962, Kennedy asked Sorensen to prepare a memorandum which would analyze the administration's relations with business and explore avenues by which those relations could be improved. Sorensen's first memo—which was used for internal purposes—said that every Democratic president faces inevitable problems in maintaining the support and cooperation of big business. Despite these inherent limitations, Sorensen suggested that it might "be desirable to launch a long-range campaign designed to soften the business hostility which reached an emotional peak during the steel price-stock market sequence of events." He then explained why:

> If business feels, *however incorrectly,* that the national climate is one of militant anti-business hostility and harassment, in which their profits are frowned upon, their labor costs increased, their views rejected and their every move subject to litigation, there is a danger that
>
> —they will be unwilling to risk new investment, but simply "batten down the hatches until the storm blows over";
>
> —the market will stay down or drop further; and
>
> *—non-business voters, influenced by the articulate voice of business that dominates their Main Street and their press, will blame*

> *their own market losses and the next recession on this Administration.*[84] [Second emphasis added.]

So there it was. It was not only a question of encouraging business investment and avoiding a further drop in the stock market; it was also a matter of ensuring that the "voters" (what happened to "the American people" as a frame of reference?) accept the administration's innocence in the decline of their economic fortunes.

Sorensen pointed out the political and policy limitations on the administration's ability to avoid these dangers. But some alternatives were suggested. Among them was the following:

> 11. *Regulation*—Can the President, or the Attorney General, or the Special Counsel, meet quietly and individually with the heads of the regulatory agencies, the anti-trust divisions, the wage-hour, Food and Drug, and other enforcement activities
>
> —to emphasize that there are times to steam ahead, to pursue, to be zealous, and there are times to be cooperative and understanding (and the latter is more appropriate now)
>
> —to explore what they can do or refrain from doing (can the SEC tone down its investigation? Is the anti-trust division encouraging treble damage suits? Has the NLRB given public emphasis to those of its decisions that favor management? Are there broad new areas of investigation planned that can be postponed? Can a conference be called of the businessmen and practitioners involved to consider new ways of proceeding?)[85]

Sorensen seemed to be suggesting here, in effect, that the federal governmental agencies compromise their enforcement of their respective statutory charters. This probably was not the first time a White House aide suggested such interference with the administrative and regulatory agencies (which are largely pro-business to begin with). But this memo does indicate how Sorensen was willing to sacrifice principles of good government—namely the presumably neutral enforcement of the regulatory laws—in order to enhance the administration's standing among the voters. And it shows how one aide's judgment was tarnished with excessive loyalty to the President's political fortunes. But Kennedy was not one to casually dismiss the importance of his own political fortunes: he basically accepted Sorensen's advice.*

---

*With Kennedy's approval, Sorensen drafted a "talking paper" for a cabinet meeting on July 26, 1962, concerning the administration's relations with business. In essence, the paper suggested steps which the Cabinet officers might take to improve those relations. The paper included the following passage:

The loyalty which Kennedy demanded and received from his White House staff helped to account for the third dominant trait which characterized that staff: an assumption of supervisory control over much of the work of the cabinet departments and in fact, the whole federal bureaucracy. Kennedy had considerable faith in his White House staff. He knew they were, almost without exception, men (there were no women assistants) of considerable intelligence who understood the nuances of making sound political judgments. And while he did not know some of them intimately at the time of their appointment to the White House staff (Dutton and Bundy are two examples), he knew enough to believe that each would remain true to his programs and political fortunes.

Because of this faith, and because he was primarily concerned with foreign affairs, Kennedy from the beginning relied greatly on his White House staff in matters concerning domestic affairs. He simply expected them to keep informed on developments in their assigned areas, brief him occasionally on those developments, and raise specific matters with him when presidential guidance or presidential decisions were required. Thus, cabinet officers whose jurisdiction was principally in the domestic arena—Abraham Ribicoff at HEW, Orville Freeman at Agriculture, Luther Hodges at Commerce, Stewart Udall at Interior, to name a few—maintained contact with Kennedy through one of his White House staff members. Kennedy was often accessible to these cabinet members when an appointment was requested or when events made such consultation necessary, but generally he preferred to spend his time on foreign affairs and let his staff maintain close supervision over these domestic departments.

"Yes, there was a concentration of power in the White House staff," White House aide Lee White told me. "The President expected his staff to handle the job and often referred matters to them. Many cabinet officers bridled because they felt they were not getting sufficient attention from the President." As one example, White cited Ribicoff. "He

---

5) *Enforcement attitudes*—most Departments have some law enforcement responsibilities affecting business: Food and Drug, Wage and Hour, Internal Revenue, Anti-trust, Meat Inspection, etc. Care can be taken to make certain that these offices are not engaged in unnecessary harassment, overzealous hostility or unhelpful remarks to those responsible businessmen with whom they come in contact.

"The Administration and Business," 3 (July 25, 1962), Files of Theodore Sorensen, John F. Kennedy Library, Box #29. See Sorensen, *Kennedy* 459–69 (1965).

Whatever the attitudes of businessmen prior to this cabinet meeting, within one month the situation was hardly discouraging. A Gallup poll of August 19, 1962, found that only 19 percent of the country's businessmen perceived the administration as antibusiness while 68 percent did not. Among the public at large, only 14 percent of the public saw the administration as antibusiness; 65 percent did not.

would call to speak to the President about an important matter and get a call back from Sorensen. Abe had been a big political figure in his own right. He had been governor of Connecticut. He had pride. And he didn't like that treatment." Interior Secretary Udall, on the other hand, accepted his limited access philosophically. "Kennedy was not terribly interested in natural resources and didn't really know much about the problems of conservation. Interior was simply not among his major priorities," Udall remarked to me. "But I felt I had broad discretion to act, and he gave my efforts strong support whenever I needed it." Within these confines Udall successfully pursued his own interests in strengthening the nation's conservation programs, its national park system, and other measures designed to protect natural resources.

In any event, Kennedy's attitude with respect to domestic departments and agencies was perhaps best reflected in a conversation he had with Fred Dutton concerning an administrator for one of the federal regulatory agencies. Almost from the beginning, the administrator continually came to Kennedy to discuss the specific issues and problems of his agency. Kennedy did not consider those issues and problems a priority matter. After several of these visits, Kennedy called in Dutton and said, "Now look, from now on I don't want that guy coming into this office. If he's got a problem, he'll have to write a memo to you, and then you take care of it."[86]

There were two basic exceptions to this general policy of relying on the White House staff to supervise the domestic departments and agencies: Douglas Dillon at Treasury and Arthur Goldberg at Labor. Kennedy had a great deal of respect for these two men. He was well acquainted with their backgrounds (Dillon as a New York banker and former high official in the Eisenhower administration; Goldberg as a nationally renowned labor lawyer); and he had considerable confidence in their skills as thinkers and decision-makers. For their part, Dillon and Goldberg were very aggressive in their relationships with Kennedy. Wherever possible, they dealt with him directly rather than go through the intermediary efforts of a staff. As an example, Kennedy might suggest to an aide that the two of them meet with Dillon to resolve a particular problem. As soon as Dillon was informed of the meeting, he would frequently call Kennedy directly and resolve the matter without waiting for the meeting with the staff person.

Kennedy's reluctance to immerse himself in domestic matters did not generally extend to international affairs. In Kennedy's eyes, foreign policy necessarily assumed priority over domestic policy. ("Domestic policy can only defeat us," he used to say. "Foreign policy can kill us."[87]) But being new to the presidential office, Kennedy initially felt it unwise to entrust these important questions to his White House staff.

Instead he thought it more prudent to rely on the foreign policy "experts," the people who staffed the intelligence community's bureaucracy. "If someone comes in to tell me this or that about the minimum wage bill," Kennedy once remarked to Arthur Schlesinger, Jr., "I have no hesitation in overruling them. But you always assume that the military and the intelligence people have some secret skill not available to ordinary mortals."[88] This attitude changed substantially after the Bay of Pigs fiasco.

In considering whether or not to approve plans for the invasion, Kennedy understood that this was not a minor matter. He realized that the United States was being asked to align itself politically and militarily with an armed invasion of a small Caribbean country. It was, in short, an important question. And for the answer he turned to the experts in the intelligence community.

The intelligence experts at the CIA, the Defense Department, and the State Department unanimously assured him that America's vital interests were at stake and that, with American military support, the invasion would succeed in toppling the Castro regime (mainly because the local population would rise up in arms to support the invaders). This advice not only coincided with Kennedy's campaign promises to train Cuban refugees for an invasion; this advice also coincided with his own natural inclination to strike a posture of toughness with the Soviet Union's attempts to expand its sphere of influence. He was therefore inclined to accept the advice. Those on his staff with whom he consulted—principally McGeorge Bundy—agreed that the advice was sound.

Kennedy mentioned the idea to Dean Acheson, who bluntly told him that the proposal was "disastrous." Kennedy was also contacted by Senator J.William Fulbright, chairman of the Senate Foreign Relations Committee and a man whose opinions Kennedy greatly respected. Fulbright gave Kennedy a memorandum opposing the proposed invasion. "To give this activity even covert support is of a piece with the hypocrisy and cynicism for which the United States is constantly denouncing the Soviet Union in the United Nations and elsewhere," Fulbright wrote. "This point will not be lost on the rest of the world—nor on our own consciences," he continued. "The Castro regime is a thorn in the flesh; but it is not a dagger in the heart."[89]

Kennedy was impressed with Fulbright's arguments and asked him to repeat them at a meeting with Secretary of State Dean Rusk, McNamara, and Thomas C. Mann and Adolf Berle, two State Department officers who handled Latin-American affairs. None of these men agreed with Fulbright. Believing that his advisers' judgments deserved greater weight, and accepting the assurances of the CIA and the Joint Chiefs of Staff that the invasion would succeed, Kennedy approved

American air support. The rest, of course, has already been related. The Cuban exiles were quickly killed or captured by Castro's superior forces, the popular uprising in Cuba never materialized, and the United States was roundly condemned in international circles for its participation in the affair.

Although Kennedy publicly accepted responsibility for the American participation, in private he bitterly complained to his wife and others close to him that many of these so-called "experts" had let him down. Their information was faulty, he said, and their judgment was poor.* He resolved that he should not fall into the same trap again. And he believed that one real assurance against that danger was to involve more trusted aides in the decision-making process.

Within a short time after the Bay of Pigs invasion, Bundy established a system independent of the bureaucracy to secure raw data and other intelligence information from the field. He also assumed an expanded role as Kennedy's adviser in national security matters. Bundy was not the only one whose role changed after the Bay of Pigs. Perhaps no two people were trusted more by Kennedy than his brother Robert and Sorensen. Although each had had only limited experience in foreign policy matters, Kennedy nonetheless believed that their sense of judgment would overcome any such limitations. He therefore asked that each of them also keep involved in national security matters by reading reports and attending appropriate meetings.

These organizational changes signaled the beginning of a new skepticism on Kennedy's part, a skepticism which would make it difficult for him to again rely exclusively on the "experts." This skepticism was particularly apparent during the Cuban missile crisis in October 1962. Anxious to formulate an effective response to the placement of Soviet missiles in Cuba, Kennedy chose not to depend on any bureaucratic agency or committee. He instead created his own advisory board—later legitimized as the Executive Committee of the National Security Council—to provide him with information, ideas, and alternatives for action. This Executive Committee was not made up from government organization charts. It consisted of selected people, in and out of gov-

---

*Bundy, as Kennedy's adviser for national security affairs, was especially upset about the failure of the invasion. Feeling he had disappointed Kennedy, Bundy drafted a letter of resignation for Kennedy to accept at any time. "You know that I wish I had served you better in the Cuban episode," Bundy wrote, "and I hope you know how I admire your own gallantry under fire in that case. If my departure can assist you in any way, I hope you will send me off—and if you have difficulty, you will still have this letter for when you may need it." Letter from McGeorge Bundy to John F. Kennedy, undated, President's Office Files, John F. Kennedy Library. Kennedy never accepted the letter of resignation.

ernment, whose advice Kennedy respected—Sorensen, Bundy, Robert Kennedy, Lovett, Acheson, McNamara, Dillon, and others.

Kennedy's reaction to the Bay of Pigs fiasco was quite understandable. Fallibility is an inherent trait of all humans and of the governmental bureaucracies which they fashion. Having learned to accept this fallibility in the intelligence community, it was only natural that Kennedy should sense the importance of seeking out people who not only had access to information but also people whose judgment was sound and whose loyalty to him was beyond question. Many who satisfied these latter criteria were on the White House staff, and, from this perspective at least, it made sense to involve them more in national security affairs.

But this response was not without its risks. Indeed, by conferring major responsibilities on his White House staff for both domestic and foreign affairs, Kennedy accelerated a trend which culminated in the Watergate scandals under Nixon. For by giving his White House staff these responsibilities, Kennedy gave his stamp of approval to the idea that governmental power can and should be concentrated in the White House rather than in the appropriate executive departments; he gave credence to the notion that anonymous White House aides rather than cabinet officers could and should exercise control over governmental programs and policies.

This development was, to say the least, at odds with the Brownlow Report which provided the impetus for an enlarged White House staff; according to the report, White House assistants were to help the President, not supplant the executive departments as the forum for decision-making. The development was also at odds with the principle of accountability which underlies any democratic government: these White House aides were not confirmed by the Senate; and they could not be held publicly responsible for the programs and policies they supervised (indeed, they were protected from having to give testimony in Congress by the doctrine of executive privilege).

This is not to lay principal blame for Watergate at Kennedy's feet. The growing concentration of power in the White House was only one of many factors which explain those abuses. It is especially difficult to pin much blame on Kennedy because, for all his effort to master the federal bureaucracy by centralizing policy in the White House, he often found himself holding the short end of the stick.

Grappling with the Bureaucracy

The somnolence of the federal governmental bureaucracy is legendary. Almost since the turn of the century, presidents have bemoaned the frustrations they must endure with a system which seems neither responsive nor responsible. William Howard Taft once listened patiently as an aide continually referred to "the machinery of government." Later Taft laughingly remarked to a friend, "You know, *he* really thinks it *is* machinery."[90]

There was at least one major difference between the bureaucracy to which Taft was referring and the one Kennedy had to control: size. Since the early 1900s—and especially after FDR's organizational revolution—the federal bureaucracy had grown by leaps and bounds. In 1961 it consisted of nine major departments, 104 bureaus, 12 sections, 108 services, 51 branches, 631 divisions, 19 administrations, 6 agencies, 4 boards, 6 commands, 20 commissions, 19 corporations, and 2.5 million employees. Many presidential decisions and directives would ultimately have to shift their way through this vast bureaucracy if they were to have the support and efforts of the individuals who would implement them. As Kennedy would soon find, however, the entire bureaucracy neither operates by the President's direct command nor is totally subject to his careful scrutiny. Many people were career servants. They did not owe their jobs to him and their futures were not tied to his; they were there before he arrived and most would remain when he was ready to leave. For better or worse, then, the bureaucracy was something Kennedy would have to live with—or, as the case may be, tolerate.

Kennedy's personality and attitudes did not lend themselves to using the formal bureaucratic structures in making decisions. He did make clear at the first cabinet meeting that he wanted an open and candid discussion of the issues.But it also became clear within a short time that he did not intend to use the cabinet meetings as a regularized forum for making decisions. Such meetings usually made Kennedy restless. They often turned on generalities when he was most interested in specifics; and they were conducted in a formal setting whereas he preferred to operate in an informal manner. Accordingly, he kept abreast of the cabinet members' work primarily through summaries prepared by his staff (who received weekly reports from the major departments and agencies).

As I have already indicated, this arrangement made many cabinet officers unhappy—especially those whose jurisdictions did not coincide with Kennedy's natural interest in foreign affairs. And even then there were sometimes problems. Secretary of State Dean Rusk—whose principal responsibility *was* foreign affairs—often played a small role in major policy decisions. To some extent, this snag was a function of Rusk's personality. An able, hardworking man, Rusk's relations with Kennedy were rather formal (Kennedy always addressed Rusk as "Mr. Secretary" or "Mr. Rusk," thus making him the only cabinet member who was not on a first-name basis with the President). This formality could not endear Rusk to a President whose demeanor was marked by informality. Rusk, moreover, was not aggressive; unless asked, he was reluctant to volunteer his opinions on problems or issues. At the height of negotiations over the American response to the Berlin situation in 1961, for example, Sorensen inquired what Rusk's views were; Kennedy replied that he didn't know.*

Other cabinet members found that politics often mattered more than personality in making decisions. Luther Hodges, the new secretary of commerce, was one of the first to appreciate this. A businessman from North Carolina, he frowned on those who viewed Commerce as an institutionalized prostitute for the special business interests; he did not subscribe to the view of Eisenhower's secretary of defense, Charles Wilson, who commented that "what's good for General Motors is good for the country." "You will never hear from me," said Hodges soon after his appointment, "that this country should do this or that simply because business wants it. What is good for General Motors may, or may not, be good for the country."[91]

True to his word, Hodges moved to make some changes in the Business Advisory Council, a coalition of private businessmen created under FDR to work with the Commerce Department. Hodges felt that the council was weighted too much in favor of big business and that its relations with the government were a little too cozy; rumors of secret deals were rampant and, he believed, all too often true. He therefore appointed new members from the smaller businesses and directed that the council's meetings be open to the public. Such heresy was not easy for the business members to swallow. They protested, and their pleas fell on sympathetic ears in other corners of the new administration. At the urging of Treasury Secretary Douglas Dillon, Kennedy tacitly endorsed the council's decision to reject Hodges' actions and continued to rely on that body for business advice. Politics apparently assumed priority over principle here; but it did not take long for the roosters to come home to roost.

Kennedy thought his conciliatory line here and elsewhere would appease big business and bring them within the New Frontier's fold. Af-

---

*Robert Kennedy offers some additional detail as to why President Kennedy began to rely more on Bundy than on Rusk in foreign policy matters. In his study of the Cuban missile crisis, *Thirteen Days*, Robert Kennedy notes that Rusk failed to chair the Executive Committee, as was probably his prerogative as the chief foreign policy officer (since President Kennedy often did not attend the meetings). Rusk also failed to attend many of these meetings, Robert Kennedy further notes, because of previous diplomatic commitments. One wonders what appointment could have been so important as to outweigh the secretary's presence at these crucial meetings.

ter all, he had openly sided with business against his own secretary of commerce. In New York City later that year, Kennedy addressed the National Association of Manufacturers. He openly acknowledged that these representatives of business had not been his staunchest allies in his drive for the presidency: "I recognize that in the last campaign, most of the members of this luncheon group today supported my opponent, except for a very few—who were under the impression that I was my father's son."[92] Kennedy said he hoped that his first actions as president had dispelled any notion that his administration was antibusiness.

No doubt, Kennedy's reversal of Hodges did help to dispel that notion. Indeed, many businessmen probably accepted the idea that Kennedy was their friend. Certainly the Business Council had reason to believe this—and the chairman of that council was none other than U.S. Steel Board Chairman Roger Blough, the man who one year later thought that Kennedy was "understanding" enough to accept an increase in the steel prices. In other words, Kennedy's decision to placate business interests (at the expense of better government and Hodges's credibility) probably contributed to a climate in which Blough and other businessmen believed that Kennedy really was, after all was said and done, his father's son.

The experience with Hodges did not mean Kennedy would always disregard the views of his cabinet. In many, if not most, situations, he valued their advice and directly solicited it. The case of the mental health legislation is illustrative. A presidential panel filed a report in October 1962 outlining the tragedy of the millions of Americans who suffered from mental retardation or some other mental disability. Within a month, Kennedy asked HEW Secretary Anthony Celebrezze, Labor Secretary Willard Wirtz, and Veterans Administrator James Gleason to study the panel's recommendations and propose appropriate actions for the federal government. Their detailed response in November 1962 became the basis of administration legislation enacted in 1963 to create community mental health centers.[93] Other cabinet officers—especially Defense Secretary McNamara, Dillon, and Goldberg—also found their initiatives and opinions to be a principal determinant of presidential decisions.

But no cabinet officer commanded more influence with Kennedy than his brother, Robert, the attorney general. Robert Kennedy really was, as popular rumor had it, the second most powerful man in the country. As manager of his brother's senate and presidential campaigns, Robert had established himself as an individual who placed his brother's interests above all others, and the President appreciated it. He relied greatly on Robert's judgment. This, as noted earlier, was why Robert was asked after the Bay of Pigs venture to participate in foreign policy decisions. But Robert's most telling impact was perhaps in civil rights.

The Kennedys came into office without much understanding of or feeling for the plight of America's blacks. To be sure, John Kennedy had made many campaign speeches lashing out at the discrimination and hatred which threaded the nation's race relations. But these statements were based more on principle than on empathy; Kennedy could lecture about equal treatment under the law, but he did not really sense the desperation and outrage that characterized the black individual's experience. The same was true of Robert Kennedy. Recalling his first months as attorney general, he said, "I did not lie awake at night worrying about the problems of Negroes."[94]

All this began to change shortly after Robert Kennedy began to discharge his responsibilities as the nation's chief law enforcement officer. The Freedom Rides, the mob violence in southern cities, the harassment of federal officials, and the stubborn resistance of the South's politicians brought home to Robert Kennedy the pains of racial discrimination in America—and the difficulties in eradicating it. The message became especially clear after John Siegenthaler, an aide to the attorney general, suffered a concussion in Alabama from the blow of a policeman who was breaking up a crowd of peaceful demonstrators. Burke Marshall, then the assistant attorney general for civil rights, remembered how all this affected Robert Kennedy. "The more he saw," said Marshall, "and this was true of me as well, the more he understood. The more you learned about how Negroes were treated in the South, the more you saw of that, the madder you became. You know he always talked about the hypocrisy. That's what got him. By the end of a year he was so mad about that kind of thing it overrode everything else."[95]

Kennedy talked to the President about these matters frequently. President Kennedy listened intently, but being somewhat removed from the battlefield he did not feel it the way his brother did. The President's reaction was also molded by his political instincts. He believed far-reaching action, and especially the introduction of legislation, was politically unwise. But he gave his brother a virtually free hand in responding to the problem (even allowing the attorney general to have Senate Majority Leader Mansfield introduce a bill in 1962 which would curtail the discriminatory use of literacy tests to block the registration of black voters).

The situation came to a head in the spring of 1963. Federal courts ordered the admission of two blacks to the previously all-white University of Alabama. Governor George Wallace's defiance of the order reflected the ugly mood which pervaded all of Alabama. Mobs of whites gathered to stone the black demonstrators, and the mobs found sympathetic accomplices in the policemen who used dogs and fire hoses to turn the blacks away.

Robert Kennedy explained to his brother in emotional terms that this was not merely a crisis of law enforcement; it was first and foremost a moral crisis. Arguing against Ted Sorensen and other White House aides, the attorney general implored his brother to address the nation on this matter. The time for patience and delay had long since passed, Robert Kennedy said; hundreds of years of oppression and indignity could not be assauged by promises of future action. Who among us, he asked rhetorically, would willingly change the color of his skin from white to black? President Kennedy listened and seemed sympathetic. He, too, had begun to understand the bitterness of the black man's life and, most importantly, the obligation of the federal government to act now.

Convinced that his brother would address the nation on the matter, the attorney general prepared a draft speech for him. "To this day," the draft intoned, "and to a far greater extent than many of us may be willing to admit, the Negro has remained less than free within our shores.This cannot, should not and must not be allowed to continue. The day is long gone when we could reasonably ask the Negro to be 'patient,' or explain to him that we must all 'move slowly.'" For most blacks, the draft continued, the American dream seems to be "a cruelly mocking illusion." The black individual suffers from chronic unemployment, cannot have his children attend schools of his choice without federal troops, vote for the public officials of his choice without harassment, or eat at the restaurant of his choice. "Let no glib specialists confuse the issue by seeing it primarily as a tangle of legal problems, or economic problems, or political problems, or social problems," the draft observed. "It is all of these, but above all—and very clearly—it is a moral problem."[96]

After considering this draft speech and having the editing suggestions of Sorensen, President Kennedy spoke to the nation on television on June 11, 1963. The mark of his brother was clearly evident. "We are confronted primarily with a moral issue," Kennedy declared. "It is as old as the scriptures and is as clear as the American Constitution." He then explained why:

> The heart of the question is whether all Americans are to be afforded equal rights and equal opportunities, whether we are going to treat our fellow Americans as we want to be treated. If an American, because his skin is dark, cannot eat lunch in a restaurant open to the public, if he cannot send his children to the best public school available, if he cannot vote for the public officials who represent him, if, in short, he cannot enjoy the full and free life which

> all of us want, then who among us would be content to have the color of his skin changed and stand in his place? Who among us would then be content with the counsels of patience and delay?[97]

In many ways, this experience reflected Kennedy at his best. The willingness to listen, to learn, and then commit himself to action. And, of course, the whole process was facilitated by the fact that the attorney general was his brother.

It was not always so in dealing with other levels of the bureaucracy. The difficulties are almost always compounded when a president tries to secure information and inspire action below the cabinet level. There is a natural tendency among bureaucrats to be cautious when talking with *the* President of the United States. The glamour and aura of the White House Oval Office seem to dampen the fire of minds and mute the force of opinions. All too few have the courage (or sense) to speak frankly when giving information and their views. Conformity and timidity are the guideposts.

To some extent, Kennedy understood this, and, as a general rule, he was anxious to avoid the pitfalls of relying on advice which was shaped not by facts but by a desire to say what the President wanted to hear. A President who wants candor and action from the bureaucracy will often need persistence and a little bit of luck. Sensing this, Kennedy often tried to push his administrators to get the information and candid opinions he felt he needed. "The tempo of this administration is fantastic," sighed Budget Director David Bell. "The President is a fellow who has a foot-long needle in you all the time."[98] Such perseverance sometimes enabled Kennedy to pierce the bureaucratic glaze and extract an individual's closely guarded views. One clear example was Kennedy's discussion with Winthrop Brown, the ambassador to Laos, in February 1961.

In their preinauguration meeting, Eisenhower had warned Kennedy that the most critical problem awaiting him was the guerrilla war in Laos. The communist Pathet Lao was gaining ground quickly, the American-supported General Phoumi Nosavan was unable to command the support of his troops or the local population, and the dispatch of American troops might soon become necessary. This concerned Kennedy greatly, and he was particularly eager to talk with Brown, who had been appointed to the Laotian ambassadorship by Eisenhower.

When he arrived at the Oval Office, Brown was greeted warmly by Kennedy. After a few pleasantries and some picture-taking, they settled down to discuss Laos. Kennedy let loose a series of questions which made Brown realize that the President had been well briefed on the subject. Instinctively, Kennedy wanted to know about the individuals who helped to shape events in Laos. "What kind of people are these people: Souvanna and Souphanouvong and Phoumi and the King and Kong Le?" Kennedy asked. Brown wanted to tell Kennedy exactly what he thought: that the American reliance on Phoumi was misplaced, that the neutralist leader Souvanna Phouma was the only one who could win the allegiance of the people. But he held back—the ambassador, he thought, should reflect policy, not try to mold it. Kennedy continued his line of questioning. Concealing his own opinion, Brown replied, "Well, sir, the policy is . . . " Kennedy cut him off. "That's not what I asked you. I said, 'What do you think, you, the Ambassador?' " Later Brown recalled how he responded to this direct appeal to his personal views:

> I told him exactly what was on my heart. Somehow or other I had the feeling that I could say anything that I wanted and it would be like the confessional, that it would go to the President and he would use it and evaluate it or not use it as he saw fit, but that it would never be used against me and it would never go any further.[99]

It is not entirely clear how far Kennedy did carry this information. But there is little doubt that Brown's responses helped convince Kennedy ultimately that the best resolution of the Laotian problem was to support a neutralist government under Souvanna Phouma.

Kennedy was not always so adept at reaching into the depths of the bureaucracy for accurate information and candid opinions. In planning the Bay of Pigs invasion he was, as noted earlier, too quick to accept the information and advice of the so-called "experts." Afterwards Kennedy realized his oversight. He had accepted opinions on almost blind faith. He had not conducted any independent investigation. He had not really encouraged people to question assumptions, to assemble all the facts, or to analyze the logic of the plan. He resolved that it should not occur again. And to some extent this resolution did govern his future relations with the bureaucracy.* In meetings or discussions

---

*Kennedy did appoint an independent commission to investigate and report on the failures of the Bay of Pigs invasion. The commission consisted of Robert Kennedy, Maxwell Taylor, CIA Director Allen Dulles, and Admiral Arleigh Burke. As Louise FitzSimmons has written, however, it would have been difficult to expect much from this commission:

> As two of the members of the commission [Dulles and Burke] were among those most directly concerned, it is hardly surprising that the inquiry was confined to a study of the details of the operation; the basic premises were apparently never questioned. Robert Lovett, who was called to testify before the commission, recalls the

with the bureaucrats he would not usually reveal his own thinking—there was too much danger that he would then hear only what others thought he wanted to hear. And he would not wait until the various bureaucratic groups and factions had ironed out their differences; he would invite discussion, debate, argument, and doubt before an individual's opinions became crystallized. He did not want unanimity of opinion which simply reflected an agreement among the bureaucrats not to air their differences before the President.

Thus, when considering the use of American troops in Laos, Kennedy did not meet with the Joint Chiefs as a group at first. In planning the Bay of Pigs invasion, Kennedy did not know that some of the Joint Chiefs had doubts about the military feasibility of the plan. He understood the reasons for this: some were reluctant to express their doubts in front of the other Joint Chiefs. In considering a response to the Laotian questions, Kennedy therefore asked each chief to submit his individual views in writing before any collective meeting. Kennedy was not startled to find disagreement among them. Having received this conflicting advice, as Morton Halperin has pointed out, "it was harder for Kennedy to make a decision to intervene but it also meant that he did not make a decision under a mistaken impression that there was a unified military view either for or against the intervention."[100]

The Bay of Pigs experience likewise reinforced Kennedy's earlier notion that a president could not administer the huge bureaucracy merely by isolating himself with the top echelon. In making decisions concerning the invasion he was basically content to involve only the Joint Chiefs of Staff, the CIA directors, the secretaries, and appropriate assistant secretaries of State and Defense. People who had the most intimate knowledge of Cuba—the Director and Deputy Director of Caribbean and Mexican Affairs—were ignored.[101] People who had intimate knowledge of the State Department's intelligence program—like Roger Hilsman, director of the Bureau of Intelligence and Research—were likewise ignored. And although the invasion raised fundamental questions of international law (the United States did belong to an international group, the Organization of American States, which seemed to prohibit the invasion), the State Department's legal adviser, Abram Chayes, was also excluded. The lesson was clear. Bureaucracies, like glaciers, move ever so slowly, and often there can be no movement in the right direction without first pushing the bottom levels a little. Ken-

---

"somewhat embarrassing setup" of having to present to the head of the CIA and a member of the Joint Chiefs criticism of their operation and judgments.

FitzSimmons, *The Kennedy Doctrine* 62–63 (1972).

nedy subsequently spent a good deal of time on the telephone calling people who had the information he needed or were responsible for implementing a decision he had made or wanted to make. He did this, Kennedy once explained, because "I think there is a great tendency in Government to have papers stay on desks too long, and it seems to me that is really one function. After all," he continued, "the President can't administer a department, but he can be a stimulant."[102]

Often these presidential calls to the lower levels of bureaucracy were placed in a fit of pique. Anger and annoyance are quite frequently the real incentive for a president to pick up the telephone to call someone at a subcabinet level. Roger Hilsman recalled, for example, how one day during the Cuban missile crisis he was surprised to find the President's voice on the other end of the telephone. Irritated, Kennedy had called to inquire how a particular congressman had been able to receive—and then leak to the press—confidential information relating to the government's response to the Soviet buildup of missiles. Although flustered at the time, Hilsman felt afterwards that his activities were continually under the watchful eye of the President.

For all this concern with motivating the bureaucracy, Kennedy was not entirely successful. His much heralded (and much overrated) "talent search" for new people had not really changed the face of the bureaucracy. Many of the government servants were not the best and brightest, and, more importantly perhaps, many were not loyal to him. As Graham Allison has made so clear in his study of the missile crisis, bureaucrats are often more concerned with serving their parochial interests than with serving the president's interests. It naturally follows that "where you stand depends on where you sit."[103] Thus, in his campaign, Kennedy had spoken of changes in foreign policies, especially those involving the underdeveloped nations. But as Walter Lippmann commented several months after Kennedy's inauguration, "there are still strong bureaucratic interests in the State Department, the CIA and the Pentagon which are as opposed to a change in policy by President Kennedy as were the French generals in Algeria to a change by De Gaulle."[104]

Kennedy recognized this and, especially in matters of defense and foreign policy, he was anxious—sometimes too anxious—to mollify the bureaucratic interests. In developing the Defense budget, Kennedy realized that the Joint Chiefs always made excessive demands and in some cases, like the new, expensive B-70 bomber, he would draw the line. But often the line was drawn after the Chiefs had extracted commitments that exceeded the bounds of reason. There was, for example, the White House meeting where Defense Secretary McNamara presented what appeared to be a tightly reasoned and highly statistical analysis to support a large increase in the number of nuclear missiles.

White House science adviser Jerome Weisner then presented his own careful analysis to show that the nation's security interests could be adequately protected by far fewer missiles. I cannot accept that, McNamara said. The reason: he had already promised the Joint Chiefs that the administration would not reduce the number of missiles to be built below the figure already proposed (and, he added, Congress would not accept less either). Statistics and reason, in short, meant little here, and Kennedy knew it.

Kennedy's willingness to appease the Joint Chiefs here did not speak well of his willingness to do what he thought was best for the country. On many other occasions, his submission to bureaucratic pressures was not entirely a matter of choice. For often those pressures simply reflected the sluggishness and sterility that often plague large organizations. It took the State Department almost six weeks, for instance, to respond to a Soviet aide-mémoire on Berlin which Khrushchev gave to Kennedy when they met in Vienna in June 1961. ("Damn it," Kennedy once remarked, "Bundy and I get more done in one day in the White House than they do in six months in the State Department.")[105] And sometimes these delays complicated the President's ability to make the choices he thought best.

An unfortunate but telling instance of this was portrayed during the Cuban missle crisis. In 1961, Kennedy directed Secretary of State Rusk to begin negotiations to remove obsolete Jupiter missiles in Turkey. One year later, Kennedy was extremely angered because the missiles were still in Turkey and no steps had been taken toward dismantling them.* Their continued existence allowed for some excruciating moments when—at the height of the crisis—Khrushchev offered to remove the Soviet missiles in Cuba if the United States would remove the missiles in Turkey, since many of these latter missiles were less than a hundred miles from the Soviet border. Wanting to avoid any public retreat from what he saw as the central issue—the deceit of the Soviet Union in trying to expand its sphere of influence—Kennedy publicly rejected any *quid pro quo* exchange. In private, however, Robert Kennedy told Soviet Ambassador Anatoly Dobrynin that the Presi-

*Kennedy's anger here was probably not because he was surprised. He had made repeated requests to the State Department to have the missiles removed. The department balked because they were afraid the removal of the missiles would cause political problems with Turkey. Exasperated, Kennedy did not pursue the matter. When the Turkish missiles became a focal point of debate during the crisis, he was annoyed with himself for not pursuing the matter more closely, and he was annoyed with the system. As Robert Kennedy said in his account of the missile crisis, "The President believed he was President and that, his wishes having been made clear, they would be followed and the missiles removed." Robert Kennedy, *Thirteen Days* 95 (1969). See Abram Chayes, *The Cuban Missile Crisis* 96, n. 43 (1974).

dent had already ordered the removal of the Turkish missiles and that they would in fact be removed after the matter of the Cuban missiles was resolved.*

In dealing with the bureaucracy Kennedy frequently found that its resistance often reflected something more than an inability to act quickly; sometimes it indicated an effort to subvert the President's policies and decisions. The attempt to resolve the problem of the two million Palestinian refugees in the Middle East was a case in point.

The Palestinians were a people whose fate had been left hanging when the United Nations sanctioned the division of the Palestinian territory into Israel and Jordan in 1947. They were (and are), in effect, a people without a home, and this has always been both a symbolic and real source of Arab hatred for Israel (although the Arabs, with far more land than Israel, could do more to help the Palestinians). Under the prodding of Mike Feldman, Kennedy approved an American initiative—under the auspices of the UN—to break the logjam on the refugee problem by asking Israel and the Arab states to accept a certain number of refugees for settlement in their respective countries. Safeguards were included so that Israel would not have to worry about being overpopulated with Palestinians. After secretly negotiating with Prime Minister Ben-Gurion and Foreign Minister Golda Meir in Jerusalem, Feldman secured Israel's acceptance of the plan. Arab acceptance also seemed quite possible.

Shortly before the UN meeting in New York at which the plan was to be publicly introduced, Golda Meir called Feldman to tell him that the plan had been changed and that Israel would not accept it now. Feldman was perplexed; to his knowledge, the plan being readied in New York was the same one he had presented to the Israelis in Jerusalem. After some inquiries, Feldman found that the State Department (whose pro-Arab bias was well known in government circles) had—unbeknownst to him or Kennedy—made sixty-two changes in the plan to make it more palatable to the Arabs. Thus did the bureaucracy work its will independently of the White House. Kennedy and Feldman were of course quite angry. But the plan was allowed to die, when the Arabs—apparently unappreciative of the State Department's efforts—objected to it and made any redrafting futile.

These experiences with entrenched bureaucratic interests were, needless to say, quite frustrating to Kennedy. Time and again he

*In this light, perhaps the State Department bureaucracy should have been thanked for its sluggishness. After all, by promising to remove the Turkish missiles, Kennedy committed himself to an action to which he was already committed. But Khrushchev may have seen the appearance of a *quid pro quo* exchange, and this may have persuaded him and his advisers that the Cuban missiles could be removed without the Soviet Union's losing face.

seemed unable to master the maze of government, to make it responsive to his touch, to the decisions which he thought should guide government policy. In many respects, Kennedy's efforts to overcome these obstacles deserve a high rating; the efforts, however, were only of limited success.

Despite these many frustrations and failures, Kennedy understood that he alone had the responsibility for decision. The soundness and effectiveness of his decisions might well depend on the thousands of faceless people spread throughout the bureaucracy; but the administration was publicly identified under only one name, and it was his. He alone would be held accountable—by the American people, the Congress, and the world—for his administration's decisions.

The Bay of Pigs fiasco had taught him, moreover, that the responsibility for decision is not easy to accept. It continually troubled him that his decision—or indecision, as the case may be—indirectly caused the deaths of many of the invading Cuban exiles. It was a sobering experience. By coincidence, a cabinet meeting was scheduled on the morning of the invasion. Kennedy came in, explained what happened, why it was done, and what went wrong. Having finished his monologue, he left the cabinet room almost immediately and went onto the outside terrace. Robert Kennedy rose and went outside to join the President for a few minutes. Then he was alone. Fred Dutton, who was there, remembered it was a "moving thing." "In terms of the cabinet," said Dutton, "he took full responsibility. What became his public posture was no different from his private discussion there. . . . Even with the Cabinet there at a moment like [that], he didn't say that they were to avoid criticism; he didn't give them a public line they were to take."[106] Later Kennedy was informed by Pierre Salinger that a cabinet member was about to hold a press conference to announce that the failure belonged to the CIA and the Joint Chiefs rather than to the President. "Call that (expletive deleted)," Kennedy exploded, "and tell him to shut his mouth. I'm the President and I'm responsible for any errors of this administration."[107]

Kennedy was, of course, simply acknowledging a fact of political life. The responsibility was his whether he wanted it or not, whether he acknowledged it or not. But it is somewhat refreshing—unfortunately—to see a president recognize facts that are evident to everyone else.

Kennedy's new sensitivity to responsibility was evident in subsequent actions. The missile crisis in 1962 provides one illustration. The guilt of the Bay of Pigs fiasco was still fresh in Kennedy's memory. In the 1962 crisis, Kennedy sought opinions but took every precaution to ensure that the final decisions remained in his hands. Although his Executive Committee aired the possibilities of attacking or blockading

Cuba, it was Kennedy who ultimately decided on the quarantine. He moreover maintained close contact with his administrators in supervising the implementation of the quarantine: when a United States Navy reconnaissance plane spotted a Lebanese freighter chartered by the Soviet Union to carry goods to Cuba, the information was immediately relayed to Kennedy, who subsequently returned an order to board and search the boat for war matériel. In a similar manner, Kennedy maintained close surveillance over the negotiations for the Test Ban Treaty in Moscow in 1963. Although Kennedy placed great faith in Averell Harriman, his personal representative in Moscow, Kennedy communicated daily with Harriman to discuss the format and content of the impending agreement. He did not want to regret later an omission or act that might have strangled the hopes for this covenant.

Involving the Congress

The president's relations with Congress, no less than his relations with the bureaucracy, are important in obtaining the information and executing the decisions which effective leadership requires. To some extent, the reasons are obvious. Much of the president's leadership is dependent on legislation or some other congressional action. The legislative process is a complex one which requires the cooperation of many people both in and out of Congress. But one point is almost always beyond question: the legislative tree will yield more fruit to the president who solicits the advice and works closely with the appropriate legislative leaders on both sides of the aisle.

But there are other reasons for involving the Congress in the formulation and execution of presidential decisions. To begin with, senators and congressmen often have information which can be of considerable use to a president. Many legislators deal with particular issues for many years and soon become experts in their own right. Anyone who wanted to know about the practices of America's pharmaceutical companies in the early 1960s, for example, would have done well to consult with Estes Kefauver, a senator from Tennessee; as a result of extensive congressional hearings which he had chaired in the late 1950s, Kefauver became something of a walking encyclopedia on the development, pricing, and advertising of drugs.

Congressional representatives can also give the president a better feel for the public moods and opinions. Each legislator represents a constituency far smaller than the president's. Hopes for reelection—which come once every two years for members of the House and once every six years for members of the Senate—generally require the legislator to keep his fingers constantly on the pulse of his constituents. This close contact can give the legislator—and, in turn, the president—a better understanding of the issues which most concern the public, the governmental policies they are most anxious to see adopted or changed, and the governmental programs they believe would most satisfactorily resolve their problems.

There is at least one other reason for involving the Congress in the making of presidential decisions, even those whose implementation does not require congressional action: a legislator who is involved in the making of a presidential decision is less likely to hamper its implementation. This is not to suggest that presidential consultation guarantees a legislator's support of a presidential decision; but such consultation does increase the chances of such support and, in any event, is likely to diminish the heat of any opposition. This is no small danger. A determined and knowledgeable legislative opponent can make matters very difficult for the implementation of a presidential decision. He can make public speeches which place the president on the defensive; or, if he is a chairman of a committee or subcommittee, he can conduct hearings which expose the deficiencies of the president's decision. Lyndon Johnson's repeated failures to involve Congress in the making of decisions concerning the Vietnam War, for example, no doubt help explain why Senator Fulbright initiated extensive public hearings on the matter under the auspices of the Senate Foreign Relations Committee; and those hearings, which were nationally televised, probably did much to mobilize public doubts about American participation in the war.

The politics of consultation here are, in part, deeply rooted in the psychology of Congress. Anyone who has worked on Capitol Hill or observed it closely knows that it consists of 535 individuals with very large egos. Some, of course, may be larger than others; but modesty is a little-known quality in Congress. Almost every legislator likes to believe (and in some instances needs to believe) that his or her opinions are important, that he or she has the knowledge and judgment to know what's best for the country. Perhaps nothing soothes the peacock's feathers more than a telephone call from the White House soliciting the legislator's advice. And the goodwill created by this presidential deference can often be reaped in other matters as well.

It is extremely difficult to describe and analyze the president's interactions with the 535 members of Congress on every issue. It is not only a question of time. It is also a question of complexity. The president's relations with Congress depend frequently on the ever-changing circumstances and events which envelop a president's tenure. Different occurrences not only affect individual congressmen in different ways, but might also have different effects on that congressman's relations with the president. In short, a president's relations with Congress—like almost all human relationships—are often quite fluid. Despite these obstacles toward a comprehensive analysis, it is possible to perceive some basic qualities which dominated Kennedy's relations with Congress.

Friendliness was one such quality. Even as a congressman and senator, Kennedy enjoyed amicable—although rarely intimate—relations with most of his colleagues, regardless of how closely their political views coincided with his. Thus, no one stood further to the right of Kennedy's political views than Goldwater; yet Kennedy was quite fond of Goldwater and often engaged in light banter with him.* Kennedy maintained these friendly relations with Congress after he entered the White House. There was virtually no one in the national legislature whom Kennedy could not talk to, or would not talk to if the need arose.

The need arose quite frequently, for example, with respect to Senator Everett Dirksen and Representative Charles Halleck, the Republican leaders in the two Houses of Congress. Because his congressional support for major legislation was almost always precarious, Kennedy was often consulting with Dirksen or Halleck or both. Kennedy recognized that such consultations were usually beneficial in obtaining information as to how to draft legislation which would attract some Republican support. Thus, in laying the foundation for the introduction and passage of civil rights legislation, Kennedy took care personally and repeatedly to solicit the views and cooperation of both Dirksen and Halleck. These personal efforts did not go unappreciated. Several years after Kennedy's death, I discussed his congressional relations with Dirksen in the Senate Minority Leader's huge and rather ornate office in the Capitol. "John Kennedy was easy to talk to," Dirksen told me. "When he had difficulties, he had no hesitation about calling me up for help. He always felt free to talk with me. And I can never remember, after having spoken with him or having seen him and trying to help him, that I did not receive a phone call or a note thanking me."[108]

Kennedy recognized the political benefits of being cooperative with Dirksen and Halleck. And he was willing to sustain the appearance of cooperation even when their requests exceeded the bounds of reasonableness. One case in point concerns the retention of Marcus Raskin on the White House staff. Raskin was a bright and quite liberal young man

---

*There was the time, for instance, when both were senators, that Kennedy was asked to preside over the Senate. He consented on the understanding that he could leave by 6 P.M. to keep a previous appointment. The only senator on the floor was Goldwater, who continued to speak past 6 P.M., although he knew Kennedy wanted to leave. Kennedy was growing more and more restless, and Goldwater, in a good-natured way, was enjoying his colleague's discomfort. Finally Kennedy sent him a note: "Do you always have to be such a shit?" Goldwater laughed and, realizing the joke was over, concluded his speech. Interview with Jack Bell, Oral History Project, John F. Kennedy Library, p. 12.

who served as Bundy's assistant on arms control and disarmament matters. He had been recruited from the House of Representatives, where he served as an aide to Congressman Robert Kastenmeier. While serving on Capitol Hill, Raskin had coauthored two liberal books[109] which questioned the assumptions of the Cold War and the desirability of continuing a massive buildup in America's defense arsenal. The books had not yet been published when Bundy interviewed Raskin for the White House position. Because the forthcoming books did not coincide with Kennedy's views, Bundy asked Raskin to remove his name as one of the authors (Bundy apparently assumed that it would be embarrassing to Kennedy to have an individual on his White House staff who wrote books criticizing positions which he had endorsed). Raskin complied with Bundy's request (much to his later regret) and joined the White House staff in the spring of 1961.

Despite the fact that Raskin's name was removed from the books, Dirksen and Halleck later learned that this young White House aide had in fact contributed to the writing of them. Being fervent Cold War warriors themselves, Dirksen and Halleck approached Kennedy and informed him that, in their view, it was unseemly to have this young radical "nonbeliever" on the White House staff. Anxious to assauge the Republican leaders about his own commitment to waging the Cold War, Kennedy bowed to their request and had Raskin transferred almost immediately to the Bureau of the Budget's staff. Kennedy's decision did not mean that all his staff served at the pleasure of the Republican congressional leadership. As McGeorge Bundy wrote to me—in a carefully worded statement which avoided comment on the specifics of the Raskin incident—"if the Republican Congressmen had governed the decision-making about staff in the Kennedy administration, there are many of us who would not have lasted the course."[110] There were probably other factors which made Raskin vulnerable (such as his ready willingness to criticize the militancy of the administration's foreign policies). But by seeming to accede to Dirksen and Halleck's recommendation that Raskin be transferred, Kennedy helped to foster an impression that, on some occasions at least, he was willing to sacrifice his staff to placate the wishes of congressional leaders.

The deference accorded to Dirksen and Halleck here was not unique. On many other matters, Kennedy was anxious to appease those in Congress whose support he considered critical to the success of his legislative program. And being eager to placate these powerful legislative leaders, Kennedy often yielded to their opinions and advice—even, sometimes, when it went against his judgment as to what was best for the country. Judicial appointments provide a prime illustration. In a time of burgeoning civil rights litigation in the courts, the legislators from the southern and border states were quite concerned about Kennedy's appointments to the federal bench. Kennedy understood the political score: ten of the fifteen committee chairmanships in the Senate belonged to individuals from that region of the country. Kennedy was therefore reluctant to lose the legislative game by adhering to the principle of appointing the most qualified people.

Thus, when Senator Robert Kerr of Oklahoma, perhaps the Senate's most powerful figure, recommended the nomination of Luther Bohannon to a judgeship, Justice Department officials explained to Kerr that Bohannon had received negative reports from the FBI and the American Bar Association. "Young men," Kerr replied, "I was here a long time before you came. I'm going to be here a long time after you go. I stand by my recommendation."[111] That reasoning was clearly enough to persuade Kennedy, and Bohannon was duly appointed (although, contrary to everyone's expectation, he turned out to be a strong pro-civil-rights judge.)*

Such deference was not accorded to every congressman and senator. Those who commanded little influence in the halls of Congress were frequently ignored—not out of malice but usually because of indifference. Gaylord Nelson, for instance, was first elected to the Senate in 1962 after serving as governor of Wisconsin for four years. Nelson knew Kennedy casually from the latter's days of campaigning for the presidency in 1959 and 1960. But, serving his first year in the Senate in 1963, Nelson did not enjoy the power wielded by Kerr and some others. The difference was telling. The White House did not show Nelson the same deference accorded to the Kerrs and Eastlands. Matters reached a breaking point with the appointment of John Gronouski as postmaster general in the summer of 1963. Gronouski had served in the Wisconsin state government when Nelson was governor. As a result of this experience, Nelson had come to know—and distrust—Gronouski. Nelson consequently expressed considerable surprise when White House aide Mike Manatos called him at home one evening to inform him that Kennedy was about to announce Gronouski's appointment to the cabinet.

Nelson's surprise was certainly justified. Normal courtesy requires a

---

*Kenneth O'Donnell and Dave Powers recounted a similar experience which illustrated the administration's deference to congressional barons. One day early in the Kennedy presidency, Attorney General Robert Kennedy met House Speaker Sam Rayburn and inquired about the delay in the enactment of some Justice Department legislative bills. Rayburn, in turn, reminded the attorney general of Rayburn's recommendation to have sixty-year-old Sara Hughes appointed to a federal judgeship in Texas. Kennedy, who was then thirty-six, replied that she was really too old to be appointed. "Son, everybody looks old to you," said Rayburn, "Do you want those bills passed, or don't you?" The next day Hughes was nominated for the judgeship. Kenneth O'Donnell and Dave Powers, *Johnny, We Hardly Knew Ye* 8 (1972).

president to check with a state's Senate delegation before making an appointment which, as in Gronouski's case, requires Senate confirmation. Nelson later recalled his reaction to Manatos's information: "I just told him they could take that appointment and go jump in the lake, as this was about the third time in a row that I hadn't been consulted on appointments affecting Wisconsin."[112] Nelson's angered response resulted in a quickly arranged meeting with Kennedy, a meeting which ended with Nelson acquiescing to Gronouski's appointment and Kennedy agreeing to visit Wisconsin on his forthcoming conservation tour across the country.

Kennedy's experience with Nelson and other congressional representatives at the bottom of the pecking order did not reflect Kennedy's insensitivity to the collective power of Congress. In drafting legislation and in planning strategies to have it enacted, Kennedy was ever mindful—sometimes too mindful—of the importance of considering the information and opinions of the appropriate legislative leaders. Every Tuesday morning (except when Kennedy was out of town) a breakfast meeting was held at the White House with the legislative leaders to discuss the pending program or developing issues. Kennedy, having considered a summary book prepared by his White House staff the night before, would usually initiate the conversation by discussing a matter of particular importance or interest to him. He would then sit back and listen intently to the ensuing debate, generally interjecting only to ask a new question or raise a new matter.

Kennedy usually found these meetings to be of great benefit. But he also knew that they were not enough. Maintaining the cooperation of Congress also required additional meetings with individual legislators on matters which fell within their committee jurisdictions. A case in point concerns Kennedy's decision to introduce legislation reducing the personal income tax and effecting certain reforms in the tax laws. Kennedy believed that this legislation would resolve two problems of particular concern to him: the need to provide the dragging economy new incentives for growth (to be provided by the increasing purchase power of the consumer through the tax cut), and the need to rectify the injustices of tax laws which enabled individuals with large incomes to escape (legally) with a minimal income tax.* When Kennedy first considered the idea in 1962, he asked his aides to check with Wilbur Mills,

---

*Once, in the summer of 1963, Kennedy entered a helicopter on the White House lawn to take him to Air Force One for a trip across the country. Upon entering the helicopter, Kennedy told the few congressional representatives and cabinet officials waiting to travel with him that he had just been reviewing the income tax returns of J. Paul Getty and H. L. Hunt, two of the richest men in the country. It was just outrageous, said Kennedy, to find that these two wealthy men had been paying only a negligible income tax.

Chairman of the House Ways and Means Committee. Since Mills's committee would have to approve the legislation, his views were of obvious importance. Mills, however,was not enthusiastic about reducing taxes while there remained a deficit in the government's budget. Mills's opposition was made clear to Kennedy in a memo which he received from Larry O'Brien, his chief congressional lobbyist. According to O'Brien, Mills could find "no public interest in a cut and others he has talked to agree—in his view, little or no political plus and serious possibility of extremely adverse reaction to deficit increase." Anxious to understand (and perhaps change) Mills's reactions, Kennedy often invited him to the White House. But Mills had no hesitation in personally expressing to Kennedy his opposition. "I doubted very frankly, and so stated," Mills later recalled, "that he could get a tax reduction through the Congress. I told him frankly that I did not think it wise, and that I did not think I could support it."[113] Primarily because of the opposition of Mills and other influential congressional leaders, as well as the absence of sufficient public support, Kennedy did not push for the legislation in 1962.

In opposing the tax legislation, Mills had made clear that he would be receptive to it in the next Congress if certain conditions were met (such as limiting government spending). So when the new Congress convened in January 1963, Kennedy revived the proposal again. But he still was not inclined to ignore Mills. Quite the contrary. He met frequently with Mills and other congressional leaders. He likewise asked his aides to keep him informed of other congressional sentiment on the legislation in the hopes that some accommodation could be reached (an accommodation which seemed to point toward relaxing the emphasis on the tax reform; this was in great part to mollify congressional critics who did not want to antagonize the wealthy individuals and large business interests, the principal source of funds for so many congressional campaigns).

The experience with the tax legislation was similar to the efforts in securing congressional opinions on a foreign assistance act, Medicare legislation, and other major administration proposals. Another typical case involved Kennedy's Alliance for Progress program for Latin America. This program, publicly proposed by Kennedy in March 1961, was designed to provide our southern and less developed neighbors with substantial economic and technical assistance. Because American relations with the Latin-American countries had deteriorated considerably in recent years, Kennedy attached great importance to this program and was particularly anxious to have it enacted by Congress.

Congressional passage, however, was by no means assured. A specific point of controversy involved Castro's rule in Cuba and, in general, the growth of communism in Latin America. Castro had promised not only to adhere to communism but also to export his revolution to his neighboring countries. This, needless to say, was cause for much alarm on Capitol Hill. The idea of living with communism ninety miles from American shores was anathema to most congressional representatives. Congressional debates and his own conversations with congressional representatives soon made Kennedy realize that the Alliance for Progress program would not attract sufficient congressional support if the Latin-American countries did not indicate a willingness to join the fight against the spread of communism. Part of Kennedy's response was a proposal for a Caribbean Defense Council. But Kennedy was definitely concerned. In late August 1961, he wrote to Dick Goodwin, one of his closest advisers on Latin-American affairs, that "it is going to become increasingly difficult to get the money from Congress unless we can find some interest on the part of the other Latin American countries to do something about Communism."[114]

There is little doubt that this concern—coupled with Kennedy's own genuine concern about the spread of communism in Latin America—inspired the administration to pressure the Organization of American States to take some action to demonstrate Latin America's commitment to fight communism. Responding to this heavy American pressure, the OAS Foreign Ministers voted 14–7 in January 1962 to institute immediately an arms embargo in trade with Cuba and to exclude Cuba from the Inter-American System. This action was taken despite the fact that the OAS charter did not provide for the latter sanction and, indeed, seemed to prohibit it. But in the interests of appeasing Congress one could not withhold action because of such "formalities." Congress was certainly not very concerned with the question of whether the OAS action was legally justified. It was concerned only with action, and the OAS resolution, as well as other administration measures, provided the necessary assurances that Latin American would join us in the struggle with communism. The Alliance for Progress program was formally adopted by Congress as Title VI of the Foreign Assistance Act and signed into law by Kennedy on August 1, 1962.

This same desire to work with Congress was evident in other areas of foreign policy. In negotiating the Test Ban Treaty in 1963, for example, Kennedy was particularly concerned that he not repeat Woodrow Wilson's mistakes in trying to secure Senate approval of the Versailles Treaty and American participation in the League of Nations. Kennedy therefore took every precaution to ensure that the Senate was a full partner in the making of decisions concerning the treaty. Appropriate congressional committees were continually briefed by Secretary of State Rusk. William Foster, Director of the Arms Control and Disarmament Agency, briefed senators individually. And Kennedy himself spent hours on the telephone speaking with individual senators, explaining how the treaty would be a step toward controlling the arms race without compromising the United States' security. But Kennedy did not wish to rely exclusively on these personal briefings and discussions. A tentative draft of a treaty (the one considered at Geneva in 1962) was sent to the Senate Foreign Relations Committee two weeks before the negotiations were completed (a move which Senator George Aiken, a senior Republican member of that committee, called "sound strategy"). And when the agreement was completed, Kennedy appointed a bipartisan group of senators to accompany Rusk to Moscow for the final ceremonies of signing the treaty,. During the subsequent Senate hearings and debates on the treaty, Kennedy maintained close contact and assuaged the senators' most pressing concerns by assuring them that the Unitd States could withdraw from the treaty if the Soviet Union violated it, that the United States could still use nuclear weapons to defend itself against attack, and that ratification would not imply that the United States had recognized East Germany, an anticipated signatory of the treaty. These intensive efforts paid off. When the treaty came to a vote, the Senate approved it by an overwhelming margin of 80–19.

It would be erroneous to conclude from these experiences that Kennedy consulted congressional leaders before taking any major action in domestic and foreign affairs. To a large extent, the marriage between Kennedy's White House and the Congress was one of necessity rather than convenience. In those instances where Kennedy involved Congress in the making of presidential decisions, it was generally because he believed that to ignore Capitol Hill was counterproductive. Where a program or presidential decision required enabling legislation or some other congressional action, this strategy of course made perfect sense. But in those instances where Kennedy could act alone, or believed he should act alone, congressional representatives often were neither seen nor heard.

Thus, the only legislator Kennedy consulted in planning the Bay of Pigs invasion was Fulbright (and he correctly argued against it). Some legislators expressed the hope that Kennedy would do better next time in consulting them (Mansfield said, for example, that he, too, would have urged Kennedy to abandon the Bay of Pigs invasion if his views had been solicited). Alas, in the making of decisions in the foreign policy area, these suggestions largely fell on deaf ears. Kennedy usually regarded Congress as a necessary evil, and the more often he could do without it, the better off he thought he would be.

When Kennedy made arrangements to exchange the prisoners captured during the Bay of Pigs invasion for drugs, medical supplies, and tractors, Congress was again ignored. Many legislators were particularly piqued by Kennedy's assurance to the American donors that their gifts would be tax exempt. As Arthur Krock later wrote in the *New York*

Times, the legislators felt that Kennedy's prior experience in Congress "should have told him to consult the fiscal committees of Congress on the legality of the ruling before he gave it. And it seemed to many also that his failure to do so marked a defect in judgment."[115] There was, of course, nothing illegal or otherwise improper in Kennedy's failure to consult Congress here; the Executive Branch issues tax rulings all the time with barely a whisper from Capitol Hill. But in an important and controversial tax ruling such as this one, Kennedy's discretion would not have been limited—and his position could have been bolstered—if he had solicited some congressional views.

Criticism of Kennedy on this score did little to inspire him to change his ways. During the Cuban missile crisis, he again ignored Congress completely in deciding on the American response (not even Fulbright was invited back). Later, administration officials explained the exclusion of Congress by contending that the legislators would have demanded a more forceful action than the imposition of a quarantine and that this would have denied Kennedy the flexibility he needed to resolve the crisis in a peaceful manner. In support of this rationalization, these officials noted that in a meeting with Kennedy one hour before his public announcement of the quarantine, many of the twenty congressional leaders present (including Fulbright) argued that the President should take stronger military action.

This explanation is somewhat specious. To begin with, the congressional leaders' reaction was very understandable. They had been totally ignored and had not had time to consider all the facts. As Fulbright pointed out in a Senate speech eleven years later, the meeting with Kennedy "was essentially a formality. President Kennedy's purpose in calling the meeting was to inform Congress of his plans rather than to seek advice. It was not a consultation so much as it was a briefing."[116] Fulbright also observed that the congressional leaders' response to the situation was comparable to the initial reaction of the people on the Executive Committee: they, too, had generally favored forceful military action at first. But the committee—unlike Congress—had almost one week of constant debate to decide that a less forceful action was more appropriate. (It is noteworthy that, after Kennedy's national television address, many of the congressional leaders telephoned Kennedy to tell him that they now understood the situation better and supported his response completely.)

In any event, Kennedy's methods remained unchanged. As long as he regarded congressional involvement as discretionary, he was prone to do without their company. This led to another snafu when Kennedy arranged to have commercial exporters sell the Soviet Union surplus wheat in the early fall of 1963. Kennedy regarded the move as an economic blessing for the United States which coincided with his view that peaceful interaction with the Soviet Union should be increased and tensions relaxed. But, again, congressional action was not required and again congressional leaders were not involved in the making of the decision. When asked at a press conference whether he expected any political repercussions from the exchange, Kennedy said, "Well, I suppose there will be some who will disagree with this decision. That is true about most decisions. But *I* have considered it very carefully and *I* think it is very much in the interest of the United States."*

There is no question that Kennedy's willingness to ignore Congress in these situations enabled him to make decisions more efficiently. But efficiency is not the sole criterion for judging the soundness of decisions or the effectiveness of leadership. Indeed, it is a criterion of limited importance in assessing governmental decisions made under our constitutional system. That system embodies the doctrine of separation of powers—shorthand for the postulate that coordinate branches of government are to share power and check each other's exercise of it. As Supreme Court Justice Louis Brandeis commented many decades ago, "The doctrine of separation of powers was adopted by the Founders of the Constitution in 1787, not to promote efficiency but to preclude the exercise of arbitrary power."[117]

The doctrine of separation of powers remains applicable in situations involving foreign policy as well as in domestic policy. Indeed, the Congress has several well-defined constitutional powers which suggest that the Founding Fathers expected Congress to play a leading role in the conduct of foreign affairs.** By ignoring Congress in many foreign policy decisions, Kennedy may not have violated any particu-

---

*John F. Kennedy, *Public Papers of the Presidents* 768 (1963) [emphasis added]. Kennedy knew that opposition to the decision already existed. At a meeting with congressional leaders prior to the press conference, House Minority Leader Halleck criticized it so vigorously that Mansfield—a man famous for his mild manner—became quite angered and bluntly told Halleck that he was being discourteous to the President.

**Under Article I, section 8 of the Constitution, Congress is empowered:

To regulate commerce with foreign nations . . . ;

****

To define and punish Piracies and Felonies committed on the high Seas, and Offenses against the Law of Nations;

To declare war, grant Letters of Marque and Reprisal, and make Rules concerning Captures on Land and Water;

To raise and support Armies . . . ;

To provide and maintain a Navy;

To make Rules for the Government and Regulation of the land and naval Forces;

To provide for calling forth the Militia to execute the Laws of the Union, suppress Insurrections and repel Invasions;

To make all Laws which shall be necessary and proper for carrying into Execution the foregoing Powers, and all other Powers vested by this Constitution in the Government of the United States, or in any Department or Office thereof.

lar provision of the Constitution. Indeed, many of his actions could find precedent dating back to George Washington. (When the House of Representatives asked Washington in 1795 for documents concerning the negotiation of the Jay Treaty with Great Britain, he politely told them it was none of their business—unless they chose to impeach him.) Other presidents in the twentieth century had followed Washington's lead. Theodore Roosevelt, for instance, had the Panama Canal built not because of Congress but in spite of it. And Harry Truman decided to dispatch troops to Korea in 1950 without waiting to determine whether Congress would support the decision.

Kennedy could look to these and other cases to justify his treatment of Congress. But repetition alone does not establish the wisdom of a practice. Here, moreover, precedent also existed to support inclusion of Congress in the making of foreign policy. There were frequent occasions, for example, when Franklin D. Roosevelt consulted congressional leaders about decisions (such as in the destroyer deal in 1940) which he could easily have made alone in the confines of the Oval Office. And Dwight Eisenhower's foreign policy decisions were often presaged by extensive discussions with Senate Majority Leader Lyndon Johnson, Speaker Sam Rayburn, and other members of Congress.

These precedents were well known, even to Kennedy. But there still should have been no surprise when Kennedy excluded Congress from foreign policy decisions. Time and again during his congressional years and his presidential campaign he had made clear his belief that the president had the power to make such decisions—even initiate war—without involving Congress. Everyone knew this (or at least should have after the missile crisis), but virtually no one did anything about it. There was, for instance, no substantial move in Congress after the missile crisis, whether by legislation or some other procedure, to restore congressional involvement in the war-making process. In any event, there is no question that Kennedy's decisions reinforced the notion that the president alone has the responsibility to formulate and execute the nation's foreign policy. However reasonable Kennedy's decisions, he therefore contributed to a climate in which succeeding presidents believed their authority to shape foreign policy—even to wage war 10,000 miles away in Southeast Asia—was self-contained. There would be hell to pay for that climate soon after Kennedy's presidency expired.

Just as there were risks in ignoring Congress in the making of foreign policy, so were there risks in disregarding the views and interests of foreign leaders. In fact, in some cases the risks were greater where foreign leaders were concerned. An offended congressional representative could sulk and withhold his vote or conduct a hearing; an offended foreign power could deny economic or political benefits to the whole

United States or, under some circumstances, threaten to involve the United States in armed conflict.

Deciding with Foreign Powers

Until the 1940s, America's involvement in international affairs was sporadic. World War II changed all that. America emerged from the war as the dominant political, military, and economic force in the world. And throughout the late 1940s and 1950s, the basic theme of American foreign policies was a containment of Soviet influence. Truman's decision to dispatch troops to South Korea in 1950; the decision to aid Turkey and Greece against internal subversion in the late 1940s; the establishment of SEATO, CENTO, and other multinational pacts; Eisenhower's decision to assist (and later abandon) efforts to assist Egypt in the construction of the Aswan Dam—all these and almost every other major foreign policy decision were premised largely on the extent to which they would advance the United States' position in waging the "Cold War" against the Soviet Union and its satellite countries.

The bipolarization between the Soviet Union and the United States in the 1950s began to show traces of deterioration by 1961. Not only had China risen as a communist power to be reckoned with, but also the forces of nationalism were slowly supplanting the forces of the Cold War on almost every continent. In Western Europe, years of prosperity and peace had heightened each nation's—and particularly France's—desire to demonstrate its independence of American hegemony. In Africa, many colonies being granted independence were more concerned with achieving political and economic stability than with staking out a position in the Cold War. And in many parts of Asia, indigenous groups were engaged in guerrilla warfare to free the local populations from rulers whose legitimacy was tied inextricably to the imperialism and colonialism of the past.

These developments, of course, did not remove the Soviet Union or the Cold War as matters of concern for American policy-makers. But the divergent nationalistic trends did complicate Kennedy's responsibilities as the principal organ of American foreign policy. Policies and programs could not be tied exclusively to the Cold War and still be effective. The world, in short, could not be viewed through bipolar lenses; it was more akin to a kaleidoscope now.

To a great extent, Kennedy appreciated the growing complexity of America's international relations. As a frequent world traveler, he understood that rhetoric and abstract principles could not solve a nation's concrete problems. And he recognized that a fear of the Soviet Union would not necessarily inspire another nation to support the United States' foreign policy decisions. Kennedy's perceptions here were made clear in a special message personally delivered to a joint session of Congress on May 25, 1961. While reaffirming his commitment to wage the Cold War, Kennedy also emphasized that America's foreign policy decisions would have to account for a broader vision. "Experience has taught us," said Kennedy, "that no one nation has the power or the wisdom to solve all the problems of the world or manage its revolutionary tides—that extending our commitments does not always increase our security—that any initiative carries with it the risk of a temporary defeat—that nuclear weapons cannot prevent subversion—that no free people can be kept free without will and energy of their own—and that no two nations or situations are exactly alike."[118]

In Kennedy's eyes, the diversity within the world underscored the need to account for another nation's perspective in formulating sound decisions. Whatever the nature of the political system under which they operated, Kennedy recognized that every foreign leader was, first and foremost, a politician who, like an American president, had to contend with an amalgam of factions, interests, and principles within his own country. These forces, in turn, shaped a foreign leader's perspective and helped to delineate the limits of his options. It was therefore important that Kennedy understand those forces. And it was equally important that foreign leaders understand Kennedy's perspective and the political limits on his options.

There is much sense in this personal approach. International politics, no less than domestic politics, is to some degree a function of human nature. Prejudices, ideals, attitudes and other personal variables are always at work; and they often dictate the actions of an individual nation. Much can be gained, consequently, by having leaders and their principal subordinates get to know each other personally. People who know each other are more likely to understand each other's interests, ideas, and opinions. Sensing this value of personal relationships—and spurred on by a natural curiosity to know something about those who exercised political power in other dominions of the world—Kennedy generally tried to sustain personal relationships with the leaders of most nations, regardless of whether they were allied to the United States, unaligned with either the United States or the Soviet Union, or an adversary of the United States.

Establishing these personal relationships was perhaps easiest with the leaders of the allied nations. Most of these leaders had come into power in the 1950s and had had an ongoing relationship with Eisenhower. Nonetheless, Kennedy wanted to make his own mark. Early in his presidency, he therefore arranged to go to Europe to meet with British Prime Minister Harold Macmillan (with whom he developed a close relationship despite the twenty years' difference in their ages), French President Charles de Gaulle, and West German Chancellor

Konrad Adenauer. He also met frequently with leaders of the Latin-American countries (except of course Castro) and made well-received trips to Mexico and South America. In general, he left the White House doors open to leaders of those nations who counted themselves among America's committed friends. And to help ensure continuity in these relationships, Kennedy maintained lengthy personal correspondence with many of the leaders and frequently talked with some (such as Macmillan) on the telephone.

This close contact with many of the allied leaders often enabled Kennedy to make foreign policy decisions which accounted for the interests and opinions of our allies. Speaking of Latin America, Costa Rican President Francisco Orlich commented, "During the Kennedy administration, we were able to feel for the first time that Hemispheric policy was multilateral. . . . President Kennedy was the first to take Latin-American thought into account in forming his policies."[119] This multilateral approach was evident in other areas as well. Thus, in developing a position to advance in negotiating the fate of Berlin with the Soviet Union, in deciding whether to resume nuclear testing, and in developing trade agreements, Kennedy was generally well briefed on the positions of our European allies. Likewise, there is little doubt that Kennedy's refusal to send American troops to Laos stemmed in part from the views of our allies. Kennedy wrote both Macmillan and de Gaulle personal letters inquiring as to whether they would be willing to dispatch troops to Laos if the United States did. Macmillan's response suggested a great reluctance to do so, and de Gaulle gave a categorical no. These answers gave Kennedy pause and helped to convince him that the best solution was one negotiated at the conference table rather than on the battlefield.

This is not to suggest that Kennedy fully understood our allies' positions or heeded their wishes in every matter. American relations with Brazil deteriorated under Kennedy in part because Brazil's leaders felt the United States expected too much in the way of social reform and was too niggardly in providing economic assistance. And Portuguese leaders were embittered by Kennedy's decision to publicly oppose Portuguese policies toward its African colonies. In some cases, Kennedy's disregard of an ally's interests was more accidental than conscious. The Skybolt affair was a classic instance.

In 1960, Macmillan met with Eisenhower at the presidential retreat at Camp David. Both as a matter of national pride and sound politics, Macmillan was anxious to have American support in the establishment of an independent nuclear force for England. Eisenhower agreed to have the United States completely fund the research and development of the Skybolt missile, an air-to-surface missile with an 800-mile range. After the missile was developed, the United States would make it available to England for use on its RAF planes. In exchange for this American commitment, Macmillan promised the United States the use of the Holy Loch port for the stationing of American nuclear submarines. Macmillan returned from Camp David quite pleased with this agreement, confident that it would not only ensure England an independent nuclear force but also bolster his own political position.

Soon after Kennedy entered the presidency, Macmillan sought—and received—assurances that the new Democratic administration would honor the commitment made by its Republican predecessor. But soon questions began to arise as to the wisdom of the commitment. Secretary of Defense McNamara and Budget Director Bell both believed that the costs of the Skybolt missile would be far greater than expected and that the benefits would be far less certain. In early November 1962, after several months of consideration, Kennedy agreed with his advisers that the Skybolt contract should be canceled. Realizing this would have enormous political consequences for England, Kennedy instructed McNamara to inform the British so that an alternative could be prepared before the cancellation received publicity. But Kennedy left it at that. He did not pursue the matter to find out what Macmillan's response was or what alternative action by the United States would dampen the political repercussions. Later Kennedy told Arthur Schlesinger, Jr., "[Macmillan] should have warned me of the dangers to him—we would have come up with a solution before publicity—he should have had [British Ambassador David Ormsby] Gore come in."[120] But Kennedy understood that his decision would not make Macmillan happy; and since the United States was retracting its part of the agreement, the burden was on Kennedy to offer a substitute.

In any event, it was not long before this political dynamite exploded. In a nationally televised interview, Kennedy acknowledged that "the British feel very strongly about" Skybolt. But he informed the viewers—and the world—that the development of the Skybolt missile would be a mistake: ". . . we are talking about $2.5 billion to build a weapon to hang on our B-52s, when we already have billions invested in Polaris, and Minutemen, we are talking about developing now Titan III and other missiles. There is just a limit to how much we need, as well as how much we can afford to have a successful deterrent. . . . [We] don't think that we are going to get $2.5 billion worth of national security. Now, I know there are others who disagree, but that is our feeling."[121]

Coincidentally, Macmillan had been planning to spend the days immediately before Christmas with Kennedy in Nassau. On the plane trip to Nassau, Kennedy conferred with Ormsby-Gore (Macmillan was flying separately from England) to find a solution to the problem. They agreed to resurrect Skybolt on the condition that England and the

United States would split the costs of development fifty-fifty. But Macmillan would have no part of that agreement. In his televised remarks Kennedy had already cast substantial doubt on the efficacy of Skybolt. How could Macmillan agree to spend British pounds on a missile that was now believed to be valueless? There was, in short, no way to resurrect Skybolt: "the lady had already been violated in public."[122] After some hurried (and harried) consultations, Kennedy agreed to give England some Polaris missiles which were to remain under the control of the NATO Command unless England needed them for a national emergency. Macmillan returned home scarred but pleased.

Macmillan's pleasure was short-lived, however. The Nassau agreement reinforced de Gaulle's suspicions that England was more committed to the United States than to Europe. Three weeks after the agreement was concluded, de Gaulle held a press conference in which he announced France's veto of British entry into the Common Market and rejected Kennedy's offer to participate in the arrangement worked out with Macmillan; France, he said, would develop her own nuclear deterrent.

The Skybolt affair—although not policy-making at its best—was really a miscalculation.* There were other occasions when Kennedy's disregard of an allied leader's opinions was deliberate. De Gaulle, for example, tried to warn Kennedy in his May 1961 visit to Paris that it would be a drastic mistake for him to commit the United States to an involvement in the quagmire of Vietnam. In his memoirs, de Gaulle recalled this part of their conversation:

> It was above all on the subject of Indochina that I pointed out to Kennedy how far apart our policies were. He made no secret of the fact that the United States was planning to intervene. . . . Kennedy gave me to understand that the American aim was to establish a bulwark against the Soviets in the Indochinese peninsula. But instead of giving him the approval he wanted, I told the President that he was taking the wrong road.
>
> "You will find," I said to him, "that intervention in this area will be an endless entanglement. Once a nation has been aroused, no foreign power, however strong, can impose its will upon it. You will discover this for yourselves. For even if you find local leaders

*Kennedy was particularly concerned about the failure of communication between England and the United States in the Skybolt affair. He therefore asked Columbia government professor Richard Neustadt to study the matter and report back to him. Neustadt submitted a report in the fall of 1963. On November 20, Kennedy told Bundy that he wanted to see Neustadt after he returned from his trip to Texas. See Richard Neustadt, *Alliance Politics* (1969).

who in their own interests are prepared to obey you, the people will not agree to it, and indeed do not want you. The ideology which you invoke will make no difference. Indeed, in the eyes of the masses it will become identified with your will to power. That is why the more you become involved out there against Communism, the more the Communists will appear as the champions of national independence, and the more support they will receive, if only from despair.

"We French have had experience of it. You Americans wanted to take our place in Indochina. Now you want to take over where we left off and revive a war which we brought to an end. I predict that you will sink step by step into a bottomless military and political quagmire, however much you spend in men and money. What you, we and others ought to do for unhappy Asia is not to take over the running of these States ourselves, but to provide them with the means to escape from the misery and humiliation which, there as elsewhere, are the causes of totalitarian regimes. I tell you this in the name of the West."[123]

Kennedy listened to de Gaulle (as he would later listen to Indian Prime Minister Nehru argue against American intervention in Vietnam). But in time it would become clear that he did not accept de Gaulle's advice (although Kennedy might have recalled it when he began to rethink his Vietnam policies in the later summer of 1963).

At times, Kennedy did not even want to consider the advice of allies before making a decision that might affect their interests. The Cuban missile crisis provides a clear example of this. In considering the response which should be made to the placement of Soviet missiles, Kennedy looked only to his own advisers. Allies were contacted only after he had decided that a quarantine of war matériel was the most appropriate response—despite the fact that this move could result in armed hostilities which would necessarily involve our allies. Accepting the suggestions of his advisers, however, Kennedy did convene an emergency meeting of the OAS to have the quarantine become an official action of that international organization.* Our European allies were contacted by Dean Acheson, Kennedy's personal representative, only on

*Sometime early in September 1962, Kennedy conferred with some Justice Department and State Department aides to consider what the United States' response should be if the Soviet Union did install offensive missiles in Cuba. Norbert Schlei, an assistant attorney general, had prepared a draft statement which mentioned the Monroe Doctrine—a unilateral declaration by President Monroe which said the United States would oppose the intervention by European powers in Latin-American affairs. The Doctrine was initially intended to help protect the independence of the Latin-American countries—and the United States—from their former colonial rulers. Schlei later remembered Kennedy's

the day that Kennedy publicly announced the quarantine. While this prior briefing did help to preserve a measure of allied unity, its timing made some—especially de Gaulle—feel that the United States, in the end, would do what it thought best, regardless of the interests and opinions of its allies. And—despite Kennedy's eagerness for close personal relations with America's allies—sometimes that was true.*

Kennedy's desire for personal relations was not limited to our allies. He sought out the leaders of the emerging nations as well, so that he might better understand their problems and goals. The limits of our influence and goodwill, he felt, would be significantly measured by our capacity to grasp the perspectives of the leadership in these underdeveloped nations. In essence, Kennedy desired to impart an attitude of cooperation rather than one of command. And to achieve this end, he placed great faith in his personal dealings with national leaders. During his first months in office, he conferred with several African representatives, including Sékou Touré of Guinea, Kwame Nkrumah of Ghana, and Julius Nyerere of Tanganyika. He also talked with other leaders of the neutral nations, such as Nehru of India, Sukarno of Indonesia, and Tito of Yugoslavia. And in these meetings, Kennedy was

---

reaction when he read that part of the draft which referred to the Monroe Doctrine. "'The Monroe Doctrine,' he snapped at me, 'what the hell is that?' I mumbled some answer about its legal significance, but it was clear that whatever it was or meant, he didn't want to mention it in his statement." Quoted in Abram Chayes, *The Cuban Missile Crisis* p. 133.

Kennedy's reaction was a sound one. The legitimacy of the Monroe Doctrine had been discredited by decades of misuse. Many presidents—especially in the first half of the twentieth century—had invoked the Monroe Doctrine to justify American military invasions of Latin-American countries—not to prevent intervention by European powers but to defend American interests. Latin Americans saw the Doctrine merely as a thin disguise for the hated "Yankee Imperialism." In any event, the Monroe Doctrine was a unilateral declaration by the United States which could hardly provide a sufficient legal justification for a forceful American response to the installation of Soviet missiles in Cuba.

*The French reaction to Kennedy's announcement of the quarantine was reported as follows:

> President de Gaulle, who received Mr. Acheson's report late yesterday afternoon, considered himself to have been "informed but not consulted." In consequence, there was no formal French statement of solidarity to match the one issued in London. Instead, the closest thing to an official French position was a statement by Pierre Baradue, spokesman for the French Foreign Ministry. He spoke in Brussels in the name of the foreign ministers of the six countries of the European Economic Community, or Common Market, who studied the Cuban situation there today. He said that the ministers "expressed comprehension of the United States position in the Cuban affair and of the measures taken by the Government of Washington." He added that the ministers "are naturally preoccupied with the possible developments of that affair."

Doty, "Lack of Talks Annoys Paris," *New York Times*, Oct. 24, 1962, p. 1.

often able to convey a genuine interest in each leader's problems and a sincere willingness to account for each leader's concerns in shaping American policy. After his meeting with Kennedy, for example, Sukarno said he found that ". . . behind [Kennedy's] easy-going manners there was a keen mind in constant search for new and better ideas. Although this first visit was brief, we had long conversations on various issues and I was most happily impressed by his fresh and uninhibited approach towards the inherent problems of growth faced by the developing countries of Asia and Africa."[124]

To help further this dialogue among leaders, Kennedy also tried to create the impression that his ambassadors were individuals who had close ties with the President, William Attwood, who served as Kennedy's ambassador to Guinea, believed that Touré "probably thought I had more access [to Kennedy] than I actually had. Nevertheless, it was quite useful; it helped me in my job. Kennedy did this, as far as I could see, with most ambassadors and strengthened their hand by giving leaders of the countries they were accredited to the feeling that they could communicate directly to the White House."[125] Overall, African political leaders sensed that Kennedy and his advisers truly cared about African interests. Speaking in 1965, Tom Mboya, economic minister of Kenya, said, "I don't want to say very much about the present [Johnson] administration, but this is what some people feel is lacking in the present administration—this personal approach to things; contact with people at a personal level became one of the main stamps of the Kennedy administration insofar as foreign policy in relation to Africa was concerned."[126]

In trying to convey this personal interest to African leaders, as well as to leaders of other unaligned nations, Kennedy did not rely exclusively on his ambassadors or periodic personal meetings with foreign leaders. Effective diplomacy, he believed, required more frequent direct contact between the leaders than that. He therefore tried to maintain contact with these leaders through personal letters which traveled outside normal diplomatic channels. Typical was the correspondence Kennedy initiated with leaders of the thirteen Arab nations.

During his campaign, Kennedy had promised to do what he could as President to bring the Arabs and Israelis together in direct negotiations. This, he said, was the best means of achieving a stable peace in the Middle East.The promise could not be easily fulfilled. The animosity between the Israelis and Arabs was deep-seated. And the Arabs had strongly resisted any suggestion that they negotiate directly with the Israelis. Kennedy nonetheless believed it worthwhile to make an attempt to crack the impasse. As part of this effort, he decided to write a personal letter to each of the Arab leaders. He wrote a basic draft that was revised as much as ten times to ensure that it created the right impression. And then Kennedy asked that a variation of this basic text be adjusted to fit the individual problems of the particular leader; he did not want each Arab leader to receive the same letter. Myer Feldman, who worked with Kennedy in preparing these letters, later remembered the care that Kennedy placed in each:

> He wanted to give the impression that he was seeking a dialogue with them, a continuing dialogue, and that they should feel free to write to him personally and not even through regular State Department channels. And, he wanted to show that he was sympathetic to all their legitimate aspirations. At the same time, he did not want to give the impression that he was siding with them in their conflict with Israel. So the effort was made to achieve a nice balance between the two. Variations in the texts of each of the letters he looked at very carefully. Indeed he discussed the variations in some of the letters with me just to make sure that they would feel that this was a personal interest, and that this would get them involved in the discussions with us.[127]

The letters did not lead to direct negotiations between the Arabs and Israelis. But they did help to improve American relations with the Arab states. And the results sometimes showed. There was, for example, a minimum of criticism from Arab capitals when Kennedy decided to provide Israel with Skyhawk missiles and development aid, and Kennedy himself attributed the relatively quiet Arab response to the goodwill generated by this correspondence. The importance of Kennedy's correspondence with the Arab leaders was later acknowledged by John Badeau, Kennedy's ambassador to Egypt. The new administration had a fresh approach to diplomacy, Badeau wrote,

> in which American prestige and judicious pressure would be used to open ways of escape from some of the area's impasses. The President's frequent and personal correspondence with Arab chiefs of state was one expression of this approach. His letters were clear and substantive, speaking to current issues and stating the American position with frankness. Yet they were never condescending or preemptory. To an unusual degree, President Kennedy was sensitive to the political problems faced by Arab leaders and took these into account in his dealings with them. A consummate politician, he understood the necessity of dealing with the reality of other people's situations, using discussion, persuasion, and the search for mutual interest to keep a question open until it could be moved toward some resolution.[128]

Kennedy's sensitivity to Arab problems, though, did not make the Arabs subservient to American interests in the Middle East. Thus, when Kennedy recognized the new republican government in Yemen in 1962, he expected (and was assured by President Gamal Nasser) that Egypt would withdraw its troops from Yemen. But instead of withdrawing troops, Nasser only sent in more. The reasons from Nasser's perspective were easy to understand. The Yemen autocracy had been overthrown by a military group allied with Nasser. He, in turn, was anxious to ensure their continued success. As long as fighting continued between the rival factions, Nasser was willing to do almost anything militarily to support his allies. And this self-interest overrode any concern of Nasser's to placate Kennedy. However understandable Nasser's actions, they did not sit well with Kennedy. American recognition of the republican regime served Nasser's own interests, and Kennedy expected Nasser to fulfill his reciprocal promise to withdraw the troops and bring the hostilities to an early end. Nasser's failure to fulfill that promise annoyed Kennedy and led him to regard Nasser as completely untrustworthy.*

Kennedy's frustrating experience with Nasser did not dampen his faith in personal relationships as a basic foundation of sound diplomacy. Indeed, the depth of this faith was suggested in his eagerness to maintain a personal relationship with the leaders of America's foremost adversary, the Soviet Union. From Kennedy's perspective, this desire was entirely reasonable. He had no illusions about defeating the Soviet Union in a military war or of converting their totalitarian system to a democratic one. But he believed that the tensions between the two countries could be eased if they understood and accounted for each other's interests in any decisions they made.[129]

In this light, it is not surprising that Kennedy responded favorably when America's ambassador to the Soviet Union, Llewellyn Thompson, informed Kennedy that Soviet premier Khrushchev was interested in a personal meeting—not to negotiate specific matters but to enable them to become better acquainted. After discussing the matter at length with his top aides, Kennedy agreed to meet with Khrushchev in Vienna in the beginning of June 1961. Although he did not expect to resolve any major issue, Kennedy believed that both could benefit by the personal encounter. "I had read his speeches and his published policies," Kennedy later said.

> I had been advised on his views. I had been told by other leaders of the West . . . what manner of man he was. But . . . it is my

---

*Kennedy was also annoyed at the State Department for urging American recognition of the new republican regime without first seeking to obtain some reciprocal action from Nasser.

duty to make decisions that no adviser and no ally can make for me. It is my obligation and responsibility to see that these decisions are as informed as possible, that they are based on as much direct, firsthand knowledge as possible. I therefore thought it was of immense importance that I know Mr. Khrushchev, that I gain as much insight and understanding as I could on his present and future policies. At the same time, I wanted to make certain Mr. Khrushchev knew this country and its policies. . . . I wanted to present our views to him directly, precisely, realistically, and with an opportunity for discussion and clarification.[130]

The meeting did have a profound effect upon Kennedy's later decisions. He emerged from the meetings shaken ("somber" was how he described his mood to news reporter William Lawrence). Khrushchev had harangued him, bullied him, and made Kennedy feel that there was virtually no chance for a political accommodation between the United States and the Soviet Union on the many problems which divided them. Believing that he had to demonstrate his "toughness" to Khrushchev, Kennedy—while not entirely abandoning his faith in peaceful negotiations—felt obligated to emphasize his willingness to defend American interests by armed force. Kennedy's actions in the Berlin crisis in 1961 and the Cuban missile crisis in 1962 can be partly explained by this attitude.

Kennedy overreacted to Khrushchev's antics at the Vienna meeting. But the meeting did lead to continued personal correspondence between the two adversaries, which proved to be quite helpful in the ability of each to assess the actions of the other. During the missile crisis, for example, Kennedy and Khrushchev exchanged several letters in which each made personal pleas to the other for a peaceful resolution of the crisis. Responding to Khrushchev's argument that the quarantine of Cuba was illegal and should not be honored, Kennedy wrote,

> . . . I am concerned that we both show prudence and do nothing to allow events to make the situation more difficult to control than it already is.
>
> I hope that you will issue immediately the necessary instructions to your ships to observe the terms of the quarantine, the basis of which was established by the vote of the Organization of American States this afternoon. . . ."[131]

After the exchange of several letters, Khrushchev wrote a long, rambling and somewhat emotional note. He stressed the risk of a miscalculation which could produce the war both wished to avoid. And then he offered the contours of what proved to be the final settlement:

I propose: we, for our part, will declare that our ships bound for Cuba are not carrying any armaments. You will declare that the United States will not invade Cuba with its troops and will not support any other forces which might intend to invade Cuba. . . .

. . . If you have not lost command of yourself and realize clearly what this could lead to, then, Mr. President, you and I should not now pull on the ends of the rope in which you have tied the knot of war, because the harder you and I pull, the tighter this knot will become. And a time may come when this knot is tied so tight that the person who tied it is no longer capable of untying it, and then the knot will have to be cut. What that would mean I need not explain to you, because you yourself understand perfectly what dread forces our two countries possess.

Therefore, if there is no intention of tightening this knot, thereby dooming the world to the catastrophe of thermonuclear war, let us not only relax the forces straining on the ends of the rope, let us take measures for untying this knot. We are agreeable to this.*

In exchanging letters with Khrushchev here, Kennedy was particularly anxious to make his position clear and, at the same time, not unduly circumscribe Khrushchev's flexibility in making decisions. Robert Kennedy, who played a critical role in determining the United States' actions during the crisis, later described his brother's concern that he and Khrushchev understand each other:

During the crisis, President Kennedy spent more time trying to determine the effect of a particular course of action on Khruschev or the Russians than on any other phase of what he was doing. What guided all his deliberations was an effort not to disgrace Khruschev, not to humiliate the Soviet Union, not to have them feel they would have to escalate their response because their national security or national interests so committed them.

This was why he was so reluctant to stop and search a Russian ship; this was why he was so opposed to attacking the missile sites. The Russians, he felt, would have to react militarily to such actions on our part.

---

*Letter from Soviet Premier Nikita S. Khrushchev to President Kennedy, October 26, 1962, President's Office Files, John F. Kennedy Library, reprinted in 69 *Dept. of State Bull.* 645 (Nov. 19, 1973). The matter became somewhat complicated when Kennedy received later in the day a more belligerent letter—perhaps written by Kremlin officials and not Khrushchev personally—which made no reference to this proposal. At the suggestion of his brother, Robert, Kennedy decided to ignore this second letter and accept the proposal outlined in the first. See Robert Kennedy, *Thirteen Days* 101–102 (1969).

* * * * * * * * * *

> Each decision that President Kennedy made kept this in mind. Always he asked himself: can we be sure that Khrushchev understands what we feel to be our vital national interest? Has the Soviet Union had sufficient time to react soberly to a particular step we have taken? All action was judged against that standard—stopping a particular ship, sending low-flying planes, making a public statement.[132]

People can argue—and have argued—that the missile "crisis" was of Kennedy's own making because he initially relied on armed force instead of normal diplomatic channels to force a withdrawal of the Soviet missiles from Cuba. Whatever the validity of this argument (and it does have some validity), it does not affect the genuineness of Kennedy's belief that his decisions should account for the facts which shaped Khrushchev's perception of the matter and the internal pressures which limited his options in dealing with it.

In the end, Kennedy's great faith in and use of personal diplomacy proved quite useful to him. It broadened his perspective, brought him into contact with information, ideas and opinions which could only redound to his benefit. And there is no question—as in the case of the missile crisis—that these personal relationships were sometimes of great value in resolving specific problems. His understanding of other leaders likewise helped him to know when—as in cases of Laos, Yemen, or the Congo—an issue was more appropriately handled by an international organization or a multinational conference.

But, more often than not, Kennedy's meetings with foreign leaders were informational exchanges between peers rather than consultations between colleagues. Kennedy, in other words, did not often involve foreign leaders in the actual making of decisions. If discussions with his advisers convinced him that a particular course was in the United States' interests, it was rare that he would reverse himself after discussing it with a foreign leader. There were few occasions when Kennedy tried to hammer out a policy or decision after close consultations with a foreign leader. Vietnam is perhaps only a more celebrated example of this.

To some extent, Kennedy's methods here were understandable. After all, the American president does have a responsibility to protect and advance American interests; and in fulfilling that responsibility, he is neither required nor always expected to attract support from foreign leaders. And sometimes for good reason. A foreign leader's first concern is almost always his own country. And frequently the support of foreign leaders can be achieved only by compromising principles or positions which may be vital to American interests. Indeed, for all his charm and apparent open-mindedness, Kennedy often found it difficult to persuade foreign leaders to adopt policies which suited American interests. Toward the conclusion of his first year in office, for instance, James Reston wrote in the *New York Times* that

> it is hard to remember a year in which there were so many splashy meetings of world leaders with so few tangible results. President Nkrumah of Ghana was President Kennedy's first major visitor of the year, and after what was billed as a successful conference Nkrumah went home and not only oriented his policy toward Moscow but established a kind of bush-league dictatorship at home. The Kennedy-De Gaulle meeting in Paris in May was proclaimed a triumph and was followed almost at once by one of the most quarrelsome periods of U.S.-French relations since the war. When the President met Nikita Khrushchev in Vienna early in June their talks were officially described as "useful," whereupon the President returned to Washington and called up the reserves. There were many others, now largely forgotten, which no doubt improved personal relations among the leaders for a few days, but the last of the really "successful" talks was with Prime Minister Nehru of India who went home and ordered the invasion of Goa.[133]

In one sense, Reston's comment reflected an unfair criticism of Kennedy's leadership. It is unrealistic to expect that a short meeting, even when buttressed by personal correspondence and ambassadorial attentions, can induce a foreign leader to shape his nation's policies to accommodate another nation's views. Cooperation in international affairs requires much more than that; it generally requires, at a minimum, diligent staff work and a favorable political climate so that nations can understand how the benefits of cooperation will exceed the costs to their individual self-interest. On the other hand, Reston's comment implicitly underscores a basic point about presidential leadership: the ability and will to make sound decisions alone is insufficient to ensure success. All the consultation in the world is of limited value without a commitment to lead, a drive to secure support for policies designed to achieve peace, justice, and prosperity. And Kennedy's willingness to exercise public leadership in both foreign and domestic spheres is the subject of the next chapter.

CHAPTER 3

John F. Kennedy as a Public Leader

The Presidency is not merely an administrative office. That is the least of it. It is more than an engineering job, efficient or inefficient. It is pre-eminently a place of moral leadership. All our great Presidents were leaders of thought at times when certain historic ideas in the life of the nation had to be clarified.

Franklin Delano Roosevelt

The President's Role as a Public Leader: An Historical Perspective

"The buck stops here," read the sign on President Truman's desk. That slogan—now almost a cliché among political commentators—still symbolizes the essence of one presidential responsibility: the need to provide public leadership. Over the decades of American history, and especially in the twentieth century, the people of this country—and, indeed, the world—have come to expect that the president's decisions will be the cutting edge in resolving the problems of the present and in removing the concerns for the future. Polls by the American Institute of Public Opinion since the 1930s have made plain that the overwhelming majority of the American people want their president to be decisive in thought and bold in action. They want him to have the insight to explain the issues, the capacity to weigh alternative solutions, and the foresight to choose wisely.

It is, of course, an almost impossible prescription to fulfill. There are enormous limitations—political, economic, social, and psychological—with which the president must deal in trying to attain any established goals. These limitations, however, are not likely to dilute the public's expectations of their president. The reasons are not difficult to understand. In a complex society with intricate governmental networks, the president stands—singular and exposed—at the pinnacle. In the public's eyes, the limitations are easily discounted. The obstacles to action are minimized. And the difficulties in choosing wisely are readily dismissed. As with many ideas, the wish for presidential action is often father to the thought of a president's capability. People frequently and mistakenly equate presidential initiative with presidential influence; they erroneously equate the presidential power to propose with the power to command.

However irrational the public's expectations may be, a president ignores them at great risk. As Fred Greenstein has written,

> In the case of the central, energizing institution in the modern American political system, the Presidency, the very strength that accrues to the President by this singular visibility and his capacity to become the receptacle of widespread personal hopes and aspirations carries with it, in the clarity of post-1965 hindsight, an obvious weakness: if things go wrong, who else is there to blame? The depression becomes "Hoover's depression;" the "mess in Washington" becomes Truman's or Nixon's, even before a proper assessment of responsibility has taken place.[1]

In short, the buck may stop at the president's desk, but there is rarely any assurance as to what it will buy.

Watergate has not changed this dynamic of our political system. Many legislators, commentators, analysts, and priests of political thought wrung their hands in despair over the Nixon presidency. Most agreed that Watergate arose because too much had been expected of the President. And in expecting too much, the Congress and the public (but not the courts) had showed the President too much deference.* He had been allowed to accumulate and exercise a vast array of political powers which escaped the check of the Congress, the public, and the courts. It was not healthy for our constitutional system. Almost everyone—even those in Nixon's own party—wanted to impeach him.

The jet carrying Nixon back to California had not yet landed before the process began to repeat itself. Gerald Ford was anointed as president in a simple but dignified ceremony in the East Room of the White House. Ford was not known as a man who could easily fill the presi-

*In almost every judicial case concerning the extended exercise of presidential power—impoundment, wiretapping, the dismantling of congressionally mandated agencies (like OEO)—the decision went against President Nixon.

dential shoes. His reputation painted him as a man of limited intellectual capabilities. Lyndon Johnson, not one to be restrained in judging others, had said many years earlier that Ford, a former football star at the University of Michigan, had played too much football without his helmet on; and another Washington rumor had it that Jerry Ford could not chew gum and simultaneously walk across the street because he could not do two things at once (and after Ford made the blunder of pardoning Nixon, the word quickly spread in the Senate cloakroom that Ford had started to chew gum again). Ford's reputation as a man of limited intellectual capacity was complemented by a lack of achievement: in twenty-five years in Congress he had not authored a single piece of legislation enacted by Congress; and as House minority leader for almost ten years, his only moment of "glory" was an ill-conceived attempt to have Supreme Court Justice William O. Douglas impeached in 1970 in part, Ford said, because Douglas had an article published in *Evergreen,* a radical magazine which featured a picture of a partially nude woman in the same issue that carried the Douglas article.

Gerald Ford, in other words, assumed the presidency without any indication that he possessed the capacity for presidential leadership. Yet the public and the Congress instinctively looked to this mortal to resolve immediately the complex problems of our nation's economy, problems which were reflected in the 12 percent annual rate of inflation, a stock market which was sinking fast, a rapid decline in housing starts, and shortages in vital natural resources. As a member of one senator's staff at the time, I remember the frustration at witnessing this folly. Five hundred and thirty-five legislators awaiting the President's word—even though some, such as Congressman Henry Reuss, were economic experts in their own right. Collectively, these individuals had the resources and the power to propose programs to deal with the sagging American economy. All they lacked was the will. It was almost enough to make one believe in anarchy. And when Ford finally announced his economic program on October 8, 1974, many in Congress and elsewhere were quick to criticize it as too weak. As James Reston wrote from Washington the next day, "President Ford has now defined the economic crisis of the nation and proposed a catalogue of remedies. The question now is whether the solutions he proposed are equal to the crisis he defined, and the fear here is that he didn't bite the bullet but nibbled it."[2]

Whatever the merit of Ford's economic proposals, one point is clear: the public still expects—and needs—a president who will provide strong, dynamic leadership. They are simply reluctant to look anywhere else. The historical irony is that the Founding Fathers probably did not expect the president to play this strong role in shaping public policies and programs. Indeed, there is ample evidence to demonstrate that the president's powers were designed to be subordinate to the Congress's in providing national leadership.*

To begin with, the Constitution outlines in some detail the broad powers which Congress is to exercise over national affairs. Among other responsibilities, the Congress is authorized to lay and collect taxes, coin money, regulate interstate and foreign commerce, to declare war, to raise and support armies and navies, and, in a catchall clause, "to make all laws which shall be necessary and proper for carrying into execution the foregoing powers, and all other powers vested by this Constitution in the Government of the United States, or in any Department or Office thereof."[3] In contrast, the president's powers are not defined in the same detailed fashion; and, in fact, the language may be read to mean that the chief executive's powers are not as comprehensive as the Congress's.

The president, for example, is charged to "take care that the laws shall be faithfully executed. . . ."[4] He is also designated as commander in chief of the armed forces and is given the power to appoint (with the advice and consent of the Senate) public ministers, ambassadors, and federal judges. He is also empowered to negotiate treaties with foreign powers (again with the advice and consent of the Senate). But these powers were envisioned as largely executive and, except in the case of repelling a sudden attack,** did not enable the president to make policy decisions.[5]

The president's constitutionally defined powers in the legislative area also seem circumscribed. He is directed to give Congress information "from time to time" on the State of the Union, is empowered to recommend legislation for Congress's consideration, and is authorized to veto legislation enacted by Congress (although Congress can override the veto by a two-thirds vote in each House). But the language of the Constitution does not require or even suggest that the president is to be a *public* leader who will communicate directly with the people and represent their collective interests in lobbying for the enactment of

---

*A detailed discussion of the history of the Constitution and the intention of the Founding Fathers is beyond the scope of this book. Some excellent examinations of this history are found in Louis Fisher, *President and Congress* (1972); Emmet John Hughes, *The Living Presidency* (1973), and Arthur Schlesinger, Jr., *The Imperial Presidency* (1973).

**Congress was given the exclusive power to declare war. Originally, the draft Constitution empowered Congress "to make war." At Madison's urging, the language was changed to "declare" war. According to Madison, this was done to leave "the Executive the power to repel sudden attacks." James Madison, *Notes of Debates in the Federal Convention of 1787* 599 (1966). See Hughes, *The Living Presidency* at 37–38.

legislation. Indeed, the president's powers in leading the public seemed so niggardly to some of the Founding Fathers that there was genuine apprehension that the Congress could easily overwhelm the chief executive and usurp his prerogatives. After all, Congress would be the principal defender of the people's rights. Congress would also consist of many individuals who, because of their limited constituencies, would be closer to the people. The convergence of these factors, it was believed, would enable Congress to overpower the executive's initiatives. This apprehension was expressed by Gouverneur Morris, John Mercer, and others at the Constitutional Convention in 1787. James Wilson, for instance, feared that the "natural operation of the Legislature will be to swallow up the Executive."[6] And in *The Federalist Papers*—the essays designed to explain and urge ratification of the Constitution—James Madison voiced concern that the Congress's proximity to the people could be an insurmountable advantage in any confrontation between the legislature and the other branches of government in resolving political issues:

> The members of the executive and judiciary departments are few in number, and can be personally known to a small part only of the people. . . .The members of the legislative department, on the other hand, are numerous. They are distributed and dwell among the people at large. Their connections of blood, of friendship, and of acquaintance embrace a great proportion of the most influential part of the society. The nature of their public trust implies a personal influence among the people, and that they are more immediately the confidential guardians of the rights and liberties of the people. With these advantages, it can hardly be supposed that the adverse party would have an equal chance for a favorable issue.[7]

The presidencies of Andrew Jackson, James Polk, and Abraham Lincoln made plain that a determined and resourceful chief executive could overcome those handicaps in providing national leadership. In each of those cases, the President interpreted his constitutional powers broadly; and in each case, the President used those powers to sidestep Congress and act decisively in imposing his will on the nation in solving specific problems. But those cases were anomalies. Throughout most of the nineteenth century, Congress remained the dominant branch of government. Thus, in 1885 Woodrow Wilson wrote in his classic work. *Congressional Government,* that the "actual form of our present government is simply a scheme of Congressional supremacy. . . . Congress [is] the dominant, nay, the irresistible power of the federal system. . . . The President [is] the first official of a carefully graded and impartially regulated civil service system . . . and his duties call rather for training than for constructive genius."* (Wilson's reverence for "Congressional" government would fade shortly before *he* became President.)

The congressional supremacy of which Wilson spoke so highly began to wither soon after Theodore Roosevelt entered the White House. Viewing the president as a "steward" of the people who should advance his view of the public interests, Roosevelt assiduously courted the congressional leaders so that they would be amenable to his legislative recommendations. For the first time, a President played a major inside role in the formulation of legislation on a continuing basis.

The changes inaugurated by Roosevelt flourished under Wilson. He came to the presidency determined to be a national leader who would speak for all the people—not only in the inner sanctum of the White House but in the halls of Congress as well. Shortly before his election to the presidency, Wilson had written of the President, "His is the only national voice in affairs. Let him once win the admiration and confidence of the country, and no other single force can withstand him, no combination of forces will easily overpower him. His position takes the imagination of the country."[8] Wilson drove himself, his aides, and the members of Congress to enact his legislative proposals. It was quite a successful reversal of roles. The principal source of legislation and leadership was now the President—not the Congress.

It would be naïve (and misleading) to suggest that this legislative metamorphosis simply reflected the force of an individual President's personality. Other factors—such as the growing complexity of the economy, the emergence of a social progressive movement among the electorate, and the willingness of many congressional representatives to defer to the President's recommendations—were also at work. But whatever the explanation, the President's responsibility for leadership—especially in time of national need—was well established. During the tenures of Warren Harding and Calvin Coolidge, there were few real tests of the President's ability and willingness to fulfill that re-

---

*Quoted in Edward S. Corwin, *The President: Office and Powers* 26–27 (1957). As civil war loomed on the nation's horizon in 1860, for example, President James Buchanan informed Congress that he would deal with the problem as he saw fit because the President "is the direct representative on earth of the people of all and each of the sovereign states. To them, and to them alone is he responsible while acting within the sphere of his constitutional duty and not in any manner to the House of Representatives." The House was angered by this proclamation of presidential pomposity and quickly passed a resolution asserting the (then) traditional view that the President was subordinate to the Congress in national affairs: "The President is not, in any respect superior to the citizen, merely because he is bound to discharge more numerous duties; and he is not coequal with that branch of Government which helps to impose and define those duties." Quoted in Marcus Raskin, *Notes on the Old System* 117, 119 (1974).

sponsibility.Those were years of peace and prosperity for Americans—and most were content to have the federal government leave well enough alone. It was a wholly different matter soon after Herbert Hoover was inaugurated as president in March 1929.

A Quaker from Iowa, Hoover seemed eminently qualified to provide public leadership. An engineer by profession, he was able to apply his genius for organization in supplying food for starving populations in war-torn Europe between 1914 and 1920. His reputation as an efficient and humanitarian administrator led Harding to appoint Hoover as his Secretary of Commerce, a position Hoover retained until his election to the presidency. As the head of the Commerce Department, Hoover became renowned for being able to enlist the voluntary cooperation of the business community in governmental policies which helped advance the country's economic fortunes (and, not surprisingly, those of the business community as well).

Hoover entered the White House with broad popular support (having carried forty states in the election). But he did not regard his popular support as an invitation to involve the federal government in correcting social or economic injustices. His personality and experience rejected any suggestion that the government should try to shape a country whose philosophical underpinnings were individualism and free enterprise. He believed that the president should be a strong leader—but only in reinforcing those principles and ensuring that the government was operated in an efficient manner. This deep belief in governmental restraint coincided with his view that the president should not try to control the legislative process. As he explained in his memoirs, he did not feel it was the president's role "to blast reforms out of" Congress. Instead, he said, "I felt deeply that the independence of the legislative arm must be respected and strengthened. I had little taste for forcing Congressional action or engaging in battles of criticism."[9]

Hoover's attitudes toward public leadership were well suited to a nation which basked in the rays of economic prosperity. But those attitudes proved to be a severe handicap when the thunder of depression rocked the nation. The rapid decline of the stock market, which began on that "Black Thursday" in October 1929, soon signaled the deterioration of the American economy. Businesses folded, banks went bankrupt, mortgages were foreclosed, workers were laid off—and the people were losing confidence in their ability to weather the economic storm. Hoover did not see this economic collapse as an invitation for governmental intervention to revive the economy and help satisfy the people's material needs. Rather, he saw it as an opportunity to reinforce the basic principles of individualism and free enterprise; and he believed it underscored the president's obligation—not to act but to inspire the people's confidence in themselves.

As the unemployment rolls mounted in January 1930, Hoover proclaimed that the rate of unemployment had been turned back. In May he said that he was convinced that "we have now passed the worst and with continued unity of effort we shall rapidly recover." In June he told a group of White House visitors, "The depression is over."[10]

These words were of little consolation to most Americans, however. Between March 1930 and January 1931, unemployment in the nation's nineteen largest cities increased 149 percent. And as unemployment soared, public faith in Hoover dropped. The reasons were not difficult to understand. Hoover was not providing the leadership which the people needed and expected of their president. And Hoover's ineptitude here was readily apparent to—and scorned by—the vast majority of Americans. As Walter Lippmann commented at the time,

> My own notion is that a close examination of Mr. Hoover's conduct in critical matters will disclose a strange weakness which renders him indecisive at the point where the battle can be won or lost. . . . [T]his weakness appears at the point where in order to win he would have to intervene in the hurly-burly of conflicting wills which are the living tissue of popular government; that he is baffled and worried and his action paralyzed by his own inexperience in the very special business of democracy.[11]

This kind of criticism increased the pressures on Hoover to provide direct federal relief for Americans. Realizing that something more had to be done, Hoover responded to these pressures and, working quietly behind the scenes with his administration and Congress, labored to have the federal government provide certain limited relief. But Hoover would not publicly renounce his oft-stated conviction that people should rely on themselves and not the federal government to resolve the economic crisis. He would not publicly abandon his view that relief from the federal government, based on a broadening of its powers, was degrading to the individual recipient and simply not proper leadership. In effect, Hoover refused to assume a burden that he felt rightfully belonged to the individual citizen and to the local and state governments. As he addressed the public in 1931, with almost one-fourth of the nation's labor force unemployed, there was little solace in his words:

> where people divest themselves of local government responsibilities they at once lay the foundation for destruction of their liberties. . . . At once when the government is centralized there arises a limitation upon the liberty of the individual and the restriction of individual opportunity . . . can lead but to the superstate where every man becomes the servant of the State and real liberty is lost.[12]

Hoover failed to realize, however, that a philosophical defense of laissez-faire could not supply needed jobs or bolster the country's broken self-confidence. Many, if only out of desperation, actively sought the guidance and action of the federal government. But in accepting renomination by the Republican Party in 1932, Hoover blindly believed that he articulated the national consensus when he again publicly rejected the possibility of massive action by the federal government: "It is not the function of the [federal] government to relieve individuals of their responsibilities to their neighbors, or to relieve private institutions of their responsibilities to the public, or of local governments to the States, or of State Governments to the Federal government."[13]

In the end, Hoover's stubborn resistance to broad federal action proved to be the cause of his political demise. In the 1932 campaign, Democratic presidential candidate Franklin D. Roosevelt did not propose a concrete program to end the depression; but he, unlike Hoover, understood the people's longing for a president who was not afraid to act, and so FDR emphasized this theme in his campaign. The results were telling: Roosevelt carried every state in the nation except six. "If any one attitude lost the election in 1932," wrote Harris Gaylord Warren in his study of Hoover, "it was Hoover's refusal to use federal resources in direct relief."[14]

But Hoover's leadership failure reflected not only a reluctance to provide massive federal action to relieve the misery of the millions of distraught Americans who were unemployed or living on subsistence wages; his failures also represented a reluctance to emphasize to the public the limited action that he had taken to resolve their problems. These actions included a proposal enacted by Congress to establish a new Farm Relief Board to help relieve farmers of the burdens of an uncertain market, provision of federal loans from the Reconstruction Finance Corporation for failing businesses, a proposal enacted by Congress to raise tariffs in order to protect American industries (but which actually proved to be counterproductive), and other measures. Hesitant to publicize these efforts (and thus appear to contradict his own expressed philosophy), Hoover offered the public mind little ground for believing that he was doing anything except to issue pious platitudes on the virtues of self-reliance. As the conservative columnist William Allen White wrote,

> President Hoover is a great executive, a splendid desk man. But he cannot dramatize his leadership. A democracy cannot follow a leader unless he is dramatized. A man to be a hero must not content himself with heroic virtues and anonymous action. He must talk and explain as he acts—drama.[15]

As a student of history, Kennedy surely appreciated this lesson of

Hoover's presidency. He would not be as reluctant to advertise his virtues and leadership to the American people—although many would question how much virtue there was in Kennedy's leadership.

The President's opportunities and obligations to provide public leadership expanded with the development of the broadcast media. Radio, and then television, enabled the President to speak directly to millions of people, to explain the nation's problems and to justify the measures he had taken or would take to resolve them. Radio was only a fledgling enterprise during Hoover's tenure, and he never fully recognized the political benefits which could be reaped by the President's use of it. Indeed, Hoover's most memorable use of national radio was the occasion when announcer Harry Von Zell made this introduction: "Ladies and Gentlemen, the President of the United States, Hoobert Heever."

Roosevelt, on the other hand, saw radio as a potent medium of communication which could further his efforts to corral public support for the President's policies and programs. This was of particular importance in the President's ability to overcome congressional resistance to his proposals. As Roosevelt himself commented,

> Time after time, in meeting legislative opposition . . . I have taken an issue directly to the voter by radio, and invariably I have met a most heartening response. Amid many developments of civilization which lead away from direct government by the people, the radio is one which tends on other hand to restore direct contact between the masses and their chosen leaders.[16]

The opportunity for—and impact of—this direct communication was enhanced by television. Not only the President's voice but his image as well could be brought into every individual's living room. This, in turn, increased the President's ability to undercut the Congress's power to oppose the President's proposals or to check the President's exercise of power. The President could appear simultaneously and for free on all three television networks at any time he chose, in any format he chose, to discuss any issue he chose. (Never has a presidential request for television time been denied by the television networks.) A presidential television appearance was and is an event in itself. It could command the attention of millions of American people. Once on television, the President could shape events of national importance. He could announce dramatic new undertakings, bold initiatives to reassure the American people, or simply report to them. The prestige of the presidency, as well as the President's ability to speak with a solitary voice (as opposed to the usually disparate voices of the opposition) gave him an almost insurmountable advantage. As a result, the public was increasingly isolated from Congress and vice versa. As early as

1952, the Supreme Court itself recognized that the President's unlimited access to radio and television could weaken the Congress's ability to check the exercise of presidential power:

> In drama, magnitude and finality the President's decisions so far overshadow any others that almost alone he fills the public eye and ear. No other personality in public life can begin to compete with him in access to the public mind through modern methods of communications. By his prestige as head of state and his influence on public opinion he exerts a leverage upon those who are supposed to check and balance his power which often cancels their effectiveness.[17]

It is true, of course, that members of Congress and the opposition party were not entirely excluded from the television airwaves. But, with very few exceptions, these appearances were on newscasts and interview programs. Moreover, unlike presidential appearances, congressional and opposition appearances did not allow the congressman or political opponent to address the public directly on any issue he wants, for as long as he wants, in any format he wants, at any time he wants, or simultaneously and for free on all three major networks. Most of the appearances of members of Congress and the opposition party on newscasts lasted about 15 seconds. On an interview program, most of which were scheduled for early Sunday afternoon (the time at which viewing audiences are the lowest), the appearance could last for 30 minutes. Collectively, these appearances did not provide Congress or the opposition party with much of an opportunity to communicate directly with the people and balance the impact of the President's appearances. As Senator Fulbright put it, these appearances can "at most convey bits and snatches of [the speaker's] point of view," creating "an impression of cranky carping at a heroic and beleaguered President."[18] More importantly, spokesmen for the administration—from cabinet officials to White House aides—also appeared with great frequency on these programs and probably balanced out congressional and opposition spokesmen. Thus the decisive factor in major political struggles remained an unfettered and unlimited presidential access to the airwaves.*

Perhaps no case better illustrates the power of presidential television

---

*Richard S. Salant, President of CBS News, is among those who have acknowledged the great disparity between presidential and congressional television appearances. In a speech, Salant observed that the views of the President's congressional opponents are internally balanced and not intended to persuade or to urge congressional action. "Further," said Salant, "the participants in these broadcasts do not have the advantages which the President has—the live, unedited appearance, the direct presentation free of journalist's questioning, the simultaneous appearance on all networks, and the control of

than President Nixon's policies concerning the Vietnam War. Nixon would surely have lost the 1968 presidential election if he had promised four more years of fighting at a cost of millions of dollars to the American taxpayers, a major increase in American casualities, geographic expansion of the war, increased bombing of North Vietnam, further denuding of South Vietnam's forests and the destruction of its major cultural centers—to say nothing of the front page pictures of a horrified American teenager weeping over the body of a Kent State college "bum" who lay dead from American bullets fired by American soldiers.

Yet all of this, and more, came to pass. And through it all, President Nixon continued to command the support of the American public, easily defeating every opposition initiative to change his policies—even to the point of watching football on TV while the streets of Washington and many other American cities teemed with those who had no recourse but to the ritualistic "moratoriums" and rallies of the last decade.

Nixon's skillful and carefully timed use of television was a principal factor in his ability to retain the support of the majority of Americans through all of this. Aside from press conferences and news programs, Nixon made twelve television addresses on Vietnam during his presidency. Each of these addresses was made during prime viewing hours (7–11 P.M.); and each was carefully timed to announce dramatic actions or to overshadow other events which might undermine public support for his policies. Just prior to the peace moratorium in November 1969, for example, Nixon gave a nationally televised address on Vietnam which was viewed by 72 million people—9 million more than had voted for all candidates in the 1968 presidential election. In his statement, Nixon emphasized that public dissent could only hinder his efforts to secure peace in Vietnam:

> And so tonight—to you, the great silent majority of my fellow Americans—I ask for your support. . . . The more support I can have from the American people, the sooner [peace can be won]; for the more divided we are at home, the less likely the enemy is to ne-

---

timing and place in the broadcast schedule." Remarks of Richard S. Salant before the Journalism Foundation of Metropolitan St. Louis, May 1, 1972.

It is significant that when Congress was provided direct access to the television networks to air the Senate Watergate hearings and the House Judiciary Committee's impeachment hearings, the power and public standing of Congress increased dramatically. See Gallup, "Rating of Congress Rises Sharply," *Washington Post,* September 6, 1974, p. A2. Much of the explanation for this rise rests, of course, on the nature of Nixon's abuses and Congress's unique responsibility to respond to them (through impeachment). But there is no question that public support for Congress, and the corresponding lack of support for Nixon, can in great part be tied to the broadcast of the congressional hearings.

> gotiate at Paris. Let us be united for peace. Let us also be united against defeat. Because let us understand: North Vietnam cannot defeat or humiliate the United States. Only Americans can do that.[19]

The effect of this address was aptly summarized by Ray Price, one of Nixon's speechwriters. "Judging by the results," said Price, "it was the most effective use of TV that's ever been done. You had the massively accelerating peace movement. But after the speech, the balloon just fizzled."[20]

Television was such a potent force that it could be used successfully to garner public support even when the people did not fully understand the President's actions. Thus, on April 30, 1970, Nixon announced on prime-time television that American troops would invade Cambodia to help that country destroy sanctuaries utilized by the North Vietnamese and Vietcong. Shortly before the speech, Gallup polls had shown that less than 10 percent of the public favored an American invasion of Cambodia. After Nixon's speech, 51 percent of those interviewed "approved" of Nixon's handling of the Cambodian situation—even though 53 percent said "we should not" send American troops to help Cambodia.

These and other developments demonstrated the power of presidential television. Indeed, a recent Twentieth Century Fund Report concluded that the President's use of television enabled him to emasculate the check which Congress could have exercised over his Indochina policies:

> Although a great many factors have influenced public opinion on this [Indochina War] issue—certainly the most complex and volatile foreign policy controversy in many years—Presidential television played a significant role in maintaining public support for the President's position and in enabling him to withstand Congressional attempts to limit his discretion in dealing with Vietnam developments.[21]

The Twentieth Century Fund Report also outlined the historical and constitutional significance of the use of television by every president since Truman:

> An intricate set of Constitutional balances limiting the powers of each of the three governmental branches added force to the separation of government functions.These political and constitutional relationships served the country well for many years. Television's impact, however, threatens to tilt that delicately balanced system in the direction of the President.[22]

Television, then, was and is a force which can alter the balance of power in our constitutional scheme. Reforms are clearly needed. Television should not be a club which the president (or perhaps in future times, the Congress) can wield to beat another branch into submission. The availability of television, however, does underscore the third criterion of presidential leadership: a president must use his office to educate the public on the vital issues of the day, involve them in the resolution of those issues, and, in general, lead them in the direction he thinks necessary to safeguard their interests and protect their futures.

Now, as when John Kennedy entered the White House, there is no simple formula or method to satisfy this criterion. Once he recognizes an issue as an important one which merits concentrated governmental attention, the president can use a variety of means to communicate with the public and lay the proper foundation for the governmental response. But regardless of how he proceeds, a starting point is the president's own recognition of his responsibilities to provide public leadership. A president must remember that he does not exist in a vacuum. However clear his concept of the presidency, and however sound his decisions, he must be sensitive to the attitudes and needs of the citizenry. He must forge his policies and programs in such a way as to make his purposes clear and his goals meaningful.

More often than not, crisis and conflict will provide the opportunity to provide this leadership. For, human nature being what it is, it is in crisis and conflict that people's concentration is greatest, their willingness to listen most acute, and their interest in the outcome most clearly expressed. Scholar James MacGregor Burns is among those who have explored the elements of presidential leadership, and his conclusions support this thesis. In his book *Presidential Government*, Burns explained that the presidency is a powerful institution which enables the occupant to influence events and causes of national importance. "Yet power alone is inadequate," Burns wrote.

> It must be linked with purpose. Ultimately it must embody a Jeffersonian thrust toward the most elevated goals of man; it must express the single central vision of the hedgehog. But purpose in turn is steeled not amid agreement, adjustment, conformity, but in crisis and conflict; it was out of crisis and conflict that Roosevelt, Nehru, Lenin, Churchill, and other great leaders of this century emerged.
>
> A great society needs not consensus but creative leadership and creative opposition—hence it needs the sting of challenge in a society rich with diversity and in a politics rich with dissent.[23]

In short, the president must lead the people and not merely be a mirror of their opinions and interests.

This is not to suggest that the president should ignore those opinions and interests. Indeed, he would do well to pay close attention to the impact his policies and programs have on the public. For it is the people who will collectively voice their judgment of the president as well as determine which congressmen and senators will share power with him in Washington. And the public's opinions of the president's programs and policies will often determine the level of support the president can expect in Congress.

An awareness of the people's influence is not tantamount to a representation of them as a single, unified body of one opinion. Quite the contrary. The president's sensitivity to public opinions and interests is especially important because they reflect considerable diversity; accounting for them will be no easy matter. The difficulties here are compounded by the fact that each individual is subject to many moods, diverse thoughts, and, quite often, overlapping interests. It is for this reason, as Grant McConnell has written, that "no election is ever a simple reflection of the preference of the people for one man (or one party) instead of the other; it is instead a composite register of the desires, frustrations, and aspirations of millions of individuals or an almost limitless number of matters. Some of these topics are concrete, some are general, and some are so deeply emotional they are beyond rational discussion."[24] This situation was in fact emphasized by the 1960 and 1964 presidential elections. How many voted for or against Kennedy merely because he was a Catholic? Or did some people vote for Kennedy simply because his youth and wit were unusual for a presidential candidate? Or did some believe that he would be more faithful than Nixon in waging the Cold War (after all, it was Kennedy, and not Nixon, who had spoken in the famous televison debates of providing American assistance to Cuban exiles who wanted to free Cuba of Castro and Communism). Four years later, could Lyndon Johnson's unprecedented triumph be attributed to a belief that he was the rightful heir to a fallen president? Or were his peace platform for Vietnam and the continuing economic growth within the country more instrumental to his victory? And how many voted *against* Barry Goldwater, the Republican candidate?

The difficulty in assigning meaning to votes in a presidential election highlights the lack of ideology of American politics. For the most part, American citizens do not have any established criteria by which to formulate consistent judgments of their government. This point was underscored by political scientist Robert Lane in his study of the "common man" in 1959. Anxious to penetrate the dynamics of political thinking in America, Lane conducted extensive interviews with fifteen people in a medium-sized city in the East (which he identified only by the fictional name of "Eastport"). These people represented a political and socioeconomic cross section of America. Lane found that an absence of ideology, or any fixed standards, impeded the individual's ability to know whether the government had fulfilled its responsibilities:

> The man of Eastport has no cathedral building in his air space to raise his sense of importance and mission; he is not engaged anywhere in a struggle against want or fear or squalor in such a way as to engage his mind and take him out of himself; he is not, like the Italian Fascists . . . rebuilding a glorious Roman history; what shall he do that will call out the greatness in him? Against the background of great purpose he might measure the political system and say whether or not it is just. But he has no way to conjure up such a vision; and hence no way to take measure of his society.[25]

While Lane's conclusions obviously reflect the time and circumstances of his study (Eisenhower was then President), his analysis does penetrate a frequent handicap of America's citizenry in making political judgments. The convergence of their anxieties, fears, hopes, and experiences often preclude an ability to analyze objectively the intended meaning of a president's words and the actual impact of his actions. There was, for instance, a natural reaction among many to inflate the meaning of Kennedy's fluent rhetoric and to attach unfounded significance to those words after his death; the accomplishments of his New Frontier were often measured by phrases instead of by concrete results.

The inability of many individuals to take measure of their society has not prevented them from developing and maintaining expectations of their government. For the most part, these expectations are tied to the immediate surroundings of an individual's life. He interprets his government's actions, and hence evaluates his president, in terms of what is happening to him. Whether this interpretation is well founded or irrational may become irrelevant if individuals maintain and continually act on it. Indeed, as Richard Neustadt has pointed out, the enemy of a president's influence with the public is unreality: "the groundless hopes, the unexpected happenings, the unaccepted outcomes that members of their public feel in daily life and relate somehow, anyhow, to That Man in the White House."[26]

The divisions and vacillations of the public opinions, as well as their frequent haziness, subsequently illuminate the essence of the president's responsibilities as a public leader: if he is to maintain their support, in Congress and at the polls, the president must learn the people's moods and needs and somehow respond to them with legislative proposals and executive direction. In the age of mass education and mass communication, the importance of this task cannot be underestimated. People today are more sophisticated in their understanding of the issues; they are more knowledgeable about the process of government (especially after the televising of the Senate Watergate hearings and the House impeachment hearings); and they are more likely to describe a president in terms of his ability to handle specific issues. This point has been stressed in recent polls on the American public's response to presidents and political issues.[27]

The need to provide leadership is particularly crucial in the president's relations with Congress. Because it is inherently a conservative institution and rather jealous of its prerogatives, especially with respect to the president, the Congress will hesitate to accommodate a president unless he is supported by a public educated on the issue. For congressmen and senators, like all elected officials, must maintain the good favor of their constituencies if they are to retain their respective political offices. Consequently, a president who drifts too far from the trends of public thinking may find himself legislatively frustrated.

Theodore Roosevelt was one President who recognized the need for public support if his programs were to be enacted. He came to the presidency determined to be an active leader, a chief executive who would use his position to push through Congress legislation that reflected his view of the public needs. But Roosevelt did not define these public needs in the isolation of his White House office. He traveled around the country making speeches on the major issues and his views on how to resolve them, always taking note of public reactions. He raised these same issues with reporters in conferences and private meetings, hoping that their stories would generate support for his proposals. (It is also noteworthy that Roosevelt was the first president to establish press offices in the White House.) All these efforts were invaluable to Roosevelt. They enabled him to understand better the public's needs and also to lay the foundation for his programs and policies. In pushing for legislation to regulate railroads, for example, he also took time to crisscross the country explaining the problem and the need for the legislation.

Having his hand on the pulse of his countrymen, Roosevelt also better understood the limits of his legislative initiatives. As one analyst later observed, Roosevelt "was able to anticipate and articulate the half-expressed wishes of the majority of Americans. His Square Deal was not a systematic theory or program. Rather, it was a vague, middle position between radicalism and reaction, and this was what most Americans seemed to want."[28] In other words, Roosevelt recognized the fluidity and ambiguity of public opinions; and he knew that public opinion would not always support enactment of legislation which seemed responsive to the public needs. Compromise then became an acceptable legislative strategy in Roosevelt's eyes. In some areas, such as in the regulation of railroads, he simply felt that the public would not demand and the Congress would not enact a measure as strong as he would like (compromise here led to enactment of the Hepburn Act). Joe Cannon, Speaker of the House during Roosevelt's tenure, indicated the gist of Roosevelt's attitude toward congressional relations: "He was a good sportsman, and accepted what he could get so long as the legislation conformed even in part to his recommendations."[29]

In the end, Roosevelt's view was that a president should be a strong advocate of public interests as he saw them. But he also realized that, in our political system, the strength of his advocacy would depend greatly on his ability to secure and retain public approval for his actions. This attitude was summarized by Roosevelt in a letter that he wrote to Senator Henry Cabot Lodge as his tenure neared its end. "I have a very definite philosophy about the Presidency," said Roosevelt. "I think it should be a very powerful office, and I think the President should be a very strong man who uses without hesitation every power that the position yields; but because of this fact I believe that he should be sharply watched by the people [and] held to a strict accountability by them."[30]

It was Woodrow Wilson's sad fate not to appreciate the wisdom in Roosevelt's remark. When the tide of public opinion favored reform legislation during his first term, Wilson was a strong leader who could prevail among the legislators on Capitol Hill to respond to the public demands. The result was a string of legislative measures which advanced the cause of progressive reform initiated by Roosevelt. It was not quite the same in Wilson's second term, especially as World War I drew to a close in the fall of 1918.

In response to a German request for peace conditions, Wilson initiated negotiations with the other allied countries and Germany to explore the possible contours of any peace agreement.[31] Wilson had already made his "peace program" clear in speeches before Congress and other audiences.* As these peace negotiations began, the Republican congressional leaders began to criticize Wilson's efforts. The Re-

---

*Before the war's end, Wilson made four major speeches outlining his program for peace. The most important speech—personally delivered to Congress on January 8, 1918—detailed fourteen objectives of the post-war peace. Among other goals, the fourteen points included the right of self-determination for nations, open diplomacy, freedom of the seas, and the creation of a league of nations. See the discussion of Woodrow Wilson in Chapter 2.

publicans' concern focused not only on the substance of Wilson's peace program but, perhaps more importantly, also on the constitutional role of the Senate in the treaty-making process. By secretly negotiating with the Germans without the Senate's participation, the Republicans said, Wilson was violating the spirit if not the letter of the Constitution.

Outraged by these Republican attacks, Wilson decided to take his case to the people. The midterm congressional elections were approaching, and Wilson was anxious to transform them into a national referendum on his peace program. On October 25, 1918, Wilson appealed to the country to retain the Democratic majorities in both houses of Congress. Such a vote, Wilson said, would make clear whether "you have approved of my leadership and wish me to continue to be your unembarrassed spokesman in affairs at home and abroad . . ."[31] He identified his Republican critics as individuals who wanted to undermine his administration's control of the war effort and create disunity in the United States. In this state of affairs, said Wilson, the midterm elections had a special significance:

> The return of a Republican majority to either House of the Congress would . . . be interpreted on the other side of the water as a repudiation of my leadership. . . . It is well understood there as well as here that the Republican leaders desire not so much to support the President as to control him.[32]

Had Wilson not been blinded by his own self-righteousness, he would have seen the folly of such an appeal. Midterm elections generally turn on local issues, and he had no reason to believe that the public would understand the special significance that he attached to the elections. The result: the Republicans won enough victories to become the majority party in both Houses (thus enabling Senator Henry Cabot Lodge, Wilson's archenemy, to become chairman of the Senate Foreign Relations Committee). But this personal defeat at the hands of the public did not cause Wilson to doubt the depth of his support among the people. His self-righteousness was made of steel. He traveled to Versailles in 1919 to negotiate the peace treaty under the impregnable assumption that he, not the Congress, could best represent the people's interests. "Senators do not know what the people are thinking," he told an aide in Paris. "They are as far from the people, the great mass of our people, as I am from Mars."[33] This wooden attitude proved to be a critical flaw in Wilson's attempts to secure Senate ratification of the Versailles Treaty which he negotiated and which carried with it his dream of American participation in the League of Nations.

With Lodge leading the way, most senators said that they would vote to ratify the treaty, but only if it contained reservations and amendments to protect certain American interests. Wilson would have nothing to do with most of these reservations, and he bluntly told the senators so. The people, Wilson said, supported the treaty and the Senate would sooner or later have to bow to the people's will. The problem was that Wilson was somewhat isolated from the people and had lost touch with the nuances in the public's views. True, the people did support the treaty; but numerous polls and newspaper reports made it clear that the overwhelming majority of the public favored a compromise treaty with some reservations.

When the Senate continued to balk, Wilson decided to go to the people. Though weak and exhausted from his unceasing efforts to secure Senate concurrence, Wilson began in September 1919 an eight thousand-mile journey to the western states to urge the people to support the treaty he had personally negotiated in their behalf. At every stop he discussed each point of contention and explained why reservations could not be accepted. And at every stop he emphasized in emotional terms the importance of the treaty in ending war as an instrument of national policies. "Ah, my fellow citizens," he remarked in one speech,

> do not forget the aching hearts that are behind discussions like this. Do not forget the forlorn homes from which those boys went and to which they never came back. I have it in my heart that if we do not do this great thing now, every woman ought to weep because of the child in her arms. If she has a boy at her breast, she may be sure that when he comes to manhood this terrible task will have to be done once more.[34]

Wilson's speeches were received enthusiastically by the crowds that came to hear him. But this favorable response did not necessarily signal public endorsement of Wilson's position. A presidential appearance was an unusual event, which attracted the curious and the faithful alike. And the applause which followed in the wake of Wilson's rhetoric may have reflected the carnival atmosphere in which people wanted to express the approval of the man who was, after all, their President. As *Harvey's Weekly* observed of the crowds' reaction, "some people would applaud a declamation of the binomial theorem or a proposal to repeal the Decalogue."[35] In other words, from an objective point of view, it would be difficult to attach much meaning to the crowd's positive response (especially since most people already endorsed the treaty in some form; the issue, in Wilson's mind, was the far more subtle question of whether there should be reservations).

Shortly after making a speech in Pueblo, Colorado, Wilson suffered a stroke and his speaking tour was brought to an end less than a month after it began. He returned to the White House a sick man, but a President who was convinced that the people supported his position on the treaty. Believing that his was the voice of the people, he refused—even in his crippled state—to tolerate suggestions that the treaty could be saved in the Senate if only he accepted reservations. No, said Wilson, the people had spoken and their will would soon smother the opposition in the Senate. The problem was that the voice of the people's will which Wilson heard was spoken only in his mind and was not available to the Senate. As Professor Thomas Bailey commented,

> Not only was Wilson enfeebled in body and weary in mind; not only was he embittered in spirit and unstable in emotion; not only did he have false notions about the public's views on reservations (that Pueblo applause would not stop); not only was he out of touch with the currents of public opinion and with Democratic leaders in the Senate; not only were his few informants carefully instructed to withhold views that might shock him into a relapse; but the guardians of his bedside continued to censor his mail. This, though desirable from a medical point of view, was . . . perhaps disastrous from a political point of view.[36]

Unwilling to compromise until the end, Wilson was unable to secure Senate concurrence for the treaty for which he had labored so long and so hard.

The lesson of Wilson's failure is clear. A president must keep informed of public attitudes and have some sense of whether his views will coincide with the public's. The need for the president to understand public moods is especially important when developments and events portend shifts in the government's direction. Events and policies must be placed in context, and the foundations must be carefully laid for any new departures.

Perhaps no President understood this better than Franklin D. Roosevelt. He usually recognized the importance of a public educated on the issues. As Arthur Schlesinger, Jr., observed, "What he really cared about was high politics—not politics as intrigue, but politics as education. Nothing government could do mattered much, he deeply believed, unless it was firmly grasped by the public mind. He once said, 'I want to be a preaching President—like my cousin.' "[37]

The fireside radio chats which Roosevelt inaugurated were a direct outgrowth of this conviction. By speaking directly to the people, Roosevelt hoped to lay the foundation for his initiatives and explain the meaning of his proposals. He therefore used simple, often colloquial terms and concrete examples to explain his point. Referring to the first fireside chat in 1933, for instance, in which Roosevelt announced a bank holiday, Will Rogers wryly commented, "Roosevelt explained the banking situation so well even the bankers understood it."[38]

Given his emphasis on public education, Roosevelt was usually reluctant to forge a new program unless he was convinced that the public would understand it and support it. Thus, although Roosevelt decided as early as 1933 to recommend enactment of a social security program, he deferred introduction of the actual proposal in Congress until January 1935. In the interim, he used press conferences, two radio fireside chats, and numerous speeches to educate the public on the soundness of the idea and, at the same time, to discount public fears that social security was an alien, socialist measure which would have no place in our democratic system.

On the other hand, Roosevelt was not above retreating from a position if he thought it did not command sufficient public support. The famous "quarantine speech" in 1937 is a case in point. Concerned about his public standing after the defeat of his court-packing plan, Roosevelt began a tour of the country to touch base with the people and to reassure himself about his ability to lead them. In Chicago, FDR decided to broach a new subject—the international dangers posed by the hostilities in China and Europe, hostilities which Roosevelt feared would almost inevitably involve the United States at some point.

Although the United States had an official policy of neutrality toward these international conflicts, and while isolationist sentiment still ran strong in the country, Roosevelt felt obliged to discuss the United States' responsibility in trying to contain the fighting. "The peace-loving nations must make a concerted effort in opposition to those violations of treaties and those ignorings of humane instincts which today are creating a state of international anarchy and instability from which there is no escape through mere isolation or neutrality," he said. These hostilities in Asia and Europe were "threatening a breakdown of all international order and law," he continued. The responsibility of the United States was clear. "When an epidemic of physical disease starts to spread," FDR declared, "the community approves and joins in a quarantine of the patients in order to protect the health of the community against the spread of the disease."[39] Although Roosevelt did not specify exactly what he intended to do, the thrust of his remarks was unmistakable: quarantine the aggressors, isolate them from the community of nations so that the dread disease of war would not spread.

The reaction of the public was swift—and devastatingly adverse. Congressmen accused Roosevelt of violating the United States' policy of neutrality. The American Federation of Labor quickly adopted a resolution opposing American involvement in foreign wars. And throughout the country, opinion polls and newspaper editorials made plain that the people most definitely did not want to become involved in foreign conflicts, even if the action taken by the United States was designed to curtail the fighting. "It's a terrible thing," Roosevelt said later to Sam Rosenman, his trusted aide, "to look over your shoulder when you are trying to lead—and to find no one there."[40] Realizing that his policies would be doomed to failure without public understanding and support, Roosevelt retreated and refrained from discussing the matter further.

By 1940, the situation worsened on both war fronts. But the dangers were particularly acute for England, a close ally of the United States. British Prime Minister Churchill pleaded with Roosevelt to loan England the use of some old American destroyers. Without them, Churchill said, England's fate would be precarious and the success of Hitler's advance almost assured. Churchill's plea to FDR of course fell on sympathetic ears. But Roosevelt, always mindful of the politics of a situation, again felt obliged to consult with congressional leaders and, perhaps most importantly, to explain to the people the importance of leasing American destroyers to England. At a press conference in December 1940, he announced the idea of leasing to England American destroyers which that country could use in her defense. Knowing that the reporters would be the intermediary through which his plan would be explained to the people, Roosevelt took care to use the simple, concrete illustration that he had used so successfully in the past. "Suppose my neighbor's home catches on fire," said Roosevelt,

> and I have a length of garden hose four or five hundred feet away. If he can take my garden hose and connect it up with his hydrant, I may help him to put out his fire. Now what do I do? I don't say to him before that operation, "Neighbor, my garden hose cost me $15; you have to pay me $15 for it." What is the transaction that goes on? I don't want $15—I want my garden hose back after the fire is over. All right. If it goes through the fire all right, intact, without any damage to it, he gives it back to me and thanks me very much for the use of it.[41]

That, in short, was the basic principle underlying the Lend-Lease program. And that same principle was explained when Roosevelt made a fireside chat to discuss Lend-Lease later that month. And it was a principle which the public could easily understand and support. The Lend-Lease program begun by FDR on his own initiative was eventually included in a legislative enactment.

This was but one of the innumerable instances in which FDR displayed his sensitivity to public thinking and made plain his obvious talent for influencing that thinking. Accepting the importance of public opinion, Roosevelt was often able to push the people in the direction he thought they should go. Harold Laski was among those who appreciated Roosevelt's role as an educator; Roosevelt, Laski approvingly wrote in 1940, "had dramatized the issues upon which men know their lives to depend." The people had been taught to understand and share "the emotions of a drama in which each spectator felt himself associated with the fortunes of the actors involved."[42] But perhaps no one more than Roosevelt himself recognized his own skill at dramatizing leadership—as he once boasted to Orson Welles, they were the two best actors in the nation.

Lend-Lease further illustrates the paradoxical quality of the President's role as a public leader: to emphasize the President's ability to interpret the needs of his public is not to employ popularity as the sole measure of his effectiveness. For in a democratic society, where change occurs rather slowly, there are fewer risks in defending the status quo than in proposing change. But this is not always sound strategy, even for a politician. A president who continually risks little can usually sustain little hope of accomplishing much. A president who merely reflects a collage of public opinions will rarely be able to push for needed changes or inspire the public support essential to the successful implementation of those changes. In short, it is not always wise to rely on public opinion as the sole measure of the merit of a program or policy. In his highly perceptive book *The Public Philosophy,* Walter Lippmann observed in 1955 that popular opinions were a weak gauge for devising effective public strategies, especially in matters relating to foreign policy or national defense:

> The unhappy truth is that the prevailing public opinion has been destructively wrong at the critical junctures. The people have imposed a veto upon the judgments of informed and responsible officials. They have compelled the governments, which usually knew what would have been wiser, or was necessary, or was more expedient, to be too late with too little, or too long with too much, too pacifist in peace and too bellicose in war, too neutralist or appeasing in negotiation or too intransigent. Mass opinion has acquired mounting power in this century. It has shown itself to be a dangerous master of decisions when the stakes are life and death.[43]

I do not share Lippmann's almost total distaste for the influence of public opinion in foreign policy or any other matter (it was not public opinion, after all, which initially put American money and troops into Vietnam); but he does underscore one point essential to any effective presidency: a leader should not always procrastinate in making the decisions he believes necessary to protect the nation's interests or to avoid future problems. Sometimes, such procrastination enables a problem to fester, to develop until its expanded complexities require more time and energy than was originally needed. Surely Roosevelt must have reflected on this as he urged the Lend-Lease program on Congress in 1940. Kennedy likewise understood that further delay in the adoption of a moratorium on nuclear-weapons testing could have grave portents for the near future. It also should be added that popularity achieved by avoiding decisions is rarely sustained in the long run, for the political constituencies tend to support those who meet their needs in the present, not those who have succeeded in the past.

In essence, then, popularity acquired at the expense of decision can sometimes entail a renunciation of responsibility and a diminution of influence. Public opinions are not always synonymous with the public interests; and popularity is not always synonymous with power and may frequently conflict with it. A president who views his principal role as trying to satisfy everyone, moreover, will probably end in satisfying no one. As George Washington explained it when he commanded the fledgling nation's armed forces, "To please everybody is impossible; were I to undertake it, I should probably please nobody."[44] Resting the direction of his programs and policies exclusively on public opinion, in other words, a president will probably find that he is building his political future on ever-shifting sands. For the outlook of the individual citizen, or group, is limited by his daily needs and his position in society; rarely will his expectations of the president account for the other, and often conflicting, demands made on the chief executive. A president who acts from his privileged perspective, though, does not preclude eventual public support: "a President who asserts the presidential perspective and disturbs the status quo will always engender criticism. . . . He must be able to win a consensus without waiting for one."[45] Certainly Woodrow Wilson, through his party caucuses and political maneuvering, demonstrated this ability early in his first administration by winning approval of his progressive legislation. While there was growing support for reform in the nation, Wilson was able to exploit it beyond its apparent limits.

Succeeding to the presidency with little preparation, Harry Truman faced a more difficult task in 1946. With the war-weary public yearning for a return to the economic freedoms of the prewar years, Truman pressed for a continuation of the Office of Price Administration in order to arrest impending inflation. For almost six years the OPA, with all its bureaucratic red tape and legendary inefficiency, had done much to check inflationary forces. By 1946, prices had increased only 30 percent over the 1939 prices (a feat which was considered all the more remarkable when it was remembered that prices had jumped more than 100 percent during World War I when there was no OPA).

Price controls made sense to the public when the nation was prepared to make material sacrifices for the war effort. But who in his right mind wanted such controls in peacetime? Harry Truman. Until America's productive resources could make an adjustment to the needs of a peacetime economy, Truman believed that continuation of the OPA authority was necessary to prevent runaway inflation. Without OPA, Truman believed, prices would rise drastically at once. In his State of the Union message in January 1946, he therefore asked Congress to extend the OPA for at least one more year.

Almost immediately Congress was deluged by protests from every sector of the country. Businessmen of every stripe and industry wanted no part of price controls. They had made their sacrifice during the war; now they wanted to enjoy the immense profits that increased prices would bring. Slowly the consumers became educated to the dangers of an economy without price controls. But their education was too slow and the lobbying efforts of the business communities too intense. Congress, believing that it truly represented the will of the country, passed a bill extending the OPA—but attaching to it amendments which virtually stripped the agency of its enforcement powers. Truman, to say the least, was not anxious to sign the bill; he knew it would not be effective and, having signed the measure he had requested of Congress, he would be blamed for the resulting inflation. At a subsequent White House meeting, however, Senate Democratic Majority Leader Alben Barkley explained to Truman that he really had no choice. "Harry, you've got to sign this bill," Barkley said. "Whether you like it or not, it's the best bill we can get out of this Congress, and it's the only one you're going to get."[46]

After the meeting, Truman went over to Paul Porter, the OPA administrator, and Clark Clifford, the White House special counsel. Both had been working on a veto message in the event Truman decided not to sign the bill. Cabell Phillips described the ensuing conversation:

> "You heard all of that?" [Truman] asked them.
>
> "Yes, Mr. President," Porter said haltingly. "And I really feel I ought to tell you that if you do sign this bill, I don't feel I could honestly stay on as OPA administrator."
>
> The thin lips spread in the familiar, puckish smile.
>
> "What the hell makes you think I'm going to sign it? You fellows are writing a veto message, aren't you? Well, get to it. And I want a

thirty-minute speech to go on the radio with tomorrow night to tell the people why I vetoed it." [47]

The death of the OPA produced the result that Truman expected: prices increased instantly and, more important to his political fortunes, most of the people blamed Congress. It was all a matter of knowing when to ride the waves of public opinion in Congress and knowing when to say no. And that is often the crux of the President's responsibility as a public leader.

John F. Kennedy: The Commitment to Lead

Neither the public opinions nor the public interests are static. While he might profit from the lessons in public leadership offered by his predecessors, John Kennedy would have to interpret public opinions and uphold public interests for which the past might not provide an analogy. Certainly the past would have its impact on the dilemmas he would face and the options he would possess. The past would also have varying effects on his advocates and on his adversaries as well as on those who would be touched by his decisions. But the past would not determine how John Kennedy would lead his constituencies in the present or prepare them for the future. John Kennedy's performance as a public leader, in other words, would be shaped by his ideals and his decisions.

Long before he entered the White House, Kennedy had made clear the importance he attached to the role of active leadership in a democracy. In *Why England Slept,* he had examined in some detail the responsibility of England's leaders for that country's state of unpreparedness in meeting the mortal dangers of Hitler's Nazi juggernaut. Kennedy believed that those leaders could not be held entirely accountable for deficiencies in England's policies—there were too many other complex political and economic forces at work to place the blame exclusively on the shoulders of a few individuals. But Kennedy argued forcefully that in the prewar years the leaders had failed miserably in fulfilling their two primary responsibilities: the obligation to educate the public about the imminence of armed conflict; and the obligation to make hard decisions to build up England's defense arsenal and otherwise make the nation secure against foreign attack.

Kennedy placed particular emphasis on the leader's educational role. England's citizenry, he argued, resisted any suggestion that the peace they enjoyed was ephemeral; and not being educated on the illusion of their faith, the people of course were unwilling to support any action—such as a defense buildup—which reflected a fear that war was near.

When war finally did strike, the people were naturally unprepared psychologically and militarily.

The problems of public education were not confined to England in the prewar years, however. Kennedy stated clearly that this was a problem endemic to all democracies—including the United States—where leaders, to continue in office, had to reflect public opinion to a large extent. Since the public would always prefer to avoid the fear and sacrifice in preparing for war, the democratic leaders would be greatly handicapped in the efforts to ensure that the nation had the means to be secure. Thus, in England the

> people for a long time would not have tolerated any great armaments program. Even though Churchill vigorously pointed out the dangers, the people were much more ready to put their confidence in those who favored a strong peace policy. The result of their attitude is that a democracy will always be behind a dictatorship. In a dictatorship, a vigorous armaments program can be carried on, even though the people are deeply hostile to the idea of going to war. The rigidly controlled state press can then build up a war psychology at any time. In contrast, in a democracy the cry of "warmonger" will discourage any politician who advocates a vigorous arms policy. This leaves armaments with few supporters.
>
> ****
>
> I say, therefore, that democracy's weaknesses are great in competing with a totalitarian system. Democracy is the superior form of government, because it is based on a respect for man as a reasonable being. *For the long run,* then, democracy is superior. But for the short run, democracy has great weaknesses. When it competes with a system of government which cares nothing for permanency, a system built primarily for war, democracy, a system built primarily for peace, is at a disadvantage. And democracy must recognize its weaknesses; it must learn to safeguard its institutions if it hopes to survive.[48]

And to Kennedy, a primary safeguard of democratic institutions were strong leaders willing to educate the public about matters it would prefer to ignore.

This respect for strong democratic leadership, no doubt, influenced Kennedy in some of the decisions he made while serving in Congress. His vote for the St. Lawrence Seaway plan in 1954[49] and his speech on Algeria in 1957[50] surely reflected a legislator who was willing to incur public criticism for the sake of supporting a policy which he deeply believed to be in the nation's interests. His appreciation for strong leadership also underlay his homage to ten courageous senators in

Profiles in Courage. In his eyes, the clearest test of a leader's convictions and strength was a willingness to accept public rebuke (and perhaps electoral defeat). Indeed, speaking at Harvard shortly after the book's publication in 1955, Kennedy stressed that democratic politicians are forever "dragging the anchor of public opinion";[51] it was therefore the rare politician who could cut the chains of public opinion to do what he thought was right.

Kennedy repeatedly emphasized the importance of vigorous leadership as he approached the 1960 presidential campaign. In many of his cross-country stops, he would recall the plight of England in the prewar years and speak of the need for an American president who would prepare the people for the (largely unspecified) challenges of the 1960s. In Tulsa, Oklahoma, on September 16, 1959, for example, he observed that "this is not a time to keep the facts from the people—to keep them complacent. To sound the alarm is not to panic but to seek action from an aroused public. . . . No, my friends, it is not we who are selling America short—not those of us who believe that the American people have the capacity to accept the harsh facts of our position and respond to them."[52] In Rochester, New York, two weeks later he again sounded this theme, this time referring explicitly to the English people's refusal to heed Churchill's admonitions in the 1930s about the dangers of Nazi Germany:

> Unfortunately for the British, Churchill had inherited the fate of Cassandra—the mythical daughter of Priam to whom the god Apollo had first given the gift of accurate prophecy but, later angered, then ordained that her prophecies would never be believed. Like Cassandra, Winston Churchill was neither believed nor beloved for his warnings of danger and his calls for sacrifice at a time when the hopes for relaxation were high.
>
> Here, too, our hopes for relaxation are high. But the hard facts of the matter are that we here in the United States, in the year 1959, cannot escape our dangers by recoiling from them—or by being lulled to sleep.[53]

In a far-ranging interview with Harper's editor John Fischer on December 9, 1959, Kennedy returned again and again to the broad challenges the people would face in the 1960s—establishing a peaceful coexistence with the Soviet Union, strengthening our military arsenal for possible conflict, defending Berlin, aiding the underdeveloped countries, stimulating the American economy, and funding new domestic programs. His language was particularly strong in discussing the foreign policy challenges. The Eisenhower administration, Kennedy told Fischer, "has not faced up to these and other problems squarely—nor have they been willing to tell the American people the frank truth about them—if they themselves know the truth—what they mean in terms of real dangers and what it will take to ease those dangers. And the worst of all," Kennedy continued, "they will not leave behind sufficient military power to enable us to deal with these situations—Berlin, Quemoy-Matsu, and all the rest—from a position of strength—not strength for war alone but for peace." His presidency would view the role of public leadership differently, Kennedy said: "I think a new Administration must be willing to tell the people the truth, and place the real dimensions of our crisis before them."[54]

Kennedy continued to pursue this theme after he announced his candidacy for the presidency on January 2, 1960. Less than two weeks after that announcement he made a major address before the National Press Club in which he gave a detailed explanation of his concept of the presidency. And he left no doubt that, in his view, the American chief executive should be a vigorous leader who would educate the public about the issues but who, in the end, would accept the responsibility of decisive action to protect the people's interests—even if it meant inviting their disapproval.

"During the past eight years," Kennedy began, "we have seen one concept of the Presidency at work. Our needs and hopes have been eloquently stated—but the initiative and follow-through have too often been left to others. And too often his own objectives have been lost by the President's failure to override objections from within his own party, in the Congress or even in his Cabinet." This was not the kind of leadership Kennedy felt the public wanted. "They demand a vigorous proponent of the national interest," Kennedy declared, "not a passive broker for conflicting private interests. They demand a man capable of acting as the commander-in-chief of the grand alliance, not merely a bookkeeper who feels that his work is done when the numbers on the balance sheet come out even. They demand that he be the head of a responsible party, not rise so far above politics as to be invisible—a man who will formulate and fight for legislative policies, not be a casual bystander in the legislative process."[55]

The passive leadership of an Eisenhower, Kennedy continued, would be especially ill suited for the 1960s. The times would instead require a decisive president who would actively involve himself in the politics of the vital issues:

> In the decade that lies ahead—in the challenging, revolutionary sixties—the American Presidency will demand more than ringing manifestoes issued from the rear of battle. It will demand that the President place himself in the very thick of the fight, that he care passionately about the fate of the people he leads, that he be will-

> ing to serve them at the risk of incurring their momentary displeasure.[56]

The significance of the speech was not lost upon the assemblage of reporters and other press people who listened to it. As James Reston observed the next day, Kennedy "was highly critical of the President in the full knowledge that the President is at the height of his personal popularity." In the country's present mood, said Reston, this criticism involved many political risks for Kennedy, "but right or wrong, he has at least started to discuss serious issues in a major arena where they cannot be ignored or brushed off. . . . And he is saying frankly that if the people want the kind of leadership President Eisenhower has given them, they better not choose the Senator from Massachusetts."[57] And as syndicated columnist David Broder remarked in later years of Kennedy's National Press Club speech, "There was nothing timid about his approach to power but he understood that the exercise of power was legitimate only when those he sought to lead understood and approved the purposes for which it was used."[58]

Kennedy continued to invoke this theme of presidential leadership as the campaign progressed. Almost always he was emphasizing the critical obligation of the president to be truthful about the problems which confronted the nation and the measures that would be necessary to meet them.

In a Senate floor speech which was billed as a major explanation of his views on foreign policy, for example, Kennedy stressed that the "next President will confront a task of unparalleled dimensions. But this task will not be his alone. For just as he must offer leadership and demand sacrifices—it is the American people who must be willing to respond to these demands."[59]

This theme reached a new crescendo when Kennedy accepted the Democratic Party's presidential nomination at Los Angeles. In his speech, Kennedy observed that the nation stood "on the edge of a New Frontier." But he quickly added that the

> New Frontier of which I speak is not a set of promises; it is a set of challenges. It sums up not what I intend to *offer* the American people, but what I intend to *ask* of them. It appeals to their pride, not to their pocketbook. It holds out the promise of more sacrifice instead of more security. Beyond that frontier are unchartered areas of science and space, unsolved problems of peace and war, unconquered pockets of ignorance and prejudice, unanswered questions of poverty and surplus.
>
> It would be easy to shrink from that frontier, to look to the safe mediocrity of the past. . . . But I believe the time demands inven-

> tion, innovation, imagination, decision. I am asking each of you to be pioneers on that New Frontier.[60]

Thus, the promise of Kennedy's leadership was forged. A President beckoning the people to new frontiers, horizons that remained largely undefined but which in any event would call forth the decision and action that the people had come to expect of their President. He would not shroud his leadership in secrecy and high intrigue, moreover. No, he would be a president who appreciated the leader's role as a public educator, who would confide in the people and discuss with them the available alternatives for solution. And once having made the critical choices, Kennedy's President would honor them—even in the face of growing popular opposition. Speaking at the New York City Coliseum two days before the election, Kennedy summarized these ideas which he and his running mate, Lyndon Johnson, had tried to stress during the campaign. Exhausted from endless days of politicking in which he often had less than four hours' sleep, Kennedy was at the brink of collapse. But he was exhilarated by the crowds that greeted him in New York, and he was eager to rise to the occasion, to respond to the emotions that lit the sea of faces before him. "We want to be a President and Vice President," he declared,

> who have confidence in the people and who take the people into their confidence, who let them know what they are doing and where we are going and who is for his program and who is against.
>
> ****
>
> In short, we believe in a President and in a Vice President who will fight for their legislative programs and not be a casual observer of the legislative process, a President who does not speak from the rear of the battle but places himself in the thick of it, committed to progress and to great programs and ends.[61]

A President committed to educating the public. A leader who would be the spokesman for high principles and the defender of progressive programs. It was ideal—and a bit too much. These campaign statements can and should be considered as the crux of Kennedy's promise for leadership. They did, after all, set a mood which many citizens probably relied on in casting their votes. But the statements could not be taken entirely at face value. For Kennedy was a politician. In seeking the nation's highest political office, he was not prone to understatement, to say the least. And his past record should have given much pause to anyone who thought Kennedy's commitment to leadership was open-ended. There had been many numerous occasions—such as his support of the southern senators' view of a key provision of the Civil Rights Act of 1957—which revealed his instinct to compromise for the sake of preserving political support.

It is in this context that one must weigh the impact of the final presidential vote on Kennedy's promise of leadership. Of more than 68 million votes cast, less than 120,000 separated Kennedy from Richard Nixon. The narrow margin of his victory greatly disturbed Kennedy: The enthusiastic reactions of large crowds, the accounts of the traveling reporters, and the estimates of his own campaign staff had encouraged him to believe his victory would be substantial. Now his expectations had been dashed (and his pride a little hurt). He did not have the popular mandate he expected to secure. It puzzled him and it troubled him. And it introduced considerable caution in his thinking.* How could he pursue the ideas and programs he had promised, he thought, if the public's preference for him was so uncertain? (In a postelection editorial, the *New York Times* expressed its view that "it is a good thing that the election was so close. It should serve as a restraining force, as a reminder to the Kennedy Administration that it should proceed with caution and that it has no mandate to embark on drastic changes of policy, either foreign or domestic."[62])

Kennedy would not of course publicly abandon the principles of leadership which he had articulated so eloquently during the campaign. Indeed, as the date of his inauguration approached, he reaffirmed them. In a speech before the Massachusetts State Legislature less than two weeks before he moved into the White House, Kennedy outlined the standards by which history would measure his success in providing leadership:

> First, were we truly men of courage, with the courage to stand up to one's enemies, and the courage to stand up, when necessary, to one's associates, the courage to resist public pressure as well as private greed?
>
> Second, were we truly men of judgment, with perceptive judgment of the future as well as the past, of our own mistakes as well as the mistakes of others, with enough wisdom to know what we did not know, and enough candor to admit it?

---

*The caution in Kennedy's first months as President was apparent to much of the public. At the start of the new administration in January 1961, Gallup conducted a survey to determine public expectations. Of those interviewed, 39 percent thought Kennedy would move to the left politically, 29 percent thought he would stay in the middle and 14 percent thought he would move to the right (18 percent had no opinion). After three months, the figures changed dramatically; 33 percent thought he would move to the middle, 25 percent thought he would move to the left, and 16 percent thought he would move to the right (26 percent had no opinion).

> Third, were we truly men of integrity, men who never ran out on either the principles in which we believed or the people who believed in us, men whom neither financial gain nor political ambition could ever divert from the fulfillment of our sacred trust?
>
> Finally, were we truly men of dedication, with an honor mortgaged to no single individual or group, and compromised by no private obligation or aim, but devoted solely to serving the public good and the national interest?[63]

This was a stiff measuring rod. And as he embarked on his presidential journey, Kennedy would soon understand as he never did before that it was a difficult standard to satisfy. And that presidential experience would also reinforce something he had already suspected: it is always easier to criticize the quality of leadership when someone else is President.

Leading the Public

In a windswept and snowbound Capitol on January 20, 1961, John F. Kennedy took the oath of office and laid before the public the guideposts of his forthcoming administration. In his inaugural address, Kennedy recalled the revolutionary heritage of the United States and declared that his generation of descendants would be "unwilling to witness or permit the slow undoing of those human rights to which this nation has always been committed, and to which we are committed today at home and around the world." In many ways, this was a veiled gesture toward the communists who seemed to threaten the survival of individual freedom. But Kennedy left nothing to the imagination in describing the United States' determination to resist those threats:

> Let every nation know, whether it wishes us well or ill, that we shall pay any price, bear any burden, meet any hardship, support any friend, oppose any foe to assure the survival and the success of liberty.[64]

He then spoke of our commitment to cooperate with America's allies, to help the underdeveloped nations break the chains of poverty, and to help defend our Latin-American neighbors (except Castro of course) from subversion. He also spoke of the special dangers which surrounded the United States' relationship with the Soviet Union. We would arm to the hilt to protect ourselves, Kennedy said, but we would also be willing to explore with the Soviet Union the possibilities of controlling the arms race in order to minimize the risk of nuclear war. It was a broad, sweeping review of the nation's hopes. Like virtually all previous inaugural addresses, it was designed to set the tone of the new administration rather than set forth detailed plans of how the announced goals would be reached. But in meeting the new administration's commitments, Kennedy reminded his audiences that they, more than he, would have to bear the burdens of his leadership:

> And so my fellow Americans: ask not what your country can do for you—ask what you can do for your country.
>
> My fellow citizens of the world: ask not what America will do for you, but what together we can do for the freedom of man.
>
> Finally, whether you are citizens of America or citizens of the world, ask of us here the same high standards of strength and sacrifice which we ask of you.[65]

In later years, many would reexamine the premises of this inaugural address and question the wisdom of its conclusions, particularly the open-ended commitment to engage the United States in every corner of the world where subversion and hostilities seemed to wear the mask of communism. At the time, however, this commitment surprised virtually no one; it was simply a restatement of the positions Kennedy had enunciated over and over again during his campaign and, indeed, throughout most of his years in Congress. The commitment, moreover, was very responsive to the concerns of the American people. Polls showed, for example, that 60 percent of the public was acutely concerned about the nation's defense, that 74 percent of the public found the Cold War issues "alarming," that 68 percent believed that the Soviet Union wanted another war, that 50 percent feared the spread of communism to friendly nations, and that only 39 percent of the people believed that the United States was better prepared than the Soviet Union for immediate war.[66]

Given these concerns and the general mood of the country, the eloquence and firm resolve of Kennedy's inaugural address were widely praised.* But few people were perceptive enough to raise the questions

---

*The next day the *New York Times* editorialized that "the world is also taking note of President Kennedy's dedication to the survival and success of liberty at any price, of his determination, if there are negotiations, to negotiate from strength, not weakness, and to that end to build up America's armed might. Indeed, there are voices, especially in Paris and Vienna, which hold that Premier Khrushchev will find President Kennedy both tough and resourceful in resisting Communist wiles and ambitions. And many see in that possibility the best chance for his success."

New York Times, January 21, 1961, p. 20.

posed by James Reston. He commented that the inaugural address deserved the praise it received for its style and content. But the speech, Reston mused, was "something more than a graceful television performance in the snow. . . . It would be interesting to know whether all the people who praised all this are willing to go along with the sacrifices implied, particularly those who praised him in the United States."[67]

The pervasive peace and prosperity in which the United States had bathed during the 1950s surely justified Reston's reflections. The nation was not engaged in any sustained military combat anywhere in the world. And, despite periodic recessions, the majority of Americans enjoyed a style of living higher than that anywhere else and, in fact, higher than most of them expected. A few simple statistics suggest the level of this affluence. By 1960, 88 percent of the nation's families, almost 44 million in all, owned television sets; one-fourth of all homes in 1960 had been built since 1950; white-collar jobs now outnumbered blue-collar jobs; and with the advent of installment buying, many people, but especially those in the middle and upper classes, were able to enjoy more luxuries.

The abundant affluence of the many helped the nation smother the problems of the few. Thus, the migration of the Negroes to the North (only 52 percent of the nation's blacks lived in the South in 1960) perhaps made racial discrimination more widespread; but it also tended to mute the demands for civil rights with the North's self-righteous claims of equal opportunity and accessible wealth. Similarly, the penetrating questions about social problems raised by those such as John Kenneth Galbraith in *The Affluent Society* produced more curiosity than concerted action. Rather than focusing on the fermenting ills which would explode upon the nation in the 1960s, the public's attention was drawn more to events such as the 1959 "kitchen debate" between Vice-President Richard Nixon and Soviet Premier Khrushchev—a debate concerned with comparative living standards. And when Eisenhower demurred at becoming involved in the Little Rock School crisis in 1957—a crisis which tested the Supreme Court's decision to end racial segregation in public schools—there was little public pressure to induce any doubts on the President's part as to the prudence and morality of his course. Only when mob violence threatened the lives of the city's populace did Eisenhower feel constrained to act—and his decision to dispatch federal troops to the scene was made with a certain resentment at becoming involved in what he regarded as essentially a state matter.

Prosperity, in short, had not obliterated the nation's problems; pronounced wealth had merely obscured the dimensions of the problems and weakened the people's resolve in solving them. The American public was considerably blind to the shortcomings of its political institutions and secure in its illusions. J. D. Salinger's *The Catcher in the Rye,* an extremely popular book at this time, characterized this national mood with disarming insight (even though the book was written in the 1940s). Here was Holden Caulfield, an adolescent haunted by the inequalities and the contradictions of American life, a boy whose empathy for others was equally matched by a realization that American society was hypocritical and often cruel. Yet Holden's reaction was withdrawal rather than involvement; his fate was a mental institution rather than a political organization. He eventually suffered a nervous breakdown because he could not accept a society to which most Americans had adjusted.

This, then, was America as John Kennedy assumed the presidency. He spoke of crises; but as Theodore White wrote, the public which voted for Kennedy sensed only an obscure crisis, a "crisis locked in the womb of time, swelling uncomfortably in embryo, crisis whose countenance was still unclear."[68] *New Yorker* columnist Richard Rovere was another analyst who recognized the problem. "President Kennedy today," Rovere said, "is attempting to meet a challenge whose existence he and his associates are almost alone in perceiving."[69] The explanations for these comments were easy to understand. On one hand, Americans surely understood Kennedy's concerns about racial inequality, economic stagnation, and the forces of communism (especially the Soviet Union). But like the English people in the 1930s, Americans did not share their leader's sense of urgency about the problems of the future. The crises of which Kennedy spoke seemed unclear because there was no tangible disaster which induced real fear; there was no obvious emergency to arouse the people's emotions and demand their efforts. Even the Cold War with the Soviet Union had slipped into the abyss of nuclear deterrence and frozen policies; it became a way of life as much as a threat to our security. As the newly independent nations became prominent in the world theatre they threatened to draw the United States and the Soviet Union into armed conflict. But the people seemed unmoved by these possible developments. As William Manchester observed, "Cold War, unlike war, doesn't generate much heat at home."[70]

The public's general response to world developments was restricted instead to token reactions. For example, in the 1950s most Americans evidenced little concern for the progress of their educational systems (the federal government's expenditures on education averaged less than $1 billion annually in the late 1950s, while the defense budget exceeded $40 billion). Suddenly, with the successful launching of the Soviet sputnik in 1957, the pressure mounted—not for a broad attack on the educational systems' deficiencies, but to provide ample support for the training of scientists to match the Soviet effort. The result, then, was not comprehensive legislation meeting the neglected needs of the country's youth; rather, the Congress passed the National Defense Education Act, a bill largely limited to aiding those students in the physical sciences. This was but one instance of the public's selective detachment from their future, of their failure to respond to the country's expanding needs.

The same passivity was evident in public attitudes toward the developing nations or those who needed American assistance. In a grand wave of rhetoric, Kennedy's inaugural address had reaffirmed in clear terms America's commitment to help those nations in a spirit of brotherhood. But the spirit was not widely shared among the general populace; most people simply did not care that much. Most could not understand the relation between Africa's future and the United States' security, between the living standards in Latin America and the United States' economy. Although the American presence was spread throughout the world, the horizons of the average American citizen did not extend much beyond the boundaries of his homeland. Reston had touched this nerve of the people when he wrote shortly before Kennedy's election that there was considerable resistance among the public

> to exhortations from the preachers, professors, columnists, and editorial writers of the nation. For unless I miss my guess, the Americano, circa 1960, is in no mood to rush off on his own initiative to "emancipate the human race," or to set any new records as the greatest benefactor of all time, or engage in any of the other crusades mapped out for him in Cambridge, Massachusetts.[71]

All this underscored to Kennedy the importance of his role as a public educator. He knew that many of his programs and policies would find little success if they were not understood and supported by the American people. He was therefore receptive to arguments that he initiate campaigns to acquaint the public with the vital issues and his proposals to resolve them.

This is not to suggest that Kennedy exploited every opportunity to crisscross the country pontificating on the issues of the day. Quite the contrary. He was always concerned lest his explanations of specific problems or his pleas for support of specific solutions fall on deaf ears. After Eisenhower appeared on one television network in the fall of 1961 to criticize the administration, Kennedy was informed that the program had finished a poor third in audience rating behind the programs on the other two networks. "People forget this," Kennedy told

Arthur Schlesinger, Jr., "when they expect me to go on the air all the time educating the nation. The nation will listen after a Vienna. But they won't listen to things which bore them. That is the great trouble."[72]

Kennedy, in short, was terrified of overexposure, especially on television. He believed that there were only so many times he could go to the people to discuss an issue which demanded their attention and to explain a response which required their support.* If there was a crisis (such as the Cuban missile crisis) or a major development (such as the signing of the Test Ban Treaty in 1963), he would not hesitate to use the television to report to the nation. He also believed that it would be useful to have his press conferences televised live so that the public would have that much more insight into the problems the country faced and the ways in which he intended to deal with them. And he would on occasion grant informal television interviews with both American and foreign newsmen.

Many of these techniques were significant innovations: no previous President had ever had his press conferences broadcast live (this caused some serious concern among Kennedy's staff who, at least in the beginning, feared that he might disclose classified information or make a serious political blunder which would be witnessed by millions of Americans); and no previous President had ever conducted an informal television interview with three network newsmen as Kennedy did in December 1962. For all these innovations, Kennedy's use of television was far more cautious than his immediate successors'. In retrospect, this seems a little strange. After all, it was Kennedy—not Johnson or Nixon—whose mystique was his adaptability to the television screen. But Kennedy was always inhibited, as FDR was, by the fear that too much exposure would decrease the impact of each individual appearance.**

Kennedy, in short, was very selective about the issues he would

---

*Kennedy was not alone in expressing this fear. Franklin D. Roosevelt, famed for his expertise in public education, once explained why he did not use the radio as much as he wanted. "People tire of seeing the same name day after day in the important headlines of the papers, and the same voice night after night over the radio," FDR said. "Individual psychology cannot, because of human weakness, be attuned for long periods of time to constant repetition of the highest note in the scale." Although Roosevelt was well known for the frequency of his "fireside chats," in twelve years in office he actually held only thirty—or an average of less than three per year.

**In his first nineteen months in office, for instance, Kennedy made fifty television appearances occupying 30.25 hours; Lyndon Johnson made thirty-three appearances for 12.50 hours and Richard Nixon made thirty-seven appearances for 13.50 hours in their first nineteen months in office. However, the vast majority of Kennedy's appearances

focus on in his public education efforts. But once he decided that an issue was important enough to merit presidential lessons, Kennedy generally employed three principal methods: public addresses, press conferences, and his ability to stimulate newspaper and magazine articles on the issue. It was rarely that Kennedy relied exclusively on any one method in working to increase public understanding of a particular issue; usually he relied on a mixture of the three methods, as well as on private meetings with groups and organizations that had a special interest in the matter. Nonetheless, it is possible to isolate some examples which reveal the extent to which Kennedy was able and willing to employ each of the three principal methods in informing the people.

Public addresses were a frequently used tool. A typical case involved the proposal to cut taxes as a means to stimulate economic growth. A few months after the inauguration, Walter Heller, chairman of the Council of Economic Advisers, wrote a memorandum to Kennedy explaining the importance of a tax cut. Although the government budget showed a continuing deficit, Heller argued that a reduction in personal and corporate income taxes could increase capital investment, consumer purchasing power, and employment. Heller candidly advised Kennedy, though, that the public would not readily accept the idea of a tax cut while the government's budget showed a deficit: "We do not blink the problem of public understanding and acceptance of this bold program," Heller wrote; "the only chance of solving this problem would be some massive educational efforts of the 'fireside chat' type."[73]

Kennedy appreciated the need for public education here; but he was not entirely convinced that a tax cut was sound fiscal policy. To begin with, in his campaign speeches he had promised the electorate that he would strive to balance the budget. Some of his advisers—like Treasury Secretary Douglas Dillon—believed that this remained a wise goal. In time Dillon began to side with Heller, and Kennedy, too, became persuaded that the sanctity of the balanced budget did not warrant preservation. He therefore decided that the time was ripe to raise the matter in his public speeches.

In a statement at the White House Conference on National Econom-

---

were either ceremonial events, press conferences, or statements made during the daytime hours. Johnson and Nixon, on the other hand, exploited prime-time viewing hours—between 7 P.M. and 11 P.M.—to a far greater extent. In his first year in office LBJ made more prime-time television appearances than Kennedy had in three years; and in his first eighteen months in office, Nixon made more prime-time television appearances than Johnson, Kennedy, and Eisenhower *combined* in their first eighteen months in office. The reasons for this greater reliance on prime-time hours is easy to understand: the President will be able to reach many millions more people. See Newton Minow, John Bartlow Martin & Lee Mitchell, *Presidential Television* (1973).

ic Issues in May 1962, Kennedy explored the myths which often impeded a realistic and effective resolution of economic problems. And in a commencement address at Yale University the next month, Kennedy again struck at the myths which clouded the public's perception of the economic problems and the means required to solve them. Kennedy explained that

> . . . the great enemy of the truth is very often not the lie—deliberate, contrived and dishonest—but the myth, persistent, persuasive, and unrealistic. Too often we hold fast to the clichés of our forbears. We subject all facts to a prefabricated set of interpretations. We enjoy the comfort of opinion without the discomfort of thought.

One of the myths Kennedy had in mind concerned deficits in the government's budget:

> The myth persists that Federal deficits create inflation and budget surpluses prevent it. Yet sizable budget surpluses after the war did not prevent inflation, and persistent deficits for the last several years have not upset our basic price stability. Obviously deficits are sometimes dangerous—and so are surpluses. But honest assessment plainly requires a more sophisticated view than the old and automatic cliché that deficits automatically bring inflation.[74]

Kennedy's address was not well received by the business community or the country at large. Convinced nonetheless that tax reduction was an essential tool to economic recovery, Kennedy made a nationally televised address in August 1962, in which he explained the need for tax reduction and his intention to propose, among other tax measures, congressional enactment of a $13.6 billion tax cut spread over three years.

Kennedy was encouraged by the public's responses to these speeches. Immediately after the August address, for example, public support for the tax cut proposal increased 4 percent. And by October 1962, the University of Michigan Survey Research Center, one of the most reputable polling organizations in the country, found that those who viewed a tax cut favorably increased from 42 percent in 1961 to 65 percent in 1962, while those who viewed it as a "bad idea" decreased from 43 percent to 19 percent. According to the survey report, which Walter Heller showed to Kennedy, the shift in public attitudes could be tied directly to the President: "It is probable that the attribution of the proposals to the President in August, 1962, made for a somewhat greater frequency of favorable reactions, especially among people with lesser education and lower income."[75] This kind of response, to say the least, reinforced Kennedy's desire to continue his educational campaign on the idea of a tax cut. He therefore discussed it at length again before the Economic Club of New York in December 1962. And after he proposed it to Congress in January 1963, he continued to examine the matter in public speeches.

One of his last—and perhaps best—speeches on the subject was on September 10, 1963, before a business group favoring the proposal. Kennedy described the bill as "the most important domestic economic measure to come before Congress in the past 15 years." And then he proceeded to explain in great detail why. He recited statistics, studies, and past history to demonstrate that enactment of the tax cut was an essential ingredient in the nation's ability to achieve a full-employment economy and even a balanced budget (since the tax cut would ultimately increase tax revenues while enabling the government to reduce expenditures). Kennedy concluded by expressing his belief "that without a quick and assured tax cut this country can look forward to more unemployment, to more lags in income, to larger budget deficits, and to more waste and weakness in economy, and that, in my opinion, is real fiscal irresponsibility."[76] One week later, Kennedy repeated the substance of this speech—with statistics, studies, and all—in a nationally televised appeal to the American people to urge their support for the tax reduction bill. Such support, Kennedy explained, was particularly crucial since the House of Representatives was preparing to vote on the measure in the next week.

It is, of course, impossible to weigh the precise impact which these public addresses had on the public mind (the House did pass the bill for which Kennedy urged public support). But there is little doubt that Kennedy's frequent speeches on the matter helped to grease the wheels of public support and eased President Johnson's task in making the final push through Congress in 1964.

Nuclear testing was another area in which Kennedy believed action was required and public understanding essential. Both as a presidential candidate and as the nation's chief executive, Kennedy continually identified a prohibition on the testing of nuclear bombs as a major priority of his administration. In his inaugural address, for example, he committed the United States to an expansion of its defense arsenal; but at the same time he made clear his desire to bring a halt to the arms race with the Soviet Union which governed much of their relations with each other. Both the United States and the Soviet Union, Kennedy, declared, should "formulate serious and precise proposals for the inspection and control of arms—and bring the absolute power to destroy other nations under the absolute control of all nations."[77] In one of his first actions, Kennedy dispatched Arthur Dean to Geneva to resume negotiations with the Russians on a treaty to ban nuclear testing.

Despite his commitment toward attaining such a treaty, Kennedy was reluctant to rely on voluntary restraints by the United States in its arms buildup and in its own nuclear test program. The Russians, he believed, must have an incentive to engage in serious discussions to halt the arms race, and there would be no incentives if the United States acted unilaterally without demanding a corresponding restraint on the Soviet Union's part. Moreover, Kennedy was always concerned that a spirit of restraint on his part would be interpreted by the Soviet Union as weakness. This concern became particularly acute after Kennedy's meeting with Khrushchev in Vienna, when the Soviet Premier bullied Kennedy and made him feel that a rapprochement with the Soviet Union on nuclear testing or any other matter would be extremely difficult. This reinforced Kennedy's resolve to be a tough leader who could demonstrate to the Russians (especially after his apparent indecision in the Bay of Pigs) that he could stand up to the Soviet Union's bluffs—even if it meant risking nuclear war.

The Cuban missile crisis—and the nation's proximity to nuclear confrontation during those thirteen days—produced a resurgence in Kennedy's desire to seek some understanding with the Soviet Union on the use and testing of nuclear weapons. He pushed hard to have the Soviet Union accept a treaty which would be limited to banning atmospheric (as opposed to underground) nuclear testing. Kennedy was uncertain as to how the American public might respond to these overtures—after all, the first two years of Kennedy's presidency had been marked by frequent "crises" in which the duplicity and malevolence of the Kremlin was frequently held up for public rebuke. In view of these experiences and prevailing public attitudes, Kennedy wondered, would the American people support a treaty whose success would depend in great part on the good faith of the Soviet Union.

Coincidentally, Norman Cousins, the publisher of *The Saturday Review*, wrote to Kennedy at this juncture urging him to make a major speech on peace. Kennedy agreed with Cousins that the question of peace had to be raised in a new context, one which would make the American public receptive to the limited test ban treaty he hoped to negotiate with the Soviet Union. He therefore asked Sorensen to prepare a draft for delivery at the commencement exercises at American University on June 10, 1963. The final product was a landmark which ultimately represented one of Kennedy's most effective uses of a speech as a means of public education.

Kennedy explained to his audience that he had "chosen this time and this place to discuss a topic on which ignorance too often abounds and the truth is too rarely perceived—yet it is the most important topic on earth: world peace." Kennedy acknowledged that it might seem like folly to discuss peace in the nuclear age when the world appeared so complex and so beyond man's control. But Kennedy argued that the nation should persevere in its attempts to secure peace. "Peace need not be impractible," Kennedy said, "and war need not be inevitable. By defining our goals more clearly, by making it seem more manageable and less remote, we can help all people to see it, to draw hope from it, and to move irresistably toward it." In fashioning these specific and manageable goals, Kennedy urged a reexamination of American attitudes toward the Soviet Union. Admitting that the United States and the Soviet Union were brothers neither in thought nor in policy, Kennedy nevertheless reminded his audience that

> no government or social system is so evil that its people must be considered as lacking in virtue. . . . So let us not be blind to our differences—but let us also direct attention to our common interests and to the means by which those differences can be resolved. And if we cannot end now our differences, at least we can help make the world safe for diversity. For, in the final analysis, our most basic common link is that we all inhabit this small planet. We all breathe the same air. We all cherish our children's future. And we are all mortal.[78]

Given this common bond, Kennedy said it was incumbent upon the United States to pursue those areas in which agreement with the Soviet Union was possible. "The one major area of these negotiations where the end is in sight, yet where a fresh start is badly needed," he said, "is in a treaty to outlaw nuclear tests." Kennedy then announced that new high-level discussions toward that goal would soon begin in Moscow and that the United States would suspend atmospheric nuclear testing at least as long as other nations followed a similar restraint.

The speech was an eloquent appeal for the public to support a simple notion: the need to prevent war. The editorial response among the nation's newspapers and magazines was generally very favorable, and the limited White House mail on the subject also suggested that the public was inclined to go along. But Kennedy remained skeptical that he had really reached the heartland of America—a skepticism which stayed with him even after he made a nationally televised announcement to the public on July 26, 1963, that the Soviet Union and the United States had agreed to a limited treaty which would ban atmospheric nuclear testing. In the back of his mind, Kennedy also feared that his efforts to make "peace" a foundation of his presidency would make him vulnerable to right-wing attacks in the 1964 election.

These concerns stayed with Kennedy as he embarked on a tour of the western states in September to stress the value of the conservation ethic (a theme which had been first suggested to him by Senator Gaylord

Nelson). Kennedy stopped first in Wisconsin, then went on to Minnesota and Montana. At each point he discussed the importance of conserving America's resources, often invoking the spirit of Theodore Roosevelt. His rhetoric was smooth as usual, but his heart was not in it. "I'm an urban fellow," he told Nelson at one point, "and I've just never given these matters any real consideration." Conservation, moreover, was not the sexy issue ecology was to become in the 1970s; the audience reactions were polite but not overwhelming; and he was rapidly becoming bored with the whole trip.

Then, in Billings, Montana, he opened his speech by referring to the Senate's acceptance of the test ban treaty. To his surprise the audience responded immediately with a spontaneous enthusiasm which had been lacking from his earlier appearances. Always the politician, Kennedy sensed an opportunity to use his remaining addresses to commune with his publics on an issue that both apparently held dear. In his next stops he consciously raised the issue of peace and the need for the test ban treaty. The audience reactions continued to be enthusiastic, and Kennedy realized that he had struck a responsive chord among the American people.

His efforts climaxed in a speech at the Mormon Tabernacle in Salt Lake City—a presumed center of right-wing extremism in America. Kennedy entered the hall to be greeted by a five-minute standing ovation. And the crowd's enthusiasm grew as he discussed America's responsibilities in the world—to help eradicate poverty, to defend freedom, to protect diversity, and to minimize the risk of nuclear confrontation. "That is why the test ban treaty is important as a first step," Kennedy declared, "perhaps to be disappointed, perhaps to find ourselves ultimately set back, but at least in 1963 the United States committed itself, and the Senate of the United States, by an overwhelming vote, to one chance to end the radiation and the possibilities of burning."[79] The next day Tom Wicker, the *New York Times* White House correspondent, and Sander Vanocur, the NBC White House correspondent, encountered Pierre Salinger and commented that the conservation trip had exposed an idea which dominated the concerns of the American people. "Yes, you're right," Salinger replied. "We've found that peace is an issue."[80]

Kennedy's public addresses on the test ban treaty thus revealed both their effectiveness and his caution in using them as a means of public education. He accepted his obligation to speak to the American people, to explain the issues to them and the actions he was taking to resolve those issues. But in most cases—even where, as with the test ban treaty, he regarded the issue as a critical one—Kennedy was inhibited by a deep-seated skepticism that anyone would really listen. His conservation trip showed that his fears of public indifference could sometimes be misplaced. But there were many other occasions in which this skepticism seemed amply justified.

Medicare was certainly a case in point. Enactment of a bill providing medical assistance to the aged was one of Kennedy's major legislative goals when he entered the White House. It was not a new concept, but Kennedy believed it was an important one which deserved his best efforts. It was a disgrace, he thought, that citizens should reach their golden years only to find themselves unable to finance the medical care they needed. The medicare bill offered a scheme of operation comparable to the social security program whereby citizens contribute to the fund during their working years.

Despite the high priority which he accorded to it, the medicare bill was moving slowly through Congress—in fact, some in the administration wondered whether it was moving at all (the bill had been defeated in the Senate in 1961 and the prospects did not seem much brighter one year later). Convinced that it was an important issue and that the public would really be behind him if they only understood the problem better, Kennedy agreed to address a major gathering of supporters in New York City's Madison Square Garden in May 1962. The idea was particularly attractive to Kennedy since the speech would be piped into 33 other cities across the country via television. Kennedy's appeal for support was simple and direct. The issue was clear; the need for the legislation beyond doubt; the only question was whether the public could bring enough pressure to bear on their elected representatives. "I come here today as a citizen," said Kennedy, his voice moving with the rhythm of a political stump speech, "asking you to exert the most basic power which is contained in the Constitution of the United States and the Declaration of Independence, the right of a citizen to petition his Government."[81]

The speech stimulated no public reaction of any significance except a heated attack on the legislation by the American Medical Association. (When asked about the AMA response at a press conference, Kennedy replied, "Well, I read the statement and I gathered they were opposed to it." [Laughter][82]) The speech, in short, did not provide the kind of public pressure Kennedy hoped it would, and in July the Senate defeated the bill again.

This experience reinforced the natural cynicism which Kennedy had toward his ability to educate and move the public through speeches. More and more he believed he should wait until some specific event or crisis penetrated the public's apathy and made them receptive to his explanations and exhortations. From a political and educational perspective, there was often a good deal of sense in this approach. People run to the doctor usually after—not before—they become sick, and that basic instinct suggested that the people would listen to their leader only when they thought they had to. Experience almost always proves to be a more able teacher than words.

There was, however, a serious flaw in this approach—it made Kennedy even more the servant rather than the master of events. True, there was some reason for Kennedy to believe he had no other choice. But the seeming ineffectiveness of his medicare speech and other addresses may have only underscored the fact that public education is an extremely slow process which required many more similar appeals. And Kennedy's attitude ignored the fact that no two issues and no two sets of circumstances are exactly parallel and that failure in one area does not necessarily ordain failure in another area. In the end, then, Kennedy's attitude compromised his promise to be an assertive executive who would be willing to serve the people even at the risk of incurring their momentary displeasure. Too often—particularly when an important issue was controversial—Kennedy was very reluctant to address the issue in a major speech. Too often he was content to wait for a change in circumstance rather than to try to create a public receptivity or tolerance for a particular policy or program. Civil rights and Vietnam are two examples.

Kennedy's commitment to protect the civil rights of America's minorities was a major theme of his presidential campaign. But, as I have pointed out earlier, Kennedy was initially reluctant to push for legislation because he did not feel there was sufficient support within Congress or among the public (his narrow election margin was evidence of that, he thought). But this did not prevent him from having his administration exercise its independent powers to fulfill the commitment.

One clear illustration was law suits. The civil rights legislation of 1957 had given the federal government power to seek court relief in protecting voting rights. And during his tenure, Kennedy's Justice Department filed fifty-eight such voting rights suits (as compared with only ten filed by Eisenhower's Administration during a comparable time period) and with some significant results.[83] To a large extent, the Justice Department's activities here reflected the active concern of the attorney general. Kennedy fully supported his brother's efforts—even under pressure from the congressional barons. Soon after Robert Kennedy became attorney general, for example, Senator James Eastland of Mississippi, chairman of the powerful Judiciary Committee, told him, "What the Supreme Court is handing down is not the law of the land, it's the law of the case. You'll have to sue us for every Negro in the South." The attorney general reported this conversation to the President, and he wrote on a memo pad, "Get the road maps and go."[84]

Civil rights litigation and other executive action, however, did not often involve the "crises" which seem to open the general public's mind to presidential lessons. Largely for that reason, Kennedy rarely used such executive actions as a lever to make speeches about principles involved and the value of the action taken. Thus, in preparing and promulgating an executive order on housing, Kennedy preferred to keep his thoughts to himself. And it did not speak well of his success as a public educator.

During the presidential campaign, Kennedy repeatedly criticized Eisenhower for not issuing an executive order which would prohibit racial discrimination in the sale of federally assisted housing. The next president, Kennedy said, must promulgate "the long-delayed Executive order putting an end to racial discrimination in federally assisted housing;" the President could resolve this problem, he said, "by a stroke of his pen."[85] When Kennedy was elected, many people—but especially those associated with the civil rights movement—expected him to issue this long-delayed executive order almost immediately. They found instead that they had an even longer wait.

Soon after his election, Kennedy found that there were complex practical and political problems in issuing such an executive order. On the one hand, questions arose as to whether the order should be extended to cover all housing financed through banks with federal insurance or only housing which was actually financed by federal funds (as, for instance, from the Veterans Administration). While the broader order would be more effective in ending discrimination, there were doubts as to whether it could be enforced without legislation (especially since the Federal Deposit Insurance Corporation was not anxious to assume the responsibility). There was also concern that the broader order would undercut the housing market (most white people still did not want to live next door to a black) and that, in turn, would further depress the American economy which Kennedy hoped to revive.

On the other hand, there were political problems as well. Kennedy wanted to elevate the Housing and Home Finance Agency to a new cabinet department on urban affairs. And he wanted to appoint the agency's head, Dr. Robert Weaver, as the secretary of the new department. The problem was that Weaver was black. Kennedy knew that would not sit well with the powerful members of the southern congressional delegations. And he felt that congressional approval of this new department and a black secretary would be even more difficult to secure if, before the vote, he issued an executive order on discrimination in housing (whose implementation would be supervised by the new department).

On a rainy Thanksgiving Day in 1961, Kennedy met with Ted Sorensen, Larry O'Brien, and Burke Marshall at his Hyannis Port home.

Robert Kennedy was there, too, playing touch football on the lawn with family and friends. The meeting focused on civil rights matters, including the housing order. Kennedy's promise to dispose of the matter with "a stroke of the pen" was coming back to haunt him. People began sending him pens in the mail (many called it the "ink for Jack" campaign), and Kennedy kept muttering good-naturedly about that phrase "a stroke of the pen," asking who had included it in his speeches (Harris Wofford was the culprit).

In this setting, Kennedy felt it necessary to decide once and for all the scope and timing of the order (there was no question that he would issue it). Periodically, Kennedy would call to his brother out the window to come in to give his thoughts. (Marshall later commented that "it was one of the few times the president got advised, any president got advised, by an attorney general on an important matter like this when the attorney general was just dripping wet in an old sweater, coming in from playing touch football in the rain."[86]) Ultimately, the decision was made to defer issuance of the housing order until the attempt could be made to secure congressional approval of the new cabinet department on urban affairs. It was also decided that the order, when issued, would extend only to housing actually financed by federal funds. (According to Sorensen, Kennedy decided that he "should make the order as broad as we were certain our writ would run and no further."[87])

The continued delay exacerbated the disappointment of those who looked to Kennedy for leadership on this matter. Criticism of the administration's restraint in the area of civil rights began to appear regularly in the nation's newspapers and magazines. Writing in *The Nation* in March 1962, Martin Luther King, Jr., reviewed the civil rights record of Kennedy's first year in office and found little to praise: "As the year unfolded, executive initiative became increasingly feeble, and the chilling prospect emerged of a general administration retreat."[88] Finally, on November 20, 1962—almost two years after his inauguration and a few months after Congress killed the proposal for new department of urban affairs—Kennedy issued the limited executive order (which ultimately proved to be so ineffective in preventing discrimination in the sale of housing that President Johnson decided not to renew it).

Throughout this whole period, Kennedy did not make one major speech explaining the need for the housing order, the complex considerations involved in determining its scope, or the reasons for the delay. Indeed, despite his campaign promises and the importance which civil rights groups attached to an effective executive order, Kennedy promulgated it with a minimum of fanfare. He simply included it as one announcement of three which he made at a press conference.

Kennedy's failure to use a major speech here was repeated in virtually every other civil rights action his administration took—except where a "crisis" demanded some public explanation. When mob violence threatened to prevent the admission of a black to the University of Mississippi in 1962 or the admission of two blacks to the University of Alabama in 1963, he would address the nation on civil rights. But not otherwise. By confining his speeches to such crises, Kennedy lost opportunities to impress upon the public the need for concerted action by the federal government to protect an individual's right to equal treatment under the law. He allowed a substantial portion of the public to believe—despite his statements to the contrary—that the crisis demanding a federal response was largely a local matter. For the very circumstances that pierced the public's apathy also afforded most people the luxury of believing that the difficulties actually were unique to the places where the crises occurred. Consequently, when Kennedy finally decided in the spring of 1963 to announce the urgency of broad civil rights legislation, he found a public inadequately informed and largely unsympathetic.

A series of Gallup polls of public opinion amply demonstrate this point. When Kennedy announced his intention to seek civil rights legislation in a nationally televised address on June 11, 1963, only one person in five throughout the country expected racial difficulties in his community. And while 46 percent of the nation's blacks believed Kennedy was moving too slowly on civil rights, the national consensus was quite different: 36 percent of the country already thought Kennedy was moving "too fast" on civil rights, while only 18 percent thought his actions were "not fast enough." (The remainder thought he was proceeding at a proper pace or had no opinion.)

Kennedy was aware of these public attitudes and the importance of his increased efforts in public education in the whole field of civil rights. He therefore initiated a series of off-the-record meetings at the White House with educators, businessmen, lawyers, civic organizations, and other leadership groups. More than seventeen hundred people attended these meetings, an unprecedented venture in the annals of presidential public education. Kennedy and other high-ranking administration officials spoke candidly about the need for broad legislation and, perhaps of greater significance, the need for voluntary efforts by these private groups to ease the transition to an integrated society.

The meetings did facilitate voluntary integration measures and the creation of specialized groups (such as the Lawyers Committee for Civil Rights Under Law). But the meetings—however successful in these spheres—did not overcome the lack of public education over the previous two and a half years. By August, half the nation believed that Kennedy was moving "too fast" in pushing integration; only 10 percent thought he was not moving fast enough. And 56 percent of the American public believed that blacks were treated as well as whites in their communities, while only 21 percent believed that blacks were not treated very well. Kennedy's general approval rating was also slipping.

For a politician acutely concerned with his narrow election in 1960 and who still maintained some anxieties about his reelection in 1964, it was indeed heartening to see Kennedy move forward despite this lukewarm public reaction. It is, of course, impossible to isolate and weigh each of the causes for that public response; but the polls do invite serious speculation that the public's support might have been much more favorable if he had only devoted more addresses to the civil rights issues in his first two and a half years.

The same lack of public education was also evident in matters concerning American involvement in Vietnam. Although Kennedy publicly discussed such involvement at various points during his presidency, there was never any clear exposition of the American purposes for being involved and never any clear statement of the circumstances under which American involvement would be terminated. Not that Kennedy was insensitive to the need for public understanding and support for his Vietnam policy. As early as August 1961, when the more militant of his advisers were pushing for the introduction of American combat troops into Southeast Asia, Kennedy asked of White House advisers Walt Rostow and General Maxwell Taylor, "By what means can we bring to world public opinion the action of the North Vietnam [sic] in Laos and Southern Vietnam? I agree with you that the groundwork has to be laid or otherwise any military action we take against Northern Vietnam will seem like aggression on our part."[89]

Some subsequent attempts were made to educate the public and lay this groundwork. But the limited efforts made were carefully designed to provide the administration with the widest latitude. When the administration was seriously considering the introduction of American troops into Vietnam, for instance, Kennedy tried to squelch speculation in the press that the administration was actively studying that option—Kennedy believed that excessive publicity would generate too much public opposition. And so when he decided, in November 1961, to send 3,200 American military advisers to Vietnam, the action was taken without the benefit of a presidential explanation.

Kennedy was not entirely mute on the subject. In his 1962 State of the Union Message, he explained to Congress and the American people that he was determined to protect the independence of the developing countries against communist aggression. Insofar as that determination concerned Vietnam, the President said simply that a "satisfactory settlement in Laos would also help to achieve and safeguard the peace in

Vietnam" and that the "systematic aggression now bleeding that country is not a 'war of liberation'—for Vietnam is already free. It is a war of attempted subjugation—and it will be resisted."[90] But there was no adequate explanation of the American purpose to be served by resisting that aggression. Was it merely to make South Vietnam secure against foreign attack? Was it to fulfill a moral commitment which the United States had to South Vietnam? Or was it to stop a wave of communist victories which might eventually reach America's shores? Or was it all three?

Chester Bowles, who had been transferred from the State Department to the White House staff in 1961, was among those who recognized the deficiencies in the public's grasp of Vietnam and other foreign policy issues. In a memo to Kennedy on January 17, 1962—less than a week after his State of the Union Message—Bowles told Kennedy, "One of the most critical problems facing this Administration in the field of foreign policy is the great and growing gap between the harsh, complex realities with which Washington policymakers must grapple and the generally limited understanding of these realities by most Americans, including the press and the Congress." Bowles advised Kennedy that if the gap were not narrowed he "may find it increasingly difficult to take many actions in the conduct of foreign policy that are essential to our national security."[91] A short time later, Bowles strongly urged Kennedy to make a major public speech explaining American policies in Vietnam.

Kennedy was sympathetic to Bowles's suggestion. But as the Vietnam conflict progressed and the involvement of the United States increased, Kennedy did not act on it or do anything else really to clarify the situation. At a press conference near the end of 1962, he was asked about discouraging reports from Vietnam. "Well, we are putting in a major effort in Vietnam," said Kennedy. But again he did not explain why. He said only that in "some phases, the military program has been quite successful. There is great difficulty, however, in fighting a guerrilla war. . . . So we don't see the end of the tunnel, but I must say I don't think it is darker than it was a year ago, and in some ways lighter."[92] In his 1963 State of the Union Message, delivered personally before Congress, Kennedy again did not state the purpose of American involvement clearly. He observed only that the "spearpoint of aggression has been blunted in Vietnam" and that American efforts would help preserve that nation's independence.[93]

The confusion was exacerbated in September when Kennedy was interviewed in the same week by Walter Cronkite on the new CBS national television news program and by David Brinkley and Chet Huntley on the new NBC national television news program. In the CBS interview, Kennedy told Cronkite and millions of American viewers that success in Vietnam would ultimately depend on the ability of the local government to win the allegiance and enlist the efforts of the native population; but he left no doubt about his intention to maintain American involvement: ". . . I don't agree with those who say we should withdraw. That would be a great mistake. . . . We took all this—made this effort to defend Europe. Now Europe is quite secure. We also have to participate—we may not like it—in the defense of Asia"[94] (what happened to the private assurances made to Mansfield?). And a few days later, Kennedy told Huntley and Brinkley that he had no intention of reducing American aid to Vietnam. Huntley then asked whether he had any doubts about the "domino theory." "No, I believe it. I believe it," Kennedy replied. "I think that the struggle is close enough. China is so large, looms so high just beyond the frontiers, that if South Vietnam went, it would not only give them an improved geographic position for a guerrilla assault on Malaya, but would also give the impression that the wave of the future *in southeast Asia* was China and the Communists. So I believe it." [95] For the millions of Americans watching the interview, the distinct impression was left that America was fighting to preserve the independence of Asia—but the relation between that independence and American national security was still unclear.

Kennedy's failure to use public addresses, or any other means, to explain fully the American involvement in Vietnam did not deprive him of public support for his actions. Indeed, throughout his presidency, the vast majority of America's newspapers and magazines maintained almost unswerving faith in his Vietnam policies. This was true even of those periodicals which would later join the vanguard of criticism of LBJ's Vietnam policies. As early as April 1961, for example, the *New York Times* editorialized that

> Vietnam today provides a particularly flagrant instance of [subversive aggression]. What amounts to an expeditionary force of thousands of armed agents from Communist North Vietnam, operating in conjunction with local Communist partisans, is engaged in South Vietnam in a deliberate and large-scale campaign to ruin and overthrow the Southern Government through sabotage, terrorist raids, assassinations and propaganda. . . .
>
> ****
>
> The free world must unceasingly protest against and oppose Communist subversive aggression, as practiced most acutely today in Southeast Asia. To accept it as a matter of course is to hand the Communists half a victory without a fight. [96]

And after Kennedy's interview with Cronkite in 1963, the *Times* criticized him for saying that the Vietnam conflict was "their" war; it is "our war," said the *Times,* "a war from which we cannot retreat and which we dare not lose."[97]

The widespread public support for Kennedy's Vietnam policies did not reflect the complete unavailability of the true facts. Numerous reporters—including many employed by the *Times*—provided the American people with detailed accounts of the indigenous character of the Vietcong guerrillas, the South Vietnam government's inability to retain the support of its own people, and the failure of American policies to really alter the situation. When the Pentagon Papers were leaked to the press years later, many people assumed that all the significant facts of our Vietnam policies were being disclosed for the first time. (Why else would the government try to stop publication?) This assumption in turn supported a widespread belief that the public had had no access in the 1960s to the truth concerning our Vietnam policies. In fact, this was not entirely so. Richard Harwood wrote in the *Washington Post* that "[T]he substance and in some cases the precise details of virtually everything the Washington *Post* and the New York *Times* have printed from the Pentagon papers is ancient history. It was nearly all published while it was happening." The problem, said Harwood, was that "neither the public nor the congressional politicians were listening."[98]

To some extent, Harwood is right. The public never did focus its attention on what was happening in Vietnam. (George Gallup did not conduct one poll on American opinion toward the Vietnam War while Kennedy was President.) And it is here that Kennedy's unwillingness to use public addresses to educate the public was particularly unfortunate. The people did not demand a full accounting by Kennedy on the issue, and for obvious reasons: there was no single "crisis" or dramatic event which seriously raised the matter in the public's mind—or Kennedy's for that matter. This, in turn, enabled him to shape policy without having to worry too much about public opposition. Not being pressured to explain his actions, he was content to invoke catchphrases and superficial analyses. It was not the assertive and foresighted leadership which Kennedy had promised; and the American people and their Presidents would pay dearly for the lag in their education on this issue.*

Kennedy himself seemed to sense the inadequacy of his Vietnam policies. Arthur Schlesinger, Jr., saw Kennedy shortly after South Vietnamese President Diem was deposed and murdered in November

---

*This is not to suggest that better public education efforts would have necessarily stayed Kennedy's, and later Johnson's hand in conducting the Vietnam war policies. After the Pentagon Papers were published in the spring of 1971, it was well publicized that those policies had rested on false assumptions and false hopes. And yet the American people tolerated Nixon's persistent use of deadly force in Vietnam—with continuing American casualties—for almost two years.

1963. Schlesinger recalled that Kennedy was very shaken by this turn of events, that "he realized that Vietnam was his great failure in foreign policy, and that he had never really given it his full attention"[99]—or, it might be added, brought it to the public's attention either.

As the experiences with civil rights and Vietnam demonstrated, Kennedy did not rely exclusively on public addresses to communicate his views to the American public. He also resorted frequently to the press to be an intermediary through which the issues would be raised, discussed and analyzed. During his tenure, for example, Kennedy conducted sixty-four press conferences (or an average of one conference every two or three weeks). Since these affairs were televised, they enabled Kennedy to make his points directly to the American people. If the occasion arose, Kennedy would therefore use the press conference to explain a particular problem and his response to it. Another advantage of this technique lay in the opportunity for Kennedy to answer reporters' specific questions about the matter, questions that might also be on the public's mind.

In general, the press conference was used with great effectiveness. One illustration of its success involved the attempt by the major steel companies, in April 1962, to raise steel prices in contravention of an understanding negotiated by the White House. Kennedy believed the increase would undermine his efforts to check the push of inflationary pressures on the economy. He consequently used an already scheduled press conference to express his outrage and to create public support for the actions he wanted to (and did) take to persuade the steel companies that the steel price increase would not serve the public interest or *their* interests (since it would result in decreased government benefits and decreased consumer confidence). Although some questioned the measures the administration employed to reverse the price increase, the public largely understood and endorsed Kennedy's reaction. As the *New York Times* editorialized after the steel companies finally agreed to rescind the price increase,

> The whole episode has provided powerful support for President Kennedy's theory that the White House has a duty to define the public interest in prices and wages while leaving the ultimate decisions to management and labor. The recent steel wage agreement provided no excuse for higher steel prices, and the President served the nation well by rebuking the major companies for shattering four years of price stability.[100]

Kennedy's press conference appearances were not always this successful in securing public support for his policies in specific matters. In trying to arrange a peaceful resolution of the conflict in Laos, for instance, Kennedy relied almost entirely on his press conferences in 1961 and 1962 to explain why it served American interests best to accept in Laos a neutral government which would include communist elements. While he would sometimes mention the problems in Laos in his major addresses, Kennedy never made one public speech devoted to an explanation for his policies in Laos.

There could be no doubt about the need for such an explanation. The policy toward Laos was something of a watershed in United States foreign policy—never before had an American President publicly endorsed creation of a neutral government with communist representatives. Not surprisingly, then, the basis of Kennedy's policy was subject to much criticism. There was vigorous disapproval in the media and in Congress of giving an American sanction to any government which included communists (although there was equally strong opposition to any policy which would result in sending thousands of American combat troops to Laos).

Kennedy's excessive reliance on press conferences here was a mistake. Although they created an impression among viewers that Kennedy was a capable, cool, and witty leader, the press conferences were usually broadcast in the late afternoons and were not seen by the much larger audiences an evening performance would have attracted. Moreover, the press conference—even with the charts which Kennedy often used to make his point—simply does not provide the drama of a major address made directly to the American people; it therefore is usually less effective in impressing the public with the need for a particular policy.

It may have been in Kennedy's political interest to downplay his Laotian policy (after all, dramatizing the issue would carry the risk of generating that much more public opposition). But the public reaction to his policy made at least one point clear: whatever the President's forum, there were limits on his ability alone to lay the foundation for public understanding of government policies and programs. Kennedy understood this, and it led him to try to use the press as an adjunct of his informational campaigns.

This is not to suggest that Kennedy would grant any reporter's request for information possessed by the government. Indeed, Kennedy was often very selective about the information he would publicly disclose, especially early in his administration. Like most presidents, he was simply reluctant to provide the news media with material which might become the bases of press criticism.

In March 1961, Arthur Schlesinger, Jr., wrote a memo to the President warning him about the dangers of this narrow approach. "There is increasing concern among our friends in the press about the alleged failure of the Administration to do as effective a job of public information and instruction as it should and must," Schlesinger wrote. He noted that Joseph Alsop, Walter Lippmann, Lester Markel of the *New York Times* and others were planning to express their disenchantment with the administration on this score and that it did not speak well of the President's efforts in public education. Schlesinger therefore urged Kennedy to instruct his administration officials to speak more openly with representatives of the news media, especially in domestic affairs. "Obviously this is a difficult matter," Schlesinger concluded. "One can't just open up the government to make Joe Alsop happy. But some kind of selective openness should be sought after."[101]

Kennedy was sensitive to this kind of criticism. But it did not entirely overcome his belief in government by secrecy, particularly where national security was concerned. Thus, he continually complained about the accounts of the Berlin negotiations being reported by Flora Lewis of the *Washington Post* and Sydney Gruson of the *New York Times*. Their explanation of the American positions did not always paint the administration in a favorable light, and this annoyed Kennedy to no end. They've got their facts all wrong, he would say, and they simply don't understand the political context in which we must work. Peter Lisagor of the *Chicago Daily News* once suggested to Kennedy that "the negotiations on Berlin wouldn't be so fouled up by Sidney [sic] Gruson and Flora Lewis if your Administration would open itself up and give the facts to the press here interested in them." But Kennedy would have none of that in a matter so sensitive as the fate of Berlin. "When the time comes, when the events ripen, when the situation grows to the point when we can conveniently and wisely release the facts," he told Lisagor, "we will give you the facts. You will get the facts in good time. Just trust us, be patient with us, and we will let you have the facts."[102]

This kind of condescension was hardly befitting a President who had promised to be frank with the American people about the "true dimensions" of the problems which confronted them. On many other occasions, on the other hand, Kennedy did frequently try to open channels of communication between the press and himself. He studied the circulation figures of America's periodicals. And he knew that the press played a basic role in shaping public attitudes; for the press helped establish the context in which issues would be debated and (hopefully) resolved by his administration. Where possible, he therefore tried to make himself accessible on a private basis to the press, to explain his attitude toward the major problems and to answer the questions which the media representative might have about the programs he had fashioned or would fashion to deal with those problems. "Press requests for legitimate information that used to stop at the desks of subordinates," *New York Times* columnist Arthur Krock wrote in November 1961, "are being fielded to the President in greater numbers than previously when he alone can supply authoritative answers and the news conference channel is not shortly available. And Mr. Kennedy's evaluation of the merit of such questions is fair and even generous."[103]

Kennedy did not approach his relations with the press in a disinterested manner. Although he knew it could not always be so, he wanted them to describe the issues as he saw them, to convey the sense of priorities which he had established, and to share his enthusiasm for the programs which his administration had proposed.* Many methods were employed to try to have the press educate the public along lines which the administration considered favorable. Among them were two-hour confidential meetings which Kennedy held monthly with selected publishers of a state. Identified as "Operation Publisher" within the White House, these meetings were described by journalism professor William L. Rivers as the "boldest and most successful instrument of Kennedy's press policy." The utility of these sessions was aptly suggested by the comment of one Republican publisher:

> Everything is handled in such an informal manner you feel at ease. The President asked us for our opinions on a number of matters. He told us he liked to have as much background as possible before making a decision. The President speaks so frankly about things that you get a feeling that he trusts you and is taking you into his confidence.[104]

It is doubtful that Kennedy really confided very much in these meetings. But there is little doubt that they helped to spur the kind of news coverage he sought.

Kennedy did not only resort to large, general meetings such as these to encourage a response from the press that would suit his own needs. More often than not, he relied on his close relationships with many of Washington's reporters and columnists to plant stories that would serve his interests. One area of which this was true was the economy. Upon assuming office, Kennedy was eager to reduce the 6.9 percent unemployment and stimulate economic growth in a nation still suffer-

*Sometimes Kennedy's efforts to communicate with the public extended beyond the usual use of the media. He was, for example, particularly eager to have John Frankenheimer make the movie *Seven Days in May,* a story about the Joint Chiefs' attempt to depose the President. Kennedy thought the movie would be a good warning to the nation about military extremism and told the director that he would go to Hyannis Port on those weekends when Frankenheimer wanted to shoot on location at the White House.

ing from the stagnation of a recession. As the months wore on, he became increasingly frustrated by his inability to develop public and congressional support for many of his economic policies. In this situation, he turned to the press and encouraged them in private to write about the economy. When Gilbert Harrison of *The New Republic* attended a White House function, for example, Kennedy approached him and said, "Now look, why aren't you writing something more about our economy?" Harrison replied that his magazine was planning an article on economic problems in a month or two. "That's too late," Kennedy responded. "You've got to do it now."[105] Kennedy was equally insistent with other journalists and the results were telling. As Hugh Sidey, White House correspondent for *Life* magazine, recalled, Kennedy "urged his friends in journalism to write more about the national economy, and in the final months of 1962 there was a mysterious outbreak of stories about balance of payments, new ideas for reporting the budget and the need for tax reduction and reform, and many were traceable back to the President."[106]

Kennedy employed this technique in other issues which he considered vital, such as international trade and nuclear testing, and this often helped create an atmosphere which he believed would facilitate public acceptance of his policies and programs.

However much Kennedy appreciated the importance of the press on these occasions, he was not always willing to accept the press's independence in making decisions on the information they would provide. If he had the freedom to suggest what they should discuss, he also felt he had the prerogative to tell them sometimes what they should not discuss. More often than not, the reasons were political. After the steel price increases were rescinded at Kennedy's urging, for instance, he was particularly sensitive about his future relations with the business community. He did not want the nation's businessmen to feel that the steel price affair implied a new mood of administration vindictiveness toward them. Consequently, he became concerned when he learned that a forthcoming CBS television news program was scheduled to include interviews with Walter Heller and Secretary of Commerce Luther Hodges which were critical of the steel industry. On the morning of the day the program was to be broadcast, CBS officials received a telephone call from a high White House aide who was with Kennedy in Palm Beach. "I am calling for the President," said the aide. "He would like these two interviews [with Heller and Hodges] dropped from the program."[107] After arguing, in vain, that the interviews would not hurt the administration politically, the CBS officials agreed and the interviews were withdrawn.

According to George Herman, then White House correspondent for

CBS News, CBS's action here was motivated by a concern that broadcast of the interviews would really antagonize Kennedy and jeopardize CBS's access to administration news sources. However justified this concern, the episode did not speak well of the news media's courage in defending its own rights and responsibilities. And it showed that Kennedy was willing to exploit his position to force the self-censorship of a press that was supposed to be free of government restraint. Nor was this an isolated incident. There were many other occasions in which Kennedy tried to discourage the printing or broadcasting of information which would create political difficulties. The best-known example is the reporting on Vietnam. Kennedy was continually irritated by the dispatches of Malcolm Browne and Peter Arnett of the Associated Press, Neil Sheehan of the United Press International, David Halberstam of the *New York Times,* and others who reported from Vietnam that the American effort had not enhanced the legitimacy of the South Vietnamese government or improved the prospects for peace and that, in fact, the war could easily continue for another ten years. Kennedy's irritation with these stories grew so strong that in 1963 he suggested to *New York Times* publisher Arthur Ochs Sulzberger that he transfer Halberstam to a less politically sensitive post. At another time, Kennedy had Washington lawyer Clark Clifford successfully persuade Philip Graham of the *Washington Post* not to publish a critical piece about the communications satellite agency, a quasi-government corporation set up by administration legislation. This was hardly the appropriate attitude for a President who, as a presidential candidate, had promised to provide the American people with the harsh facts about the consequences of American policies.

Sometimes Kennedy believed that legitimate national security interests warranted his requests for "restraint" on the part of the press. Immediately before the Bay of Pigs invasion, for example, he asked the *New York Times* to squelch a story which would have revealed the details of the plan. And when Gilbert Harrison inquired of Arthur Schlesinger whether *The New Republic* should publish a piece that also described the invasion plans with pinpoint accuracy, Schlesinger consulted with Kennedy and replied that it would be in the nation's best interests to stop publication. (Unbeknownst to Schlesinger, the author of the piece independently asked Harrison to withdraw it.)

Despite these attempts to censor accounts of the planned invasion, there were numerous press stories reporting the CIA training of the Cuban exiles in Guatemala and other facts which probably alerted Castro that something was afoot. Privately, Kennedy complained afterward that the invasion could not have succeeded when the whole world knew about the action being contemplated before it was actually executed. This reaction was reflected in his public comments as well. At a meeting of the American Newspaper Publishers Association in New York City two weeks after the invasion had fallen apart, Kennedy explicitly asked "every publisher, every editor, and every newsman in the nation to re-examine his own standards, and to recognize the nature of our country's peril." Although there had been no formal declaration of war, Kennedy said that the Cold War nonetheless posed a very real threat to the security of the nation:

> Our way of life is under attack. Those who make themselves our enemy are advancing around the globe. The survival of our friends is in danger. . . .
>
> If the press is awaiting a declaration of war before it imposes the self-discipline of combat conditions, then I can only say that no war ever posed a greater threat to our security. . . .
>
> . . . For we are opposed around the world by a monolithic and ruthless conspiracy that relies primarily on covert means for expanding its sphere of influence. . . .

In this context, said Kennedy, it was incumbent on every newspaper to ask not only "Is it news?" but also another question: "Is it in the interest of the national security?"[108]

Kennedy's plea for self-censorship on the part of the press was not, to say the least, well received. And for good reason. Newspapers and magazines lambasted the administration for seeking to weaken one of our political system's lasting strengths: a free and independent press. It was one thing to ask the press to withhold publication of specific information whose disclosure would expose the nation to attack or some other hostile action by a foreign power or somehow endanger lives; it was quite another thing to propose, as a general principle, that the press refrain from publishing stories which would reveal the facts—and with them the defects—of the administration's policies and actions in foreign affairs. Later, Kennedy recognized that he had overreacted to the press accounts of the Cuban invasion. "I should have realized," he told Kenneth O'Donnell and Dave Powers, "that there is no way of keeping a clandestine operation like this one a secret in a free democracy. And that's as it should be."[109] For all this remorse, Kennedy's old habits died hard. When Alfred Friendly of the *Washington Post* and James Reston of the *New York Times* learned of the planned quarantine of Cuba in October 1962, Kennedy personally requested—and received—assurances that their stories would not be published until after he had made his public announcement of the measure. To do otherwise, Kennedy argued, would have deprived the United States of the advantage of surprise in forcing a withdrawal of the Soviet missiles.

In the final analysis, then, Kennedy was very concerned with public education—but often only if it proceeded along lines which would not complicate his choices or, on occasion, disturb his political standing with select groups. Kennedy's efforts in public education were also inhibited by his fear of mass emotion as a lever by which to secure public support for his policies and programs. As Richard Neustadt observed, "What Kennedy also had was a distaste for preaching, really for the preachiness of politics, backed by a genuine distrust of mass emotion as a tool in politics."[110] Kennedy feared mass emotion principally because he knew that it was often irrational and could sometimes lead to excesses which were counterproductive (liberal criticism on his stand toward Joe McCarthy had sensitized him on this point).

Kennedy's ideas of public leadership were thus strongly fixed by his interpretations of history. Realizing that public comprehension of issues and ideas occurs slowly, Kennedy was persuaded to rely more on Congress than on the momentum of mass support. Such reliance was certainly justified, in part, by the nature of American society in the early 1960s. There seems little doubt, however, that Kennedy's reliance on Congress as the middleman to public leadership invoked a continuing check to policies which Kennedy considered crucial to the public's interests.

Leading the Congress

Providing leadership in Congress is no easy matter. Ensconced within the offices of Capitol Hill are 535 individuals—each with his own view of the nation's priorities, his own biases, and, perhaps most importantly, his own independent source of power. Seeking agreement by a majority of these individuals on a single piece of legislation—especially one which has broad impact on a wide variety of competing interests—will often require skillful negotiation. The President's difficulties in setting the nation's legislative agenda are compounded further by the very organization of the Congress. Anyone familiar with the operations of Capitol Hill can attest to the considerable power individual committee chairman wield over the fate of any legislation. On occasion, a determined and substantial group of congressional representatives can force the chairman to conduct hearings and report a bill to the floor. The reforms of the 93rd and 94th Congresses have made committee chairmen less dictatorial and more responsive to other committee members. But these reforms have not changed the situation entirely. From my own experience, I can recall numerous times when a bill on a major issue, supported by a majority of the Senate and an overwhelming majority of the public, languished in committee because the chairman opposed the measure and simply refused to act on it.

These problems in moving the Congress were particularly acute when John Kennedy entered the White House. In personally delivering the State of the Union message to a joint session of Congress on January 30, 1961, Kennedy said he spoke "in an hour of national peril and national opportunity. Before my term has ended, we shall have to test anew whether a nation organized and governed such as ours can endure. The outcome is by no means certain."[111] To most of the congressional representatives in attendance, this was probably news. For if the American political system was endangered, the source of the threat was not entirely clear. To them, as to their constituents, the problems confronting America were complex, and in some cases severe; but nowhere was there any tangible crisis that suggested the problems would paralyze and even engulf the American form of government.

It was equally clear to Congress that Kennedy had no public mandate to push for enactment of his legislative proposals, which included some far-reaching reforms. His selection over Richard Nixon as President had been by one of the narrowest popular margins in the nation's history. And there was no indication that his campaign views had inspired public support for congressmen and senators who shared them; indeed, twenty-two liberal congressmen who might have supported Kennedy's legislative program were defeated in their bids for reelection. The predominant mood in Congress was perhaps captured best by one Democratic congressman who told the *U.S. News and World Report,* "The people in Congress do not feel that they owe the President anything. A good many of them were elected in 1960 in spite of his presence on the ticket rather than because his name was there. They feel that they have more of a mandate for their point of view than he does for his program."[112] The 1960 congressional elections, in short, seemed to reflect a people that were more or less satisfied with their lives and not at all eager to see their President lobby Congress for the major changes proposed in the platforms of the Democratic Party. As Arthur Krock observed, "The close division of the popular vote will act as a restraint on legislation to carry out the extreme social-economic programs pledged by the Democrats."[113]

Kennedy's first encounters with Congress demonstrated the prophetic quality of Krock's comment. In meetings conducted shortly before his inauguration, Kennedy pressured House Speaker Sam Rayburn to propose that the membership of the House Rules Committee be expanded from twelve to fifteen members. Since the Rules Committee usually had the final say over whether a bill came to the floor for a vote, it was obviously important to have a majority sympathetic to the President's program. But that majority could not be secured unless the membership was expanded to allow Rayburn to stack the committee with members who would offset the existing conservative majority. Rayburn releuctantly agreed to fight for the proposal. And while Kennedy personally did little lobbying, everyone understood that the proposal was the new President's first test as to the willingness of the House to follow his leadership.* The proposal was adopted, but by a discouragingly close vote of 217 to 212. Although this assured Kennedy a favorable Rules Committee on most of his proposals, the close vote also suggested that it would be tough going once the measure got to the floor.

At the same time that the House was voting to expand the Rules Committee, the Senate was voting (by a close 50–46 margin) to retain the cloture rule. This rule assured that a determined minority in the Senate could prevent a vote on a bill which they opposed; debate could be terminated only upon the concurrence of two-thirds of those present. All this signified that controversial proposals—such as civil rights legislation—would not find smooth sailing in Congress.

Pressures to preserve the status quo magnified the weaknesses in Kennedy's personal style in dealing with members of Congress. Kennedy did not have Lyndon Johnson's fascination with the legislative maneuverings of Capitol Hill. He accepted the President's responsibility to act as a legislative leader (a responsibility which he felt Truman and Eisenhower had not properly met); and he would give Larry O'Brien and others on his congressional liaison staff all the time they requested on legislative matters. But he was unwilling to use the cajolery, the arm-twisting, and emotional appeals which LBJ later used so successfully in pushing Kennedy's legislative program and his own Great Society proposals.

Johnson felt comfortable dealing with legislators. Having spent

---

*In his first press conference, only days before the vote on the proposal, Kennedy was asked about his position. Kennedy said that under the Constitution each House of Congress has the power to decide its own rules and that he would not interfere with that process. "But it's no secret," he said, "that—I would strongly believe that the Members of the House should have an opportunity to vote themselves on the programs which we will present. . . . For example, we have the housing bill which is going to come before the Congress this year. We have an aid-to-education bill. We have legislation which will affect the income of farmers. Shouldn't the Members of the House themselves and not merely the members of the Rules Committee have a chance to vote on those measures? But the responsibility rests with the Members of the House," he added quickly, "and I would not attempt in any way to infringe upon that responsibility. I merely give my view as an interested citizen. [laughter]" John F. Kennedy, *Public Papers of the President* 11 (1961). In fact, Kennedy made only a couple of telephone calls to congressmen, insofar as I can determine. Larry O'Brien says he made one to Harold Cooley, dean of the North Carolina delegation; Frank Thompson, Jr., told me that Kennedy also called Robert Jones of Alabama.

twenty-three years in Congress as a representative or senator, he was intimately acquainted with its procedures and the people who roamed its halls. They were his colleagues, his friends, individuals who had shared his burdens as well as his liquor. The bonds were close, and he would not readily tolerate criticism from these people.* And, if the need arose, he would not hesitate to invoke their friendship to extract the support he wanted. Often he would invite a recalcitrant congressional representative and his wife over for dinner, reminisce about the political battles they may have fought together, fill him with food and drink, and then, as the evening was drawing to a close, place his arm around the legislator and say in tones which left no doubt about the answer, "I can count on your vote this week, can't I?" On other occasions, when there was not enough time (or room) to hold such social gatherings with key congressmen and senators, Johnson would not hesitate to summon a congressman to the White House or call him on the telephone and literally plead for his support on a bill that was coming up for a vote. "The country needs this measure," he would say, "and I am asking you, I'm begging you to put your local problems aside and look at the national interest. Don't desert your President in this time of national need."

LBJ's impressive string of legislative victories demonstrates the effectiveness of this approach. But it was one which was totally alien to Kennedy's method of lobbying Congress. He generally did not want to spend his time socializing with congressmen and senators, except when a specific White House function was planned.** And he was not willing to use his presidential perspective to plead with a congressman or a senator to support a presidential program. Ralph Dungan, who served on Kennedy's staff in the Senate and in the White House, found that "Kennedy's Congressional relations were marked by a formality and stiffness which, I believe, stemmed from the fact that he had never

---

*In the summer of 1967, Senator Thruston Morton of Kentucky criticized Johnson for delaying the dispatch of federal troops to Detroit, a city which had succumbed to vicious race riots. Morton suggested that there might be political reasons for the delay. Michigan Governor George Romney was a potential Republican presidential candidate, and the riots in Detroit did not make him look good. After Morton made this critical comment, Johnson quickly telephoned the senator and reportedly said, "How could you do this to me? We've been buddies for twenty years."

**One experienced lobbyist for Democratic programs told me that, in his view, one of Kennedy's great drawbacks in dealing with Congress was Jacqueline Kennedy. "She wouldn't entertain, wouldn't have any part of politics," the lobbyist said. "She just wasn't interested. And she made no bones about the fact that she didn't like politicians and didn't want them interfering with her private life. Jackie Kennedy was no asset at all."

really felt comfortable as a member of the legislature, nor did he personally identify with it. He was unwilling to pay the dues, so to speak, and felt something of an aloofness, if not disdain, for the legislative body."[114]

Kennedy's cool relations with Congress also reflected his somewhat fatalistic view that flattery and arm-twisting would be to no avail. "There's nothing that can be done about a man from a safe district," he used to say. "He'll vote the way he wants to." [115] From this perspective, it was not wise to expend his resources and time on a matter which did not promise victory (his whole upbringing cautioned him against fighting for matters he did not think he had a chance to win). "There is no sense," he once said, "in raising hell, and then not being successful. There is no sense in putting the office of the Presidency on the line on an issue, and then being defeated."[116] On most occasions, he therefore wanted to hoard his limited presidential capital for those matters which he deemed really important and which offered some hope of success.

This is not to suggest that Kennedy refused to meet with congressional representatives except under favorable conditions. Quite the contrary. He met in private frequently with senators and congressmen of all stripes on a wide variety of issues. But, more often than not, these meetings were not devoted to emotional pleas or ringing exhortations for the legislator's support. They were, as Larry O'Brien said, "soft sell sessions" in which Kennedy would explain his case for the proposal in a rational fashion and hope that the legislator would see the light as the President saw it. But he would not put the legislator on the spot by asking if his support could be expected. According to O'Brien, who ably headed the congressional liaison staff, "Kennedy rarely asked a member for his vote on a specific piece of legislation."[117] One illustrative case concerned Kennedy's attempts to secure the support of a powerful congressman on an agricultural subsidy bill the administration was trying to push through Congress. The congressman had never voted for such legislation, but Kennedy wanted to make an attempt nevertheless. He asked New Jersey Congressman Frank Thompson, Jr., to bring the other legislator to the White House one late afternoon for drinks. At the appointed hour, Kennedy made his pitch for the bill. As Thompson related the incident to me, the congressman listened to the President and then said, "Fuck it! I have never voted for an agricultural bill and I am not going to vote for this one. So why don't we just sit here and enjoy our drinks." With that, Kennedy threw his head back in laughter and then dropped the matter.

Kennedy's lack of aggressiveness in legislative matters was very apparent to the congressional representatives. "Kennedy didn't use drive," Senate Minority Leader Everett Dirksen told me in 1967. "He relied on persuasion and the force of his personality. Johnson has the empiricist quality—he glories in driving things through by twisting arms. Kennedy tried to rely entirely on the basis of the intrinsic merit of the request." When I asked Senator Hubert Humphrey, then the assistant Democratic Senate leader about this, he also replied, "No, Kennedy did not do the same kind of arm-twisting that Johnson did, to use your term." Senator Allen Ellender, one of the South's potent power brokers in Congress, likewise commented that "Kennedy was not as aggressive as he could have been, and personally I may be in error about this, but personally it's my belief that if Kennedy had lived, the program that Johnson afterwards put through would have never been enacted. . . . He was a little shy; he wasn't forward." [118] And Congressman Otto Passman, another southern baron whose position enabled him to undercut Kennedy's proposals for foreign aid, once related to me that he much admired Kennedy because he was a sincere individual who respected Passman's different views on the foreign aid program.

Senator Mansfield believed that Kennedy's deference to congressional views revealed him as "a man of great historical understanding" who "recognized the line which divided the executive from the legislative." [119] Perhaps. But whatever the characterization, there is no question that Kennedy's methods of legislative leadership restrained his hand in pushing measures which he regarded as too controversial and where he considered the prospects of defeat too high. And this restraint would be exercised even if it involved a matter where the need for legislation was pressing and Kennedy's commitment to act explicit. Civil rights legislation is the prime example.

Throughout his campaign Kennedy had made clear that he would use the full scope of his presidential powers to help right the wrongs of racial discrimination. Most assumed this included the proposal of legislation—mainly because Kennedy himself had spoken of the executive *and* legislative civil rights measures he would take as President. Moreover, the Democratic Platform on which he campaigned pledged the Democratic nominee to work for civil rights legislation. And during the campaign, Kennedy had asked Senator Joseph Clark of Pennsylvania and Congressman Emanuel Celler of New York to develop some civil rights legislative proposals.

After the campaign was over, Kennedy remained ever conscious of the commitments he had made on civil rights and other matters (in fact, he had his staff prepare books detailing the promises he had made during the campaign). Even before the inauguration, however, hints were being leaked from the new President's organization that he would initially rely more on executive powers than on the enactment of legislation to strike at racial discrimination. (NAACP director Roy Wilkins likened this to a quarterback announcing before a football game that he would not use a forward pass.) Despite this reluctance to push for civil rights legislation, Kennedy instructed Mike Feldman less than a month after the inaugural to work with Senator Clark and Representative Celler in drawing up legislation "to implement the civil rights commitments of the platform"; but Kennedy assumed that the administration would "have the fight next year after the hearings."[120]

As time progressed, Kennedy became more and more concerned about the wisdom of pushing for civil rights legislation during his first term. Under any circumstances, he knew it would be a bitter battle with the outcome not at all certain. He was also anxious to conserve his political capital with the Congress for other important legislative battles (such as on the Trade Expansion Act) where the chances of success loomed much brighter. All this anxiety was heightened in 1962 when the Senate could muster only forty-three votes (twenty-four shy of sure victory) to cut off debate on Mansfield's bill to end racial discrimination in the states' application of literacy tests for voters. Many legislators, such as Humphrey, continued to believe that Kennedy should propose comprehensive legislation. ("It wouldn't have hurt," Humphrey said, "and it might have helped.") But Mansfield—whose advice Kennedy greatly respected—told him that the Senate would "never again" pass civil rights legislation under a Democratic President because too many Republican votes were needed to get cloture. (Mansfield's concern with the Republican members of Congress was justified. After the administration's civil rights bill was introduced in the spring of 1963, one Democratic senator approached Dirksen in private, telling him the Democratic votes were lined up and asking whether the Republican votes were secure. "It's easier to line up votes on your side of the aisle," Dirksen replied. "I have to deal with some real sons of bitches.")

The pressures on Kennedy to introduce legislation, however, were increasing. Despite some successes in the courts and in the administrative agencies, progress in fighting racial discrimination was agonizingly slow on most fronts. Almost ten years after the Supreme Court's landmark decision in *Brown v. Topeka Board of Education,*[121] for example, desegregation in the South's public schools was moving at a snail's pace. Of the 2,900 school districts in the seventeen southern and border states, approximately 900 were "desegregated" (which meant they included at least one black and one white student) in 1961. By 1963, approximately 1150 schools were desegregated, but the number of black students attending schools with whites had increased from 6.9 percent only to 9.2 percent.

Public accommodations were another area in which executive action proved unsatisfactory. Although the Justice Department continued to file an unprecedented number of lawsuits to desegregate bus terminals, airports, railroad stations, and other public facilities, the stranglehold of racism remained firm. Neither the freedom rides of 1960 and 1961 nor the initiation of the lawsuits persuaded the white governors to open up their cities' doors and facilities to black and white alike. This refusal to treat blacks equally in public accommodations perplexed and angered Kennedy. Burke Marshall, who frequently discussed these matters with Kennedy, remembered that the "public accommodations section, that just made him mad really. He thought it was just outrageous to refuse to serve people because of their race. . . . He couldn't understand why anyone would want to refuse service to a Negro."[122] Indeed, when matters flared up into racial riots in Albany, Georgia, in the spring and summer of 1962, Kennedy could not understand why the white leaders then refused even to meet with the black leaders to discuss how the situation might be resolved peacefully. "Let me say that I find it wholly inexplicable," he said at a press conference in the summer of 1962, "why the City Council of Albany will not sit down with the citizens of Albany, who may be Negroes, and attempt to secure them, in a peaceful way, their rights. The United States Government is involved in sitting down at Geneva with the Soviet Union," he added. "I can't understand why the government of Albany . . . cannot do the same for American citizens."[123]

This, then, was how Kennedy looked at the civil rights issues. He did not view them in terms of laws violated or constitutional rights abused. He considered these issues almost exclusively in terms of their impact on human beings and what they reflected of human nature. It was not really a question of whether a black had a legal right to use the same restaurant or rest room as a white; it was a matter of human decency. And in his mind it was not really a question of whether racial segregation of public schools violated the Constitution's Equal Protection Clause; it was more a question of whether black children would have the same opportunity as white children to learn and to master professions of their own choosing.

The slow progress in civil rights matters was not a closely guarded secret either within the administration or among the public. And in both spheres pressures continued to mount for the President to take more drastic measures. In the Justice Department, for instance, there were frequent debates in 1962 and 1963 as to whether the President legally could, and politically should, simply suspend federal assistance to those states, such as Mississippi, where an official policy of racial discrimination was blatant and rampant (this, in fact, led to the creation of a department file entitled "Stick-It-To-Mississippi"). After all, the argument went, why should the federal government subsidize a practice that openly violated the Constitution and offended human sensibilities?

This argument had been advanced to Kennedy in a detailed legal memorandum submitted by the NAACP in the early months of 1961. And in April 1963 the Civil Rights Commission also recommended to Kennedy that he withhold federal funds from those states which used the funds in a racially discriminatory manner. Kennedy recoiled from the NAACP's advice in 1961, and he did the same when the Commission endorsed it in 1963. (They "ran away from it like it was a rattlesnake," said Roy Wilkins.*) In Kennedy's view, the President could not constitutionally withhold federal funds appropriated by Congress without congressional authorization and, in any event, he saw the power to withhold funds as a dangerous weapon for a president to use unilaterally. At one press conference in April 1963, Kennedy said flatly that he did not have the power to withhold funds and that "it would be unwise to give the President of the United States that kind of power because it could start in one State and for one reason or another it might be moved to another State which was not measuring up as the President would like to see it measure up in one way or another."[124] As he explained at another press conference a few days later, he was simply afraid that a president could use the power to achieve purposes other than an end to racial discrimination.[125]

These fears, and Kennedy's general reluctance to introduce broad, substantive legislation, began to fade as the racial riots in Alabama worsened.** He recognized that executive action alone was inadequate to deal with the magnitude of the problem. In late May 1963, after discussing the matter with his top White House advisers, Burke Marshall, and Robert Kennedy, he decided—largely on the attorney general's advice—that substantial civil rights legislation would have to be introduced. The congressional battles he had so much wanted to avoid would now have to be risked. There was simply no other way. He was

---

*However, Kennedy did accept in large measure the Civil Rights Commission's 1961 recommendation that federal funds be withheld from colleges that engaged in racial discrimination. In 1962, Kennedy approved the addition of an anti-discrimination clause in contracts for those colleges who received funds under the National Defense Educational Act. See memorandum from Harris Wofford to President Kennedy, January 23, 1962, President's Office Files, John F. Kennedy Library.

**Kennedy did propose civil rights legislation in February 1963. But virtually all of the civil rights leaders regarded these as very limited proposals. Basically, the proposals concerned discriminatory use of literacy tests by states in voter registration, the statutory extension of the Civil Rights Commission, and financial aid for schools in the process of desegregation.

convinced that the legislation would just have to be proposed—not because he thought his chances of success had improved but because he thought it was something he had to do.*

Having finally accepted his obligation to propose comprehensive legislation, Kennedy also recognized his special responsibility to provide the legislative leadership that would be necessary if there were to be any real hope of enactment. He met often with Mansfield to discuss strategy and the probability of success. Mansfield was skeptical, but Kennedy wanted him to push ahead. "You've got to get it done," Kennedy said. "It's the heart of the matter. These people are entitled to this consideration, and I'm depending on you to see that what I recommended is passed."[126] Mansfield prepared memoranda for Kennedy, outlining the details of who should introduce what, how it should be moved through Congress, and that, if necessary, he was "prepared to keep the Senate in session until January 1964."[127] On the basis of the advice of Mansfield and others, as well as his own knowledge, Kennedy also worked closely with the Republican leaders, especially Everett Dirksen, Charles Halleck, and William McCulloch, the ranking Republican in the House Judiciary Committee (which had jurisdiction over the legislation). One other person whose advice Kennedy frequently solicited on the civil rights legislation was Vice-President Johnson, and this requires some further explanation.

Whatever the reason for Kennedy's selection of Lyndon Johnson as his running mate in 1960, it was not because of a close personal relationship between them.** Both as a senator and as President, Kennedy's

---

*The principal sections of this comprehensive legislative proposal, which was introduced in the middle of June, included the substance of the February legislation as well as provisions which would ban racial discrimination in public accommodations, authorize the attorney general to initiate public school desegregation suits under certain circumstances, authorize the withholding of federal funds from programs which were operated in a racially discriminatory manner, extend the life and expand the powers of the Civil Rights Commission, establish a Community Relations Service to help mediate racial problems in particular communities, provide a statutory charter for the President's Committee on Equal Employment Opportunity, and provide additional funds for manpower training programs.

**Sorensen, who advised Kennedy on the selection of the vice-presidential nominee at the 1960 Democratic Convention, said the decision was based on LBJ's stature and the votes he could attract in the South: "As runner-up in the Presidential balloting (409 votes compared to Kennedy's 806), as leader of the party in the Senate, as candidate of the area most opposed to Kennedy, as spokesman for a large state that would be difficult for Kennedy to carry, Johnson was the strongest potential running mate and the logical man to be given 'first refusal' on the job." Sorensen, *Kennedy* 164 (1965). In explaining his choice to Gaylord Nelson, then governor of Wisconsin and a progressive leader concerned about the choice of LBJ, Kennedy did not emphasize Johnson's qualifications; he cited instead the great pressure that Johnson and House Speaker Sam Rayburn were ap-

relations with Johnson were rather formal and distant. Personal contact between them was not frequent, and their exchanges were not characterized by the easy conversation and light banter which marked Kennedy's relationships with his closer advisers. Kennedy nonetheless respected Johnson's views, particularly on civil rights, and appointed him chairman of the Committee on Equal Employment Opportunity, an executive group designed to increase minority employment opportunities in the federal government and with government contracters. Kennedy became deeply concerned about the federal government's efforts in this area, but he generally tried to leave Johnson a free hand in running the committee. Johnson, in turn, worked conscientiously to fulfill his responsibilities; and often he would tell Kennedy about the growing bitterness he found within the black community—not only because of job discrimination but also in response to the other indignities blacks were forced to endure in housing, schools, and other matters.[128]

After Kennedy decided to propose comprehensive civil rights legislation in the spring of 1963, he made a concerted effort to solicit Johnson's advice on the proposal. Initially, Kennedy dispatched Sorensen to discuss the matter with the Vice-President. (The attorney general simultaneously sent Burke Marshall to see Johnson for the same purpose.) Although Johnson had doubts about the political wisdom of introducing such legislation (he was afraid it could not pass and would succeed only in alienating the southern congressional leaders), he readily gave his opinions as to what the bill should include. From his perspective, it was essential that the bill incorporate far-reaching measures to improve the educational and employment opportunities for blacks. Kennedy considered these views carefully and discussed them with Johnson personally. And there is no doubt that those views had an impact. Sorensen, for example, credits Johnson with being largely responsible for the bill's inclusion of job training and vocational education provisions as well as a provision proposing a community relations service in the Justice Department to help mediate racial problems.[129]

Johnson's impact extended beyond the legislation, however. In response to the Vice-President's concerns, Kennedy himself dashed off a memo to Labor secretary Wirtz and HEW secretary Celebrezze in ear-

---

plying to have Johnson nominated for vice-president. "How successful could I be as President of the United States," Kennedy rhetorically asked Nelson, "if I had Sam Rayburn, the Speaker of the House, and Lyndon Johnson, the majority leader of the Senate, against me?" Interview with Gaylord Nelson, Oral History Project, John F. Kennedy Library, p.6. It is doubtful that Kennedy made his decision solely on this basis, but the comment does suggest that other factors may have been at work.

ly June 1963 to inquire about the administration's other efforts to improve employment opportunities for the country's black community. "The Vice-President feels, on the basis of his experience with the Committee on Equal Employment Opportunity, that the Federal Government should and could be doing much more to relieve Negro unemployment by additional and intensive job training programs for the unskilled, the illiterate and those on public welfare," Kennedy said. "I would like the two of you and your respective staffs—in consultation with the Vice President, to the extent that he is available—to review the adequacy of existing programs and current proposals to the Congress. . . ." Kennedy then asked the two Cabinet secretaries to report to him within six days the results of the study and specific recommendations for executive and legislative action.[130]

Johnson also attended most of the off-the-record White House meetings held that spring with community leaders concerning voluntary desegregation efforts. And sometimes he spoke at these meetings. "I thought he was very effective on occasion," Burke Marshall later said of Johnson's comments at these meetings. "Particularly I thought with the lawyers, you know, which you would not necessarily think would be his meat. I thought he was very effective, very good. . . . He spoke out of his own experience, he spoke as a Southerner, and he spoke of it as just a question of what was right."[131]

All this reflected not only Kennedy's reliance on Johnson; it also revealed Johnson's deep commitment to civil rights, a commitment which would become even clearer when Johnson, as president, labored hard to push Kennedy's civil rights bill through Congress. It is, of course, impossible to know whether Kennedy would have enjoyed the final success of Johnson in having the legislation enacted substantially intact in June 1964 (although Kennedy did lay much of the groundwork for Johnson—by October the House Judiciary Committee had approved the legislation). In any event, Kennedy was the one who broke the ice, and it showed that he could provide the legislative leadership on this issue which he had promised the electorate in 1960.

There were other occasions when Kennedy provided legislative leadership without waiting for his hand to be forced by events. Tax reduction as well as mental health and mental retardation legislation were two areas in which these initiatives ultimately proved successful. Another basic field in which presidential direction was offered involved international trade.

In the midst of the depression in the 1930s, President Roosevelt recognized that high protective tariffs impeded the nation's economic recovery by limiting our trade with foreign nations. At his urging, Congress had passed the Reciprocal Trade Agreements Act of 1934, which gave the President limited authority to negotiate a reciprocal reduction of tariffs with other countries on specific articles. This presidential authority was due to expire on June 30, 1962. Kennedy could easily have secured a congressional extension of that authority. But he wanted to expand it to facilitate an even greater reduction of tariffs on whole categories of products and to give him the necessary power to deal with the growing economic power of the Common Market.

An expansion of that authority would be far more difficult, he knew, for most congressional representatives are always concerned that decreased tariffs mean more inexpensive imports, and cheaper imports could threaten the survival of American industries within the representative's district or state. Despite these inherent obstacles, Kennedy was persuaded, largely at the urging of House Democratic whip Hale Boggs and Larry O'Brien, that he should make the attempt to achieve broader legislation. In his first special legislative message to Congress in 1962, Kennedy therefore proposed that the Reciprocal Trade Agreements Act be extended with two basic modifications: first, the President would have authority to reduce tariffs by 50 percent in whole categories of products, and, second, the President would have authority to eliminate tariffs altogether on those trade items where the United States and the Common Market controlled 80 percent of the market.

Kennedy argued that these changes would help stimulate economic growth in the United States as well as help offset the Soviet Union's growing trade with noncommunist nations (the specter of communism rarely lurked far away in justifying any foreign policy measure). But perhaps most importantly in Kennedy's eyes, enactment of the trade expansion bill would solidify the partnership of the United States with the European community. "The two great Atlantic markets will either grow together or they will grow apart," Kennedy told Congress. "The meaning and range of free economic choice will either be widened for the benefit of free men everywhere—or confused and constricted by new barriers and delays."[132]

Kennedy regarded the trade expansion bill as his top legislative priority in 1962. Some believed, as I do, that this was a political miscalculation. Arthur Schlesinger, Jr., explained to me, as he had written in his book, that he and other advisers argued vigorously with Kennedy that it was more important for him to concentrate his energies on other, more controversial matters—such as education, medicare, or civil rights—which would have more meaning for the American people than the trade bill. And other advisers, as well as some congressional members, cautioned Kennedy that a large part of the bill's effectiveness was dependent on England's entry into the Common Market—a condition which would require the acquiescence of the mercurial French president, Charles de Gaulle.

Kennedy nonetheless pushed ahead on the trade bill. He understood that the economic benefits, although substantial, would not be that significant. But, as a politician, his thinking focused on the political importance of the trade bill: an attempt to revive a sagging partnership between America and her European allies. As Sorensen recalled, "The President was never intimately interested, in my opinion, in the economics of trade, certainly not as much as he was interested in the politics of trade."[133]

Kennedy met frequently with congressional representatives, discussing the political and economic significance of the bill, negotiating certain provisions which might be of particular concern to a congressman or senator's constituency, and reassuring all that the bill's enactment would not endanger the viability of American industries. And the most assiduous efforts were made by Kennedy to secure the support of the appropriate legislative leaders, especially House Ways and Means Chairman Wilbur Mills, Senate Finance Committee Chairman Harry Byrd, and the very powerful Senator Robert Kerr of Oklahoma (who also sat on the Finance Committee). These intensive lobbying efforts bore fruit. The House passed the bill in the late summer of 1962 by a vote of 298–125, and the Senate passed it by a vote of 78–8.*

Kennedy's success in obtaining the enactment of the trade bill, or any other legislation, did not always or merely reflect his ability to persuade an individual legislator of the merits of the legislation. In congressional affairs, as perhaps with other business relationships, success in one matter is often dependent on collecting debts from other matters. Trade-offs are sometimes made whereby support is given for one bill in exchange for support on another. Sometimes the trade-off is explicit; other times it is implicit. But in legislative matters, it is often a factor to some extent.

Kennedy understood this and accepted it. He realized that his legislative leadership on some administration proposals would find less resistance from certain legislators if he acquiesced to other measures which those legislators deemed important. And he was, within limits, willing to play this game. There was the time, for example, when Charles Daly, a member of O'Brien's congressional liaison staff, wanted Kennedy to sign a bill to keep a particular congressman within the administration's fold. Kennedy read the bill and said, "Chuck, I just want to be sure you understand that this bill is a goddamn boondoggle." Daly replied that he knew that. As Kennedy signed the measure

---

*The exaltation of victory faded quickly, however. In January 1963, de Gaulle vetoed England's entry into the Common Market, thereby undercutting the President's ability to negotiate a reduction in tariffs with the Common Market countries. After that development, Kennedy lost much of his interest in international trade.

he responded, "Well, as long as you know that, and I know that, I think that's important."[134]

On occasion, the trade-offs involved compromises on fundamental matters. This, in turn, invited justified criticism that Kennedy was too willing to bargain away the public interest. The administration's handling of the communications satellite bill in 1962 is a case in point.

Kennedy always regarded the United States' development of communications satellites as a technological advance of major importance to the United States and the world generally. By making it possible to televise events and programs across the vast expanse of oceans and continents, the communications satellites could facilitate closer contact with nations separated by great distances. The satellites could also be used by the United States and other nations (especially the developing ones in Asia and Africa) to provide educational programs for great numbers of people who might be located hundreds of miles from the point of broadcast. In his first statement on communication satellite policy in the summer of 1961, Kennedy therefore declared that, in formulating institutional arrangements to develop and operate the satellites, the "public interest objectives [should] be given the highest priority."[135]

Kennedy nonetheless recommended that the ownership of the satellite program be private rather than public. This annoyed many legislators, especially Senators Russell Long of Louisiana, Estes Kefauver of Tennessee, and Wayne Morse of Oregon. They argued that a great deal of power and monetary profit was involved. Even with the safeguards proposed by Kennedy, they said it was myopic to expect a private corporation to give priority to the broad public interests. And, since the federal government would be investing billions of dollars in research and development, it did not make sense or good policy to consign the fruits of that investment to a privately owned corporation.

Kennedy was sympathetic to these arguments. But he was reluctant to proceed as those senators proposed. To begin with, he was anxious that the satellite program be enacted as soon as possible, but in any event within a year. As with many other major programs, he was afraid of being outdistanced by the Russians. And he was not about to lose that race by spending vast amounts of time haggling over the form of ownership. White House aide Lee White, who advised Kennedy on this matter, was one who recognized the importance of this factor. "Kennedy had been told, and I think he believed," White remarked to me, "that establishment of the communications satellite operation should be done right away, because if we didn't do it, the Russians would beat us. So he was not that much concerned with the issue of public versus private ownership. He was basically concerned with the practical problem of getting the thing set up as quickly as possible and beating the Russians."

Aside from this concern with the Soviet Union, Kennedy had two basic political problems. One was the business community. Private business groups (spearheaded by the American Telephone and Telegraph Company) were eager to control and reap the benefits of the satellite program. Not without some justification, the business groups argued that they had expertise in these matters and could operate the program more efficiently than the government. Whatever the merit of the argument, Kennedy did not want to alienate the business community, and this concern helped convince him to endorse a proposal that high administration officials privately conceded was "pro-business."[136]

But another, perhaps more important political problem was Senator Robert Kerr, one of the Senate's most powerful figures. Kennedy needed Kerr's support on many other measures—such as the Trade Expansion Act—which Kennedy viewed as crucial to his legislative program. And Kerr was pushing strenuously for a communications satellite corporation that would be privately owned. Kennedy did not want to buck Kerr on this point, and so he felt constrained to recommend something which would at least bear some semblance to Kerr's bill. In later discussing this legislative battle, Senator Mansfield remembered that Kennedy "became involved because of the fact that Senator Kerr pushed the bill and the Administration just couldn't get out of it." Although the administration proposal did not have "the wholehearted approval of the President," Mansfield explained why Kerr's views commanded so much influence in the White House:

> . . . we had to depend upon Kerr for a lot of legislation which came up that year because that was the year in which he was the strong man in the Senate. Much of the important legislation came out of the Finance Committee and without his support and leadership on these proposals we might have met with failure. As it was, because of his support and leadership, we were uniformly successful.[137]

Thus believing Kerr's support to be so essential, Kennedy worked with those senators who successfully terminated the filibuster being led by Long, Kefauver, and Morse for public ownership of the satellite program.* This paved the way for congressional passage of the ad-

*When cloture was voted on August 14, 1962, by a vote of 63–27, it represented the first time in thirty-five years that the Senate had voted to cut off debate. And it made many critics wonder out loud why the administration could secure cloture on a matter protecting business interests but not on a matter protecting people's civil rights.

ministration's bill. The measure was signed by Kennedy on October 11, 1962.

The trade-offs and compromises made with respect to the communications satellite bill were evident in other areas as well. During the campaign, Kennedy had made enactment of a minimum wage bill one of his priority legislative goals in 1961; and he pointed to the nation's 150,000 laundry workers (most of whom were black) as epitomizing the need for his leadership in securing that minimum wage legislation: "As long as the average wage for laundry women in the five largest cities is 65 cents an hour for a 48-hour week," he declared in Buffalo in September 1960, ". . . there is a need for our party."[138] Yet when the minimum wage bill was debated in the House of Representatives in the early months of 1961, Kennedy accepted an amendment which exempted laundryworkers from the bill's coverage. ("It washes laundries clean out of the picture," Representative Carl Vinson of Georgia gleefully told his colleagues.) From Kennedy's perspective, this compromise was necessary to obtain a favorable House vote on the whole bill. (The administration also argued, with some justification, that an increased minimum wage for laundry workers would accelerate automation in the industry and result in increased unemployment for them.)

And when he proposed in February 1961 that Congress enact a broad program of federal aid to education—another priority legislative goal for his first year as President—Kennedy made clear that he was adamantly opposed to any federal aid to parochial schools: "Well the Constitution clearly prohibits aid to the schools, to parochial schools," he said at a press conference a few days after submitting his education proposal. "Aid to the school is—there isn't any room for debate on that subject."[139] To a large extent, this clear statement of principle reflected more a political than a constitutional judgment on Kennedy's part. In campaigning to be the first Roman Catholic president of the United States, Kennedy had faced the religious issue squarely and said that his religious views would not affect his performance as chief executive; now he felt obligated to demonstrate the point by excluding any consideration of aid to parochial schools. Indeed, at a White House meeting with his advisers, Kennedy said he agreed with Congressman Frank Thompson, Jr., the sponsor of the administration's bill, who had said that, politically, it was better for the education bill to be defeated without aid to parochial schools than to pass with it. However much he may have agreed with Thompson's reasoning, it was also clear that Kennedy was anxious to have the bill enacted. For when his public statement of opposition ignited a vigorous, outspoken response by the Catholic Church and its supporters in Congress, Kennedy made a tactical retreat: at a press conference a week later, he said that Congress could debate the question of special purpose loans to parochial schools; his earlier remarks, he observed, had concerned only across-the-board grants to elementary and secondary schools.

In these and other situations, Kennedy was trying to deal with the political realities as he saw them. It is difficult to determine whether his compromises in these and other situations were really necessary to secure enactment of the particular legislative proposals.* But it would not be fair to infer from these compromises that Kennedy was entirely passive in his relations with Congress. On certain matters that he considered crucial, he was often willing to use the executive branch's resources to press Congress to accept his recommendations intact. Otto Passman, chairman of the House Appropriations Subcommittee on Foreign Aid, found, for example, that his proposals to cut the administration's foreign aid bill did not go unchallenged in 1961: "While I was presenting the subcommittee report in the full committee meeting, administration agents continued to place phone calls to committee members in the room. In the same meeting, letters from an Assistant Secretary of State to the members of the committee, all calling for more funds, were actually slipped under the door."[140]

And even when he expected congressional resistance, Kennedy was sometimes willing to take the initiatives which he had promised the electorate would be the mark of his legislative leadership. This was especially so toward the end of his tenure when his self-confidence began to grow. Thus, shortly before his death Kennedy authorized Walter Heller and Ted Sorensen to develop legislative proposals to be proposed in 1964 which would constitute a broad attack on poverty in America. Kennedy had read Michael Harrington's book *The Other America* describing the "invisible" poor people in the United States; and he was particularly impressed by Heller's memos which pointed out that the levels of poverty in America were being reduced at a rate slower than under Eisenhower.[141] Kennedy then accepted his duty to work for legislation which would help remedy the problem (although, in an apparent attempt to make these poverty proposals broadly acceptable to the American people and their representatives in Congress,

---

*The minimum wage bill was passed in the 87th Congress (1961–1962); the education bill was not. It has been argued that exempting laundry workers from the minimum wage bill was unnecessary and that the "retreat" on federal aid to parochial schools really complicated Kennedy's task in having Congress approve his recommendations on education. See Tom Wicker, *JFK and LBJ: The Influence of Personality on Politics* 25–148 (1968).

Kennedy also told Heller to include something in the proposals for middle-class Americans).

For all his initiatives and compromises, however, Kennedy's success with Congress was quite limited. He did secure enactment of or lay the groundwork for some important legislation—in trade, taxation, foreign aid, mental health, civil rights, and other matters. And when an administration proposal came to a vote on the floor of either the Senate or the House, Kennedy often saw his recommendation approved (Congress supported Kennedy's proposals on roll-call votes on the floor 81 percent of the time in 1961 and 85.4 percent of the time in 1962).

The problem was Kennedy's great difficulty in overcoming the opposition of the congressional barons who controlled the legislative committees. They were all men senior to him both in public service and in age (the average committee chairman was thirty years older than Kennedy). And both by temperament and political philosophy, few of them were receptive to the proposals emanating from the other end of Pennsylvania Avenue. As William Manchester observed in 1962, "Franklin Roosevelt was thwarted by nine old men. Kennedy must deal with a Congress full of them."[142] A measure of the committee chairmen's influence—and their disagreement with Kennedy—is reflected in some simple statistics. In 1961, only 48.4 percent of Kennedy's 355 specific legislative requests were approved; in 1962, only 44.6 percent of his 298 specific legislative requests were approved; and in 1963, only 27.2 percent of Kennedy's 401 requests were approved—at that time the lowest approval rating ever recorded by the prestigious publication *Congressional Quarterly.**

In many instances, Kennedy made little effort to overcome the near-

---

*Of these 1963 requests, ninety-one had received no action, thirty-four were rejected in committee or on the floor but could have been raised again, and twenty-eight were rejected finally.

To place Kennedy's record in context, it should be noted that Eisenhower had never made more than 234 specific legislative requests in any one year. In his best year (1953), 64.7 percent of his proposals had been approved by Congress; in his worst year (1960), Congress approved only 30.6 percent of his requests.

It should also be emphasized that the quality of Kennedy's legislative leadership cannot be gauged solely in quantitative terms. In a memorandum to Kennedy in September 1962, Larry O'Brien maintained that Congress had already approved seventy of the administration's 107 "major" proposals, as compared with Congress's approval of twenty-nine of Eisenhower's sixty-five "major" proposals in his first two years of office. O'Brien's list, of course, excludes an accounting of those measures—such as on civil rights and tax reduction—which Kennedy had not yet introduced because, among other reasons, congressional opposition had already been made clear. Memorandum from Lawrence F. O'Brien to President Kennedy, September 10, 1962, President's Office Files, John F. Kennedy Library.

omnipotence of the committee chairmen. But he knew the situation could only get worse if the 1962 midterm elections resulted in the defeat of some of his congressional supporters. He therefore traveled 19,000 miles in the fall of 1962 campaigning vigorously for congressional candidates who supported his legislative program. Many of his senior advisers had argued against this presidential involvement because midterm elections usually turned on local issues totally divorced from the Washington scene. (In a long memo studded with historical references, Schlesinger also pointed out that presidential campaigning had had only negligible effect on previous midterm elections.) But Kennedy viewed the matter differently. In a speech at the University of Pittsburgh, he observed, as he had in numerous other forums throughout the country, that "it is the responsibility of a President of the United States to have a program and to fight for it. . . . I do not believe that in this most critical and dangerous period that Presidents . . . should confine themselves to ceremonial occasions, ornamenting an office at a time when this country and this world need all of the energy and the action and the commitment to progress that [they] can possibly have."[143]

The 1962 congressional elections—which usually result in losses to the President's party—turned out well from Kennedy's perspective. The Republicans gained only two seats in the House and lost four in the Senate. So it appeared that the Congress of 1963 would be very much like the Congress of 1961. But as time would show, the new Congress was in fact far more resistant to the President's leadership. And this fact did not escape the attention of observers of national politics. One week before Kennedy's death, James Reston commented that Congress "has seldom appeared more futile, divided, confused, and morally indifferent than it does these days. It is not its legislative leadership alone that is so spotty—after eleven months there is still no indication that it will deal effectively with the problems of unemployment, education or civil rights—but its attitude toward public criticism is even worse." And, said Reston, the President had little basis to believe that matters would change for the better in the near future: "Representative government itself is increasingly the object of ridicule in the capital, but the men who have the power to improve it are either indifferent or helpless."[144]

The congressional impediments to the President's leadership loomed especially large in domestic affairs. By nature and history, Congress was far more able and willing to exercise restraints over the programs Kennedy proposed to deal with the material needs of the American people. Although legislation was often needed to implement the President's foreign policy decisions—whether through the appropriation of federal funds or the acceptance of treaties or some other measure—Congress was far less able or willing to restrict the President's actions or shape his policies in foreign affairs. But greater congressional abstinence here did not assure the effectiveness of Kennedy's leadership in international spheres.

Providing Leadership in World Affairs

International relations and world affairs are generally far removed from the average American's daily thoughts and concerns. Although most people have definite opinions on broad topics—the Arab oil embargo, the need to contain communism, or the importance of protecting American industries from inexpensive imports—few Americans dwell on exactly how basic policies should be formulated and implemented. And, unless some specific, dramatic event (such as the bombing of Pearl Harbor) commands their attention and emotions, the American people are, within limits, very malleable. They are extremely tolerant of a president's foreign policies, whatever they may be, so long as there is some plausible explanation for them and the costs to the American public are not too stiff.

The broad tolerance afforded the president in foreign affairs in some respects provides him with expansive opportunities to act in secret and to fashion policies without securing the same kind of public support which is usually necessary when he wants to obtain enactment of a domestic program. This is a natural development. The effective conduct of foreign policies is not often conducive, either practically or politically, to the popular constraints of a democracy. Alexis de Tocqueville took note of this in his classic study of the United States in the early nineteenth century:

> As for myself, I do not hesitate to say that it is especially in the conduct of their foreign relations that democracies appear to me decidedly inferior to other governments. . . . Foreign politics demand scarcely any of those qualities which are peculiar to a democracy; they require, on the contrary, the perfect use of almost all those in which it is deficient. . . . Democracy can only with great difficulty regulate the details of an important undertaking, persevere in a fixed design, and work out its execution in spite of serious obstacles. It cannot combine its measures with secrecy or await their consequences with patience. These are qualities which more especially belong to an individual or an aristocracy.[145]

The freedom with which a president forges the nation's foreign policies, of course, increases the chances that he will abuse his powers. The Founding Fathers recognized this risk. "The management of foreign relations," James Madison once wrote to Thomas Jefferson, "appears to be the most susceptible of abuse of all the trusts committed to a Government." This was so, he said, because information relating to foreign policies could "be concealed or disclosed, or disclosed in such parts and at such times as will best suit particular views."[146] The selective manner in which American presidents disclosed information about the Vietnam War demonstrates the prophetic quality of Madison's observation.

If Vietnam is proof that presidential powers can be abused, it also shows that the freedom to abuse power does not ensure the effectiveness of a president's leadership in world affairs. For a president's success in the international arena is even more dependent than in the domestic arena on people and events which are not easily moved by his hand. Ideals, circumstances, and other sovereigns compete with the president in his efforts to shape world politics—and often the competition proves to be too much.

John Kennedy appreciated these limitations on the President's ability to provide leadership in international affairs. Despite the glib comments which often dotted his campaign speeches, he knew that the world would not be totally responsive to an American president's touch. His sensitivity to these limitations was perhaps heightened after his first few months in the White House—a time during which he saw the Bay of Pigs invasion end in disaster, personally confronted the Russians' intransigence at Vienna, and struggled to help establish a neutral government in Laos. Speaking at the University of Washington in November 1961, Kennedy reminded his audience that

> we must face problems [in foreign affairs] which do not lend themselves to easy or quick or permanent solutions. And we must face the fact that the United States is neither omnipotent nor omniscient—that we are only 6 percent of the world's population—that we cannot impose our will upon the other 94 percent of mankind—that we cannot right every wrong or reverse each adversity—and that, therefore, there cannot be an American solution to every world problem.[147]

The limitations on the President's conduct in world politics did not dampen Kennedy's great enthusiasm for foreign policy matters. Even as a congressman and a senator (who sat on the Senate Foreign Relations Committee), he had a tremendous fascination with the interplay of foreign nations and foreign peoples. (Before he became President he told Sorensen that, if he had to make a choice for a cabinet post, he would most prefer to be secretary of state.) Indeed, McGeorge Bundy estimated that Kennedy spent most of his time in the first couple of months on national security affairs, and after a year it was reported that the President was spending 80 percent of his time on foreign policy matters, a trend which did not diminish much during the remainder of his presidency.

It is beyond the scope of my purposes to catalogue and analyze each of Kennedy's actions in conducting the United States' foreign policies. However, it is possible to isolate and assess some basic themes which dominated his foreign policy concerns. To be sure, almost every policy Kennedy adopted and almost every action he took in foreign affairs was calculated with an eye toward the communist menace, and especially the Soviet Union. Although other factors were, of course, considered—and sometimes preeminent in his thinking—he almost always accounted for how a particular action or policy would affect the nation's relations with the Soviet Union and in protecting the world from what he saw as communist subversion.

One of the major elements of Kennedy's leadership in world affairs, for example, was his keen interest in expanding the depth and mobility of the nation's military arsenal. Throughout his congressional years and presidential campaign, Kennedy had repeatedly stressed the importance of developing a weapons arsenal which could be used to defend the nation against attack, an arsenal that would be so strong that it would in fact deter an attack by any adversary (principally the Soviet Union). Thus, in Washington on September 20, 1960, Kennedy spoke of the need for a rapid increase in the nation's nuclear and conventional arms. "Only then," he said, "can we get Mr. Khrushchev and the Chinese communists to talk about disarmament, because having the second best defensive hand in the 1960's will be like having the second best poker hand."[148] Kennedy's focus on the so-called "missile gap" during the Eisenhower years was another outgrowth of this concern. Kennedy's emphasis on military preparednesss was so strong that Hanson Baldwin, one of the most respected reporters on military affairs, commented six days before the 1960 election that Kennedy "has put himself on the side of the military 'realists.' His election would seem to mean major changes and a larger defense budget."[149]

Much as expected, Kennedy carried through on his promise to pursue a military buildup. In his inaugural address he said of the nation's adversaries, "we dare not tempt them with weakness. For only when our arms are sufficient beyond doubt can we be certain beyond doubt that they will never be employed."[150] To fulfill this pledge, Kennedy requested and received additional billions of dollars in military appropriations from Congress. These added funds were used to increase not only the nation's nuclear strike strength but also the conventional forces.

Kennedy had often criticized Eisenhower's principal reliance on "massive retaliation" as a military deterrent—the notion that we needed only a strong nuclear force to protect our interests and dissuade the Soviet Union from attacking the United States. In Kennedy's eyes, this "strategic monism" had serious deficiencies: how, he asked, could the United States defend against attacks by combat troops in Europe or communist subversion in Asia without simultaneously risking a nuclear holocaust? The United States needed a wide range of military arms and forces which would enable it to respond to limited wars without resorting to nuclear weapons. As he wrote in the *Saturday Review* in September 1960,

> The notion that the free world can be protected simply by the threat of "massive retaliation" is no longer tenable. . . . Responsible leaders in the West will not and should not deal with limited aggression by unlimited weapons. . . . The central task of American and Western military policy is to make all forms of Communist aggression irrational and unattractive.[151]

The need for this military adaptability, Kennedy believed, was particularly great in fighting guerrilla warfare in the jungles of Asia. He was impressed by the argument of General Maxwell Taylor, Chairman of the Joint Chiefs of Staff under Eisenhower, that the nation should have the capability of a "flexible response," especially given the communists' sponsorship of guerrilla wars in which nuclear arms and conventional forces would be of limited utility. (Taylor resigned in protest in part because Eisenhower declined to accept his advice on this point.) Much to his pleasure, Kennedy moved into the White House only to find that the Eisenhower Administration had in fact prepared a tentative plan for the United States to create counterinsurgency forces for South Vietnam. The plan, of course, made sense to Kennedy and he approved it. Responding to the arguments of Taylor and his own biases, Kennedy also revived the Special Counter-Insurgency Forces of the United States Army and equipped them with green berets to signify the high status that would now be accorded to them.

All these early actions reflected attitudes which Kennedy brought to and nurtured in the White House. One must not only have strength; one must be willing to use it. Otherwise, the strength would not deter the adversary's hostile actions, and threats to use your military strength would not be taken seriously. "We increase our arms at a heavy cost," he said toward the end of his first year in office, "primarily to make certain that we will not have to use them. We must face up to the chance of war, if we are to maintain the peace."[152] Militance consequently was a major arm of Kennedy's foreign policies. He would consider using and make clear his willingness to use varied levels of armed force in any conflict which seemed to threaten vital American interests anywhere in the world. The Bay of Pigs, Berlin, Vietnam, and the Cuban missile crisis were among the fruits of this policy.

Even after the missile crisis had been resolved and the test ban treaty signed, Kennedy did not abandon his faith in a strong military arsenal and a willingness to use it to persuade an adversary that peace was a more profitable course. In remarks which he had prepared for delivery at the Trade Mart in Dallas on November 22, 1963, Kennedy had chosen to emphasize this theme once again. In discussing the nation's defense policies, Kennedy was to tell his audience, "Above all, words alone are not enough. The United States is a peaceful nation. And where our strength and determination are clear, our words need merely to convey conviction, not belligerence. If we are strong, our strength will speak for itself. If we are weak, words will be of no help." Kennedy planned to recall his forceful responses to the communists in Berlin, Laos, and Cuba and observe that "our successful defense of freedom was due not to the words we used, but to the strength we stood ready to use on behalf of the principles we stand ready to defend." This strength, he was to say, had been improved greatly under his presidency: a 50 percent increase in Polaris submarines, a 75 percent increase in Minuteman missiles, a 50 percent increase of strategic bombers on fifteen-minute alert, and a 100 percent increase in the total number of nuclear weapons available to the nation's strategic alert forces. These statistics, he was to say, did not account for the vast increases in our airlift capacity to Europe or the vast increases in our military assistance to friendly nations all over the world. Kennedy was to conclude that these statistics demonstrated that the United States did have the strength to respond to threats to the nation's security, threats which remained ever present: "Our adversaries have not abandoned their ambitions, our dangers have not diminished, our vigilance cannot be relaxed. But now we have the military, the scientific, and the economic strength to do whatever must be done for the preservation and promotion of freedom."[153]

Despite this almost obsessive concern with strengthening the nation's military muscle, Kennedy did not view armed might as an end in and of itself. He saw it as a means—not only to defend the peace, but also, in an ironic sense, to lay the foundation for efforts to control the use of arms. For he knew, both from reading history and witnessing it himself in Europe and in Indochina, that armed force was a stopgap measure which did not really eradicate the conditions which made war possible.

In his first message to Congress on defense matters, he stressed this point—even while requesting increases in the military arsenal. "The basic problems facing the world today," he said, "are not susceptible to a military solution. Neither our strategy nor our psychology as a nation—and certainly not our economy—must become dependent upon the permanent maintenance of a large military establishment. Our military posture must be sufficiently flexible and under control to be consistent with our efforts to explore all possibilities and to take every step to lessen tensions, to obtain peaceful solutions and to secure arms limitations."[154] And even while he was preparing to send 3,200 American military advisers to Vietnam in the fall of 1961, Kennedy had real reservations about the use of troops and planes to combat the problems of an explosive nationalism in Southeast Asia. "They want a force of American troops," he told Arthur Schlesinger at the time. "They say it's necessary in order to restore confidence and maintain morale. But it will be just like Berlin. The troops will march in; the bands will play; the crowds will cheer; and in four days everyone will have forgotten. Then we will be told we have to send in more troops. It's like taking a drink. The effect wears off, and you have to take another."[155] This attitude no doubt helped explain why Kennedy was reluctant to send combat troops to Laos or Vietnam and why in 1963 he rejected the advice of McGeorge Bundy and Henry Cabot Lodge, Jr., then the American ambassador to South Vietnam, that he initiate a selected bombing campaign in North Vietnam.

But his commitment to peace did not rest entirely on his reluctance to use armed force in certain instances. During his later Senate years and in the presidential campaign, he had said that any American president should give priority to disarmament and control matters. And when the Soviet Union and the United States agreed in 1958 to adopt a voluntary moratorium on nuclear testing, he applauded the action, saying that the dangers of nuclear testing "loom very large indeed in human and moral terms. Moreover, there is still much that we do not know—and too often in the past we have minimized these perils and shrugged aside these dangers, only to find that our estimates were faulty and the real dangers were worse than we knew."[156] As a presidential candidate, Kennedy therefore promised that, if elected, he would not be the first to break the moratorium by conducting atmospheric tests and that he would not conduct underground tests without exploring all reasonable opportunities to secure an agreement.

Kennedy never really regarded a disarmament agreement with the Soviet Union as a goal which could be achieved early in his tenure. Although he appointed the prestigious and hard-nosed Republican John J. McCloy as his chief adviser on disarmament matters, and while he believed that a disarmament agreement with the Soviet Union would be a fundamental step toward ensuring world peace, he was very skeptical that the Russians were willing to take that step. (In fact, at one meeting at Hyannis Port in the summer of 1961, Kennedy hurt Adlai Stevenson, who was arguing forcefully for a new disarmament proposal, by saying that he understood the "propaganda" effect of such a move—thus implying to Stevenson that he did not really care about disarmament.)

Kennedy thought the prospects for achieving a comprehensive nuclear test ban treaty were much brighter. Despite some snags at past negotiations under Eisenhower—especially the question of on-site inspections to ensure compliance with the ban—Kennedy believed the Russians would be receptive to realistic proposals to halt nuclear testing. Not only did the Russians have the same interests in avoiding a nuclear fallout, but an agreement signed by other nations would help discourage other countries from developing nuclear weapons and challenging the nuclear superiority of either the Soviet Union or the United States. Arthur Dean, the new American negotiator, was immediately dispatched to Geneva with refined proposals. But he soon found that the Russians were not as receptive as Kennedy had hoped—the American proposals for supervision were rejected outright since they did not reserve to the Soviet Union an absolute veto power. Despite this hardening of Russian attitudes, Khrushchev assured Kennedy at Vienna in June 1961 that the Soviet Union would not be the first to break the moratorium on nuclear testing. Believing that agreement was still possible, Kennedy ordered Dean back to Geneva with a new set of proposals and instructions "to outsit, outtalk and outlast the Russian negotiators (in what Dean had once privately called 'the bladder technique' of diplomacy) until he could find out for certain whether any glimmer of progress was possible."[157]

Meanwhile, Kennedy was under considerable pressure to resume nuclear testing, at least underground. The American public favored it by a better than two-to-one margin, and powerful voices within the Congress, the Pentagon, and the Atomic Energy Commission were telling Kennedy that the United States would forego its nuclear superiority over the Russians if it did not begin a new series of tests. Kennedy was not one to dismiss such predictions casually. He empaneled a group of leading scientists to study the matter and questioned them closely about the possible benefits of any new testing. The scientists were divided on the question and Kennedy, believing that the benefits were too uncertain and the political costs too high, postponed any decision—until the Soviet Union announced at the end of August that it would resume atmospheric nuclear tests on September 1.

Kennedy was annoyed and greatly disappointed with the Soviet decision. Khrushchev had given him his word, and now this. After some hasty consultations with British Prime Minister Macmillan (and after the first Soviet tests were conducted), Kennedy and Macmillan proposed to the Soviet Union an immediate halt to all atmospheric nuclear testing. The Russians rejected the proposal outright. Kennedy prepared to take action. He would not order atmospheric tests (there was no clear indication that they would be that much more fruitful than underground tests). But he felt that he had to do something. He could not let the American people, other nations, and most especially the Soviet Union believe that he could be deceived and made to look like an indecisive leader who could not stand up to the Russians. The resumption of underground nuclear tests seemed to be the only alternative, and on September 5 Kennedy ordered that that alternative be adopted. At a meeting later in the day on U.N. matters, Stevenson expressed his regret about the decision to resume testing. "What choice did we have?" Kennedy snapped back. "They had spit in our eye three times. We couldn't possibly sit back and do nothing at all. We had to do this." "But we were ahead in the propaganda battle," Stevenson remarked. "What does that mean?" Kennedy retorted. "I don't hear of any windows broken because of the Soviet decision. The neutrals have been terrible. The Russians made two tests *after* our note calling for a ban on atmospheric testing. Maybe they couldn't have stopped the first, but they could have stopped the second. . . . All this makes Khrushchev look pretty tough. He has had a succession of apparent victories—space, Cuba, the thirteenth of August [the Berlin Wall], though I don't myself regard this as a Soviet victory. He wants to give out the feeling that he has us on the run. The third test was a contemptuous response to our note. . . . Anyway, the decision has been made. I'm not saying it was the right decision. Who the hell knows? But it is the decision which has been taken."[158]

The Russian atmospheric tests and the resumption of underground tests by the United States only increased the pressures on Kennedy to order atmospheric tests. But, in January 1962, Sorensen wrote a memo to Kennedy pointing out that the public was evenly divided on the matter and that the majority of newspapers across the country wanted a resumption of atmospheric tests only for the most compelling reasons (he quoted or paraphrased editorials from some leading newspapers to make this point). Sorensen concluded by advising Kennedy that "your reservoir of goodwill (77%) is higher than that which enabled Eisenhower to withstand similar pressures from the same people who wanted him to resume while the Geneva talks were in progress."[159]

The pressures on Kennedy continued to mount, however, He was being told that the underground tests had produced only marginal results and that, while in the short run there was no immediate need to test in the atmosphere, in the long run such tests would be necessary if the United States were to keep abreast of Soviet developments. Under this pressure, Kennedy agreed—despite the persistent and vigorous entreatings of Macmillan—to resume atmospheric testing in the late spring of 1962. (Macmillan was later described as "a sad and embittered man" who said that Kennedy's decision would "shatter the hopes of millions of people across the earth."[160])

Kennedy's decision did not signify a renunciation of arms control as a major bastion of his foreign policy. He still had hopes that something could be worked out. In August 1962, he decided to send Arthur Dean back to Geneva with two sets of proposals for a test ban treaty: a comprehensive ban on all nuclear tests, and another proposal limited to a prohibition of atmospheric tests (implementation of the latter agreement would not require on-site inspections). The Cuban missile crisis galvanized the Soviet Union into becoming more responsive. In December 1962, Khrushchev wrote Kennedy a letter proposing that new energies be devoted to the negotiation of a nuclear test ban treaty. "It seems to me, Mr. President," the Soviet Premier said, "that the time has come now to put an end once and for all to nuclear tests, to draw a line through such tests." As a show of compromise, Khrushchev said the Soviet Union would accept two or three on-site inspections in a comprehensive treaty. Kennedy—who had been pushing for many more inspections—countered with an offer of eight. Although this was disconcerting to Khrushchev (who apparently believed that the United States would accept his offer), the ground was laid for initiating substantive discussions. Certainly the desire for success was mutual. Having brought the nation so close to war in the missile crisis, Kennedy was more anxious than ever to secure the test ban agreement because he thought it would help reduce the tensions of the Cold War (as well as eliminate the health hazards of nuclear fallout). "It may sound corny," he told Chester Bowles at the end of May 1963, "but I am thinking not so much of our world but the world that Caroline will live in." Even if he could "muster only ten votes in the Senate," he said he was determined to recommend adoption of the treaty.[161]

Despite the importance he attached to the subsequent agreement with the Soviet Union in July to ban all atmospheric nuclear tests, Kennedy was under no illusion that it represented the end of the adversary relationship with the Soviet Union. He viewed the treaty instead as a significant, if largely symbolic, move toward a relaxation of Cold War tensions. Sorensen remembered that Kennedy "took pains—partly for political reasons, perhaps, but also because it was his substantive belief—to warn the Administration and the general public against any smug feeling that the millennium had arrived and that everything would be rosy in our relations with the Russians from here on out.

. . . While he hoped for further agreement, he remained to the end extremely cautious in his expressions of optimism and extremely anxious not to lower our guard, even though tensions were, hopefully, lessened."[162] Senator Mansfield, who worked closely with Kennedy in devising the strategy to obtain Senate acceptance of the treaty, likewise found that Kennedy

> regarded it as a small step. He said something to the effect that if you're going to travel a mile, you've got at least to take that first step. He didn't expect great things of it, but he thought it might increase the thaw, might open paths which hitherto had remained closed, and might mark a beginning in a better relationship between the Soviet [Union] and ourselves. Most important of all, he thought it might give mankind as a whole some hope of not being subjected to nuclear destruction or radioactive fallout.[163]

Whatever the ultimate significance of the treaty, Kennedy remained convinced that his firmness—in Berlin, in Cuba, and in ordering a resumption of nuclear tests by the United States—had paved the way for it.* Without demonstrating his toughness, Kennedy believed, the Russians would have had little incentive to meet at the conference table. There is probably no way to prove beyond a doubt that Kennedy was right or wrong. The human condition is so complex that it is almost always difficult to explain the cause and effect of human behavior with precision—especially when it involves the assorted mix of politics, science, and emotions that was present in the efforts to secure a test ban treaty.

Nonetheless, there is reason to believe that Kennedy may have missed the mark and actually complicated his task in obtaining the treaty. By usually resorting to a "tough" posture in international developments, he may have encouraged the Russians to become even more intransigent in their refusal to negotiate in 1961 and 1962. For his

---

*Since the United States and the Soviet Union could not agree on the number of on-site inspections that would be adequate to supervise a ban on underground tests, the test ban treaty adopted did not ban underground tests. It has been argued that failure to include underground tests had two adverse consequences: first, it legitimized the use of underground tests (the United States in fact increased its underground testing program between 1963 and 1970); and, second, it removed the public pressure for a further agreement prohibiting underground tests. See Richard Walton, *Cold War and Counterrevolution: The Foreign Policy of John F. Kennedy* 157–60 (1972). Both points have some validity. But it is difficult to assign the consequences directly to Kennedy. He accepted the limited test ban treaty because, among other reasons, he thought it was the most he could get politically, and that it was important to accept a limited treaty instead of waiting for agreement on a comprehensive treaty. It is almost impossible to determine in hindsight whether that belief was justified. But, in any event, the failure of subsequent American and Soviet leaders to negotiate another agreement on underground tests is their responsibility, not Kennedy's.

firmness may have persuaded many Soviet leaders that he was a reckless warmonger who could not be trusted. Khrushchev told John McCloy in the summer of 1961, for example, that he was under a great deal of pressure from the hard-liners in the Kremlin to resume testing (much as Kennedy was under pressure from the Pentagon and elsewhere to resume testing) and that Kennedy's belligerent tone in his July 1961 speech on the Berlin crisis made those pressures almost impossible to resist. Kennedy did not always look at matters from this perspective (he felt he had been "burned" too many times). Throughout almost the entire course of developments, Kennedy therefore interpreted Soviet intentions in the worst possible light and then acted accordingly. As James Reston observed in an astute comment on Kennedy's decision to resume atmospheric tests in the spring of 1962, "the decision to test came down not primarily to a scientific but, essentially, to a philosophic point. The President had to decide not on the basis of unquestioned facts but on informed guesses whether to assume the worst of Soviet motives or the best, and in the end he decided that he had to assume the worst."[164]

Trying to understand and account for foreign leaders' motivations was equally important to Kennedy in another major area of his foreign policy initiatives: the desire to develop a full political and economic partnership with the United States' allies in Western Europe. In the aftermath of World War II, the United States had responded generously to Europe's defense and economic needs. The Marshall Plan had provided war-ravaged countries with the capital and technical assistance to move toward economic recovery; and the establishment of the North Atlantic Treaty Organization in 1949 had given Europe the umbrella of the American nuclear deterrent to protect against the apparent dangers of Soviet aggression.

By 1961, the need for American economic assistance had diminished—Europe had prospered in the 1950s and had become a powerful economic force in its own right. This development had been furthered by the creation of the Common Market in 1957, an economic union of France, West Germany, Italy, Belgium, the Netherlands, and Luxembourg. Many theoreticians in Europe and the United States, such as Jean Monnet and George Ball, Kennedy's Undersecretary of State for Economic Affairs, saw the Common Market as the embryo of the eventual formation of a European political union which would be able to compete on an equal footing with the United States in both economic and political affairs. In the meantime, the Common Market erected trade barriers with the non-Market countries (including the United States) by increasing tariffs while reducing tariffs for trade among themselves.

The strength of the NATO organization had also begun to wane when Kennedy assumed office. Although the United States continued to maintain a large contingent of American troops under the NATO command in Europe, and while the American nuclear strike force was still available to NATO (under strict American controls), questions had been raised in both Washington, D.C., and the European capitals about the distribution of responsibilities. The United States, on the one hand, felt that the European communities were not fulfilling their obligations to provide NATO with troops and financial support; this, in turn, meant that the United States was assuming a disproportionate share of the burdens with increasing strains on the American balance of payments.

Although the Europeans still viewed the Soviet Union with some apprehension, the situation seemed to have been stabilized, and most regarded a Soviet attack on Europe with conventional forces as highly unlikely. In this state of affairs, the Europeans regarded the nuclear deterrent of NATO as the only defensive tool of any consequence, and that deterrent was under the control of the United States. Pressures grew within European circles for the European nations either to acquire their own nuclear deterrent or to share in the control of the NATO deterrent (otherwise, some said, the defense of Europe would continue to depend on the American willingness to risk nuclear warfare—and who could say that the United States would want to assume that risk in protecting a European country from aggression).

Kennedy was sensitive to these economic and political questions. In his first State of the Union Message, he acknowledged the divisions and made clear his basic desire to strengthen the Atlantic alliance. "In Europe our alliances are unfulfilled and in some disarray," he said. "The unity of NATO has been weakened by economic rivalry and partially eroded by national interest. It has not yet fully mobilized its resources nor fully achieved a common outlook. Yet no Atlantic power can meet on its own the mutual problems now facing us in defense, foreign aid, monetary reserves, and a host of other areas; and the interests we share are among this Nation's most powerful assets."[165]

To revitalize the alliance, Kennedy moved in two complementary directions. First, he decided that he would support efforts to strengthen the Common Market and, in particular, England's desire to join that organization. This policy was fraught with economic risks for the United States, Kennedy knew; England's membership in the Common Market would increase the trade barriers for the United States and help the Market move into trading areas dominated by the United States. But Kennedy, ever the politician, was more concerned with the politics of the matter. He believed that the growth of the Common Market would bolster Europe's economic and political security, and this would make economic and political cooperation among the allies that much easier.* So when Kennedy met with French President Charles de Gaulle in Paris in May 1961, he raised the question of British entry into the Common Market. As the most dynamic political force in the European community, it was obviously necessary to have de Gaulle's support. And while the French general remained uncommitted, Kennedy left with hopes that de Gaulle would eventually accede to British membership (de Gaulle was concerned that England could not break her special relationships with the United States or the Commonwealth nations).

The second direction in which Kennedy moved to revive the Atlantic alliance involved control of the NATO forces, especially the nuclear deterrent. Kennedy was always concerned about the proliferation of nuclear weapons and so was not anxious, to say the least, to see any European nation acquire its own nuclear force. But he did understand the European desire for greater control over the NATO forces and, in particular, the nuclear deterrent. It was in this setting that Kennedy gave new life to an idea which had been originally conceived in the Eisenhower Administration: the multilateral force (MLF). The sponsors of the idea envisioned that submarines and ships armed with polaris missiles would be placed under joint control of NATO nations (with the United States still retaining the veto over their use). Kennedy mentioned the idea in Canada in the spring of 1961, and this gave new momentum to those in the administration who supported the idea. Kennedy, though, was not that enamored of the proposal and, since the United States would not relinquish its ultimate control, did not see why the Europeans would favor the proposal either.

In any event, the need for continued cooperation between the allies in economic and defense matters remained a central element of Kennedy's foreign policy. In an Independence Day address in Philadelphia in 1962, Kennedy spoke of the need to strengthen the Atlantic partnership (a "Declaration of Interdependence" he called it) for the benefit not only of the allies themselves but also the developing nations who required the economic and technical assistance which the United States and Europe could provide. As he explained at a press conference the next day:

> As I said yesterday, the first task is for Europe, in its own way and according to its own decisions, to complete its organization. When a decision is reached in regard to Great Britain's joining, which we

---

*Kennedy also pushed the Trade Expansion Act in 1962 so that the economic ties between the Common Market and the United States could be strengthened and the political alliance solidified.

> hope this summer, then, of course, this work will move ahead at a more accelerated pace. . . .
>
> * * * *
>
> My concern is that the relationship between Europe, using it in the single sense, and the United States, be intimate. . . . And, I'm hopeful that we can reach accommodations on the economic relations of trade, and also the problem of currencies and all the rest; on the problem of military policy; and then that we can emphasize, which I suggested yesterday, that we look outward.[166]

Kennedy's hopes of intimate relations with Europe were not to be realized in his presidency. In January 1963, de Gaulle vetoed British membership in the Common Market and simultaneously rejected the American offer of the polaris missiles which Kennedy had also offered Macmillan in the wake of the Skybolt affair. (France would develop and control her own defenses.) De Gaulle's actions irritated and puzzled Kennedy. He simply could not understand why the French leader—who was anxious to restore France's great role in history—would willingly rebuild his country on the ruins of the Atlantic alliance, an alliance that had served all the nations well for so many years. Charles E. (Chip) Bohlen, the experienced diplomat who was then the American ambassador to France, wrote from Paris that little could be done to improve the situation. "I can see no particular moves that we can make," he said, "beyond going on with day to day questions and matters as they come up."[167]

Kennedy could not accept the matter that fatalistically. He invited de Gaulle to visit the United States in the winter of 1964 (de Gaulle accepted) and, in a moment of exasperation, once called the French President directly on the telephone, only to come away more perplexed about the general's motivations. "I came to the conclusion," Kennedy told the French writer Jean Daniel on a sunny Washington afternoon in October 1963, "that General de Gaulle's strategy, which is rather incomprehensible to me, requires a certain amount of tension with the United States. It would seem that only through this tension is it possible to restore to Europe the desire to think for itself and renounce its torpid dependence on American dollar aid and political guidance!"[168]

If Kennedy had difficulties understanding the motivations of the nation's adversaries and European allies, he was, curiously enough, far more able to grasp those of the leaders in Latin America and the Third World, many of whom were aligned with neither the United States nor the Soviet Union. From his numerous world travels while he served in Congress, Kennedy had acquired a deep appreciation for the forces of nationalism that burned in Latin America, Africa, Asia, and elsewhere.

"We shall not always expect to find them supporting our view," Kennedy said of the developing nations in his inaugural address. "But we shall always hope to find them strongly supporting their own freedom. . . ."[169]

Kennedy also believed that it was in the United States' interests to help these countries remove the yoke of poverty even if they remained politically neutral. In proposing to Congress a reorganization of the American foreign aid program in March 1961, for example, Kennedy urged that substantial increases be made in American assistance to the developing nations. This assistance, he said, could thwart the advance of communism and thus help protect the United States' security. "But," he added, "the fundamental task of our foreign aid program in the 1960's is not negatively to fight Communism: Its fundamental task is to help make a historical demonstration that in the twentieth century, as in the nineteenth—in the southern half of the globe as in the north—economic growth and political democracy can develop hand in hand."[170]

All this represented a shift from the policies fathered in the Eisenhower Administration by Secretary of State John Foster Dulles, who saw foreign aid only as a tool to strengthen America's hand in fighting communists and who could not accept a nation's neutrality in the Cold War (he called neutrality "immoral"). The first test of Kennedy's commitment to this new policy to support a neutral nation's independence came early in his presidency. In fact, it was waiting for him when he arrived at the White House.

In July 1960, Belgium granted independence to the Congo, its former African colony. Within days a representative of the new Republic of the Congo, headed by President Joseph Kasavubu, was seated in the United Nations. From the beginning, Kasavubu made it clear that he would not commit the Congo to alliance with either the United States or the Soviet Union. All was not tranquil for the infant nation, however. Within a month the country split into three principal sections: Kasavubu's legitimate government; Patrice Lumumba's radical, procommunist faction; and that of conservative Moishe Tshombe in the copper-rich area of Katanga. With these three factions poised to destroy each other, the United Nations dispatched a peace force of fifteen thousand soldiers consisting largely of Indian troops. Matters became complicated when Lumumba, who had been receiving arms assistance from the Soviet Union, was assassinated in February 1961. Most suspected the complicity of Tshombe in the assassination. The Soviet Union urged the U.N. to take immediate military action against Tshombe and said that it would take matters into its own hands if the U.N. did not act quickly.

This situation posed some delicate problems for Kennedy. A large portion of the American public, the Congress, the State Department, and the Western European nations regarded Tshombe as a shrewd anticommunist leader who would protect the Western economic interests in the Congo's highly profitable copper mines. On the other hand, Kasavubu had been recognized by the U.N. as the legitimate head of State, and most of the emerging nations regarded him as the rightful leader of the new African country. All eyes were therefore on Kennedy to see whether he would support the U.N.'s recognition of the neutralist Kasavubu.

Kennedy understood the significance of the United States' position as a barometer of whether the new administration would really respect the independence of the neutral nations. And he knew his position would indicate whether he would make good on his campaign promises to lend the full weight of American prestige to the United Nations. At his fourth press conference, immediately following Lumumba's death, Kennedy left no doubt that he would fulfill his commitment. "The United States has suported and will continue to support the United Nations presence in the Congo," he said. "The United States considers that the only legal authority entitled to speak for the Congo as a whole is a government established under the Chief of State, President Kasavubu. . . ." With respect to the Soviet Union's threatened action, Kennedy added that the United States would support the U.N. fully in "opposing any attempt by any government to intervene unilaterally in the Congo."[171]

Kennedy never deviated from this endorsement of the U.N. and the Kasavubu government over the next two years, rebuffing pressures within the United States and Europe that he accord Tshombe some legitimacy.* By the beginning of 1963, the U.N. forces had overcome Tshombe's resistance and the Congo was reunified. Much of this was possible because of the United States' support. And there is no question that Kennedy's policy convinced many within the developing nations that he was sincerely dedicated to protecting the U.N. and the prerogative of a new nation to remain neutral.

The same dedication to helping foreign peoples achieve economic and political independence was also evident in Kennedy's relations with Latin America. He was sensitive to the deterioration of American

*In 1962, Kennedy rejected Tshombe's request for a visa to come to the United States to lobby for public support. Arthur Krock, who belonged to the racially discriminatory Metropolitan Club in Washington, D.C., criticized Kennedy's action. "I'll give Tshombe a visa," Kennedy later joked at a private gathering, "and Arthur can give him a dinner at the Metropolitan Club."

relations with Latin America, a growing bitterness dramatically underscored by the stoning of Vice-President Nixon by mobs in Venezuela in 1958. In an attempt to revive and further Franklin Roosevelt's Good Neighbor Policy, Kennedy proposed the Alliance for Progress—a multibillion-dollar aid program that sought to strike at the poverty, disease, and political repression which characterized many of the Latin American nations. It was envisioned that the Alliance for Progress would draw upon technical and capital investments from both public and private sources to meet specific economic plans designed by each participating country. And it was also understood that the program's success would require each country's implementation of basic economic and social reforms to ensure that the benefits were not confined to a wealthy few. Kennedy consequently introduced the program to Latin-American diplomats in March 1961 by stating that "the completion of our task will, of course, require the efforts of all the governments of our hemisphere. But the efforts of governments alone will never be enough. In the end, the people must choose and the people must help themselves. . . . Let us once again transform the American continent into a vast crucible of revolutionary ideas and efforts—a tribute to the power of the creative energies of free men and women—an example to all the world that liberty and progress walk hand in hand."[172]

This was all fine-sounding rhetoric, but during Kennedy's presidency the program never really approached the goals that had been established for it. The capital investment in countries never flowered; there was not much private investment from American sources; there was little economic or political reform in most countries; too often American officials were too willing to accept the perspectives of the ruling classes rather than push for the changes contemplated in the program; and although a few countries did well, the overall economic growth rate of Latin America in the 1960s was not higher than earlier decades—and much of that growth was absorbed by corresponding increases in population. In part, the failures reflected the State Department's inability to match the new program's innovative spirit with aggressive, creative administrators. "The Alianza has the same trouble as the Washington Nats [a perennial last-place baseball team]—they don't have the ballplayers," Dick Goodwin wrote to Kennedy in September 1963. "There are, of course, some very good people, but there is also a tremendous amount of mediocrity in high places. . . . The reasons for this are many but include: complete lack of a good recruiting effort, impossible personnel procedures, a structure which discourages individual initiative and responsibility, a careerist mentality, and an inability to recognize mediocrity when it is seen."[173] Another flaw in the Alliance program was a fundamental assumption on which it was premised: that the political aristocracy in Latin American countries would join forces with the campesinos and workers to initiate social reforms peacefully. As Michael Harrington later observed, "That seriously overestimated the reform potential of the Latin upper classes as well as their commitment to democracy and social change."[174]

Kennedy recognized the failures of the Alliance and publicly acknowledged them at his press conference on August 1, 1963. But he remained convinced that the thrust of the Alliance was sound policy. In a long interview with Jean Daniel shortly before he died, Kennedy explained the source of his deep-seated commitment to the program:

> I believe that there is no country in the world, including all the African regions, including any and all the countries under colonial domination, where economic colonization, humiliation and exploitation were worse than in Cuba, in part owing to my country's policies during the Batista regime. I believe that we created, built and manufactured the Castro movement out of whole cloth and without realizing it. I believe that the accumulation of these mistakes has jeopardized all of Latin America. The great aim of the Alliance for Progress is to reverse this unfortunate policy. This is one of the most, if not *the most,* important problems in American foreign policy.[175]

Thus did Kennedy make clear his view that repressive policies, which eventually alienate the local population, in the end do not serve American interests. It was a theme which threaded much of his foreign policies—although pressures to meet an immediate crisis often caused him to overlook it. Even in coping with the quagmires in Southeast Asia, Kennedy recognized—as he did when he was a congressman and senator—the importance of policies which would win the support of the people. In his second State of the Union Message to Congress in May 1961, Kennedy spoke of the countries threatened by communist subversion. "We would be badly mistaken to consider their problems in military terms alone," he observed.

> For no amount of arms and armies can help stabilize those governments which are unable or unwilling to achieve social and economic reform and development. Military pacts cannot help nations whose social injustice and economic chaos invite insurgency and penetration and subversion.
>
> The most skillful counter-guerrilla efforts cannot succeed where the local population is too caught up in its own misery to be concerned about the advance of communism.[176]

And in his nationally televised interview with Walter Cronkite more than two years later, Kennedy stressed the importance of support among the South Vietnamese people in thwarting communist aggression: "I don't think that unless a greater effort is made by the [South Vietnamese] Government to win popular support that the war can be won out there. In the final analysis, it is their war. They are the ones who have to win it or lose it. We can help them, we can give them equipment, we can send our men out there as advisers, but they have to win it, the people of Vietnam, against the Communists."[177]

This kind of comment underscored the basic duality of Kennedy's attitudes toward leadership in world affairs. On the one hand, he placed great faith in the use of military might to secure peace. And on the other hand, he knew that people could not be forced to fight for governments and policies they did not believe in. Peace and the willingness to defend it were ultimately matters of heart and mind.

This duality in attitude was reflected in Kennedy's actions. Wherever and whenever he perceived threats to American interests, he almost always stood ready to resort to armed force; and yet the imminence or initiation of hostilities also encouraged him to try to draw the warring factions to the conference table, to work out agreements and programs which would remove the incentive or need to fight. In this vein, Sorensen observed that the eagle in the presidential seal has arrows clasped in one claw and olive branches in the other and that Kennedy devoted equal energies to both the use of force and the use of peace initiatives. In fact, however, Kennedy was much more prone—especially in his first couple of years—to concentrate on the use of armed force, and there is much reason to believe that that emphasis burned some of his olive branches.

Despite the many compromises, crises, and failures in foreign policy or domestic policy, Kennedy generally remained in good standing with the vast majority of his constituencies in the United States and throughout the world. Almost always there was a deep reservoir of support which enabled him to retain the prestige and influence to exploit future opportunities. It was thus not only a question of whether he won or lost but how he looked when he played the game. To appreciate fully Kennedy's performance as President, it is therefore necessary to identify the images he inspired among his supporters and adversaries, images which often determined the extent to which people would be willing to follow his lead.

CHAPTER 4

The Presidential Images of John F. Kennedy

If you once forfeit the confidence of your fellow citizens, you can never regain their respect and esteem. It is true that you may fool all the people some of the time; you can even fool some of the people all the time; but you can't fool all of the people all the time.

Abraham Lincoln

The Images of a President: An Historical Perspective

Adlai Stevenson once said that a politician is a statesman who approaches every controversy with an open mouth. Certainly that is an opinion which many people have (and sometimes rightly so) of politicians. Too often political leaders appear to speak about problems before they have thought about them, to make judgments before considering the consequences.

No president wants to be perceived in this way—especially if he is concerned about being an effective leader. The reasons are fairly obvious. In trying to solve problems, the president will often need public support on matters which most people understand only dimly, if at all. He may also need the support of congressional representatives and foreign leaders who do not share his perspective on a specific issue. Much will depend, of course, on his abilities as a public educator. But to be a persuasive teacher—to the American people, the Congress, or even the world—a president must establish an atmosphere in which people are receptive to his analysis of the situation as well as to his conclusions as to what should be done. For as in any other classroom, the responses of these students is determined not only by the relevance of the teacher's lessons to their interests but also by the respect the students have for the teacher.

In other words, the president's effectiveness will frequently depend on the ways in which he is viewed by his constituencies. If they are to unify behind him in national adversity, if they are to rally behind the programs he proposes, if they are to tolerate his mistakes and omissions, then the president must win their confidence and earn their respect. To be sure, neither confidence nor respect can guarantee the president the support of any particular individual or group on any particular issue; nor will the absence of confidence and respect necessarily preclude the support the president needs. But confidence and respect can make the president's task in securing such support that much easier. Thus the fourth criterion in measuring a president's performance: Did he develop and use images of his presidency that inspired support for his policies and confidence in his leadership?

The president's image is not divorced from the other criteria for assessing presidential leadership; indeed, that image will largely be a composite reflection of the concepts the president relies on and the decisions he makes in fulfilling his responsibilities as a public leader. Nor is image something to be scorned as a public relations matter affecting the shadow but not the substance of power; in trying to persuade others to support him—whether in seeking legislation, in confronting a belligerent adversary or in negotiating an agreement to end armed conflict among nations—the president's image will often be a critical factor in determining his success.

Images are particularly important in the president's efforts to secure the American public's support for his programs and policies. Most Americans revere the presidency. They want their president to possess those virtues to which all men and women aspire. "A President should not only not be selfish," Calvin Coolidge once said, "but he ought to avoid the appearance of selfishness. The people would not have confidence in a man that appeared to be grasping for office." Which shows that, even earlier in the twentieth century, some recognized the value of a president who does not exhibit the weaknesses or deficiencies which are the mark of human nature.

In the wake of Watergate it can be and has been argued that the president should not be viewed in this light. He is simply an individual who, by some combination of skill, circumstance, and luck, has assumed the nation's highest political office. True enough. But in any society—and especially one as complex as ours—most people are likely to expect their chosen leader to embody characteristics which the position seems to require. And to some extent, this expectation is justified. For any people have a right to want and hope that the managers of their public affairs will be individuals with intelligence, sensitivity, and a sure sense of judgment.

In the past these hopes have encouraged people to place their presidents on a pedestal. Almost from the time they are thinking beings, American children are taught to view the American president as an individual who is a cut above other mortals. A 1960 study found, for instance, that children become conscious of the president early in their lives and that they usually possess an idealized picture of him as a person who is "the best in the world."[1] The reported reaction of a twelve-year-old boy in 1970 seemed to capture the essence of this idealized notion. "The President of the United States," the boy said, "is a man or a woman or whatever who is, like, picked by the people to head the country. And they try and make the person almost perfect. I mean, if he does anything wrong, they down him . . . because if a person is going to be the head of a country like the United States for four years, he just has to be just about perfect."[2]

To a large extent, this idealized perception of the president follows an individual from childhood to adulthood. Indeed, in his study of the "common man" in 1959, Robert Lane found that Congress is usually regarded as

> . . . an oral agency—the congressman's job is one of talking and listening, often quite informally. . . . Not so the President. He *studies* matters, something he can do alone. When he is with others, he *tells* them; he does not listen. . . . Congress is responsive; the President is autonomous. . . . Congress expresses the impulsive immediate needs; the President has a longer view. . . . The President offers a chance to fulfill the life goals of the nation. Perhaps this is the reason that in normal times they write to their congressmen, if they write at all. In times of national emergency they write to the President. . . . The President is a strong arm against the outside world; he is the national protector, and has the stature to be one. He cares deeply about what happens to the nation and the people and the values for which this country stands. Part of what makes the congressmen so appealing is that they are not so seriously committed in this way; they are more human. But what makes the President appealing is that he is not "all too human" like the rest of us; . . . He is supportive of whatever small heroic qualities we have in us, at the very least, of our moral selves.[3]

The urge—and sometimes need—for people to invest their president with these heroic qualities has mushroomed with the advent of television. The heroes of the mind are transfigured on the screen. The grandeur of the civics textbook is brought to life in the privacy of each individual's living room. The imagery and fantasy of history are thus made very real. For the president is, in a way, just another one of the many heroes who appear daily in the schedule of television programs. "As a result of continual exposure to television," one experienced television political consultant has written, "we have learned to project characteristics of our television heroes to our political heroes. We want them to be articulate and also look competent."[4]

Richard Nixon certainly understood this, and it probably helps explain why his 1972 campaign slogan was "Re-elect the President" and not "Re-elect Richard Nixon."* And it helps explain why Senator George McGovern, like previous presidential candidates who tried to challenge an incumbent, had great difficulty in campaigning against Nixon.** As Russell Baker observed in a column entitled, "Nobody Here But Us Presidents," on August 15, 1972 in the *New York Times,*

> Mr. McGovern wants to run against Richard M. Nixon. Of course, he believes Mr. Nixon would be easier to beat than the President, and he's probably right.
>
> Americans tend to like the President and dislike the people who oppose him. The President is one of those universally revered modern American institutions like Mother, Friday night, the flag, burgers, progress, and plenty of free parking which everybody assumes that all decent, right-thinking citizens approve of and support. Other countries have the cult of personality; we have the cult of the Presidency. "I may not like the man or anything he does," we say, "but I respect the office."[5]

Given this intense respect (awe?) for the office, the American public has had an insatiable curiosity about anything relating to the personal lives of the president and the first family. Those with short memories believe this fixation with presidential trivia came and ended with the Kennedys, who seemed so young, so vibrant, so intriguing. Not so. The public was deeply concerned about their president's personal life before that. In fact, the high moment in presidential trivia probably came

---

*Apparently, another reason for not using Nixon's name is that the White House advertising specialists found that there was something in Nixon's name which instinctively "turned people off." See Rather and Gates, *The Palace Guard* 242–43 (1974).

**In the twentieth century, only two incumbent presidents have been defeated for reelection: Taft in 1912 (when Theodore Roosevelt syphoned off many Republican votes by forming an independent party with himself as the candidate), and Hoover in 1932 (because of the depression).

under Eisenhower when James Hagerty, the President's press secretary, made the following announcement to 400 correspondents during Eisenhower's 1959 visit to London: "I have one bit of hard news. Mr. Berding [the State Department's press spokesman] was asked this morning if the President was sleeping in a four-poster bed, and the answer is yes, and also if he had ever slept before in a four-poster bed, and the answer is also yes." This bit of "hard news" inspired the following parody by Art Buchwald:

Q. "Jim, whose idea was it for the President to go to sleep?"

A. "It was the President's idea."

Q. "Did the President speak to anyone before retiring?"

A. "He spoke to the Secretary of State."

Q. "What did he say to the Secretary of State?"

A. "He said , 'Good night, Foster.' "

Q. "And what did the Secretary say to the President?"

A. "He said, 'Good night, Mr. President.' "[6]

The public's craze for presidential tidbits continues today. How else explain feature stories in respected periodicals after Mr. Ford's assumption of the presidential office about one reporter's "thrilling" experience in staying at the White House overnight, about the new dog acquired by the President's family, or about the details (with charts and all) of Mrs. Ford's cancer operation?

The concern with the President's private life—the image he casts as a person—helps to shape the way people view him as a political leader. This fact is evidenced in the reporting of presidential elections. A study of twenty newspapers in the last four weeks of the 1968 presidential campaign found, for example, that 97 percent of all presidential qualities discussed focused on personality traits rather than the individual's ability to handle the job or positions on specific issues.[7] The irony is that perhaps no President better appreciated the importance of presidential images—in getting elected and in governing—than Richard Nixon; and yet perhaps no President failed more miserably than he in forging the images which he believed necessary to his success.

Almost everyone remembers the famous debates between Kennedy and Nixon in the closing days of the 1960 presidential campaign. More than 70 million Americans viewed those four debates on television (millions more listened to them on the radio). The distinctions between the candidates' views on the issues were not that great. But most agreed that the debates helped dispel the argument that Kennedy was too young and too inexperienced to be President, that he lacked the poise to endure the burdens of presidential decisions. Kennedy looked cool, collected, self-confident, and knowledgeable. (In fact, subsequent opinion polls showed that those who watched the debates on television thought Kennedy had the edge; those who listened to them on radio thought they came out even.) While the significance of the debates in deciding the election result has not (and probably cannot) be finally determined, the candidates themselves accorded the debates an important role. "Looking back now on all four of them," Nixon wrote in 1962, "there can be no question but that Kennedy had gained more from the debates than I."[8] Kennedy basically agreed on the importance of using television: "We wouldn't have had a prayer without that gadget."[9] And afterward Nixon explained why Kennedy secured the advantage. "At the conclusion of our postmortem," Nixon said, "I recognized the basic mistake I had made. I had concentrated too much on substance and not enough on appearance."[10]

He did not repeat the mistake when he ran for President in 1968. He made sure that his appearances on television were carefully timed and planned to foster the image he most wanted to create. He wanted to be seen as a cool, collected, self-confident, and knowledgeable leader; in a word, he wanted to look like Kennedy. He would not submit to spontaneous press exchanges at his campaign headquarters or on "Meet the Press," "Issues and Answers," and other television interview programs; there was too much risk in that. He would instead answer prearranged questions from a prearranged (and obviously sympathetic) group of citizens. And always there was the effort to present himself as a dedicated statesman, an individual above the politics of the fight.

On occasion, this led to some embarrassing moments. There was the time, for example, when Nixon and George Romney, the Michigan governor who said he had been "brainwashed" by the Pentagon spokesman in his visit to Vietnam a few months earlier, were battling for Republican votes in the New Hampshire presidential primary in February 1968. When it was reported that Romney would probably announce his withdrawal from the race at a televised press conference, Nixon told an aide that he was not interested in watching the conference, even though Romney's withdrawal would virtually clear the way for Nixon's eventual nomination. Nixon said he had more important things to do; he was above the petty politics of the matter. As soon as Romney said he was withdrawing, the aide rushed over to Nixon's private hotel suite and burst in to tell Nixon the great news—only to find the candidate staring intently at the television as Romney explained the reasons for his withdrawal.

As a President, Nixon tried to sustain the fantasy that he did not care about how he was viewed. In March 1971, Barbara Walters conducted a rare interview with Nixon on the popular morning "Today" program on NBC television. "Are you worried about your image, Mr. President?" Walters inquired. "Not at all," Nixon told her and the millions of viewing Americans. "When Presidents begin to worry about images . . . do you know what happens? They become like the athletes, the football teams and the rest, who become so concerned about what is written about them and what is said about them that they don't play the game well. . . . The President, with the enormous responsibility that he has, must not be constantly preening in front of a mirror. . . . I don't worry about polls. I don't worry about images. . . . I never have."

But that, of course, was a lie. He was intensely concerned about his image. No President before Nixon had devoted as much attention—or public money—to his image and that of his administration. In November 1970, the Executive Branch's Office of Management and Budget estimated that the Nixon Administration employed 6,144 people in public relations matters (which included congressional relations) at an annual cost of $161 million. The White House itself employed about sixty people whose responsibility was image-making (some of these people were drafted right out of Madison Avenue's advertising firms); and every Saturday morning a group of Nixon's top PR advisers—Herb Klein, Ronald Ziegler, Charles Colson, among others—gathered as the Image Committee to discuss how to make their boss an appealing figure to the American electorate.

The enormous energies expended on, and the great significance Nixon attached to, his public image were exemplified when he prepared to travel to China almost a year after the Walters interview. I remember discussing the planning of that trip with a high State Department official. He was primarily interested in the historic breakthrough of an American president (especially *this* American president) traveling to China and establishing more normal diplomatic relations with our country's vocal nemesis of more than twenty years. The White House, the official said, was interested only in the impact the trip would have on the electorate's mind. Planning for the trip, he said, was like preparing a media blitz campaign for the advertising of a major new consumer product. Travel schedules were arranged, meetings planned, and events molded to coincide with prime-time television viewing hours. Not surprisingly, one White House aide described the China trip as "one of the most exciting events in TV history."[11] And indeed it was. For several days the American television audience was treated to almost nonstop coverage of virtually everything the President and Mrs.

Nixon did or said on this historic journey. As in other matters of presidential image, Art Buchwald was able to place the whole affair in some perspective after the trip was concluded:

> It was two days after President Nixon's return from China and the family went into the living room after dinner to watch television.
>
> My wife turned on the set and said, "That's funny. There seems to be something wrong with the T.V. I can't get President Nixon on the tube. . . ." "I can't understand it," I said, "President Nixon has been coming in loud and clear on prime time every evening. But tonight all I can get is a movie, Dean Martin, and a Lucy rerun."[12]

Nowhere was Nixon's concern with image probably more acute than with the Watergate affair. Spread throughout the transcripts of his conversations in the winter and spring of 1973 is evidence of Nixon's obvious interest in the public's actual and anticipated reaction to Watergate developments. But almost always he underestimated the public's growing curiosity, as well as the potential impact of the Senate Watergate Committee hearings. At one point in the middle of April—before the committee hearings began but after John Dean, Jeb Magruder, and others had started talking with the prosecutors—Nixon discussed with H. R. Haldeman the announcement he felt obligated to make: that, as a result of "new" information disclosed for the first time to him on March 21, 1973, he was making great progress in uncovering the truth. Nixon felt he should make the announcement as quietly as possible since Watergate was, in his view, not yet really a major news item and he did not want to make it one. "Well, in the country it is not that big," Nixon told Haldeman. "It is just a little bit in the evening news and it should be handled as a news story. I am not going to go on and say, look, we are in a hell of a shape. It will be a big news story, it will be a big story for a couple or three weeks. Let's face it. . . ."[13]

In the end, Nixon's involvement in the Watergate affair invited the widespread rebuke of the same electorate that only a year and a half earlier had reelected him by one of the largest popular margins in the nation's history. The public's disenchantment with Nixon reflected not only outrage at the sordid and illegal quality of many of his administration's activities; that disenchantment evolved also from the fact that Nixon had openly tarnished the image which most people did have and wanted to have of their President. This sin was also unacceptable.

Hopefully, the lessons of Watergate and the growing political sophistication of the nation's citizenry will introduce changes in the way the president is viewed. It is vitally important for the political health of the country that people be willing to scrutinize their president as just another human being who does not possess any mystical qualities, who is capable of making fundamental errors, who is heir to the same flaws of human nature that belong to all mankind.

Regardless of whether this new attitude takes hold, people will and should continue to expect a president to reflect certain basic qualities. And whether he retains or gains support on any particular matter may well depend on the president's ability to cast an image that incorporates those basic qualities.

To begin with, the people want their president to be an individual who has a high moral standard, who deals with issues in an honest manner, and who explains them to the American public in an honest fashion. No one likes to be deceived, especially when it concerns matters of great importance to the country and perhaps even the world.

Certainly this was a basic source of Dwight Eisenhower's immense popularity as President. (Except for a year-long period during the economic recession of 1958–1959, Eisenhower's approval rating never dipped much below 60 percent.) A novice at politics, Eisenhower had been elected to office in 1952 without proposing any fundamental alternatives to Harry Truman's Fair Deal programs. Nor did Eisenhower's speeches and campaign strategies offer much indication as to whether or not he would continue with Truman's policies. But the people had been impressed with the man who had organized the Allied military effort in Europe during World War II. He possessed those personal qualities the people deemed important. As Cabell Phillips observed, the nation had "voted only for a new face—the face of a simple, virtuous, warm-hearted folk hero whose promise was not to lead but to go along."[14]

The remarkable strength of Eisenhower's image was underscored by the fact that he did not consciously try to cultivate it by courting the mass media. Indeed, he had little regard for those who reported on his activities and policies to the American people. He rarely granted private interviews with reporters; and he did not pay much attention to what they said. "Listen!" he would say if a Cabinet member referred to a telecast or newspaper editorial. "Anyone who has time to listen to commentators or read columnists obviously doesn't have enough work to do."[15]

Unfortunately, Eisenhower was reluctant to use the wedge of his popular appeal to provide leadership in solving some of the country's most troublesome problems, especially civil rights. Although the Supreme Court had declared in 1954 that racial segregation in public schools was unconstitutional, he would not lend the great weight of his prestige in making the court's determination a reality for the nation's blacks in public schools or in any other sphere. He simply refused to tell the American people that he supported the court's action and that he would use the resources of his office to help make the transition from a segregated society to an integrated society. "I am convinced," he insisted forcefully to White House adviser Emmet John Hughes in 1956, "that the Supreme Court decision *set back* progress in the South *at least fifteen years*. . . . It's all very well to talk about school integration—if you remember you may be also talking about social *dis*integration. Feelings are deep on this, especially where children are involved. . . . We can't demand *perfection* in these moral questions. All we can do is keep working toward a goal and keep it high. And the fellow who tries to tell me that you can do these things by *force* is just plain *nuts*."[16] While Eisenhower's perception of the difficulties in protecting civil rights was perhaps accurate, his reaction left much to be desired. For his frequent indecisiveness on this fundamental issue represented a serious abdication of the President's obligation to provide moral leadership, an obligation he himself understood and accepted in theory.

Lyndon Johnson, in contrast, was rarely hesitant to use the presidential office to assert leadership on matters of domestic or foreign policy. But in so doing, he created the image of a President who would dissemble, confuse, and even deceive the American people about the actions he was taking in their name. This unflattering portrait did much to undermine popular support for Johnson and to cripple his effectiveness as a national leader. And, to a large extent, it was not difficult to understand how all this came about. There was, for example, the American intervention in the Dominican Republic.

On April 25, 1965, the pro-American government of Donald Reid Cabral was overthrown by military forces in a violent coup. The military rebels made clear immediately that they wanted to bring back as their leader Juan Bosch, the leftist President who had been overthrown in 1963. After a few days of widespread fighting in which many people were killed, the American ambassador cabled back to Washington that the 2,500 Americans in the country were in grave danger, that the President should send in American troops to ensure a safe evacuation of the American citizens, and that the President might want to consider using American force to prevent the establishment of "another Cuba" under Bosch. (Although Bosch was not a communist, his extreme left political views branded him as one in the eyes of most American officials.) After some hasty consultations with a few of his advisers, Johnson made a decision and explained it to the American people on the evening of April 28, 1965, over national television. His face grave, his manner solemn, Johnson announced that the

> United States Government has been informed by military authorities in the Dominican Republic that American lives are in danger. These authorities are no longer able to guarantee their safety and they have reported that the assistance of military personnel is now needed for that purpose.
>
> I have ordered the Secretary of Defense to put the necessary American troops ashore in order to give protection to hundreds of Americans who are still in the Dominican Republic and to escort them safely back to this country.[17]

Johnson added that the American military contingent would consist of 400 marines.

The fighting continued and the prospects of Bosch's ascension to power seemed much more probable. On the evening of May 2, 1965, Johnson made another nationally televised address to announce that he was increasing the American military force in the Dominican Republic to 14,500. Only this time he had a different explanation than the safe evacuation of Americans:

> The American nations cannot, must not, and will not permit the establishment of another Communist government in the Western Hemisphere. . . . We believe that change comes and we are glad it does, and it should come through peaceful process. But revolution in any country is a matter for that country to deal with. It becomes a matter calling for hemispheric action only—repeat—*only* when the object is the establishment of a communistic dictatorship.[18]

This switch in justifications for American military intervention did not sit well with much of the American public—not so much because they did not support American actions to thwart the advance of communism as because the switch left many people concerned that Johnson was not being entirely truthful. In a lead editorial in May, for example, *The New Republic* complained that the Johnson Administration "seems deliberately to have tried to conceal what its real motives were by insisting up to the last minute that protection of US citizens was the sole reason for having sent in troops. 'There was certainly nothing like that,' said Presidential Press Secretary Reedy the morning after, when asked if the aim was to prevent a Communist take-over."[19]

Public doubts about Johnson's veracity only increased when the

American military involvement in Vietnam was escalated. And for good reason. In August 1964, Johnson had demanded before national television that Congress authorize him to take retaliatory military measures against the North Vietnamese who, Johnson said, had gratuitously attacked two American destroyers in the Gulf of Tonkin off the coast of South Vietnam; Congress dutifully complied, rallying around the American flag and passing by near-unanimous votes (only Senators Ernest Gruening and Wayne Morse voted against it) a resolution which declared that Congress "approves and supports the determination of the President, as Commander in Chief, to take all necessary measures to repel any armed attack against the forces of the United States and to prevent further aggression." Within a couple of years, facts began to emerge in public indicating that the administration had prepared draft resolutions for introduction into Congress months before the Gulf of Tonkin incident and that the American destroyers had not been attacked at all. (What were they doing there in the first place?)

But this was not all. Immediately before and during the 1964 presidential campaign, Johnson—trying to draw a clear contrast between himself and his Republican opponent, Senator Barry Goldwater—had stated over and over again that the United States would not become involved in combat operations in Vietnam under his presidency. Thus, at Eufala, Oklahoma, on September 25, Johnson told his audience, "We don't want our American boys to do the fighting for Asian boys. We don't want to get involved in a nation with 700 million people and get tied down in a land war in Asia."[20] At Manchester, New Hampshire, a few days later, Johnson added: "We are not going north and drop bombs at this stage of the game, and we are not going south and run out . . ."[21] And at Akron, Ohio, on October 21, Johnson explained what he had already made clear to the American people: "Sometimes our folks get a little impatient. Sometimes they rattle their rockets some, and they bluff about their bombs. But we are not about to send American boys nine or ten thousand miles away from home to do what Asian boys ought to be doing for themselves."[22]

All this was, to say the least, a rather misleading picture of the future. By February 1965, Johnson authorized American bombers to raid North Vietnam in retaliation for guerrilla attacks on American soldiers in South Vietnam. (Johnson later told Tom Wicker that he had selected the bombing sites in October 1964.) Later the justification for the bombing changed—it was not for retaliation so much as to pressure North Vietnam to negotiate a cease fire settlement. Johnson also began dispatching more American soldiers to Vietnam, drafting more American boys, and then sending even more soldiers to Vietnam so that the

American military contingent in Vietnam numbered 180,000 by the end of 1965, 375,000 by the end of 1966, 425,000 by 1967, and 536,000 by 1968. These were not military advisers; these were combat troops.

Questions were naturally raised about whether Johnson had lied to the American people about his real intentions in 1964 and whether he was telling the truth when he explained the shifts in his policies. In May 1965, David Wise of the *New York Herald Tribune* suggested that Johnson may have a "credibility gap" with the American people. In December 1965, Murrey Marder of the *Washington Post* offered a detailed analysis of Johnson's public standing and said that there is "growing doubt and cynicism concerning Administration pronouncements. . . . The problem could be called a credibility gap."[23] By 1966, polls showed that 65 percent of the public believed that the Johnson Administration was not telling the American people enough about the Vietnam War. The feeling was widespread that Lyndon Johnson could not be trusted. The Washington bureau chief of one large west coast newspaper told me in 1967 with a great deal of vigor, "Johnson's a liar. Johnson would lie in your face every minute of the day if he could."*

Johnson's rapidly falling stock with the American people made it more difficult for him to secure public support for his Vietnam policies, made him vulnerable to challenges from within his own party, and ultimately forced him to withdraw from the 1968 presidential race. The effect spilled over into Nixon's administration. The University of Michigan's Institute for Social Research found that, while 64 percent of the public had a high degree of confidence in the federal government in 1964, only 35 percent had the same degree of confidence in 1970. By 1971, it was also reported that 69 percent of the American public felt the Nixon Administration was not telling the American people enough about the Vietnam War. This cynicism was so deeply ingrained in the public thinking that Nixon could not ignore it. On the night of April 7, 1971, Nixon appeared on national television to speak of his administration's Vietnam policies. The "Vietnamization" program, he said, was working; American troops would continue to be withdrawn. "I can assure you tonight with confidence," Nixon declared, "that American involvement in this war is coming to an end."

*The current jokes in Washington reflected this great public distrust of Johnson. One sample: "Do you know when Lyndon Johnson is telling the truth?" the person would ask. "Well, when he goes like this"—finger beside nose—"he's telling the truth. When he goes like this"—pulling an earlobe—"he's telling the truth. When he goes like this"—pulling the chin—"he's telling the truth." Then: "But when he starts moving his lips, that's when he's not telling the truth." Quoted in Eric Goldman, *The Tragedy of Lyndon Johnson* 410 (1969).

He then paused, looked directly at his audience, and added: "But can you believe this?"[24]

In part because he did make good on his promise—however slowly—to continue to withdraw American troops, he was largely able to retain public support for his Vietnam policies. Later it would be widely reported and fully known how Nixon had actually deceived the American people about his military policies in Southeast Asia (as well as in Watergate and other matters). But in the presidential election of 1972, the full scope of the deception had not yet been uncovered. And so Nixon was able to win reelection with a landslide vote. But his victory was not entirely of his own making. He had considerable help from the image of his Democratic opponent, Senator George McGovern.

The son of a South Dakota preacher, McGovern offered the electorate a clear alternative to Nixon's domestic and foreign policies. A principal problem for McGovern, however, was not only public controversy about the substance of his policies; a more fatal problem involved the image of himself which was forged in the public mind: that of an indecisive, fickle man who could not handle his own staff let alone the enormous burdens of the presidency. "If the Senator is wondering why he is making so little personal impact on the voters," Tom Wicker wrote of McGovern in the *New York Times* on September 24, 1972, "it may well be because many people no longer can be sure of who he is or where he stands."[25] (In reporting the next day that McGovern was trailing Nixon in public support by a 62 percent to 23 percent margin, pollster Daniel Yankelovich said that one reason for McGovern's poor showing "appeared to be a pronounced view among many voters that Mr. McGovern was radical and indecisive."[26])

There were probably many reasons why McGovern created this image, and some of them are fairly obvious. In the Democratic primary campaign, for example, he proposed a new welfare program which included a $1,000 minimum income for every family; and yet on national television he admitted that he was not entirely sure how the program would work or how much it would cost the American taxpayer. Amidst the ensuing public criticism, he modified the proposal.

And then there was the whole train of events involving the selection and ejection of Senator Thomas F. Eagleton as the Democratic vice-presidential nominee. Anyone who speaks to George McGovern can understand that he had good reason to act the way he did in this affair. But the impression created in public was not sympathetic. After it was disclosed that Eagleton had been treated for a nervous breakdown, many wondered why McGovern had not taken the necessary precautions to ensure that his running mate was healthy and mentally fit to be president (never mind that McGovern had followed the same procedures used by almost all twentieth-century presidential nominees and had acted on the recommendation of many well-respected Senate colleagues). When McGovern announced that he still stood behind Eagleton 1,000 percent, it was obviously the mark of a man acting from compassion, a man who would not desert his compatriot in the face of adversity. But when the public criticism continued unabated and it was clear that Eagleton's presence on the Democratic ticket endangered the chances for victory in November, McGovern firmly and publicly pressured him to withdraw from the race. The image of indecisiveness which this move inspired was only solidified when high Democratic campaign officials later began to complain and even resign in protest because there was so much confusion as to the distribution of responsibilities in the campaign organization McGovern headed.

Throughout all this, few could doubt that McGovern was a compassionate man who deeply believed in the basic premises of the programs and policies he proposed. But, unfortunately for him, the American people want more than that from their president. They want him to be strong-willed, decisive, capable of foreseeing the consequences of his choices, and able to inspire public confidence in his leadership. Thus, a 1968 study by one political scientist found that "[in] matters of style, the public seemed concerned primarily with elements of strength. . . . Compassion was hardly mentioned."[27] McGovern did not strike the appearance of a strong leader who knew his own mind; whatever else you can say about him, Nixon did, and the 1972 electoral vote reflected this difference in image.

Perhaps no President better demonstrated the power of an image of strength than Franklin D. Roosevelt. From his very first day in office he exuded a sense of self-confidence about his legislative proposals and the ability of the nation to withstand ultimately the strains of depression. Although his programs and policies were not always as effective as he said they would be, the economy did improve and there was always hope that the future would see greater gains. In his masterful study of the New Deal, Arthur Schlesinger, Jr., touched on this quality of Roosevelt's leadership:

> His greatest resource lay not in charm of manner or skill at persuasion. It lay in his ability to stir idealism in people's souls. . . . Beyond the background of the depression and the deeds of the New Deal, Roosevelt gained his popular strength from that union of personality and public idealism which he joined so irresistibly to create so profoundly compelling a national image.[28]

He was, in a word, a leader who could be trusted to deal with the people's problems in a decisive and honest fashion. And this was a major factor in explaining his ability to secure public support for his administration's changing policies and programs. "I never met him," many people told John Gunther shortly after FDR's death, "but I feel as if I had lost my greatest friend."[29]

In the end, it has not been and probably is not necessary for a president to be loved or even liked as friend—although such feelings can rarely hurt him. It is far more important that the president be trusted and respected as an individual qualified to be the nation's chief executive in every sense of the term. And having an image that inspires trust and respect will make it that much easier for the president to enjoy the support of the American people, the Congress, and even other nations in any endeavor. Because although it often is not true, many people believe you *can* judge a book by its cover.

John F. Kennedy: Inspiring the Public

The public longing for presidential inspiration was apparent in many quarters in 1960 as Americans prepared to choose another president. Although Eisenhower remained quite popular with large segments of the population, there was an underlying feeling of stagnation, of alienation which permeated the American way of life. Americans had become an extremely mobile people—geographically, economically, and socially—and yet something was missing. Beatniks appeared in Greenwich Village, Jack Kerouac appeared in print, and the Russian sputniks appeared on the television screen. Something more was needed. In his celebrated article in *Esquire* magazine, "Superman Comes to the Supermarket"—a piece about the 1960 Democratic Convention at Los Angeles—Norman Mailer touched this exposed nerve of American life:

> Yes, the life of politics and the life of the myth had diverged too far. There was nothing to return them to one another, no common danger, no cause, no desire, and most essentially, no hero. It was a hero America needed, a hero central to his time, a man whose personality might suggest contradictions and mysteries which could reach into the alienated circuits of the underground, because only a hero can capture the secret imagination of a people, and so be good for the vitality of his nation; a hero embodies the fantasy and so allows each private mind the liberty to consider its fantasy and find a way to grow.[30]

It was in this atmosphere that John F. Kennedy was elected President of the United States. And although his margin of victory was narrow, that would soon be largely forgotten (except perhaps by some in Congress and those in Kennedy's circle who were already looking to

1964). He was now the nation's leader—a vigorous, youthful-looking one at that (who spoke with an accent then unfamiliar to the public at large)—and he would be entitled to all the physical and psychological trappings that went with the position.

John Kennedy entered office confident of his ability to be a good president and determined to communicate that self-confidence to the public. He understood the importance of a president's image. And he did not want to let the people down, not only for their sake but for his as well. Many more experienced politicians tried to caution the new leader that the job was tougher than he imagined; and while his political talents were generally conceded to be substantial, many people still wondered whether he could be an effective president. But Kennedy scoffed at such speculation. "Sure, it's a big job," he told Time-Life correspondent Hugh Sidey in the privacy of his Georgetown home a month before the inauguration. "But I don't know anybody who can do it any better than I can. I'm going to be in it for four years. . . . It isn't going to be so bad. You've got time to think. You don't have all those people bothering you that you had in the Senate—besides the pay is pretty good."[31]

It was the kind of self-assurance which would be a Kennedy trademark as President, and almost everyone inside and outside government would take note of it—the detached but confident appraisal, the cool composure, even under intense pressure. "Kennedy had something of a buccaneer attitude," I was told by one White House staff person who did not get to know him until the 1960 campaign. "From his almost aristocratic upbringing, all his fucking around, his accomplishments—it seemed he was always in control of himself and the situation." Others in government who were not close to Kennedy had much the same impression. House Democratic Whip Hale Boggs remembered that October afternoon in 1962 when Kennedy explained to a group of senators and congressmen the decision to quarantine Cuba, a decision designed to force removal of the Soviet missiles being installed. There was a great deal of tension. "And the calmest man in the whole United States of America was John F. Kennedy," said Boggs. ". . . And he was so completely convinced of the rightness of his course that there was no evidence whatsoever of strain or nervousness or of tension about the man. And this, in itself, was tremendously inspiring because when you are in a period of real crisis you look, then, to your leadership. And if your leader is nervous and upset and tense this translates itself to everyone else and you in time translate that feeling to other people. So there came from the White House during that period this sense of complete confidence . . ."[32] Undersecretary of State U. Alexis Johnson, who was a member of the group that hammered out the plan for the quarantine, agreed with Boggs. Kennedy "always gave you a sense of confidence and coolness around him," said Johnson. "It was one thing he was always able to inspire, even during the most critical periods of the Cuban affair. . . . But he certainly never gave the impression of the deep nervous and emotional energy you knew was at work within him. . . . Throughout that period, the one solid rock and the one thing that kept all of us on course was the steady, matter-of-fact way in which President Kennedy handled his meetings, and the attitude of calmness that he at all times exhibited."[33]

Much of the Kennedy self-confidence was reflected in the sharp wit and the self-deprecating humor dotting his private conversation and his public comments. There was the time in 1962, for example, when it was disclosed publicly that his younger brother, Ted, who was then campaigning for the Senate, had been involved in a cheating scandal while a college student at Harvard. "It won't go over with you WASPs," Kennedy told his close friend Benjamin Bradlee. "They take a very dim view of looking over someone else's exam paper. They go in more for stealing from stockholders and banks."[34] And after reviewing the first volume of Eisenhower's presidential memoirs, he remarked to an aide, "Apparently Ike never did anything wrong. . . . When we come to writing the memoirs of this administration, we'll do it differently."[35]

But more often Kennedy made himself the object of his sarcasm and humor. And often it reflected a certain irreverence, a reluctance to take his words or himself too seriously. Thus, at a Democratic party fund-raising dinner on the first anniversary of his inauguration, Kennedy was asked to address the assemblage of partisan donors and dignitaries. Against the advice of his senior advisers, he decided to offer a parody of the inaugural address which had been so solemnly praised and analyzed only a short time before. "I spoke a year ago today," Kennedy began,

> and I would like to paraphrase a couple of statements I made that day by saying that we observe tonight not a celebration of freedom but a victory of party, for we have sworn to pay off the same party debt our forebears ran up nearly a year and three months ago. Our deficit will not be paid off in the next hundred days, nor will it be paid off in the first one thousand days, nor in the life of this administration. Nor, perhaps even in our lifetime on this planet, but let us begin—remembering that generosity is not a sign of weakness and that Ambassadors are always subject to Senate confirmation, for if the Democratic Party cannot be helped by the many who are poor, it cannot be saved by the few who are rich. So let us begin.[36]

Kennedy was not above using such humor on occasion even to remark on his failures in providing public leadership. At a Gridiron Club dinner shortly after the Supreme Court announced its decision banning compulsory prayers in public schools, for example, Kennedy offered this comment on his education bill, which was then floundering in Congress: "The Chief Justice has assured me that our school bill is clearly constitutional—because it hasn't got a prayer."[37] This humor would not be spared from his political adversaries. In February 1961, Kennedy addressed the National Industrial Conference Board, a group composed of people who had opposed his election. The speech was a harbinger of what the public could often expect from the Kennedy style:

> It has recently been suggested that whether I serve one or two terms in the Presidency, I will find myself at the end of that period at what might be called the awkward age—too old to begin a new career and too young to write my memoirs.
>
> A similar dilemma, it seems to me, is posed by the occasion of a presidential address to a business group on business conditions less than four weeks after entering the White House—for it is too early to be claiming credit for the new administration and too late to be blaming the old one. And it would be premature to seek your support in the next election, and inaccurate to express thanks for having had it in the last one.[38]

Humor was an integral part of Kennedy's personality and this kind of comment showed that, in many respects, Kennedy was not afraid to be himself in public. But he was not unconcerned with how he appeared in public. Quite the contrary. He was almost always sensitive to the image he portrayed to the public. During the campaign he would invariably turn on the television set around 7 P.M. and watch newsclips of himself. And he would do so with a self-critical eye, trying to improve himself and the way he appeared to the public at large. Myer Feldman recalled one time in the beginning of the campaign when Kennedy turned on the television in the hotel room to watch the evening news. Included was a segment of himself discussing the Democratic party. Kennedy "became very annoyed," said Feldman. "He points to himself on the screen and he says 'party' not 'pawty,' 'party.' "[39]

This concern with television appearances continued even after Kennedy entered the White House. He was almost always interested in looking the way he thought a President should look. Thus, after he made his televised address on the Berlin situation in July 1961, Sorensen dashed off a memo to the President complimenting him ("The Berlin TV speech was without question your greatest triumph of this kind.") and suggesting some ways in which he might improve "the execution." Among other measures, Sorensen proposed reducing the heat in the room "so you need never wipe your brow," sharpening the lighting so that Kennedy could "stand out in appearance as dramatically as you did in the first debate," and having the camera concentrate on "close-ups which give a close personal feeling and also avoid the hands or arms handling the manuscript."[40]

Kennedy's concern with image was not confined to the mechanics of looking good on television. He had promised to be a vigorous, progressive President and he was anxious to make good on that promise both in substance and in form. Within his first two months, he made ten public addresses, held seven press conferences, and issued thirty-two official messages and legislative recommendations. (Eisenhower had issued only five after his first two months.) The spirit of activity was everywhere. "Washington is crackling, rocking, jumping!" TRB proclaimed in *The New Republic* at the end of March. "It is a kite zigging in the breeze."[41] McGeorge Bundy agreed: "At this point, we are like the Harlem Globetrotters, passing forward, behind, sidewise, and underneath. But nobody has made a basket yet."[42] Kennedy was pleased nonetheless. In an interview with *Newsweek* magazine, which was published in the second week of May, Kennedy assessed his first one hundred days in office and said that "he was satisfied that at least one goal he had set himself in the period had been fulfilled: to stamp his administration as activist, with a pace and tempo commensurate with the magnitude of the problems."[43]

All this did much to establish Kennedy as a confident and credible President. His public approval rating soared to 78 percent by the beginning of April, and he was well on his way toward the creation of an image which could be used to secure public support for his positions and policies. And indeed this image did prove helpful when Kennedy addressed the nation on the "crises" which seemed to arise every few months during his tenure.

Almost always the vast majority of the public was willing to believe his interpretation of events and support his announced response to them. In matters involving the Bay of Pigs fiasco, Berlin, nuclear testing, and the Cuban missile crisis, Kennedy found a public that was very sympathetic to his leadership; voices that criticized his handling of these issues were in a distinct minority. And many—including Kennedy himself—believed that that was so because the people generally respected him and accepted him as President. "I've always believed that a first impression is important," he told William Manchester shortly after the abortive invasion at the Bay of Pigs. "In press conferences I gave the impression of knowing what I was doing, and my general activity, in my judgment, stimulated confidence. Cuba could have been difficult if I hadn't done that."[44]

If Kennedy was eager to establish a mood of self-confidence, he was equally interested in having his administration viewed publicly as one receptive to new ideas, constructive criticism, and bold proposals. This was the kind of presidency he had promised the electorate; and to a large degree, he sincerely believed this to be the kind of leadership which would make his tenure a productive one. In his first State of the Union Message, for example, he told Congress and the nation that he had pledged himself and his

> . . . colleagues in the Cabinet to a continuous encouragement of initiative, responsibility and energy in serving the public interest. Let every public servant know, whether his post is high or low, that a man's rank and reputation in this Administration will be determined by the size of the job he does, and not by the size of his staff, his office or his budget. Let it be clear that this Administration recognizes the value of dissent and daring—that we greet healthy controversy as the hallmark of healthy change.[45]

Initiative and boundless energy. Dissent and daring. These traits, he firmly believed, were the mark of a progressive and confident presidency, and, above all, he wanted them to be the marks of *his* presidency. In his addresses, his press conferences, and his other public remarks he would frequently stress this theme, exhorting his audiences to speak the truth, to challenge the conventional wisdom, and to undertake new ventures. So in commemorating the twentieth anniversary of the Voice of America in February 1962, he explained to its employees that "what we do here in this country, and what we are, what we want to be, represents a really great experiment in a most difficult kind of self-discipline, and that is the organization and maintenance and development of the progress of free government. And it is your task . . . to tell that story around the world." But, he added, "you are obliged to tell our story in a truthful way, to tell it, as Oliver Cromwell said about his portrait, 'Paint us with all our blemishes and warts, all those things about us that may not be so immediately attractive.'"[46]

Perhaps Kennedy's most eloquent testament to these principles of candor and creativity was his speech at Amherst College in late October 1963 in honor of Robert Frost. In paying tribute to Frost, Kennedy said, we honor "the deepest sources of our national strength. That strength takes many forms, and the most obvious forms are not always the most significant. The men who create power make an indispensable contribution to the Nation's greatness, but the men who question power make a contribution just as indispensable, especially when that questioning is disinterested, for they help determine whether we use power or power uses us." And there lay Frost's significant contributions: "He brought an unsparing instinct for reality to bear on the platitudes and pieties of society. . . . This is not a popular role. If Robert Frost was much honored during his lifetime, it was because a good many preferred to ignore his darker truths. Yet in retrospect, we see how the artist's fidelity has strengthened the fibre of our national life." And in this context, said Kennedy, "I see little more importance to the future of our country and our civilization than full recognition of the place of the artist."[47]

It is easy—and somewhat fashionable today—to disparage these kinds of statements as the imprint of a President who was more adept at pushing a pen than in moving the nation. But Kennedy's public appeals to reason and innovation did have a visible impact both within his administration and among the public at large. People from all over the country, excited by the prospect and challenge of the new administration, flocked to Washington to join the federal service in 1961. And once there, many found that, despite the inherent limitations of moving the government in any direction, the President was indeed open to new ideas. Speaking from his experience at the State Department, Roger Hilsman observed that "President Kennedy established this climate of receptivity at the beginning of his administration very quickly. His actions showed that he was reading people's memos, and he called up the 'little' men on the phone, all of which created an excitement that the bureaucracy had not known for many years."[48] This is not to say that Kennedy's attitudes transformed the bureaucracy into a compliant and effective servant of his policies. As I showed earlier,[49] the bureaucracy often remained resistant to Kennedy's leadership, and Kennedy himself was a poor administrator in many respects. But Kennedy's image did help inspire a greater dedication and sense of purpose among bureaucrats who for so long had felt divorced from the President.

The effects on the public psyche were equally telling. Kennedy's youthful, exuberant appearance and his call to new adventures encouraged those who were striking out in new areas. Norman Mailer referred to this inspirational quality in the preface to his 1964 book, *The Presidential Papers:*

> . . . We have here a book which was written in part for a man very much alive. . . . It tells the story of a President and of a Presidential time which was neither conclusive nor legislatively active, but which was nonetheless a period not without a suspicion of greatness, greatness of promise at the very least, for it was a time when

writers could speak across the land in intimate dialogue with their leader.[50]

The youth of America also seemed especially attracted to Kennedy. The proposal for a Peace Corps seemed to epitomize the idealism and hope which young people could invest in the new administration. To travel to distant lands to help impoverished people—it was the spirit of generosity and involvement that was sorely missed under Eisenhower. The reverberations of the Kennedy touch were not confined to government programs, however. It is perhaps more than coincidental that activism among college students was conceived and nurtured during Kennedy's tenure (the Port Huron manifesto of the Students for a Democratic Society was issued in the summer of 1962). "The election of John Kennedy in 1960 probably hastened the flowering of the New Radicalism," Jack Newfield wrote in *A Prophetic Minority.* "In that election the nation chose vitality over torpor, adventure over caution, hope over passivity; and this decision liberated energies bottled up for a decade. . . . Kennedy provided a friendly umbrella for the New Left to grow under, and held up a vision of social idealism, represented by the Peace Corps, which led students to take the next logical step—into SNCC and SDS."[51]

It would be misleading to suggest that Kennedy encouraged criticism of every bastion of American life or that he endorsed the radical politics that would bloom on the nation's college campuses in the late 1960s. He did not. Gallup polls throughout his presidency showed, in fact, that most Americans wanted Kennedy to follow a middle course in his politics and that most perceived him to be pursuing that middle course. Those perceptions were largely accurate. Although Kennedy would question accepted assumptions in public he would rarely support actions which would disturb the fundamental tenets of American society. He often spoke of change and progress but in truth he was frequently quite concerned about the political and economic uncertainties that change and progress would bring.

Thus, when civil rights activists Bayard Rustin, Walter Reuther, and others proposed a march on Washington in the summer of 1963 to dramatize to Congress and the country the bitter station of America's blacks, Kennedy was less than enthusiastic. Although he was increasingly sympathetic to the black man's frustrations, the violent experiences in the South made him wary of street demonstrations. "He was skeptical that it would do much good for the civil rights movement," Sorensen recalled, "and he was concerned that it might appear to be a very heavy-handed pressure-type tactic which would alienate some members of the Congress and others around the country—particularly when there was talk in the early days about sit-ins in the galleries of the House and the Senate and that sort of thing."[52]

Kennedy therefore tried to convince the leaders of the march that such a move would probably endanger the chances for civil rights legislation and perhaps even the demonstrators' safety. And at a press conference at the end of May he explained that he was considering the introduction of additional civil rights legislation "which would provide a legal outlet for a desire for a remedy other than having to engage in demonstrations which bring them into conflict with the forces of law and order in the community."[53] Martin Luther King, Jr., however, expressed wholehearted support for the march, as did the Urban League's Whitney Young and the NAACP's Roy Wilkins, both of whom had initially been cool to the idea. The march would go ahead as planned. Faced with this *fait accompli,* Kennedy accepted it and encouraged the attorney general to work closely with the march leaders in making the necessary arrangements. And at a press conference at the end of July, Kennedy made plain that he welcomed the march, which was then planned for the end of August:

> I think that the way that the Washington march is now developed, which is a peaceful assembly calling for a redress of grievances . . . they are going to express their strong views. I think that's in the great tradition. I look forward to being here. I am sure Members of Congress will be here. We want citizens to come to Washington if they feel that they are not having their rights expressed. . . .
>
> . . . You just can't tell people "Don't protest," but on the other hand, "We are not going to let you come into a store or a restaurant." It seems to me it is a two-way street.[54]

Kennedy's handling of the Washington march was symptomatic of the cautious way he handled civil rights and many other explosive issues. But this caution did not necessarily dampen the enthusiasm of the people for Kennedy and the strong leadership he appeared to represent. This was often true even for those whose interests were compromised by Kennedy's caution. Civil rights leaders—who were largely disappointed with Kennedy's actions until June 1963—continually expressed bewilderment at why Kennedy's support among blacks across the country would always remain high. Time and time again civil rights leaders would travel to speak to various communities and to criticize the administration only to find that blacks erupted in spontaneous applause at the mention of the President's name.[55] The explanation for this reaction is not entirely obscure. While Kennedy's actions might not have been everything the leaders wanted or had a right to expect, his image continued to embody the promise of change for the better. "He created a climate in which change could take place," Roy Wilkins later observed, "in which change was not regarded necessarily as a revolution, in which change was regarded as a step forward in the moral, economic, and political growth of the American ideal. . . . He made these things understandable and plausible. He gave them a flair they hadn't had before."[56] Simeon Booker, a respected black journalist, similarly commented that Kennedy gave blacks "a shot in the arm. And it wasn't through programs necessarily, but it was through a sense of freshness, a sense of new life, a hope, and he did it not only at our middle class, but he did it at the area of people in the ghettos, slums."[57]

This kind of attitude toward Kennedy suffused public thinking on most major issues (a fact which may help explain why, until the fall of 1963—after he began pushing strong civil rights legislation—Kennedy's approval rating among the public consistently remained between 60 and 80 percent). There was a good deal of hope and excitement about the future on almost every front. Problems abounded, to be sure, and Kennedy's leadership in many areas could be (and was) criticized. But people generally had a high degree of confidence in the federal government and in themselves. One series of attitude surveys showed, for example, that Americans were more optimistic about their futures at the end of Kennedy's presidency than at the end of Eisenhower's (and since Kennedy, the same surveys show that the people's optimism has decreased 50 percent).[58]

Both critics and admirers believed that much of the optimism could be tied to Kennedy. Michael Harrington, author of *The Other America*, and one who was often dissatisfied with Kennedy's progress in pushing social reforms, later said, "The nation was happier then. It had, God knows, problems, but they seemed solvable. . . . Since there was a President who could grow in office, who could learn from the Bay of Pigs and the missile crisis, who could come to understand that we had to move decisively as a nation in response to the just demands of black America, the mood, the political atmosphere of these United States changed in January 1961. It was that intangible which was perhaps most important."[59] Art Buchwald expressed similar views to me in his office in Washington:

> Kennedy gave you a great respect and faith in your government. He gave you an idealistic picture which we hadn't had and which was lost when he died. He ennobled government. He made you proud to be an American. He could do it with words. Those of us who were here then noticed that the town had an excitement and it had a purpose. It's undefinable but we all became part of it.

There were, of course, risks in this optimism. People often expect more than will be accomplished. Legislative proposals to remedy injustice are compromised before they are enacted and, in any event, the final product often fails to be as effective as people hoped it would. New programs and policies likewise get bogged down in bureaucratic red tape, conventional wisdoms, and the resistance of influential people (including the President) who are afraid of losing their power. In either case the resulting disappointments can aggravate frustrations and ultimately heighten skepticism that conditions can be improved. Certainly the campus unrest and the civil disorders of the late 1960s can be traced in part to the widespread disillusionment when the promises of Kennedy's presidency were not fully realized.

Kennedy cannot be entirely blamed for this disillusionment. He had emphasized *ad nauseum* that it was a long, hard road—requiring many sacrifices by the public—before his administration could attain the goals it had set for itself. Moreover, as in the cases of the Test Ban Treaty and the housing order on discrimination, he frequently underplayed the significance of the steps he did take to solve specific problems. And, even more importantly, he was not standing at the helm of government when the people's frustrations spilled over into campus and civil disorders.

It is clear, on the other hand, that Kennedy's image did invite people to trust in his leadership and glory in his achievements. And there is no question that Kennedy consciously fostered that presidential image. To appreciate fully the nature of Kennedy's efforts to promote a favorable image—and thus to assess better the extent to which he should be held accountable for the disillusionment of the 1960s—it is necessary to examine Kennedy's relations with the press.

Working with the News Media

As a former newspaperman himself, John Kennedy felt a certain cameraderie with the press. He was familiar with their working habits, knew the pressures under which they almost constantly labored, and understood—both as a member of Congress and as President—how he could make their jobs more fruitful by giving them "inside" information. Kennedy's affinity for the press was also strengthened by the fact that some of his more intimate friends, such as Joseph Alsop and Benjamin Bradlee, were members of the press. But the real key to understanding Kennedy's relations with the press is his belief that the media commanded a great deal of political power. It was the media, after all, that interpreted events and judged leaders for the American people. Kennedy therefore sensed that his success as a candidate and as President would depend greatly on his ability to have the media interpret events and judge people (especially himself) in a way that would cast him and his administration in the most favorable light.

Kennedy was particularly adept at courting the press corps during the 1960 presidential campaign. Although his daily schedule was quite hectic and often lasted more than ten or twelve hours, he would always try to make himself available to the press, answering their questions, giving his views on specific issues, and sometimes complimenting a reporter on a story he or she had written (flattery which did not go unappreciated by the reporter). Conversations were often casual, full of banter and good humor. It was an enjoyable experience for most of the reporters who traveled with Kennedy and by November, as Theodore White has written, many "had become his friends and, some of them, his most devoted admirers."[60] "I know of no photographer or newsman who covered that campaign, start to finish," Laura Bergquist of *Look* magazine later said, "who didn't come away thinking he *knew* John F. Kennedy—they were no longer the press corps, but his friends. In turn, the President knew them and all their idiosyncracies."[61] Whether all the feelings of genuine friendship were mutual with Kennedy is open to question; but there is no doubt that he recognized and gladly accepted the political benefits of the favorable news reports which those feelings frequently generated.

Kennedy maintained close contacts with many press people after he entered the White House. In his eyes, their importance seemed that much greater after the election. This was understandable. His narrow margin of victory underscored to him the need to create the favorable image of a strong, decisive President—not only so he would have public support for his programs and policies but also to help get in 1964 that large popular mandate he wanted but did not receive in 1960. From this perspective, it made more sense to concentrate on the larger and more influential periodicals. Accordingly, representatives of the *New York Times*, the *Washington Post*, the *Chicago Daily News*, *Newsweek*, *Time*, and other large-circulation and important periodicals generally found it far easier to see Kennedy than someone representing a small town magazine or newspaper.

Within these confines, Kennedy remained very accessible to the press. And almost always he seemed to talk openly about matters that were on his mind, dispensing information and opinions which would give the reporter an inside view and perhaps a feature story. "Well, he was extremely easy to see," William Lawrence of the *New York Times* remembered, "and whenver you saw him, he tried to dig up a story for you."[62] Henry Brandon of the London *Sunday Times* agreed. "Well, he was the easiest person to talk to from a newspaperman's point of view," said Brandon, "and that continued even when he was the President. I think he had this marvelous gift of being absolutely frank, giving you the impression that he's telling you more than he should—and he very often did—and that you sometimes sort of looked over your shoulder whether anybody's listening and you said to yourself, 'My God, I can't tell anybody about this.'"[63] But most—including Brandon—often did report the information.

As during the campaign, Kennedy's easy manner with the press in the White House did not represent a disinterested generosity. Although he genuinely liked and trusted some of them, Kennedy was anxious to gain or retain the respect of the press people, to bring them on the administration team, and to encourage stories which would reflect that team spirit. And he wanted to use them to stimulate public interest in matters that he thought important. The economy, as I have shown earlier, was one example. And when he was anxious to ease the public tension about the Berlin situation in the fall of 1961 (tension which he helped to create), Kennedy spoke to Arthur Krock and other press people, suggesting that they praise speeches by Senator Claiborne Pell of Rhode Island and other congressional spokesmen who were discussing the approach of a *modus vivendi* with the Soviet Union on the Berlin issue. Another example involved the test ban treaty. When the Senate prepared to consider and vote on the treaty negotiated in Moscow, Kennedy was deeply concerned that the public would be skeptical about making an agreement with the Soviet Union, and he knew that such public skepticism might be reflected in the senators' decision on whether to advise and consent to the treaty. He therefore spoke to many press people about the significance of the treaty and the need to establish a favorable climate for it within the country.

Kennedy rarely made these kinds of suggestions to representatives of the broadcast media. Although he recognized the influence of radio and television, he believed that he could best use the broadcast media through press conferences and special addresses to speak directly to the American people, discarding the necessity to rely on reporters as intermediaries. The press conferences, for instance, were conducted in the cavernous State Department auditorium, with Kennedy standing behind a podium and the press seated below him. Kennedy could thus make announcements and answer questions while appearing isolated from the sea of reporters. And in answering a question, Kennedy was prone to look directly at the camera rather than at the reporter who asked it. The whole arrangement prompted Peter Lisagor of the *Chicago Daily News* to comment that reporters "became spearcarriers in a great televised opera. We were props in a show, in a performance. Kennedy mastered the art of this performance early, and he used it with great effectiveness. We were simply there as props. I always felt that we should have joined Actors Equity. Those of us that had a chance to ask questions should have charged that much extra for speaking lines."[64]

Since he regarded the press as a powerful force in politics, it was only natural that Kennedy should pay close attention to what they said and how they said it. And he combed through their words very carefully when the subject being discussed was himself or the merits of the administration's policies. This was true of both the broadcast media and the print media. "About seven P.M., or whenever the news was on television," Fred Dutton told me, "everything usually stopped in the White House. Kennedy monitored television very closely to see what they were saying about him and what he was doing." Many newspapers and magazines came under similar scrutiny, and the press knew it. Commenting on a conversation with Kennedy in October 1961, for example, Arthur Krock wrote that "the President's close reading of the newspapers was again indicated when he seized on a sentence in James Reston's piece of that day to the effect that men of Speaker Rayburn's generation didn't have their speeches ghost-written for them."[65] Merriman Smith, the veteran White House United Press International reporter, was equally impressed with the attention Kennedy and his staff gave to reading periodicals. "How they can spot an obscure paragraph in a paper of three thousand circulation two thousand miles away is beyond me," said Merriman. "They must have a thousand little gnomes reading the paper for them."[66] George Herman, then White House correspondent for CBS news, similarly told me that Kennedy "read everything, including the footnotes. In fact, he once chewed out a reporter for a footnote that was buried in a long story." Kennedy's reading of the press literature was so extensive (or, as Gilbert Harrison said, the staff work was so good) that on one occasion he called up a little-known journalist to inquire about some facts he had referred to in a book review he had written for *The New Republic*.

Very little of this reading was idle curiosity. Kennedy scrutinized newspapers and magazines because he thought they would provide him with useful information. As a national politician, he was anxious to learn about the dominant moods in the country. He was also—if not primarily—eager to see whether he was reaching the people on a particular issue and whether the press was treating him and his administration fairly. Words were weighed, tones were analyzed, facts were verified—all to determine whether the press was painting them the way they wanted to look (the old saw about Oliver Cromwell's portrait was forgotten when they evaluated the comments of the press). Thus, shortly after the steel price controversy was resolved, David Lawrence ran a long column in the *U.S. News and World Report* arguing that Kennedy had misled the country about the steel industry's high profits and the lack of any justification for the price increase. Within a day James Tobin, a member of the President's Council of Economic Advisers, prepared a detailed memo for Kennedy examining each argument in Lawrence's column and explaining why it was fallacious.

This experience with Lawrence is but one small indication of how sensitive Kennedy was to press criticism—especially when he first saw it. Even during the campaign—when his good relations with the press were obvious—Kennedy would sometimes explode at the way his campaign was being reported to the American people. Frequently, for example, Kennedy or one of his staff people would call CBS executives to complain about that network's television coverage. Indeed, at one point CBS correspondent Blair Clark, who was covering Kennedy, flew from the Midwest to New York to discuss the deteriorating situation and the dangers involved for CBS—which owned broadcast stations that needed a federal license to operate—if Kennedy should be elected; Clark was reported to have told CBS President Frank Stanton that Kennedy had said, "Wait till I'm President—I'll cut Stanton's balls off."[67]

Kennedy did not take any surgical action against Stanton after he was elected (in fact, they met on occasion on the most friendly of terms). But that remark suggested how little regard Kennedy had for a reporter's independence; freedom of the press was a concept he was prone to ignore during the campaign when it came to criticism of his statements and actions. Kennedy's sensitivity to press criticism remained very much intact after his inauguration. At first glance, his instincts led him to feel—especially on important issues—that a press person's critical remarks were based on ignorance or political malice or sometimes both. And press people who repeatedly criticized Kennedy and his administration were of particular concern. Even Arthur Krock—an old Kennedy family friend—was not immune from this presidential scorn. (William Lawrence said that Kennedy "couldn't read Krock without his blood pressure going up."[68]) And on many occasions, Kennedy was not loath to express his frustrations and to seek (usually in vain) some kind of immediate remedy.

There was the time when Kennedy watched the NBC Huntley-Brinkley evening news program carry a speech by someone who attacked the President's actions in the steel price controversy. Kennedy was irate, and he quickly called Federal Communications Commission

Chairman Newton Minow at home. (Kennedy always seemed to remember that broadcasters were regulated by the FCC.) The following conversation then ensued:

Kennedy: Did you see that goddam thing on Huntley-Brinkley?

Minow: Yes.

Kennedy: I thought they were supposed to be our friends. I want you to do something about that. You do something about that.[69]

Minow never took any action against NBC (although he did call Kenneth O'Donnell the next morning to have him tell Kennedy that "he's lucky he has an FCC chairman who doesn't do what the President tells him"[70]). But this was an outrageous example of Kennedy's insensitivity to the press's freedom. Although Minow said he could not remember another similar instance, there was no excuse for the first one.

Kennedy, however, continued to be intolerant of criticism of his handling of the steel crisis. This became evident about a month later in an incident involving the *New York Herald Tribune.* For weeks in the spring of 1962, the newspaper had been running front-page stories suggesting the complicity of Democratic political leaders in the scandals involving Billie Sol Estes, a Texas financier who was charged with unlawful manipulation of federal support programs. The coverage irritated Kennedy because he felt the insinuations against the Democrats were unwarranted and because the paper was largely ignoring a stockpiling scandal involving high Eisenhower administration officials. In other words, he thought the paper was more interested in hurting his Democratic administration than in reporting the facts to the people. In the middle of May, while the Billie Sol Estes stories were still running, the *Herald Tribune* ran a page-one Fischetti cartoon that showed Pierre Salinger—who had just returned from a much-publicized visit with Khrushchev in the Soviet Union—walking with Kennedy outside the White House and saying, "Mr. Khrushchev said he liked your style in the steel crisis." Kennedy happened to be in New York City at the time, and Salinger telephoned the *Herald Tribune*'s Washington correspondent, David Wise, who was also in New York City. "I just wanted you to know the President's reaction to this morning's *Herald Tribune,"* said Salinger. Wise asked what it was, and Salinger replied, "The fucking *Herald Tribune* is at it again."[71] Within two weeks, it was publicly revealed that Kennedy had canceled the White House's twenty-two subscriptions to the *Herald Tribune* because, according to Salinger, the President wanted to "diversify" his reading.

Kennedy's cancellation of the *Herald Tribune* was a mistake, both as a matter of principle and as a matter of politics (many rightly criticized Kennedy because he preferred a managed press to a free press). It was also somewhat unusual. In most situations, Kennedy would vent his frustrations by discussing them with an aide, and on many occasions he would simply point out to the press the errors he saw. Often he would accomplish this by calling the reporter or the periodical's publisher himself; other times he would ask a White House staff person to do it. Thus, in September 1961, when Kennedy was making legislative proposals which he believed would cut the 6.9 percent rate of unemployment, he asked Fred Dutton to write a letter to the president of *Reader's Digest* (a periodical with one of the largest circulations in the country) "challenging his statistics in the September *Reader's Digest* on unemployment that the program presented this year would cost the taxpayer 18 billion dollars annually in a few years. It is wholly untrue and we ought to make him eat it."[72] On another occasion, Kennedy saw Gilbert Harrison of *The New Republic* at a White House function. The magazine had recently run a comment on Egyptian President Nasser and the Middle East situation. Kennedy singled out Harrison and said, "Say, you ran a note a couple of weeks ago [on American policy towards Nasser]. You got that wrong. I'll tell you what I want you to do. I want you to sit down with Mac Bundy and get straight on this because the information wasn't correct."[73] Within four days, Harrison had a three-page, single-spaced typed memo from Bundy concerning the matter.

These incidents were typical of Kennedy's experience with the press. On the one hand, he made himself and his administration more accessible to the press than any other President or administration (with the possible exception of FDR); on the other hand, much of this access was a calculated effort to mold the press's reaction to Kennedy's personality, policies, and programs. To some extent, the reporters themselves recognized these qualities in Kennedy's press relations. A 1963 *Newsweek* poll among forty-three top Washington correspondents found, for example, that forty believed that the Kennedy administration was more accessible than any previous administration; but forty of those same correspondents also believed that the Kennedy administration's efforts to manage news were more intense than those of any previous administration.[74] It was, in a way, a love-hate relationship. "Kennedy had a love affair with the press," George Herman remarked to me. "He truly enjoyed their company, but he was always trying to manipulate their reporting. He viewed it as part of the friendship. He genuinely liked reporters and expected their loyalty in return. And that meant favorable stories." Journalists who failed to reciprocate the presidential friendship with favorable stories frequently were, in a sense, "exiled" from administration news sources—including, and most especially, the President himself. No one was immune from this rule of reciprocity—not even close friends like Ben Bradlee (who found himself ostracized from the Kennedy circle for a few months after he was quoted in *Look* magazine as saying that it is "almost impossible to write a story" the Kennedy brothers like. "Even if a story is quite favorable to their side," Bradlee said, "they'll find one paragraph to quibble with."[75]).

This sensitivity to press criticism rarely surfaced in public (which is one reason why the White House cancellation of the *New York Herald Tribune* made such a splash in the news). Kennedy knew that in public he had to express his respect for the press as an independent force. And he frequently obliged with appropriate comments. At a press conference in the spring of 1962, for instance, he was asked to comment on the press's treatment of his administration. "Well," said Kennedy, "I am reading more and enjoying it less—[laughter]—and so on, but I have not complained nor do I plan to make any general complaints. I read and talk to myself about it, but I don't plan to issue any general statement to the press. I think that they are doing their task, as a critical branch, the fourth estate. And I am attempting to do mine. And we are going to live together for a period, and then go our separate ways. [Laughter]"[76] Later that year Kennedy announced at a press conference that

> We have the President of Chile. We are very glad to welcome him here on his first visit to the United States.
>
> And he told me that he had a press conference yesterday and that the press in America were far gentler than they were in Chile. [Applause.]
>
> We don't want to give him the wrong impression, so I'll call on Mr. Chalmers Roberts [White House correspondent for the *Washington Post*]. [Laughter.][77]

This kind of humor, as well as Kennedy's quick mind, endeared him to much of the press. "President Kennedy, the real master of 'the game,' was a witty computer," James Reston later wrote. "He either overwhelmed you with decimal points, or disarmed you with a smile and a wisecrack."[78] But there was the personal side of it, too. Kennedy appeared to treat reporters and commentators as individuals, as people whom he liked and in whom he was sincerely interested. He would mention them by name at press conferences, would notice their absence on presidential trips and later ask why they were not there to accompany him with the rest of the press, and would often try to help them personally in their tasks (when Max Frankel of the *New York Times* requested some information in 1961 about a meeting between Kennedy and Soviet foreign minister Andrei Gromyko, for example, he soon found a personal response from the President fulfilling the request).

The short and the long of it is that many people in the press liked Kennedy, and this was sometimes reflected in the way they reported his activities to the American people. In a word, many press people allowed themselves to become willing accomplices in Kennedy's schemes to have his policies and programs described the way he wanted them described. "I think we were as smitten by the President's style and his manner, that quality of grace, really, that he had, as much as any other segment of the society," Peter Lisagor later mused, "and I think this tended to reflect as much in the press. . . . I know many of my colleagues thought the world of him, wouldn't be critical of him, you know, and really lost a bit of their professional aplomb and poise in the face of Kennedy."[79] Thus did Kennedy's conscious courtship of the press help him in his efforts to create an image of positive leadership with the American people. But if the press was helpful to Kennedy in maintaining a favorable image with the public, the press was of little benefit to Kennedy in shaping the images which the Congress had of its constitutional partner.

Moving Congress

Members of Congress do not possess identical images of the President at any time or in any circumstance. Indeed, as the representatives of diverse constituencies with conflicting interests, congressmen and senators disagree about the image of any President perhaps as often as they differ about the nature of and the solution to the nation's problems. Those images, moreover, are not static. Experience and events will alter a congressional representative's perception of the President much as they do in other personal relationships. There were, nevertheless, certain persistent attitudes which crowned many congressmen and senators' images of President Kennedy.

Because of his fourteen years as a congressman and a senator, Kennedy's was a familiar face on Capitol Hill. But that did not ensure him a favorable image among the nation's legislators. In fact, such familiarity was, in a way, a great impediment to Kennedy.

In delivering his first State of the Union Message, he told the assembled group of congressmen and senators that it was "a pleasure to return from whence I came. You are among my oldest friends in Washington—and this House is my oldest home. . . . I am confident that that friendship will continue."[80] In some respects, Kennedy had reason to speak so glowingly of his relationships with the nation's legislators. Some of them were his friends. But Kennedy knew—as did most of Congress—that he was not really an integral part of that institution and that he was never really interested in making Congress his career. In the beginning, many simply viewed him as an intellectual playboy who had catapulted himself into Congress on his father's name and money. And they sensed that he was more interested in the prestige than in the responsibilities of a congressional seat. This attitude was perhaps epitomized by one elderly senator's recollection of an incident involving Kennedy. The Senate was working into the night on legislative business, and this particular senator was presiding. "There was [Senate Majority Leader Lyndon] Johnson down there on the floor, working like hell, pushing bills through," he said. "I looked up in the gallery and there were Jack Kennedy and George Smathers sneaking out with a couple of girls. Johnson and the rest of us were still in there working while they went out on the town."[81]

In time, many in Congress came to respect Kennedy's political independence (how else explain his vote on the St. Lawrence Seaway Project or his stand on Algeria) and, especially after his management of the labor bill in 1959, his talents as well (Senator Paul Douglas later called Kennedy's handling of that bill "an amazing performance"[82]). But none of this improved Kennedy's general standing in Congress or altered the image which most had of him. He was not one to involve himself heavily in congressional affairs and wait patiently for his power to accrue through seniority. He was a man in a hurry, a politician eager to move on to bigger and better things. And after winning his Senate seat, there was only one elective goal left—the presidency. Almost from the last day of the 1956 Democratic convention (when Kennedy almost won the Democratic vice-presidential nomination), Kennedy started planning and organizing his effort to capture the White House in 1960. This effort required him to spend most of his time traveling across the country speaking with local political leaders instead of attending to his duties in the Senate. (In 1960, for example, Kennedy attended only three of the ninety-six committee sessions held by the Senate Foreign Relations Committee, of which he was a member.) And this, of course, did not endear Kennedy to many in Congress, but especially the leaders.

Kennedy never really tried to become a member of the inner circles of Congress and many of the more established figures—who also wielded great power as chairmen of the committees—resented Kennedy's election to the presidency. He was far younger than they, to begin with;* and, in their eyes, he had never demonstrated much ability as a leader. "Yes, they resented him," Congressman Frank Thompson, Jr., told me of the congressional leaders' reaction to Kennedy's election. "To them he was just a wise-ass Catholic kid." Senator Paul Douglas likewise observed that the elder statesmen in the Senate "had the feeling that here was a youngster who had come into the Senate and in eight years had parachuted into the Presidency, so to speak. And they may not have taken him as seriously as he deserved to be taken. . . . There was an element of coldness perhaps which many of the members felt towards him."[83] The AFL-CIO's chief legislative lobbyist, Andrew Biemiller, made much the same observations. "Many of the old bulls resented his coming along," Biemiller told me. "They never thought of him as a Senator's senator. He worked damn hard on his subcommittee on labor, but he didn't pitch in on the daily chores. It was obvious from '57 on that he was going to run for the President. Unlike other congressmen, he could just hop on his private plane and go anywhere he wanted to." As if to confirm these feelings among the congressional leadership at the time of his ascendency to the presidency, House Rules Committee Chairman Howard Smith bluntly told me that Kennedy "was quite young. I did not feel that he had a wide grasp of public affairs." In fact, said Smith, "I was rather surprised that he knew as much as he did."

These images of Kennedy among the congressional leadership were not, to say the least, a major plus in his efforts to secure enactment of his legislative proposals. The elder statesmen were often found grumbling in the Senate and House cloakrooms about "what that young fella was sending down here." Their instinctive negative reaction to Kennedy was heightened by the fact that he was viewed as a critic of the system they revered. Kennedy always seemed to be talking about new challenges and new obligations to correct past injustice and guard against future dangers. Such statements irritated many senior members of Congress. By speaking of past failures, Kennedy seemed to question Congress's effectiveness in dealing with the nation's problems; and by speaking of emerging crises, he seemed to suggest that the President would assume powers that the congressional leadership thought belonged to them.

---

*For example, in 1960 House Rules Comittee Chairman Howard Smith was 76; House Appropriations Committee Chairman Clarence Cannon was 80; House Armed Services Committee Chairman Carl Vinson was 76; House Banking and Currency Committee Chairman Brent Spence was 85; Senate Appropriations Comittee Chairman Carl Hayden was 82; Senate Banking and Currency Committee Chairman A. Willis Robertson was 72; Senate Finance Committee Chairman Harry F. Byrd was 72; and Senate Interior Committee Chairman James Murray was 83. Kennedy was 43.

None of this prevented Kennedy and his staff from laboring long and hard to establish a favorable climate in which to push the administration's legislative program. The staff continually consulted with appropriate legislators on specific issues and Kennedy himself often met with congressmen and senators at White House social functions or private meetings in the President's Oval Office. Through these frequent meetings, many legislators were quickly impressed with his confident manner and his apparent sincerity. His conversations were usually marked by light banter, a careful analysis of a particular problem, and how a specific legislative proposal would meet that problem. It was a direct approach, but most came away feeling that the President was an easy man to talk to and understand. (Theodore White said Kennedy was the best political conversationalist after Hubert Humphrey.) "He had a much deeper conception of the American way of life than people gave him credit for," Louisiana Congressman Otto Passman later said of Kennedy. "He was a very critical man but I think he was sincere and that he knew where he was going." House Majority Leader Carl Albert likewise felt that, in dealing with Congress, Kennedy's personality "was his greatest political asset."[84]

But, as in his courtship of the press, Kennedy knew how to make those personal touches which often made the congressman or senator believe that Kennedy was interested in him as an individual—a telephone call thanking someone for his support, an agreement to try to place a federal facility in the congressman or senator's area to help combat unemployment, or a special tour for the congressman who brought his family to the White House to see the President. Charles Daly, who worked on the White House congressional relations staff, remembered that Kennedy "was damn willing—he seemed almost unendingly willing—to give the extra courtesy to the family of the guy who had helped us." Daly recalled the time, for example, that California congressman John Moss, who supported Kennedy on most issues, was invited to the White House with his family for a ceremony in the Rose Garden. Daly mentioned to Kennedy that, if he had a chance, he should try to say hello to Moss and his family after the ceremony was over. "Well, he did more than that," Daly said. "After the ceremony, he dragged them to the porch of his office. They had their little cameras, and they took a bunch of pictures. . . . In a job where the coin is almost undefinable that sort of thing was of very direct and substantial value. Perhaps it bored the President, but he was awfully good at it."[85]

This kind of effort did pay dividends to Kennedy. When his legislative proposals reached the floor of the House or Senate, he often found considerable support among the rank and file congressmen and senators. This was true even of the conservative southern bloc. In 1961 and

1962, for example, more than half of the congressmen from fourteen southern and border states supported administration proposals at least 60 percent of the time, and almost two-thirds of those congressmen supported Kennedy at least 50 percent of the time. Many complex reasons explain why Kennedy was able to command this much support on the floors of the Congress. But there is little doubt that part of the explanation was Kennedy's success in establishing an image of a sincere, knowledgeable, and considerate President.

Kennedy was far more successful in establishing and using that image with the rank and file than with the congressional leadership. Most in that latter group remained largely unpersuaded of the President's skills or the merits of his legislative program. They continued to believe that he had no public mandate for many of his proposals and, in any event, believed he was pushing too much legislation much too fast. (Louisiana senator Allen Ellender felt this was due in part to the fact that "President Kennedy was surrounded, as all presidents are, by a lot of dreamers, by a lot of people who are not practical."[86]) The results were telling. Many of the congressional leaders consistently voted against Kennedy's proposals on the floor;* and of more importance, they blocked much of his legislation in committee, refusing to hold hearings or to report bills to the floor.

There was little that Kennedy was able to do about this resistance. He spoke with the congressional leaders frequently, both at White House functions and in private meetings. And he would also make those personal gestures which greatly impressed so many of the other congressmen and senators. One well-known example was Kennedy's surprise visit, via helicopter, to Senator Byrd's birthday party at Mount Vernon, Virginia. But these conferences and gestures left most of the congressional leaders unmoved. (Byrd, in fact, later criticized Kennedy's excessive use of his helicopter service as a waste of the taxpayer's money.) In their eyes, Kennedy was not, as Lyndon Johnson was, a part of their charmed circle, a man whom they understood and enjoyed dealing with.

So, while Kennedy was able to forge favorable images among the public at large as well as among many congressmen and senators, those

---

*This was especially true in the Senate. Thus, Government Operations Committee Chairman John McClellan voted for only 35 percent of Kennedy's proposals in 1961 and for only 43 percent in 1962; Armed Services Committee Chairman Richard Russell voted for only 31 percent of Kennedy's proposals in 1961 and for only 37 percent in 1962; Judiciary Committee Chairman James Eastland voted for only 27 percent of Kennedy's proposals in both 1961 and 1962; and Banking and Currency Committee Chairman A. Willis Robertson voted for only 37 percent of Kennedy's proposals in 1961 and for 38 percent in 1962.

images were insufficient to overcome the less favorable images which many congressional leaders had or their opposition to his legislative programs. It was often a frustrating experience for Kennedy. Time and time again he found his efforts to push Congress to be like hitting FDR's proverbial feather bed—he would hit them repeatedly with explanations and gestures only to discover that he had not moved them very much. In many ways, it was akin to the frustrations Kennedy would experience in trying to influence world politics.

The Eyes of the World

John Kennedy did not attach much importance to his image among the world's peoples. International politics, he felt, were not greatly influenced by the attitudes of a foreign nation's populace toward the American President. After the Bay of Pigs fiasco, for instance, Kennedy had lunch in the private dining quarters of the Executive Mansion with Arthur Schlesinger, Jr., and James Reston. Would the United States' prestige suffer, he was asked, if the administration abandoned its support of the Cuban rebels' cause? "What is prestige?" Kennedy responded. "Is it the shadow of power or the substance of power? We are going to work on the substance of power. No doubt we will be kicked in the can for the next couple of weeks, but that won't affect the main business."[87]

And the main business, in Kennedy's eyes, was the world's political leaders. They, of course, would have to attend to the interests and opinions of their own constituencies. But Kennedy was more concerned with impressing the leaders themselves that he was an individual who could account for the other fellow's perspective, that he was a statesman willing to reason with other statesmen in resolving their differences, and that he was an American leader who would be resolute—and willing to risk war if necessary—in defending his country's vital interests. His success in dealing with the nation's allies, its adversaries, and the Third World as well, he believed, would depend in part on his ability to inspire those images through his words and actions.

Thus, Kennedy was naturally interested in maintaining the alliances which had been forged before he entered the White House. He therefore established contact with each ally and reaffirmed his intention to continue to respect the bonds of friendship. When problems arose, he would listen and try to be accommodating. This was true of almost all of our allies, regardless of the influence they commanded in world affairs. (On nineteen different occasions, for example, Kennedy reaffirmed a pledge to Israel to help defend her in the event of an attack by the Arab nations.)

Kennedy was especially eager to restore good relations with the Latin-American countries. Because American presidents in the twentieth century had repeatedly authorized military intervention in Latin-American affairs, and since the resources of the Latin-American nations were continually exploited by American corporations, the spirit of amity had long before been replaced by Latin-American hatred for "Yankee imperialism." Kennedy understood this and decided to pursue policies which would change the image of the United States as a corporate, jingoistic machine which would treat Latin America as its own backyard. And those Kennedy policies in fact proved to be quite successful in changing that image. Dominican Republic President Juan Bosch observed that he found Kennedy to be ". . . a man as fully concerned about the fate of the Latin-American people as he might be concerned about the fate of Arkansas, Georgia, or his native state, Massachusetts."[88] (In fact, Kennedy once advised Bosch as to how he might prevent Dominican companies from being purchased by American corporations.) Brazil's ambassador to the United States, Roberto Campos, likewise commented that Brazil's President Goulart ". . . was personally struck by Kennedy's personality and liberal posture. . . ."[89] And Costa Rican President Francisco Orlich acknowledged ". . . the obvious fact that President Kennedy revealed himself from the beginning as a genuine friend of Latin Americans, as a statesman concerned about their problems and prepared to help solve them by means, and on terms, the Latin Americans could understand" and that this fact "helped establish that bond of affection that we all see between the people of my country and President Kennedy."[90] Despite its limited success, the Alliance for Progress program helped establish this great affection for Kennedy among Latin Americans. Although often frustrated with the program's slow progress (in part because they frequently refused to cooperate in developing the reforms which the program's success required), many Latin-American leaders appreciated the spirit in which the program was offered. Examining the program six years after its introduction, Herbert Matthews, a *New York Times* reporter for 45 years and a specialist in Latin-American affairs, commented, "The Alliance for Progress is an answer which was devised to meet the challenges of the Cuban Revolution—incidentally by John F. Kennedy, the only United States President since Franklin D. Roosevelt to have any understanding of and feeling for Latin Americans."[91]

Kennedy was also keenly interested in shoring up the European alliances, in making clear his willingness to accept and work with European nations beginning to regain some of the muscle that had been ripped asunder by the Second World War. After his first meetings with the principal European leaders in 1961, Kennedy favorably impressed them as a man with a sharp intellect who was indeed anxious to preserve the Atlantic alliance. French President Charles de Gaulle remarked that he had met only two genuine statesmen in his life, and one of them was Kennedy. West German Chancellor Konrad Adenauer left the White House in 1961 commenting, "I've never left this house feeling better."[92] And British Prime Minister Macmillan agreed that Kennedy was an astute leader with a quick mind. "Your President," he told an American journalist, "catches onto ideas very fast."[93]

This favorable first image was, in some degree, shaped by the fact that Kennedy seemed more akin to European politicians than his predecessors in the White House. His whole style suggested breeding; his conversations suggested a respect for the world of ideas; and his crispness revealed a certain realism. James Reston once touched on this ability of Kennedy to invite a positive reaction from European leaders. "Prime ministers and other foreign leaders liked Kennedy's style, his brevity, his conciseness, his culture and the intellectual atmosphere he conveyed," Reston told me in 1967. "This seems to rest on the fact that politicians in Europe and other nations are, for the most part, intellectuals themselves. Kennedy . . . presented a contrast to the stereotyped picture of Americans which foreigners had been prejudiced against. Lyndon Johnson typifies their image of an American who is a buffoon and uncultured, cunning and shrewd."*

Kennedy often used this style with great effectiveness. He was generally direct in his private dealings with the European leaders and other allies, openly addressing their concerns and candidly explaining his own country's interests. "His manner was always the same," French foreign minister Maurice Couve de Murville said of Kennedy. "It was very simple; it was very direct, not hesitating to say things as they were, always friendly and calm; and it was really very easy to discuss with him. It was easy, in particular, to have an objective discussion. I mean exchanging arguments and the arguments being accepted on both sides."[94] David Bruce, the American Ambassador to England, likewise observed that "the frequency and frankness" of the interchanges between Kennedy and Macmillan "had few parallels in modern diplomatic intercourse."[95] This kind of interaction helped establish a reservoir of goodwill which became very handy in those cases—such as in the Cuban missile crisis and in the Skybolt affair—when

*As if in confirmation of Reston's observations, de Gaulle once remarked that Johnson is "a cowboy, and that's saying everything. An efficient man without any style. I rather like Johnson. He doesn't even take the trouble to pretend he's thinking. Roosevelt and Kennedy were masks over the real face of America. He reveals the country to us as it is, rough and raw. If he didn't exist, we'd have to invent him."

Kennedy seemed to place American interests above those of the allies. For even then most of them were often willing to work with Kennedy and support his policies.

But there were, of course, limitations on the ability of Kennedy to use his favorable image to secure the cooperation of the allies. De Gaulle was particularly troublesome for Kennedy in this respect. Although he liked the young American President, de Gaulle was first and foremost concerned with the need to revive France's powerful role in world affairs. All the goodwill in the world could not dampen that concern. And so when Kennedy risked nuclear war with the Soviet Union over the Cuban missiles without consulting France, when he promised Macmillan the Polaris missiles after their 1962 Nassau meeting, and when he negotiated the test ban treaty with the Soviet Union, de Gaulle was less than enthusiastic. From his perspective, those actions signified Kennedy's preoccupation with American (as opposed to world) interests as well as Kennedy's desire to preserve the American hegemony by blocking France's entry into the nuclear club. Whatever his feelings about Kennedy personally, de Gaulle believed that France's political influence and military security could not be tied to America's apron strings. Even before Kennedy was assassinated, de Gaulle was therefore moving toward a decision to remove France from the American-dominated NATO alliance.

Although Kennedy was deeply troubled about the deterioration of the Atlantic alliance and was often quite frustrated in his attempts to reverse that trend, he was even more concerned about the United States' relations with the nation's adversaries, but especially the Soviet Union. The reasons for this concern are obvious. Only the United States and the Soviet Union possessed the military power to destroy all the world. China, of course, was always a potential problem. Its bellicose posturing, its ready abundance of millions of combat troops, and its apparent willingness to use them, as in Korea—all these factors made China a power to be reckoned with. But she did not have either the military or economic muscle to dominate world affairs. (China did not explode its first atomic bomb until 1964.) Only the Soviet Union, in other words, seemed anxious and able to expand its sphere of influence in every continent.

Kennedy was eager to establish an atmosphere in which the Soviet Union and the United States could live peacefully on the same planet. But he believed that that atmosphere could be created only if the Kremlin believed that he was willing to use American military forces to defend the "free world's" basic interests. Certainly this was a factor in Kennedy's decision to sanction limited American military assistance to the Cuban rebels who made the invasion at the Bay of Pigs. He did not want the Soviet Union or the world at large to disregard his willingness to stand firm, to bite the bullet of military intervention. He had, after all, campaigned on his determination to face up to the communist menace in Cuba and everywhere else in the world. As Sorensen later wrote, Kennedy was concerned "that his disapproval of the [Bay of Pigs] plan would be a show of weakness inconsistent with his general stance."[96]

The Russians, however, probably had the opposite reaction. Kennedy's support of the invasion was limited to air support, and it was quite clear that he had some grave reservations about the whole undertaking (why else would he have canceled the second air strike?). This, at least, was the interpretation of many foreign affairs specialists in the United States, including Senator J. William Fulbright, chairman of the Senate Foreign Relations Committee. According to Haynes Johnson and Bernard Gwertzman, who wrote a biography of the Arkansas Democrat based on extensive interviews with him, "Fulbright always believed that the Bay of Pigs accounted for many of the ills that afflicted America throughout most of the 1960's. He and others felt that Kennedy's poor handling of that situation caused Khrushchev to misjudge the young President as inexperienced, unsure and perhaps weak."[97]

This image of Kennedy as a reluctant cold war warrior was probably reinforced when he met with Khrushchev at Vienna in June 1961. Khrushchev dominated the dialogue, pointing out the inevitable popular revolutions which would swallow capitalism. Kennedy tried to speak of the need for peaceful accommodations; Khrushchev spoke instead of the inevitability of violent change throughout the world. Again, there is good reason to believe that Khrushchev left Vienna confident that Kennedy would not be the tough, resourceful leader he had promised to be in the 1960 campaign. George Kennan, a noted American authority on Soviet affairs and then the American ambassador to Yugoslavia, was asked to review the transcripts of the Kennedy-Khrushchev meetings; and he saw ample evidence to provide the Russians with the image of Kennedy as an indecisive and even frightened commander. "I think they thought that this is a tongue-tied young man," said Kennan,

> who's not forceful and who doesn't have ideas of his own. They thought they could get away with something.
>
> He was, I thought, strangely tongue-tied in this interview with Khrushchev and numbers of these typical, characteristic Communist exaggerations and false accusations were simply let to pass . . . instead of being replied to, being rebutted.[98]

Kennedy's actions may have been explained, in part at least, by the advice he received to ignore much of Khrushchev's harangues. But whatever the explanation, the Soviet leaders probably viewed Kennedy in a different way from that in which he wanted to be seen. Kennedy understood this to some extent, and this helped account for his actions in the Berlin crisis, in resuming the American nuclear testing program, and in facing the Russians down in Cuba in the fall of 1962. Those actions probably surprised the Russians at first (Khrushchev, who was conferring with John J. McCloy on disarmament matters at the time of the Berlin speech in the summer of 1961, expressed surprise at Kennedy's bellicose tone). And there seems little question that Kennedy's belligerent words helped inspire the Soviet Union to accelerate its own military preparedness program (thus the resumption of nuclear tests in September 1961).

But the Russians probably also retained a certain skepticism as to whether Kennedy would actually force a nuclear confrontation with the Soviet Union except in circumstances that posed a clear danger to the United States' security. For when all was said and done, Kennedy had not authorized full American military participation in the Bay of Pigs; he had not challenged militarily the construction of the wall around East Berlin in August 1961; and he had sanctioned in 1962 the establishment in Laos of a neutral government with communist representation (something the Russians knew Eisenhower would never have tolerated). From this perspective, it was quite reasonable for the Soviet Union to attempt to install offensive missiles in Cuba in the late summer of 1962. Their installation would give the Soviet Union a lift in prestige and might enchance their military position as well (although most experts felt at the time that the military advantage to the Soviet Union was small).* And it seemed unlikely that Kennedy—despite a warning issued to the Soviet Union on September 4, 1962—would use American military might to destroy the missiles or force their withdrawal.

To the extent this reasoning underlay the Soviet decision, it was a miscalculation. Kennedy's subsequent actions dispelled any notion

*There is some basis for also believing that, to some extent at least, the Russians were genuinely interested in protecting Cuba against another Bay of Pigs invasion with greater American military support. Kennedy had rejected indirect overtures by Castro to renew American-Cuban relations in some way and, in fact, had told *Pravda* editor, Aleksei Adzhubei (who also happened to be Khrushchev's son-in-law), that the United States would not tolerate Cuba's status as a Soviet satellite. In this regard, it is also noteworthy that *New York Times* reporter Tad Szulc told Schlesinger, upon returning from a visit with the Cuban premier, that "Castro indicated that he would be interested in the resumption of some form of relationship with us, provided that we agree to quit trying to 'destroy' his revolution." See Jean Daniel, "Unofficial Envoy: An Historic Report From Two Capitals," *The New Republic,* Dec. 14, 1963, p. 18; Letter from Tad Szulc to Arthur Schlesinger, Jr., June 23, 1961, attached to memorandum from Schlesinger to President Kennedy, June 26, 1961, President's Office Files, John F. Kennedy Library.

that he would shy away from using American nuclear power to defend expressed American interests. The image of Kennedy as a weak and indecisive leader thus evaporated. Indeed, he consciously chose his course of action here on the assumption—and hope—that the Soviet Union would come away perceiving him as the strong President he wanted to be. In a nationally televised interview with three network correspondents two months later, Kennedy expressed his belief that the missile crisis had made Khrushchev more aware of the dangers of the nuclear age. As for his own decisions in that crisis, Kennedy acknowledged that he was not terribly worried about the military advantage which would accrue to the Soviet Union if the missiles were installed (". . . if they were going to get into a nuclear struggle, they have their own missiles in the Soviet Union"). No, Kennedy was more concerned about the images which his inaction would foster. The installation of the missiles, he said, "would have politically changed the balance of power. It would have appeared to, and appearances contribute to reality."[99]

It was, to be sure, an appearance avoided at great risk. But having finally convinced the Russians of his determination to use military force, Kennedy then tried to convince them—through a personal exchange of letters with Khrushchev, his personal representatives at the Geneva talks, and his American University speech—that he was genuinely interested in arms control and a general relaxation of tensions. The test ban treaty is evidence that those efforts were at least partly successful.

If Kennedy had difficulties presenting the image he wanted to in his relations with Soviet leaders, he found it much easier to establish a favorable image with the leaders of the Third World. To some extent, this was because of the positions he had staked out as a senator. He was one, for instance, who had spoken of the former colonies' right to self-determination in Vietnam, in Algeria, and in Central Africa. And he had repeatedly expressed his view that the United States should help further the implementation of that principle without demanding the new nations' alliance in the Cold War struggle. All this inspired hope among the leaders of the developing nations that they would find in John Kennedy an American President sensitive to their political aspirations and willing to help them meet their countries' material needs. "The news of Mr. John F. Kennedy's election to the Presidency of the United States of America was welcomed in Cambodia," Cambodian Premier Norodom Sihanouk later wrote,

> where nerves had become somewhat frayed by the obvious determination of the outgoing Government to ignore the powerful forces making for change unleashed throughout the world, and to maintain the "status quo" cost what it might: a tendency some-

> times to be found among older men, who have failed to keep abreast of the times. The election of a President of the United States still young in years, with an intellectual's approach to the business of Government, completed by practical experience of the limitations of power, who was alive to the need for the American People to adopt a "pioneer's" approach to challenging present-day problems, gave us good grounds to hope that the American Government under his aegis would modify its rigid attitudes toward Asian aspirations . . . "[100]

To a large degree, these hopes were not disappointed. Almost from the beginning, Kennedy was seen as a compassionate and understanding leader. His defense of the United Nation's position in the Congo, his stated willingness to accept a neutral government in Laos, and his proposals to expand the American economic assistance programs—all these factors suggested a man who would live up to his promise.

Kennedy's image among the Third World leaders was bolstered further by personal meetings. Among the first dignitaries invited to the White House, for example, were the leaders of Africa's emerging nations, even those, such as Sékou Touré of Guinea, who had publicly identified themselves with communism (shortly after Kennedy's election Touré accepted the Lenin Peace Prize from the Soviet Union). In these meetings, Kennedy made clear his intention to support the economic and political independence of the developing nations. "His keen personal interest was immediately conveyed to the Heads of State who met him," said Tom Mboya, "and this almost created, as it were, not just better diplomatic relations but personal relationships between Africa and America."[101] And as with others who visited him in the Oval Office, Kennedy conveyed to these African leaders an aura of confidence and dynamism. "With Kennedy there were sparks," said Samuel Ibe, a young Nigerian diplomat. "You would meet him and 'shoo, shoo,' sparks and electricity would be shooting all over."[102] Most of the African leaders were very much impressed with this personal magnetism and, most importantly, by Kennedy's apparent concern for their countries' futures. "At the end of our talks with President Kennedy," Touré told his people after returning from a 1962 visit to the United States,

> I and the Guinean delegation expressed our satisfaction to have found in the United States President a man quite open to African problems and determined to promote the American contribution to their happy solution.
>
> We took this opportunity to congratulate the American Government for the aid which it has so generously granted to Guinea and to express to him our satisfaction regarding the firmness with

which the United States struggles against racial discrimination and for complete integration of the colored people into American society.[103]

Most Asian leaders had a similar response to Kennedy. In almost every case, they saw Kennedy as a man concerned with their economic problems and sympathetic to their political dilemmas. Speaking of Kennedy's stature among the Asian countries, Roger Hilsman, who ultimately became the assistant secretary of state for the Far East under Kennedy, said, "It is difficult to convey the appeal that Kennedy had to the emerging peoples. But anyone who knew these peoples was conscious that his popularity was unrivaled in recent times by any other American since Roosevelt. . . . I think the principal source of his appeal was that he genuinely *cared* about the emerging peoples and that he had come truly to understand them and their aspirations."[104] Regardless of whether his interest in Asia was genuine, Kennedy nonetheless was able to convey a sense of real concern for peoples struggling to achieve independence. "My definite impression was that President Kennedy was trying to accept a new order in the world based upon the independence of all nations," Indonesian President Sukarno later said, "their forceful thrust towards establishing social justice, abiding peace and the brotherhood of Man, and a new order in which international relations should no longer be merely the vehicle of pure power politics."*

Despite his favorable image among the leaders of the Third World, Kennedy found it of only limited utility in helping them with their economic needs or in encouraging them to pursue their political interests in a manner compatible with American interests. The forces of nationalism, tyranny, hunger, and poverty proved to be a set of formidable obstacles which could not be overcome by an American President's apparent compassion or his aid programs. Even in those situations where Kennedy tried to be understanding he sometimes found himself in uncomfortable positions. In 1961, for instance, Sukarno threatened war unless the Netherlands relinquished its claim to Dutch New Guinea and allowed the colony to be absorbed by Indonesia. While the colo-

---

*Interview with Sukarno, Oral History Project, John F. Kennedy Library, p. 5. Kennedy met with Sukarno within a month after moving into the White House. Even before that meeting, however, Kennedy had remarked in private conversation that Sukarno's anti-American attitude was understandable in light of the CIA's participation in an unsuccessful attempt to depose the Indonesian leader in 1958. Somehow this remark got back to Sukarno, and it encouraged him to believe that Kennedy was an honest man who could appreciate another leader's perspective. This attitude was only reinforced after Sukarno met with Kennedy in the White House.

ny's people were not ethnically tied to the Indonesian people, Sukarno claimed that the land really belonged to his country and that, in any event, he did not want the Dutch to retain a foothold from which they could try to retake Indonesia.

Although Sukarno's threat was blackmail in its most blatant form, and while Kennedy did not want to disrupt the American-Dutch alliance, he acceded to Sukarno's pressure and persuaded the Dutch to surrender their claim to the colony. While he privately condemned Sukarno's tactics, Kennedy believed that world peace could not afford another war in Southeast Asia (with one seeming to approach an end in Laos and another escalating in Vietnam). But the settlement was criticized in the American press (Arthur Krock said it was a triumph "of the threat of armed force as a means of territorial aggression"[105]); and in spite of Kennedy's indulgence of Sukarno's aggressive whims, the Indonesian leader later repudiated American friendship and established closer ties with the Soviet Union.

The encounter with Sukarno was but one example of the frustration Kennedy experienced in trying to help the developing nations attain their self-professed goals of political independence. All the charm, magnetism, and understanding of one American President could not paper over the differences in perspective or eliminate the conflicts in national interests. And this was true of Kennedy's relations with national leaders in every part of the globe.

There was a certain irony in Kennedy's limited success with the leaders. He believed that their image of him was far more important than the images which the general populaces had. And yet he was far more successful in creating support among the world's peoples than in influencing their leaders. Many people around the globe—whether in Europe, Africa, Latin America, or Asia—came to see Kennedy as the embodiment of hope for peace and prosperity in the world. To some extent, there was a serious lack of logic and factual basis in that image. But it persisted nonetheless. People who heard Kennedy give his "Ich bin ein Berliner" speech in Berlin in June 1963 felt it; and so did those who saw him in other European countries, in Mexico, in South America, and even in those places where Kennedy had never set foot. Since his country's relations with the United States had deteriorated rapidly under Kennedy, for example, Roberto Campos, Brazil's ambassador to the United States, was surprised at the grief which Brazilians expressed over Kennedy's death: "I was amazed and surprised at the degree of popular emotion that one felt in Rio, probably an emotion as strong as one could notice anywhere in the United States if not stronger, since the Latins are more demonstrative, or at least supposed to be so. There was a feeling of deep personal loss. I saw people crying in the streets."[106] For some, there was an explanation for this feeling of personal loss in foreign countries. "Kennedy exalted the image of the American Presidency around the world," former *New York Herald Tribune* White House correspondent Robert J. Donovan once told me. From traveling abroad with Kennedy and on his own, Donovan felt that "Kennedy made the Presidency elegant and vocal and powerful." It was this image that most of the world mourned after an assassin's bullet hit its mark in Dallas.

CHAPTER 5

The Aftermath

For everything there is a season and a
time for every matter under the heaven.
A time to be born, and a time to die;
a time to plant, and a time to pluck that
which is planted; . . .
A time for war, and a time for peace.
What gain has the worker from his toil?

Ecclesiastes 3:1–9

The final test of a leader is that he leaves behind him in other men the conviction and the will to carry on.

Walter Lippmann

The most appropriate description of John Kennedy's Presidency is "frustrating." He himself was very much aware of the problems he failed to solve—and sometimes even dent—as President. "When I was in the House [of Representatives]," he recalled at one point in his presidency, "I used to wonder how President Truman got in so much trouble. Now I'm beginning to get the idea. It is not difficult."

The difficulties in forging new policies and new programs, as well as his narrow margin of victory in 1960, often made Kennedy very cautious in striking new ground to meet old problems or in fashioning bold strategies to deal with emerging ones. There was a certain irony in this caution. For Kennedy's vision of the President's responsibilities was not narrow. He viewed the American chief executive as a leader who was obligated to provide clear direction in a world suffocating from complexity and conflicts of interest. The American president of the 1960s, he believed, would have to help awaken the nation and even the world to the basic values which would have to guide governmental policies if the American economy was to be revived, if racial discrimination was to be eradicated, if the political independence of new nations was to be protected, and if a peaceful accommodation between communism and democracy was to be reached. On numerous occasions, his statements both as a senator and as a president therefore included explanations of those basic values and the importance of their incorporation in public policy.

Time and again, however, Kennedy was unable to reach beyond an articulation of those basic values. Time and again his policies remained frozen in the past and seemed unresponsive to the new realities he perceived. Too often his ideals were compromised by his understanding of the American and international political systems. Thus, conservative southern congressmen could not be pushed too far in accepting progressive legislative proposals; big business interests could not be alienated if the economy was to function smoothly and if generous support was to be forthcoming in his anticipated reelection bid in 1964; and the American commitment to dictatorships in Latin America, Spain, and Southeast Asia could not be abandoned if our adversaries were to remain convinced of America's strength and if international stability was to be preserved. Perhaps in time Kennedy would have acted more vigorously in trying to rise above the barriers favoring the status quo and resisting change; but in his one thousand days in the White House, Kennedy was largely unable to move the nation or the world in the direction which he thought necessary in order to avoid the turmoil and conflict that ultimately did prevail in the late 1960s. Sensitive to his responsibilities as a steward of the people, Kennedy nevertheless was unable to achieve as much as his campaign and his rhetoric promised.

To recognize the distance between Kennedy's promise and performance as President does not satisfactorily answer the question of whether Kennedy was, in the end, an effective leader. While I was writing this book, many friends and colleagues asked what my final conclusion would be. "Was he a good President?" they would invariably inquire. My response to them, as well as to any reader who has been asking the same question, is that there is no one word or one sentence answer to that question. The reasons are somewhat obvious. To measure the ultimate effectiveness of Kennedy, or any president, is an extremely difficult task. Such measurement depends not only on the perspective and expectations of the individual judge, but also on his ability to value proportionately the various achievements and failures of the president's administration. Who can say, for instance, whether Kennedy's successes in securing new trade legislation or a limited test ban treaty with the Soviet Union counterbalanced any failures, such as the Bay of Pigs invasion or the rejection of many of his legislative proposals?

The obstacles to any precise measurement of a president's effectiveness are further compounded by the fact that many of the president's decisions will continue to affect and be affected by national policies and international politics long after he has left the White House. The passage of time may alter the consequences and hence the full meaning of any presidential decision. In the 1970s, for instance, many argued, and with some justification, that the test ban treaty—by banning only atmospheric nuclear tests—actually created a political climate in which an underground testing program could proceed at an accelerated rate. And while Kennedy repeatedly resisted proposals to dispatch American bombers and combat troops to Vietnam, he did reaffirm publicly the United States' commitment to protect South Vietnam's political independence and he did send 16,000 American military advisers to that Southeast Asian country; many later argued, again with some justification, that these actions provided Lyndon Johnson a basis from which he could increase American military involvement in Vietnam (although, as I pointed out earlier, Johnson was free to expand or restrict the American commitment as much as he wanted, and there would be plenty of advisers available to rationalize either choice).

Vietnam is also proof of the fact that the president does not have the power to transform the world to suit his policies and objectives. A president's particular goals may be undermined by events and people he cannot control; his special areas of concern may be overshadowed by forces he does not really understand: our past is dotted with presidents who found the circumstances of their respective tenures much different from what they had anticipated, less comfortable than they had wished. In this regard, most presidents, but especially those of the twentieth century, would readily concur with Lincoln's confession that events usually control the president rather than vice versa.

This does not mean that a president is powerless to influence the outcome of events or the thoughts of people; in fact, he has considerable power. Nor do the limitations on the president's control of events and people mean that he should resign his administration's policies—or the fortunes of our country—to the whim of fate. A president interested in being effective (and reelected) had damn well better use his office to foster ideals and programs that will help alleviate the concerns of his constituencies. For today most Americans expect—and rightly so—that the president will assume a major responsibility in trying to resolve the public issues which dominate their lives.

Given the inherent conflicts in interests and perspectives, criticism is inevitable. It is difficult to conceive a situation in which everyone will be entirely satisfied with the president's course of action in any sphere. Disappointments are especially likely since much of the public often vests the president with an imagined power which far exceeds his actual resources and potential influence.

A president's lack of immunity from criticism is not necessarily the curse of the office, despite presidential statements to the contrary. Public and private criticism is often a curb on the president's growing self-righteousness: it is a guide for action and yet a restraint on his enthusiasm for power. To a certain extent, such criticism can define the limits of his policies and illuminate the weaknesses of his decisions. In a word, criticism can expose the president's sensitivity to the needs and emotions of the people he must lead. Criticism can likewise indicate the intellectual and emotional makeup of the incumbent: if a president ignores pervasive criticism, it may—depending on the particular circumstances—reflect either blind self-confidence (Wilson and the League of Nations controversy) or political naïveté (Hoover's reluctance to heed public criticism over his handling of the depression); if, on the other hand, the president caters to his critics in an effort to weaken their impact on his constituencies, it may—again depending on the circumstances—reflect political shrewdness (Roosevelt and the First New Deal's cooperation with business) or lack of self-confidence (Nixon and the short-lived adventure with welfare reform).

Any probe of Kennedy's presidency should try to account for these subjective and amorphous factors of the President's tenure—his ability to absorb constructive criticism, to defend his convictions and offer direction among his many constituencies, and to retain or enlarge the dignity of his office. Given the contradictions and ambiguities involved in these considerations, evaluating Kennedy, or any president, simply in terms of being "great," "near-great,"or "poor" loses much of the meaning. It is really myopic to refer to presidents by such broad adjectives; to paraphrase Kennedy's observation of myths, such adjectives provide the security of judgment without the discomfort of a careful analysis.

To raise the difficulties in assessing a president's leadership is not to dismiss the relevance or worth of such an assessment. For an intelligent president and a discerning electorate will profit from an analysis of history. John Kennedy was no exception. Familiarized with power by a father who moved in elite financial and political circles, Kennedy's interest in history and his desire to exercise supreme political power led him to study carefully those men who had preceded his occupancy of the White House. But in spite of this preparation, John Kennedy's first experience with executive power proved to be a humbling one. He soon learned that the presidency alone did not provide adequate means to achieve the goals of his New Frontier. Too frequently he realized the wide gap between the ideal of a dynamic, creative presidency envisaged in his energetic 1960 campaign, and the complex restraints and dilemmas which formed the realities of his presidential experience. This gap and its frustrations were perhaps epitomized at the height of the Cuban missile crisis. While considering the proper response to Soviet initiatives, Kennedy was reminded that his order to the State Department to remove the obsolete Jupiter missiles from Turkey had not been executed—a failure which aggravated the risks of any decision he would make in the Cuban affair. As if momentarily paralyzed by his frustration, Kennedy commented on the inherent futility of big government, and, while making a visible effort to control his emotions, left the Cabinet room.

The Promise of JFK's Leadership

Despite the difficulties in evaluating a president's performance, an attempt should be made to forge some final judgments about John Kennedy's success in providing strong and effective leadership. But to understand such judgments, it is first necessary to account for the standards employed to render them. In considering the performance of a president, or any elected official, perhaps the most appropriate standard is the promise which he offered to those whose interests he must represent. For the promise of a president's leadership, viewed in terms of the four criteria outlined above (the president's concept of the office; the methods by which he intends to make decisions; the manner in which he intends to serve that concept and execute those decisions to lead the public; and the images he will cast among his many constituencies), should reveal not only the attitudes and goals the candidate brings to the office; that promise also should suggest the means he will use to have those attitudes reflected in public policy and to achieve those goals. In short, the promise of a president's leadership delineates in a general fashion the legitimate expectations of the electorate that confers his right to hold office.

The promise of Kennedy's leadership in 1960 was not shaped by any clarion call from the public—the material prosperity in the United States (the poor still being "invisible") and the apparent lack of crises abroad dampened the public's interest in many of the issues which would dominate his presidency. In this setting, it is not surprising that much of the campaign concerned false issues. As an example, the "burning" campaign discussions surrounding the communist shelling of the Chinese islands of Quemoy and Matsu would fade quickly after the votes were counted in 1960. The lack of fervor among the public had likewise obscured the distinctions between the two principal presidential candidates. Indeed, before the election Arthur Schlesinger, Jr., felt obliged to publish a campaign piece, *Kennedy or Nixon: Does it Make a Difference?* (he argued that it did).[1] To say the least, few political creeds seemed to be at stake in the 1960 presidential election.

Despite this absence of precise ideological and political cleavages among the American public, the promise of Kennedy's leadership was clear. The style and direction of his campaign—coupled with an understanding of his words and actions as a member of Congress—offered guidelines to shape expectations of his presidency. Essentially, the promise of Kennedy in the White House was his willingness to strike a new balance between idealism and realism. Under Kennedy's aegis, the presidency would become actively involved in the implementation of progressive ideals in a manner that would render them palatable to the institutions of government and acceptable to the attitudes of the populace. For instance, in contrast to Eisenhower's tenure, there would be a new and deep concern within the White House for civil rights and for the plight of America's disadvantaged groups. Nor would the new President's concern for the oppressed be confined to the United States. Indicative of Kennedy's promise to work for change in the world was his statement the day before he publicly announced his candidacy for the Presidency that

> Whether we like it or not, this is a time of change. As a people that set out to change the world, I think we should like it, however difficult the challenges. For no nation is at its best except under great challenge. The question for us now is whether in a changing world we will respond in a way befitting "the land of the free and the home of the brave"—whether we will be at our best in these crucial years of our world leadership—whether we will measure up to the task awaiting us.
>
> That task is to do all in our power to see that the changes taking place all around us—in our cities, in our countryside, our economy, within the Western world, in the uncommitted world, in the Soviet empire, on all continents—lead to more freedom for more men and to world peace.[2]

As this statement suggests, Kennedy's concern for oppressed peoples was interspersed with the struggle he perceived between the forces of democracy and the forces of communism. Throughout his congressional years and his presidential campaign, Kennedy emphasized that the survival of our political system required the defeat of an enemy not contained by national boundaries. This perspective was perhaps exemplified by a statement made by Kennedy at the Mormon Tabernacle in Salt Lake City in September 1960. With a swipe at Nixon's claim that he had bested Khrushchev in the famous "kitchen debate" of 1959,

Kennedy proclaimed, "Defeating Mr. Khrushchev in debate does not defeat the enemy. For the enemy is the communist system itself—implacable, insatiable, unceasing in its drive for world domination." He then added that "this is not a struggle for supremacy of arms alone—it is also a struggle for supremacy between two conflicting ideologies: Freedom under God versus ruthless, godless tyranny."[3]

Given this perceived struggle between "freedom" and "tyranny," Kennedy felt constrained to promise that his presidency would undertake new initiatives to blunt the spread of communism. This promise was most strongly reflected in his commitment, if elected President, to isolate Cuba economically and to offer American assistance to those Cuban exiles seeking to depose Castro. At Johnstown, Pennsylvania, in October 1960, for example, Kennedy observed that the newly elected administration would have to pursue five measures to protect the western hemisphere from the communist system in Cuba:

> The first thing we have to do is let the Cuban people know our determination that they will someday again be free. We did not make clear to the Cubans our devotion to freedom during the brutal regime of the Batista dictatorship—and we are not making our position any clearer under the Castro dictatorship. We have no Cuban Voice of America broadcasts in Spanish at all, and only one hour a day in Spanish beamed in general to all Latin America. We must promptly initiate a major broadcast program for Cuba in particular, and more for Latin America in general.
>
> Secondly, we must end the harassment, which this government has carried on, of liberty-loving anti-Castro forces in Cuba and other lands. While we cannot violate international law, we must recognize that these exiles and rebels represent the real voice of Cuba, and should not be constantly handicapped by our Immigration and Justice Department authorities.
>
> Third, we must let Mr. Castro know that we do not intend to be pushed around any longer and in particular do not intend to be pushed out of our naval base at Guantanamo, or denied fair compensation for American property he has seized.
>
> Fourth, we must let Mr. Khrushchev know that we are permitting no expansion of this foothold in our hemisphere—and that the Organization of American States will be given real strength and stature to resist any further communist penetration by whatever means are necessary.
>
> Fifth, and finally, we must strengthen the cause of freedom throughout all Latin America, creating an atmosphere where liber-

> ty will flourish, and where Cuban communism will be resisted, isolated and left to die on the vine.[4]

Thus did Kennedy make plain his willingness to incur military and political risks to smother communism in Cuba and elsewhere throughout the world. Nor was this willingness announced quietly in a rare moment; rather, throughout his political career and campaign Kennedy fervently and frequently stressed his fear of the monolithic communist conspiracy. Hence, there should have been no surprise that Kennedy adopted such an extreme anticommunist posture in so many specific situations after he was elected. Nor should there have been surprise that Kennedy's positions on communism were well received by the electorate. "Better dead than red" was the watchword of the public mind. (In fact, polls showed that 80 percent of the people preferred war with the Soviet Union to a life under communist rule.)

The promise of Kennedy's presidency stretched beyond specific positions on specific issues. His political career as well as his presidential candidacy embraced the general promise that his presidency would be a dynamic one, that he would consciously direct the nation's resources and pointedly involve the public's energies in an effort to rectify perceived injustice and to thwart imminent hostilities. Certainly the promise was consciously furthered by Kennedy not only in his speeches, but in his actions as well. The much publicized "talent search" immediately after his election in 1960 seemed to epitomize the attitude of the new administration. The President, it was believed, would gather the best minds in the country and harness their collective power in his quest to achieve the grand goals he had set for his presidency.

This promise of grand achievement was not open-ended. Those familiar with Kennedy's background and his speeches recognized that his commitment to cherished ideals would not be quixotic. Rather, the strength of Kennedy's idealism and dynamism would be balanced by compromise, much as it had been during his congressional years. Unlike his brother Robert, John Kennedy was not prone to wear his heart on his sleeve or to alienate his critics casually, even when their criticism bordered on the absurd. In this sense, Kennedy reflected the stereotyped mold of the politician—he knew that at some future time his success might well depend on the support or votes of his former critics. In short, Kennedy did not intend to reform or revolutionize the American form of government. He did not want to intellectualize politics and make the political parties defenders of a particular ideology. He simply wanted to inspire in American government a dedication to formulate practical solutions to man-made problems. His White House staff reflected this political stance. With the single exception of Arthur Schlesinger, Jr., Kennedy's aides were not reformers or intellectuals.* They were bright, aggressive men bred by the system and, above all, eager to see it work for them—even, sometimes, at the expense of substance and consistency.

This is not to suggest that Kennedy's actions as President were guided only by his own political fortunes (although those fortunes were accorded great importance). He was also anxious to make his mark as a leader who would be responsive to the needs of people. At an early 1961 press conference, Kennedy declined to identify his administration with any particular philosophy, saying, "I hope I am a responsible President."[5] In his eyes, this meant the formulation of programs and policies which would, among other things, help provide food for the hungry, jobs for the unemployed, equality for the oppressed, and peace for the world. But in promising to be a responsible President, Kennedy did not harbor illusions that he would solve all of the world's problems or that he would preclude the emergence of new dilemmas and conflicts. His concept of the President as a focus, rather than as the monopoly, of direction and power led him to avoid such utopian assurances. Indeed, he continually reminded his audiences that the people of the United States and the world would ultimately determine the effectiveness of his leadership—for they would have to support his policies, accept the sacrifices that might be involved, and be patient when progress seemed beyond their grasp.

But Kennedy's promise of leadership was not defined wholly by public opinion. For the overriding thrust of his congressional years and presidential candidacy was a promise to be a leader, to be a Presi-

---

*While Kennedy respected the ideas which Schlesinger could bring to the councils of government, he probably was most interested in having Schlesinger write a detailed—and hopefully favorable—account of his presidency. (Kennedy knew that the judgments of posterity very much depended on who was writing the history.) After the Bay of Pigs invasion, Kennedy said to Schlesinger, "I hope you kept a full account of that." Surprised, Schlesinger replied that he had not since Kennedy had asked that no staff person take complete notes for fear that that would inhibit freedom of expression among his advisers. "No, go ahead," Kennedy told Schlesinger. "You can be damn sure that the CIA has its record and the Joint Chiefs theirs. We'd better make sure we have a record over here. So you go ahead." This, at least, is how Schlesinger explained his decision to take the copious notes that formed the basis of his chronicle of the Kennedy presidency.

At various times after that conversation, Schlesinger urged Kennedy to tape "conversations in which you would discuss the key decisions as soon as possible after the fact with the people most directly concerned." However much Kennedy desired an accurate and favorable account of his administration, he apparently never took up Schlesinger's suggestion. See Memoranda from Arthur Schlesinger, Jr., to President Kennedy, Feb. 1, 1961; January 29, 1963; February 12, 1963; June 8, 1963; President's Office Files, John F. Kennedy Library.

dent who would acknowledge his obligation to help make progressive changes in the world and who would accept the burdens and criticisms those changes would bring. It was a promise that would surely bring him into conflict with those who resisted alterations in the status quo. Southern congressmen, for example, were as amenable to Kennedy's campaign calls for broadened federal activity in the protection of civil rights as the American Medical Association was to Kennedy's campaign proposal for medicare. But the promise of Kennedy's leadership was to adhere to controversial positions despite political resistance, to ensure that the President did not become a passive participant in the affairs of government.

JFK's Performance: The Accomplishments

As the judgments of history began to crystallize shortly after Kennedy's death, it seemed that most would remember him more for the ideals he articulated and inspired in others than for substantive achievement in either program or policy. There is some basis for this judgment. Certainly his success in moving Congress was quite limited. "He never understood his relations with Congress as well as he should have," AFL-CIO lobbyist Andrew Biemiller told me. Senator Hubert Humphrey similarly commented that Kennedy "was not a real legislative leader [and] his legislative program was not that successful." Senator Gaylord Nelson agreed with this assessment. "Kennedy reflected a lot of splendor and elegance, and fit what the Eastern establishment wanted a president to look like, but legislatively he wasn't much," Nelson remarked to me. "There was a large gap between what he appeared to be and what he was." House Speaker Carl Albert was more cautious in expressing a like judgment. In dealing with Congress, said Albert, Kennedy operated "with a lot of handicaps: he was Catholic; he was from an isolated part of the country, the extreme northeast; he was younger than many people think a President should be; he had not been a national leader, he'd [not] been an important public figure. Considering all these things, I think he did extremely well."[6] Kennedy's obvious shortcomings were not confined to Congress. There were setbacks in foreign policy as well. He did not secure a disarmament agreement with the Soviet Union, he did not "blunt the spearpoint of aggression" in South Vietnam, and he did not stabilize American relations with all the NATO allies, most especially France.

Reference to Kennedy's failures in specific instances, however, should not blind us to the significance of one of his major achievements while President: an ability to inspire confidence in the President and in the ability of the government to help resolve the issues of the day. It is easy and perhaps fashionable to underestimate the value of this achievement, for it has been so glorified by the early Kennedy chroniclers that many regard it as a myth undeserving of respect. No one can doubt that many of the Kennedy chroniclers have indeed inflated the value of the inspirational quality of Kennedy's presidency. But this was nevertheless a very real achievement of no small dimension. For the spirit of American government and public attitudes toward that government, as Kennedy so often said, have to be the bases of any sound program. People will not support and cooperate with a policy they believe to be futile or perhaps a gesture merely designed to advance the President's political standing (one example being Gerald Ford's vain attempt in the fall of 1974 to restore the economy through slogans, buttons, and a program consisting primarily of voluntary cooperation).

To understand fully Kennedy's success in earning the people's trust and in winning their confidence, one has only to survey the public attitudes fostered by the two administrations that immediately followed his. While both Lyndon Johnson and Richard Nixon made significant strides in alleviating many of the nation's problems, both presidents wallowed in a sea of public skepticism. In contrast to attitudes generally prevalent during Kennedy's administration, under Johnson and Nixon the public was extremely cynical about the President's willingness to resolve the issues of the day in good faith. This public cynicism reflects many complex factors, not all of which can be tied to the President. But there is little question that both Lyndon Johnson and Richard Nixon—by their omissions as well as by their commisions—contributed greatly to this cynicism. And there is little question that both Lyndon Johnson and Richard Nixon had more difficulty than Kennedy in securing the public's trust and support, particularly when confronted by crisis.

Even in the face of obvious failure—as in the Bay of Pigs invasion—Kennedy's standing with the public remained high (83 percent of the public approved of Kennedy's presidency *after* the Bay of Pigs invasion). Because public trust was generally forthcoming, Kennedy was able to retain the public's confidence and secure its cooperation when meeting later crises, such as when the Soviet Union installed offensive missiles in Cuba or when the civil rights disturbances in 1963 led Kennedy to seek the voluntary help of business and civic leaders in removing discriminatory practices. Neither Lyndon Johnson nor Richard Nixon enjoyed the same degree of public confidence and cooperation.

One example involves the American military intervention in the Dominican Republic in 1965. Like the Bay of Pigs invasion, American action in the Dominican Republic was motivated by the fact that a socialist leader, here Juan Bosch, assumed the reins of power in a small Latin-American country. Like the Bay of Pigs invasion, the American involvement was on a limited scale. But *un*like the Bay of Pigs invasion, the American action in the Dominican Republic was successful in attaining the stated objective: Juan Bosch's government collapsed shortly after the American action, and he was replaced by an individual more oriented toward the American viewpoint. Notwithstanding this "success," Johnson's respect and support among the public soon fell; people were confused about the justification for the American intervention, and many attributed the confusion to Johnson's shifting explanations. Johnson's problems in gaining public trust were exacerbated when he started offering different rationales for the growing American presence in Vietnam. By March 1968 only 35 percent of the American public approved of his performance as President.

Like Johnson, Richard Nixon had great difficulties in retaining the public's confidence—even before Watergate. Lacking this credibility, Nixon was not able to rely on public support, even when, as in the case of the American invasion of Cambodia in May 1970, he embarked on an endeavor which he claimed to be vital to the country's security. In that case, for example, Nixon informed a nationwide television audience that his decision was dictated by a desire to preserve the historical ideals of democracy. "We live in an age of anarchy, both abroad and at home," Nixon observed, in which there were ". . . mindless attacks on all the great institutions which have been created by free civilization in the last 500 years." In this setting, he continued, history had posed a formidable challenge to the United States: "If when the chips are down the world's most powerful nation—the United States of America—acts like a pitiful, helpless giant, the forces of totalitarianism and anarchy will threaten free nations and free institutions throughout the world." Nixon acknowledged that the decision to invade Cambodia could have adverse consequences for his political future; but where the "challenge" of history was involved, he would sacrifice such personal pleasures as a second term as President: "Whether I may be a one-term President is insignificant compared to whether by our failure to act in this crisis the United States proves itself to be unworthy to lead the forces of freedom in this critical period in world history."[7] Despite this justification, Nixon's decision to invade Cambodia released a flood of protest and criticism. Colleges closed, politicians caucused, and ordinary citizens shook their heads in puzzlement—many sharing a concern that their President was misstating the facts and unable, or perhaps unwilling, to see the dangers of, and public opposition to, another escalation in the war.

This kind of skepticism toward the wisdom of Nixon's leadership in a crisis heightened dramatically as Watergate unfolded. His approval rating plunged below 30 percent, a majority of Americans believed that their President had been involved in a criminal conspiracy to obstruct justice, and a vast majority bitterly opposed his dismissal of Watergate Special Prosecutor Archibald Cox, who was trying to gain access to the President's tape recordings. It was in this context that it was learned that the United States was placing its military forces on alert in response to threats by the Soviet Union to intervene militarily in the "Yom Kippur" war then raging in the Middle East. But much of the public remained skeptical; in their eyes, the Soviet threat and the resulting American alert were merely ploys to divert the public's attention from Watergate.

This skepticism was openly expressed at Secretary of State Henry Kissinger's press conference the morning after the alert was put into effect. "Mr. Secretary," one of the first questioners began,

> could you tell us whether the United States received a specific warning from the Soviet Union that it would send its forces unilaterally into the Middle East? Do you have intelligence that the Russians are preparing for such an action? The reason I raise these questions—as you know, there has been some line of speculation this morning that the American alert might have been prompted as much perhaps by American domestic requirements as by the real requirements of diplomacy in the Middle East. And I wonder if you could provide some additional information on that.[8]

Kissinger denied that there was a Watergate connection, but the public skepticism persisted. At his press conference the next day, Nixon was asked about the justification for the American alert. He did not understate the case; he said with a great deal of vigor that the Soviet threat posed "the most difficult crisis we had since the Cuban missile crisis in 1962."[9] The skepticism remained nonetheless, and there appeared subsequently a rash of stories and reports about how the reasons for this "crisis" had been manufactured to help bolster the President's sagging political fortunes.

A certain skepticism toward presidential decisions—especially in a crisis—is a healthy thing for our political system. A president does not have a monopoly on wisdom, and the public should never hesitate to question the soundness of any decision the president has made or plans to make. But here people were not only questioning the wisdom of the American alert; they were more seriously concerned about the very integrity of the President, about his ability to assess the situation on its merits rather than from some sinister political perspective. Some people did of course question Kennedy's response in handling a particular crisis. (Thus, some agreed with Walter Lippmann that Kennedy should have used normal diplomatic channels rather than a military quarantine to pressure the Soviet Union to remove the missiles from Cuba.) But very few doubted Kennedy's sincerity in describing a situation or his willingness to deal with it in the manner which would best serve the country's interests.

It is not enough for a president to earn the public's trust in dealing with crises, however. Of equal, if not greater, importance is the president's ability to secure the public's support and cooperation in developing policies and programs to solve the nation's fundamental problems. If a president's success in this latter sphere is to be measured by the list of legislation he gets enacted, then Kennedy's leadership cannot receive high marks; for many of his major legislative proposals—such as the tax cut, medicare, and civil rights—did not become law while he was in the White House. But if success is measured by the contribution which the President makes to the ultimate adoption of legislation or other remedies, then Kennedy's leadership was quite successful in several areas.

He was the one who first pushed and tried to educate the public about the economic benefits of a tax cut while the government budget showed a deficit; and those efforts laid much of the groundwork in the public mind and in Congress for the eventual passage of the tax cut in 1964. He was also the President who stressed the obligation of the federal government to "wage war on poverty"; and many of his administration's ideas and proposals became a basis for Johnson's Great Society programs. Likewise, although he was quite slow in urging the adoption of comprehensive civil rights legislation, he moved quickly—and with a good deal of effectiveness—once he finally decided to push for action in the spring of 1963. He conferred with aides and congressional leaders, he held private meetings in the White House with hundreds of community leaders, and he addressed the need for legislative action in his public addresses—at each point explaining the problems in human terms, the benefits of comprehensive legislation, and, above all, the importance of the public's voluntary cooperation in achieving an integrated society. Indeed, at almost every principal juncture in his tenure—in the call-up of the army reserves during the Berlin crisis in 1961, at the University of Mississippi in 1962, during the steel price dispute in 1962, and at the University of Alabama in 1963—Kennedy sought to impress upon his public the responsibilities they should share with him in the crucible of leadership. As he reminded his audience at Vanderbilt University in 1963, "This nation was not founded solely on the principle of citizen's rights. Equally important—though too infrequently discussed—is the citizen's responsibility. For our privileges can be no greater than our obligations. The protection of our rights can endure no longer than the performance of our responsibilities. Each can be neglected only at the peril of the other."[10]

Kennedy's emphasis on citizen responsibility sprang from a deep-seated belief that, under most circumstances, it would be difficult for a leader to be effective if the people did not understand or support his policies and actions. In Kennedy's eyes, it was vitally important for a president to account for public opinion at all times—to heed it when the public views were strong, and to try to change them when they seemed to resist needed changes in national policy. In this setting, one can appreciate another basic accomplishment of Kennedy's presidency: a willingness to encourage a more accommodating public attitude toward the Cold War in general and the Soviet Union in particular. The significance of this accomplishment was all the greater since it represented a shift in Kennedy's promise to conduct a tireless crusade—economically, politically, and militarily—against the forces of communism. To a large extent, but particularly in the early months of his administration, Kennedy was true to that promise. He sanctioned limited American support of the Cuban exiles; invasion at the Bay of Pigs; he engineered a substantial increase in our country's conventional defense arsenal; he expanded American involvement in the South Vietnam government's struggle with the Viet Cong; and he readied the United States for war when Khrushchev's proposed treaty with East Germany seemed to threaten the security of West Berlin. Kennedy's militant postures here reflected not only his very real fear of communist expansion. Those militant postures also reflected his concern that other nations, but especially the Soviet Union, might interpret his youth and inexperience as weakness.

Despite these fears and concerns, Kennedy's commitment to contain or eradicate communism was not as unqualified as his campaign and inaugural address seemed to indicate. He refused to sanction American involvement in the combat operations at the Bay of Pigs invasion and then reduced the cover support the United States would give to the invading Cuban exiles; he rejected proposals for expanded American military operations in Laos and eventually acceded to the establishment of a coalition government there which included members of the communist Pathet Lao; he resisted the persistent advice of the military and many of his senior advisers that he dispatch up to 200,000 American troops to assist South Vietnam in its efforts to crush the Viet Cong; and, in the last months of his life, he began to question the basic premises of his promise to lead that tireless crusade against the forces of communism.

Kennedy's growing change of heart with respect to these basic premises became clear in his speech at the American University in June

1963, a speech which Khrushchev told Averell Harriman was "the best speech by an American President since Franklin Roosevelt."[11] In that speech, Kennedy declared that he did not want ". . . a Pax Americana enforced on the world by American weapons of war," that future stability and peace required that Americans reexamine their attitudes toward the Soviet Union, and that each adversary nation must search for means to make the world safe for a diversity of political systems. The concluding passages of the speech underscored the growing reservations Kennedy had about his unqualified promise to wage battle with communism on every front:

> Let us examine our attitude toward the Cold War, remembering that we are not engaged in a debate, seeking to pile up debating points. We are not here distributing blame or pointing the finger of judgment. We must deal with the world as it is, and not as it might have been had the history of the last eighteen years been different.[12]

Kennedy's change of heart soon found expression in foreign policy decisions. Shortly after the speech the United States signed a limited test ban treaty with the Soviet Union. In September 1963, Kennedy made a decision to renounce support for South Vietnam's President Diem unless the latter effected meaningful political reforms in his country.[13] And in October 1963, Kennedy authorized the shipment of surplus wheat to the Soviet Union to help counteract a severe wheat shortage in that country. The point of these examples is not that Kennedy foreswore all challenges to communism—he did not; rather, the point is that these sentiments and actions represented a significant alteration of his promise to be an anticommunist crusader, and that, partly as a result of having altered that promise, Kennedy was able to effect a détente with the Soviet Union shortly before his death. In other words, Kennedy's eventual success in relaxing Cold War tensions with the Soviet Union can be traced, in part at least, to his willingness to compromise on an early promise to his American constituency.

JFK's Performance: The Failures

Since a president is neither omniscient nor omnipotent, it is sometimes easy for him and his admirers to contend—and not without some validity—that independent forces checked his leadership. Kennedy himself sometimes revealed a certain fatalism in deliberating the possibilities that his legislative strategies or foreign policies would enjoy success. But however complex or seemingly unmanageable the President's political environment, it cannot absolve him of his responsibility to act in the nation's best interests—even when he knows his choices may antagonize powerful interest groups. In most circumstances, Kennedy accepted this responsibility; and in most situations he recognized the long-term benefits of a leader willing to endure controversy and criticism where basic issues were involved. Yet it was in these situations that he often failed to fulfill the promise of his leadership. Joseph Kennedy's children were not accustomed to losing in any competition, and John Kennedy very much reflected this upbringing. Even as President, he was frequently reluctant to assume risks without considerable assurances of success. The interplay of this attitude sometimes enabled Kennedy's Administration to escape caustic political disputes. But it was an escape that sometimes heightened the dilemmas of his presidency and later complicated the problems encountered by his successors. Especially in areas where public support was critical—such as congressional matters—Kennedy was often hesitant to assert forcefully a position consistent with his personal values and the ideals of his campaign.

Here it would be well to recall the history of triumphant leaders, for only rarely have history's noted leaders been universally loved and admired by those who were beckoned to the leader's cause. Indeed, Machiavelli warned his prince that it would be better for him to be feared by his subjects than to be loved. In short, to be successful, a leader need not command the affection of his followers so much as their respect—the former may ensure tears at the leader's demise, but the latter is far more crucial to sustaining a leader's political strength. Thus, if a president disregards his convictions and accepts the status quo in order to preserve his Gallup Poll rating, he may later find that he has undermined his ability to propose and effect needed change.

Had he lived, Kennedy probably would have recognized the long-term consequences of his shortcomings in this respect. He was, for instance, painfully aware of the fact that in many areas he had not adequately fulfilled his promise to employ his presidential resources as the wedge to assertive leadership. Although his image as President inspired public confidence, rarely was he willing to exploit that confidence to corral support for his programs or policies. In fact, it is somewhat of an historic misnomer to identify Kennedy's image among the public as charisma. Charisma is a political force. Traditionally, charismatic leadership inspires popular support for the leader's policies and programs; charismatic leaders are able to use their image as a tool to overcome skepticism and institutional resistance, to rally the people around an effort to help the leader attain his goals.[14] Kennedy's image was infrequently used as such a tool. That his charm and wit were greatly attractive to the American public cannot be denied; that such appeal was evident of broad political support for Kennedy's policies, on the other hand, is doubtful. Much of the public simply showed little interest in the progressive reforms to which Kennedy had committed his administration. "Thus, while there is much sentiment in favor of the domestic innovations and reforms, the sentiment, by and large, is passive and diffuse," Walter Lippmann wrote on the occasion of Kennedy's second anniversary in the White House. "The people are not passionately excited about education, medical care, conservation, and urban development."[15]

All this helped to make Kennedy quite cautious in approaching solutions to controversial issues. As an example, he would not employ his presidential image to overcome congressional opposition to civil rights legislation in 1961 or 1962. He believed that any exhortation to the public to pressure Congress on this score would alienate senators and congressmen while stirring few embers among the electorate. Although Kennedy had some justification for this decision, it not only exacerbated the frustration of the civil rights movement; more importantly, it evinced a willingness on Kennedy's part to renounce the role of positive leadership for one of waiting for the appropriate public mood to take hold of the country. It was more the politics of reaction than the politics of action; and it was inconsistent with the essence of Kennedy's promise to be a vigorous President who would not be content to issue ringing manifestos from the rear of battle.

A similar inconsistency was often apparent when big business interests were involved. Kennedy was usually very cautious about doing anything which might seriously offend those vested interests or their supporters on Capitol Hill. There is perhaps no better illustration of this attitude than the administration's handling of Senator Estes Kefauver's drug legislation.

Between 1959 and 1961, Kefauver conducted extensive hearings in exploring the manufacturing, merchandising, and efficacy of drugs. The hearings revealed not only a strong monopolistic strain in the industry (90 percent of the industry's $3.5 billion in revenue went to twenty-two of the industry's one thousand firms); the hearings also showed that the American public and their physicians were being misled about the virtues of some drugs, exposed to serious (and undisclosed) health hazards in the use of others, and overcharged for almost all of them. (There were newspaper headlines across the country when the committee found that one drug's selling price represented a 7,079 percent markup over cost and another's selling price represented a 1,118 percent markup over cost.) The publicity afforded Kefauver's hearings had political reverberations; politicians openly discussed the need to control the drug industry and the Democratic Party's 1960 platform included a promise to do something about "flagrant profiteering" in that business.

Kefauver introduced a remedial bill in April 1961. With the considerable publicity given to the issue and a new, progressive President in the White House, he had much reason to hope that his bill would pass Congress. The legislation struck at each of the major problems—it restricted the industry's ability to push new "miracle" drugs which simply combined two existing drugs, required pharmaceutical firms to register with and be subjected to inspections by the federal Food and Drug Administration, increased the FDA's power to halt the public sale of questionable items, and provided for "compulsory licensing" to increase price competition.* Needless to say, this legislation was not enthusiastically received by the drug industry. And while Kennedy said in his 1962 State of the Union Message that he would recommend new food and drug laws to "protect our consumers from the careless and unscrupulous,"[16] he was not eager to identify his administration with Kefauver's bold proposals.

When the Tennessee senator learned in early 1962 that Kennedy was preparing a message on consumer affairs, he went to the White House and conferred with Mike Feldman, who was doing the staff work on the message. Kefauver asked that the administration endorse his bill and, in any event, that it not propose a separate piece of legislation which could divide energies and attention to the basic reforms incorporated within his bill. The Consumer Message was issued on March 15, 1962, (the first to be made by a President since Theodore Roosevelt). It did not, in fact, propose additional drug legislation; but it did not endorse Kefauver's either. (When pressed on this point afterward, Feldman told Kefauver that the administration fully supported his proposal; "I wish to hell you'd made that clear in the Message," Kefauver responded.[17])

Within a month, however, Kennedy apparently changed his mind about new legislation and, without consulting Kefauver, had Congressman Oren Harris introduce another drug bill which did not include some of the stronger provisions in Kefauver's bill. This, of course, did not upset the pharmaceutical industry. Meanwhile, Senator James Eastland of Mississippi, chairman of the Judiciary Committee (which had jurisdiction over Kefauver's bill), talked with Feldman about the possibilities of reporting out legislation that would conform

*The "compulsory-licensing" provision allowed the original manufacturer to retain exclusive control over a drug for three (as opposed to seventeen) years. After that, he would be obligated to license any qualified applicant to produce the drug in exchange for a royalty equaling 8 percent of sales.

to the President's recommendations without embracing the radical measures proposed by Kefauver. Eastland suggested that it would be best to work things out without Kefauver and asked Feldman to send some technical advisers from the Department of Health, Education and Welfare to a meeting with some industry representatives and some like-minded senators. Feldman accepted the suggestion, had the HEW advisers go to the meeting, and said nothing to Kefauver. The result of the meeting was a bill more acceptable to the industry. When Kefauver learned of these developments at a Judiciary Committee meeting the next day, he was irate. He went almost immediately to the Senate floor to make a speech explaining how Eastland and the administration were trying to undercut drug reform. Feldman was told of Kefauver's intention and telephoned him at once, telling him that such a speech would embarrass the administration and asking him to reconsider. Kefauver would not yield. "I haven't been so shoddily treated in twenty-three years in Congress," he angrily told Feldman, and hung up.[18]

Kefauver's impassioned statement made a deep impression on many. (Murray Kempton commented on the statement in the *New York Post* by saying, "The passion of his grievance was unprecedented, both in a man so mild and in a loyal Democrat."[19]) But the prospects for Kefauver's drug bill did not look bright—until the news of the thalidomide tragedy splashed across the country's newspapers and television screens in July 1962. Millions of Americans were told in simple terms how a dangerous drug administered to pregnant women in Germany had produced deformed babies and how the drug's sale in the United States had been prevented only because of the extra diligence of a single official at FDA. A month later HEW reported that some of the thalidomide drug had been mistakenly distributed in the United States under a different label and that the government could not locate all the doctors who had gained possession of the mislabeled drug.

All this did not sit well with the American public and the majority of their representatives in Congress. Considerable pressure welled up for a law that would regulate the drug industry effectively. Kennedy quickly grabbed the opportunity. Even before the thalidomide story was played out, he urged the Congress to enact the Harris bill since it was stronger than the new Senate bill. (He did not mention the fact that he was partly responsible for the weaknesses in the new Senate bill.) Kennedy also urged the Senate to redraft its bill and restore many of the strong provisons contained in Kefauver's original version; but the request for redrafting was made in a way that would enable the administration, rather than Kefauver, to claim major credit for the revision. The revised bill was ultimately passed by the Congress and signed by Kennedy on October 10, 1962.

It may have been, as Mike Feldman later told me, that the administration always supported effective drug reform and that there was no intention to sidestep Kefauver.* But this episode was not an experience of which Kennedy could be terribly proud. For he had not provided farsighted or courageous leadership in fighting for meaningful reforms. Indeed, it seemed that he was primarily interested in exploiting a political opportunity that had developed in spite of his lack of leadership. And his methods offended many congressmen, particularly Kefauver, who witnessed the administration's chameleonlike tactics. Kennedy's actions here were perhaps explainable in terms of political expediency and the desire for electoral support at the next election. But such positions undermined the promise of good faith and strong convictions which Kennedy brought to the presidency.

Kennedy's behavior in the drug bill fight underscored the paradoxical quality of his performance as President. Thus, his concept of the presidency led him to be impressed by the need for assertive leadership, but he was often reluctant to face the political uncertainties which would follow in the wake of the leadership. And while his concept of the presidency led him to urge change in government policies and his constituencies' attitudes, Kennedy feared that the public would not support those policies or adopt those attitudes. In making decisions, Kennedy knew that the public interests were not always synonymous with the public opinions; but acutely aware of the ups and downs of public leadership, he could not consistently decide in favor of the public interests. He wanted to eliminate the myths which impeded the optimal solutions to pressing problems, but had anxieties about his ability to communicate the more appropriate alternatives to audiences that he knew were not always attentive. And lacking the momentum and strength of public support, he was often unwilling to take on the vested interests in Congress, in agriculture, in the business community, in the South, or just about anywhere.

In the end, Kennedy was able to foster the image of a romantic who wanted to have his administration embody high ideals and elevate the prestige of professional politics; but he was a skeptic who doubted his ability to take more than that first step of a thousand-mile journey. While he created an aura of idealism to surround his presidency, he was in fact a hard-nosed pragmatist who was willing to procrastinate for the sake of tranquility and the avoidance of defeat. He genuinely

---

*In fact, there is some evidence to suggest that, to some extent at least, the administration did work closely with Kefauver. See, for example, Memorandum from Wilbur Cohen to Myer Feldman, April 20, 1962; Memorandum from Wilbur Cohen to Myer Feldman, June 29, 1962, Papers of Myer Feldman, Box #8, John F. Kennedy Library.

appreciated the need for a public fully informed on the issues of the day and on the options available to the government in any situation; but he was unwilling to use his position consistently to educate the public on the issues and, indeed, often was quite willing—as in civil rights and Vietnam—to avoid public discussion for the sake of expediency. Despite the lapses in leadership, Kennedy was deeply committed to the presidency as the steward of the people; but he understood that he would probably not achieve everything he wanted to or even everything he promised—as he characteristically and perhaps prophetically told his family midway through his term, "I had plenty of problems when I came into office, but wait until the fellow who follows me sees what he will inherit."[20]

The paradoxes which characterized Kennedy's style of leadership were not very different from the paradoxes which have marked most of the presidencies in the twentieth century. To a certain extent, most presidents have found themselves in a state of political limbo as they each sought to balance the pressures to preserve the status quo with their responsibilities to effect needed change. And like the tenures of most of his predecessors, the paradoxes of Kennedy's style of leadership allowed him to fall victim to two overriding shortcomings: a lack of farsighted strategies to serve his established goals, and, secondly, a failure to grapple with the moral and constitutional dilemmas whose resolution must be the cornerstone of truly responsible democratic leadership.

Although well-versed in history and familiar with the current political trends, Kennedy devoted little time to establishing long-range strategies which would guide his administration's policies and programs, strategies which could give more substance to the farsighted rhetoric of many of his speeches. In part, this was a matter of personality. For Kennedy, the questions usually had to be specific, concrete, and immediate. While he would often try to gauge the long-term consequences of a particular choice that he was about to make, he showed little interest in mapping out long-term plans for problems which had not yet reached crisis proportions or attracted the attention of the country.

This personal style was accentuated in the first year or so of his presidency. Lacking any previous executive experience, his first encounter with the responsibilities of the presidency was overwhelming. The pressures were more penetrating than those he had known as a senator, the information he had to digest daily was immense even for a man as well read as he, and the institutional impediments were much more pervasive than he had realized even when he had criticized them as a senator. As a result, Kennedy found himself expending most of his energies in handling the day-to-day operations of the presidency—although as he oriented himself to the burdens of the office, he began to reserve more and more time for discussions with his senior advisers and others on the priorities of his administration and the means to achieving them.

Perhaps in this vein Kennedy did not entirely appreciate the lesson of Eisenhower's style of leadership. Despite the abrasive criticism heaped on him by the liberal establishment, Eisenhower's structured approach to the presidency contained some merit—though he failed to exploit it properly. Eisenhower observed that if the President were constantly concerned with the details of the daily operation of his office, he would have little time to consider and implement the long-range goals of his administration. Eisenhower therefore delegated considerable authority to his staff and, for the most part, had only the major decisions siphoned off to the Oval Office.

Watergate has shown that there can be serious dangers involved when a president delegates too much authority without means of supervising its exercise. But if the proper balance can be struck between the delegation and supervision of authority, there is much sense in Eisenhower's admonition that a president should not become too immersed in the minutiae of government. Kennedy, however, frequently seemed to be a victim of the politics of his immediate choices. It seemed that he was always rushing to keep up with existing crises rather than planning for the future. (There was the time in the late winter of 1963, for example, when interior secretary Stewart Udall sent Kennedy a memo requesting an appointment to discuss the long-range problems relating to conservation and environmental control. After some time went by without a response, Udall telephoned O'Donnell, who asked some questions about the matter but made it clear that he had no intention of scheduling a meeting with the President which did not require Kennedy's immediate attention. Udall never got his requested appointment.)

Even at those times when he did adopt a long-range strategy, it was often colored by a political expediency which limited its value in guiding administration policy. The coalition government established in Laos under the Geneva Accords of 1962 is illustrative. For the first time, the American government formally participated in the creation of a government which had communist representation. Kennedy's response to the situation was a breakwater in American foreign policy and reflected an open-minded attitude which deserves much credit. But he realized that the coalition was an unstable one at best, that at any moment a renewal of hostilities could present him with agonizing choices. Yet Kennedy failed to give these potential dilemmas much consideration once the settlement was reached; and he failed to heed the philosophical inconsistency between his support of the coalition government in Laos and his willingness to support the repressive Diem regime in South Vietnam primarily because it was anticommunist.

The political underpinnings of the inconsistency were fairly evident. In Laos the hostilities had escalated to a dangerous point and threatened to draw the United States and the Soviet Union into open confrontation. With a crisis just subsiding in Berlin, Kennedy believed that any palatable settlement of the Laotian controversy was essential. On the other hand, he did not want to sponsor too many coalition governments in Southeast Asia lest other nations regard it as a sign of weakness. And, of course, he could rationalize the difference in policies by claiming that the Vietnam conflict was not a civil war but a case of simple aggression, that the Viet Cong guerrillas were simply an arm of North Vietnam. Consequently, Kennedy was generally unwilling to challenge the righteousness of American support of South Vietnam so long as that support proved effective in sustaining the Southeast Asian government—until the summer of 1963 when he began to sense that continuation of such support would involve great political costs with few political benefits.

A similar political expediency was apparent in Kennedy's express policy in 1961 to spend billions of dollars to place a man on the moon by 1970. The decision was certainly consistent with Kennedy's desire to support scientific progress and to encourage development of man's resources. But Kennedy viewed the space program primarily in political terms. The Russians' launching of the sputnik in October 1957 seemed to epitomize the laxity in the American will to compete with the Soviet Union on political, economic, and technological fronts. His concern only increased after the Soviet Union launched Yuri Gagarin into space in April 1961, thus making the Russians the first to place a man in orbit. Kennedy quickly dashed off a note to Vice President Johnson, who was assigned the responsibility for coordinating the American space effort. "Do we have a chance of beating the Soviets," Kennedy asked, "by putting a laboratory in space, or by a trip around the moon, or by a rocket to go to the moon and back with a man? Is there any other space program which promises dramatic results in which we could win? How much additional would it cost? Are we working 24 hours a day on existing programs? If not, why not?"[21]

In personally delivering his second State of the Union Message to Congress on May 25, 1961, Kennedy publicly set forth the goal of placing a man on the moon by the end of the decade. Here, too, he emphasized the symbolic value of such a goal. "Finally, if we are to win the battle that is now going on around the world between freedom and tyranny," he said,

> the dramatic achievements in space which occurred in recent weeks should have made clear to us all, as did the Sputnik in 1957, the impact of this adventure on the minds of men everywhere, who are attempting to make a determination of which road they should take. . . .
>
> * * * *
>
> . . . I believe that this nation should commit itself to achieving the goal, before this decade is out, of landing a man on the moon and returning him safely to the earth. . . . But in a very real sense, it will not be one man going to the moon—if we make this judgment affirmatively, it will be an entire nation. For all of us must work to put him there.[22]

Once Kennedy made the proposal, Congress responded with the necessary funds. The work continued unceasingly until, in July 1969, three American citizens made the first round trip to the moon. For all this success, Kennedy's commitment to space was a mistake. For it required the nation to invest a good deal of its attention, energy, and money in a project which would yield few returns in solving many of the more basic problems here on earth. It would have been more consistent with Kennedy's understanding of the problems confronting the nation to give such publicized priority to other goals, such as a good job and a decent home for every American by 1970. (Indeed, in April 1963, James Reston reported that labor unions were becoming critical of Kennedy because "the President says unemployment is the nation's major economic problem, but puts $5 billion into space, which produces few jobs, rather than putting at least part of this into urban transportation and housing that would create jobs."[23]) As time progressed, Kennedy became increasingly concerned with the price tag of the space effort and the wisdom of making the project such a high priority item. But aspiring to place a man on the moon was a palatable political gesture in 1961. And in Kennedy's eyes at least, it could demonstrate dramatically that he was in fact getting the country moving again.

Kennedy's failure to develop sufficient long-range strategies in other, more important areas was compounded by another basic shortcoming: a failure to grapple with some fundamental moral and constitutional principles. This failure was not uncommon. In their eagerness to preserve their political standing, most presidents have sometimes ignored the implications that their actions have on the moral and constitutional premises of our democratic government. The efficacy of presidential decisions is too often equated with the righteousness of those decisions.

Kennedy's first principal international confrontation—the Bay of Pigs invasion in Cuba—shows how the dichotomy can be obscured. Following the abortive invasion of Cuba, there was abundant criticism of Kennedy's ability to appraise the consequences of his decisions. Kennedy himself lamented the deaths and embarrassment to the United States which the invasion produced. But the criticism he responded to was that his advisers, and particularly the intelligence system, had failed to provide him with accurate information and sound analyses. The committee which he subsequently established to investigate the Bay of Pigs fiasco therefore focused on the efficiency and effectiveness of the intelligence system. The underlying and more fundamental question, however, was whether the powerful United States had a moral right to assist an invasion of a small country which was not threatening the United States. Advice as to whether the invasion would be successful was irrelevant in answering this latter question; morality is not contingent upon success.

A few in the administration sensed this. A month or so after the Bay of Pigs invasion, for instance, Chester Bowles, then the undersecretary of state, observed in his personal notebook,

> The question which concerns me most about the new Administration is whether it lacks a genuine sense of conviction about what is right and what is wrong. I realize in posing this question I am raising an extremely serious point. Nevertheless, I feel it must be faced. . . . The Cuban fiasco demonstrates how far astray a man as brilliant and well intentioned as President Kennedy can go who lacks a basic moral reference point.[24]

Unfortunately, people with Bowles's concern were among a distinct minority, the vast majority of whom (including Bowles) were not part of Kennedy's inner circle. Few presidential energies were expended deliberating the serious questions posed by Bowles. As with earlier (and later) presidents, Kennedy continued to invoke the cloak of "national security" to justify practices that ignored constitutional restraints as well as basic moral principles.

The use of wiretaps and other forms of electronic surveillance was a clear example of Kennedy's failure to grapple with these constitutional and moral limitations. The fourth amendment to the Constitution provides that the government cannot invade a person's privacy and take something without first obtaining a court warrant based on probable cause.* It was not until 1967 that the United States Supreme Court held that wiretapping was a "search" subject to the fourth amendment limitations.[25] Long before that, however, lawyers, judges, and politicians alike recognized the grave ethical and constitutional questions raised by the use of wiretaps which were not approved by a court.

In 1928, U.S. Supreme Court Justice Oliver Wendell Holmes said (in a dissenting opinion) that warrantless wiretapping was illegal but that, whatever the status of the law, the government's practice of secretly listening to private telephone conversations was "dirty business."[26] The basis of this ethical concern is plain. People should not have to worry that their private conversations are being overheard—especially by government agents who can use the information against the people involved. If individual freedom means anything, it means, U.S. Supreme Court Justice Louis Brandeis said in that same 1928 case (and also in dissent), the right to be left alone, to know that one's private affairs are protected against the intrusive eyes and ears of the government.

Ethics aside, Holmes's concern with the lawfulness of warrantless wiretaps was well placed and easily understood. The fundamental premise of our constitutional system is that all government powers are limited and that each branch of the government can be checked by one or both of the other branches. This check, it was believed, would help ensure that the government's powers would be exercised only for legitimate purposes. The power to conduct warrantless wiretaps flies in the face of this basic notion. The president's exercise of that power escapes the review—and check—of the Congress and the courts. The President (or one of his agents) can decide alone whose telephone to tap and for how long—no questions asked. As a result, presidents can use—and have used—warrantless wiretaps for purposes which bear little relation to the nation's interests. Kennedy was not the first—nor the last—President to be amused by the FBI's information on the purely private affairs of law-abiding citizens, information which was derived in great part from wiretaps.[27] It may be, of course, that there have been and will be occasions when the government has a legitimate need for wiretaps; but under our constitutional system, the government's needs alone do not define the limits of its powers. Our founding fathers were more concerned with protecting the individual against the government than

*The fourth amendment reads as follows: "The right of the people to be secure in their persons, houses, papers, and effects, against unreasonable searches and seizures shall not be violated, and no warrants shall issue, but upon probable cause, supported by oath or affirmation, and particularly describing the place to be searched, and the persons or things to be seized."

in expanding the government's tools to exercise power over the individual.[28] For that reason, they wanted a neutral court to determine whether or not the government's intended invasion of an individual's privacy was reasonable.*

Even those government officials with the power to wiretap were, at least initially, sensitive to the ethical and constitutional dangers of the government's use of such devices to spy on individuals. "While [wiretapping] may not be illegal," FBI Director Hoover commented in 1931, "I think it is unethical and it is not permitted under the regulations by the Attorney General."[29] President Franklin D. Roosevelt was another who recognized the problems. On the eve of World War II, he directed Attorney General Robert Jackson to use warrantless wiretaps to obtain information about the "fifth column" and other subversive elements in the United States. But even in authorizing this electronic surveillance, Roosevelt issued a cautionary note to Jackson. "Under ordinary and normal circumstances," he told the attorney general, "wiretapping by Government agents should not be carried on for the excellent reason that it is almost bound to lead to abuse of civil rights." He therefore urged Jackson to restrict the wiretapping "insofar as possible to aliens."[30]

After World War II, the government used wiretapping not only for national security purposes but for investigating domestic crimes as well. But in time it would be revealed that many American citizens were subject to such wiretaps even though their activities did not involve crimes or threaten the nation's security.[31]

All this wiretapping and other electronic surveillance was done without affirmative congressional approval. Roosevelt's, Truman's, and Eisenhower's Administrations attempted to have Congress authorize wiretapping; each of these attempts failed. Roosevelt and his successors (up to and including Ford) nevertheless maintained that the

---

*In 1972, the U.S. Supreme Court held that the government could not use warrantless wiretaps against individuals even when they were suspected of endangering the nation's "domestic" security. ". . . Fourth Amendment freedoms cannot properly be guaranteed," the Court said, "if domestic security surveillances may be conducted solely within the discretion of the executive branch. The Fourth Amendment does not contemplate the executive officers of Government as neutral and disinterested magistrates. Their duty and responsibility is to enforce the laws, to investigate and to prosecute. . . . The historical judgment, which the Fourth Amendment accepts, is that unreviewed executive discretion may yield too readily to pressures to obtain incriminating evidence and overlook potential invasions of privacy and protected speech." The Court declined to say whether or not it would also require a warrant when the government wanted to wiretap an American citizen who has a "significant connection" with a foreign power. *United States* v. *United States District Court*, 407, U.S. 297, 317 (1972).

President has an inherent power to use warrantless wiretaps to protect the nation's security.

Kennedy followed the footsteps of his predecessors. He recognized the inherent constitutional and ethical dangers of wiretapping. (In fact, as a congressman he introduced a bill to prohibit all wiretapping.[32]) And he would listen patiently to liberal friends who urged him to abandon the practice. But he did not fully share their concerns. He not only continued the use of electronic surveillance for so-called "national security" reasons—he expanded it.[33] And, like his predecessors, he urged Congress to adopt legislation to authorize warrantless wiretapping for national security purposes.*

Wiretapping was not the only other issue to present Kennedy with some difficult constitutional and moral questions. Indeed, such questions were most dramatically presented by the Cuban missile crisis. In announcing the quarantine and in communicating with other nations, Kennedy was acknowledged as the spokesman who had the singular power to act for the nation. But the underlying issue is whether Kennedy, as President of the United States, had the moral and constitutional right to approach the situation as he did—assuming total responsibility for the United States' forceful response to the deployment of Soviet missiles in Cuba. In other words, to what extent did Kennedy's behavior here conform to the obligations and privileges accorded his office by the Constitution and the American political system?

In light of his constitutional duties as the commander in chief of the armed forces and as the principal force behind the nation's foreign policy, a president is normally expected by the citizenry to assume a primary responsibility in preserving the national security. By 1960, moreover, there was a long line of historical commentary that supported the president's power to act on his own in meeting foreign dangers.[34] The drafters of the Constitution, after all, empowered Congress to "declare" war with the assumption that the president would be free to re-

---

*In testifying before Congress on the administration's wiretap proposal, Attorney General Robert Kennedy argued that the law was needed for two principal reasons: on the one hand, there was no *legislative* restriction on the government's power to wiretap (the Constitution was apparently overlooked here); on the other hand, the existing law did prohibit the use of wiretap information in a court—even if that information provided evidence of a crime. In 1968, Congress finally did pass a law authorizing government wiretaps with a court warrant for certain criminal purposes and allowing the use of wiretap information in court. The Congress declined to deny the President any constitutional power he may have to use warrantless wiretaps for national security purposes. See *Hearings on S. 2813 and S. 1495 before Committee on the Judiciary,* U. S. Senate, 87th Congress, 2d Session, pp. 1–46 (1962); Memorandum from Lee C. White to President Kennedy, March 12, 1963, President's Office Files, John F. Kennedy Library.

pel sudden attacks without the need to secure prior congressional approval. And it was generally accepted that the president would act in secrecy in gathering information about the activities of foreign powers. (In *The Federalist Papers*, John Jay extolled the Constitution for allowing the president alone "to manage the business of intelligence in such manner as prudence may suggest."[35])

These factors encouraged presidents to view their power in foreign affairs as self-contained, and that view was accorded legitimacy not only by the many foreign military excursions authorized by presidents but by judicial decisions as well.* In 1890, for example, the United States Supreme Court recognized an inherent presidential power to defend the "peace of the United States" through "rights, duties, and obligations growing out of the Constitution itself, our international relations, and all the protection implied by the nature of the government under the Constitution."[36] In 1936 the Court made the sweeping (and largely inaccurate) constitutional claim that the president has the "plenary and exclusive power" to be "the sole organ of the federal government in the field of international relations—a power which does not require as a basis for its exercise an act of Congress . . ."[37] And with the advent of the First and Second World Wars, the Court upheld numerous congressional and presidential actions that allowed the president broad power in meeting foreign dangers—even if the action involved a significant infringement of individual rights and liberties. (FDR's internment of 110,000 Japanese-Americans during World War II was perhaps the most offensive action to be sanctioned under the aegis of war.)

These and like judicial pronouncements made the president seem immune to external restraints in dealing with a foreign enemy. In discussing some of these cases shortly before Kennedy entered the White House, presidential scholar Edward S. Corwin wrote "that in the war crucible the more general principles of constitutional law and theory . . . become highly malleable, and that even the more specific provisions of the Bill of Rights take on an unaccustomed flexibility."[38] The President's obligation and power to act unilaterally seemed all the greater with the advent of nuclear bombs and new, technologically advanced weaponry. Russia could launch a devastating nuclear attack on the United States within minutes, and this seemed to underscore the

---

*It has been claimed that the United States has engaged in 150 wars but that only five were formally sanctioned by a congressional declaration. In fact, few of those "wars" were much more than military posturing. See Arthur Schlesinger, Jr., *The Imperial Presidency* 51–54 (1973). But the claims were pervasive and did much to perpetuate the myth that the president alone had the responsibility to act in foreign exigencies.

importance of presidential expertise and secrecy. And the public seemed to expect and hope that the President would make the most of these power advantages in protecting the United States' security.

Kennedy thus had ample precedent and justification to believe that he possessed both the obligation and the power to thwart any sudden initiative by the Soviet Union that threatened American security. Consequently, when Republican senators and congressmen publicly expressed fears in the summer of 1962 that the Soviet Union was establishing an offensive missile base in Cuba, Kennedy believed that he could not stand idly by if such charges proved to be true. And when their accuracy was confirmed in October by some high-altitude photographs, he believed he had to act. If he had ignored the installation of the missiles, he could have spared the country the risks of a nuclear confrontation with the Soviet Union. But if the American public interpreted the presence of the missiles as a threat, peace could not have guaranteed public support of Kennedy's position. Indeed, if the maintenance of Soviet missiles in Cuba instilled fear in the American public—as Kennedy believed it would—public confidence in his ability as the steward of the people, he felt, would have been seriously undermined; cooperation with the public and with other political bodies, a critical factor in any president's power to cope with a crisis, would have been extremely difficult. No doubt Kennedy believed that his view was confirmed by his meeting with twenty congressional leaders shortly before the public announcement of the quarantine. At that meeting, many senators and congressmen were critical of Kennedy's limited response and urged him to take stronger military action.

To some extent, Kennedy had expected this critical reaction from various quarters; he knew that many people—like Dean Acheson—would prefer a more forceful response, such as an American air strike into Cuba. But he had laid that option aside for at least two basic reasons. First of all, the military could not provide him with any guarantee that such an air strike would be successful; they told him, after much prodding, that a full-scale invasion (with a risk of many American casualties) might eventually be necessary. Second, he was apparently persuaded by the reasoning of his brother Robert, who had argued strenuously at the Executive Committee meetings that it was simply immoral for a superpower like the United States to execute a surprise attack on a small nation like Cuba which had not actually engaged in any aggressive behavior. (In fact, while plans for an American strike at Cuba were being proposed at one of the first White House meetings, the attorney general passed a note to the President: "I now know how Tojo felt when he was planning Pearl Harbor."[39])

Throughout these discussions, however, apparently no thought was given to involve Congress in the making of the decision. The exclusion of members of Congress here was not surprising; but it certainly was highly questionable. For the power to declare war is vested constitutionally in Congress. Only that body, collectively representing the popular will (in theory at least), could sanction the entry of the United States into armed conflict with another nation—unless there was a sudden attack on the United States (and there was no evidence of either the Soviet Union or Cuba planning such an attack).

There was, of course, no war, and so Kennedy never actually usurped Congress's power to make the final decision. But if war had resulted, it would have been a different matter. For in establishing the quarantine and in threatening to remove the Soviet missiles by military force, Kennedy stripped Congress of the freedom to decide whether armed conflict was necessary. In effect, Congress's power to declare war was so seriously diluted by Kennedy that it could only approve or disapprove of his actions.

This observation is not affected by the fact that Congress adopted a joint resolution on October 3, 1962, prior to the discovery of the offensive Soviet missiles in Cuba. That resolution, adopted without initiatives or pressure from the White House, expressed only the United States' determination to prevent the development of a situation in Cuba that would threaten the security of the United States. It did not sanction any presidential decision to emasculate or ignore Congress's constitutional power to declare war. Thus, while Congress was regularly consulted about administration policy toward Cuba before the discovery of the missiles on October 16, such consultations could not replace the President's obligation to respect the Congress's constitutional war-making power in responding to a specific situation. That Congress might have agreed with the President if consulted, or that the Congress might have approved subsequently the President's course of action, does not resolve the issue. For the test of legitimacy is not the efficacy of the President's policy; the question is whether he *alone* should represent the American people in risking armed confrontation with the Soviet Union.

In establishing the Executive Committee, Kennedy obviously sought the benefits of consultation without the inevitable delay and probable inefficiency of most congressional debates. That many viewpoints were represented at the Executive Committee's meetings, and that they were carefully considered by Kennedy before he made any decision, shows that he was anxious to consider all viewpoints and think the matter through before making the final decision.

At the moment the "crisis" was identified, however, there was no assurance that Kennedy would consult with these men or that he would consider their analyses in formulating and implementing his decisions. Furthermore, these individuals were much less qualified to represent the American people than the Congress—none was elected to office in his own right, some were not even officials of the government, and all served at the grace of the President. At no point did the American people—whose destiny Kennedy may have decided—have a real opportunity to voice opposition to his decisions, to express the belief that the gains of the quarantine did not merit the risks of armed confrontation, or to modify his course of action in any way.

In the last analysis, Kennedy's choices were limited by his interpretation of his obligations. He believed that resorting to constitutional procedures for declaring war would be disadvantageous in two respects. First, there was no immediate necessity to declare war because there had been no invasion or armed strike; and second, any deference to congressional bodies probably would have reduced needed flexibility. On the other hand, for him to do nothing, Kennedy thought, would weaken the respect he would command from Congress and the public as the crisis evolved, or in any future test of presidential leadership. Not wanting to dilute the inherent mobility and resources of his office, he felt constrained to adopt a compromise position that he hoped would avoid the conflict between the presidential and congressional spheres of duty. The quarantine allowed him to meet his obligation as commander in chief without technically encroaching on Congress's responsibility to determine whether the United States should engage in a war.

This reasoning is not sufficient where the risks include a nuclear exchange with the Soviet Union. This is not to suggest that Kennedy's avoidance of Congress at the crucial moment had no rational basis at all; but it is to question the support that his avoidance may give to future presidential decisions. For the danger of Kennedy's resolution of the Cuban missile crisis is that one human being *alone* exercised the responsibility to decide a matter that could have determined the fate of 185 million others. Surely this is one possibility that the Founding Fathers tried to guard against by bestowing upon Congress the authority to declare war (although undoubtedly the Founding Fathers never contemplated a nuclear holocaust). As James Wilson explained to the Pennsylvania Constitutional Ratification Convention, Congress was given the power to declare war so that a "single man [could not] . . . involve us in such distress."*

The Cuban missile crisis thus contains the seeds of tragedy. For like

*Here it is worthwhile to remember the Constitution provides only that "The President shall be Commander in Chief of the Army and Navy of the United States, and of the Mi-

the classical Greek drama, the Cuban missile crisis reflected a tension between two forces that could not be easily reconciled: the power of the President to protect the nation's security, and the constitutional authority of Congress to determine whether a situation demands a declaration of war. While one can understand the convergence of Kennedy's obligations and fears, one can nevertheless realize the awesome burden he assumed, a burden designed by the Founding Fathers to be shared by Congress and the citizenry in the crucible of leadership.

In terms of ensuring the survival of the American political system, the lesson of the missile crisis should be equally evident. For the contingency of inflicting mass violence on another nation—and that nation's retaliation on the United States—need not rest on irrational hysteria or accident. Rather, the system's Achilles' heel appears to be an honest error in one individual's judgment. To hypothesize, in another time and circumstance, another president might consult with only one or two advisers and conclude that the risk of war—though unfortunate—was necessary. The wheels of human destruction might then begin to grind before further analysis and debate could illuminate the source of any miscalculation. The reality of this possibility is in fact suggested by Nixon's decisions to invade Cambodia on May 1, 1970, to attempt to rescue American POWs by invading North Vietnam in October 1970, and to place the American forces on alert during the Yom Kippur War in the Middle East. In all three cases, Nixon consulted with only a few advisers before making his decision; in none of the cases was the public or the Congress consulted or informed before the implementation of the decision.

In the aftermath of the missile crisis, Kennedy paid little attention to the dangers of the President's acting alone in risking nuclear war or other armed conflicts. Indeed, he continued to use such unilateral decisions to increase the American involvement in Vietnam. Such decisions underscored the unfortunate irony of his presidency. Eager to involve the citizenry in the crucial decisions and issues of his administration, he was unable always to provide a meaningful avenue for such participation; in these instances, he frequently found it easier to resort to vague notions of executive responsibility to justify the decisions made solely within the confines of his office. And only rarely was the public aroused to protest its exclusion. Indeed, in American society,

---

litia of the several States, when called into the actual service of the United States; . . ." Article II, Section 2. In Federalist Paper number 69, Alexander Hamilton said that this power "would amount to nothing more than the supreme command and direction of the military and naval forces, as first general and admiral of the Confederacy; while that of the British King extends to the *declaring* of war and to the *raising* and *regulating* of fleets and armies—all which, by the Constitution under consideration, would appertain to the legislature."

where criticizing the President is as fashionable as it is valuable, there still remains a remarkable faith among the populace as a whole—a faith that in the ultimate tests of leadership, such as in the Cuban missile crisis, the presidency will be the focus of rational processes and morality, that the folly of man's history will somehow be avoided by an individual president's decisions.

This faith is even reflected in the War Powers legislation enacted by Congress in the fall of 1973 over President Nixon's veto.[40] Proponents of the legislation proclaimed that it would restore the proper congressional role in controlling American involvement in foreign conflicts. To some extent, this is true. The legislation requires the president to justify to Congress the dispatch of American troops abroad and, if Congress does not affirmatively approve, requires him to withdraw the troops after sixty days (or ninety days if the president claims a continuing military necessity). But at the same time, the legislation leaves the president free to conduct a foreign war on his own authority for two or three months. And it is unclear whether the legislation would circumscribe the president's actions in a situation, like the missile crisis, where the dispatch of troops to a foreign nation is not involved. (It should also be remembered that the missile crisis, from start to finish, occupied only thirteen days.)

It is all well and good for people to have confidence in their leaders; but the better part of wisdom—especially in matters of war and peace—is to place faith in established procedures. Otherwise the security and survival of the nation will in many situations continue to rest on the sound judgment of a single individual. I have no easy answer for the problem—except to say that, at minimum, there should be formal consultations with Congress whenever the president contemplates military action that may result in armed conflict with another nation. The War Powers Act does require the president to "consult" with Congress before using armed force in foreign conflicts. But the term "consult" is not defined, and in the first application of the provision—President Ford's rescue of the Mayaguez merchant ship crew from Cambodia last spring—the President interpreted the term only to require that he advise Congress of the decision shortly after it was made and the armed assault initiated. If Congress's constitutional war-making powers are to be preserved, the term "consult" must have a broader meaning than that. But, in any event, the solution will not be found until it is recognized that the problem still exists.

Conclusion

It is, of course, impossible to determine whether Kennedy would have succeeded in fulfilling the promise he offered in 1961 if he had survived two terms in the White House. It is not entirely clear how he would have responded to evolving problems and changing circumstances. But it is clear the additional five years would have allowed Kennedy to clarify and perhaps change the decisions of those first three years and pose different choices for his successors.

Kennedy's response to the hostilities in Vietnam is illustrative. His growth in the White House may have enabled him to draw upon his lessons with the Laotian settlement and the détente with the Soviet Union to realize the dangers of the growing American involvement in that conflict. As noted earlier, there is much evidence to suggest that Kennedy was in fact becoming more sensitive to those dangers. In short, in judging the soundness and foresight of Kennedy's actual decisions in exercising leadership, one should also consider the probable direction of those decisions, the degree to which they would mesh with the trends of history, and the extent to which he would grow with his experiences. For Kennedy's politics, like a nation's politics, did not know the absolute demarcations which define the end of one policy and the inception of another—demarcations which could guide analyses and facilitate indisputable conclusions. American politics is a continuum, and each president is part of that continuum.

For three years, the promises of Kennedy's performance were considerably compromised by the limitations of the presidential office and by his own attitudes. Yet after the funeral procession faded from memory, his ideals lingered on, with millions of people in this country and around the world grasping for the promise that remained unfulfilled. The finality of any judgment would, in some ways, be as tenuous as a similar analysis of Abraham Lincoln if he had died after delivering the Gettysburg Address. And as with Lincoln, the tragedy of Kennedy's untimely death was that his effect on the continuum of American politics was suspended. "He was a man who could have become great or could have failed," Norman Mailer said shortly after Kennedy's death, "and now we'll never know. That's what's so awful. . . . Tragedy is amputation: the nerves of one's memory run back to the limb which is no longer there."[41]

PREFACE TO NOTES

At one time I considered preparing a bibliography of the sources used in the research for this book. I ultimately decided against that, however. I recognized that any complete bibliography would require an inordinate amount of time and energy to develop; any other "selected" bibliography would necessarily be incomplete and perhaps misleading to anyone interested in the nature of my sources. The materials and interviews identified in the text and in the notes below should provide some indication of the breadth of the sources used. Anyone desiring a complete listing of books, articles, and other materials on John F. Kennedy and his presidential years should contact the John F. Kennedy Library in Waltham, Massachusetts. If my experience is at all representative, the library staff will be most helpful.

Unless otherwise specified, all opinion polls referred to in the book were conducted by the American Institute for Public Opinion.

NOTES

Introduction

1 William Manchester, *Portrait of a President* (1962).
2 Arthur Schlesinger, Jr., *A Thousand Days* (1965).
3 Theodore C. Sorensen, *Kennedy* (1965).
4 Ibid., p. 758.
5 Victor Navasky, *Kennedy Justice* (1971).
6 Navasky, "A Dim New View of J.F.K.," *Life* magazine, Feb. 11, 1972, p. 16.

Chapter 1: John F. Kennedy's Concept of the Presidency

1 *New York Times*, Nov. 9, 1960, p. 46.
2 Ibid., Aug. 9, 1968, p. 20.
3 See *The New Republic*, Sept. 23, 1972, pp. 5–6.
4 Quoted in Marriner S. Eccles, *Beckoning Frontiers* 336 (1951).
5 James David Barber, *The Presidential Character: Predicting Performance in the White House* 7 (1972).
6 Quoted in Richard Neustadt, *Presidential Power* 9–10 (1960).
7 Ibid., 120.
8 *The New Republic*, June 15, 1974, p. 4.
9 See Richard Hofstadter, *The American Political Tradition* 210 (1948).
10 Quoted by Wilson Sullivan in *The American Heritage Pictorial History of the Presidents*, Vol. II, p. 632 (1968).
11 See Theodore Roosevelt, *The Letters of Theodore Roosevelt* (E. Morison, ed.) (8 vols. 1951–54), Vol. I, pp. 66, 245, 459, 655, Vol. II, p. 1356, Vol. IV, p. 1328.
12 See E. Morison, "Introduction," in Roosevelt, *Letters*, Vol. V; John Blum, *The Republican Roosevelt* Ch. 3 (1954).
13 See Roosevelt, *Letters* Vol. VI, p. 1329.
14 Quoted in Joseph E. Kallenbach, *The American Chief Executive* 246 (1965).
15 Erwin C. Hargrove, *Presidential Leadership: Personality and Political Style* 21 (1966).
16 For an example of this, see Arthur Krock's description of Roosevelt's appearance before a congressional hearing in 1910. Krock, *Memoirs: Sixty Years on the Firing Line* 100–103 (1968).
17 See William Manners, *TR and Will* 225–27 (1969).
18 See Henry Pringle, *The Life and Times of William Howard Taft*, Vol. I (1964); Barber, *Presidential Character*, pp. 173–90.
19 Quoted in Barber, *Presidential Character*, p. 176.
20 See Manners, *TR and Will*, p. 226.
21 William Howard Taft, *Our Chief Magistrate and His Powers* 139–40, 144 (1915).
22 Quoted in Barber, *Presidential Character*, p. 180.
23 See ibid., 175.

24 See Ray S. Baker, *Woodrow Wilson: Life and Letters,* Vol. I, pp. 37–39 (1927); E. B. Wilson, *My Memoir* 57–58 (1938).
25 Arthur Link, *Wilson: The New Freedom* 64 (1956).
26 William Binkley, *The Man in the White House* 136 (1958).
27 Lloyd George, *Memoirs of the Peace Conference,* Vol. I, pp. 140–42 (1939).
28 See A. & J. George, *Woodrow Wilson and Colonel House* 261–62 (Dover ed. 1964).
29 Baker & Dodd (eds.), *The Public Papers of Woodrow Wilson,* Vol. I, pp. 537–52 (1925).
30 Quoted in Thomas A. Bailey, *Woodrow Wilson and the Great Betrayal* 184 (1945).
31 Ibid., 277.
32 Frank Freidel, *Franklin D. Roosevelt, The Apprenticeship* 73 (1952).
33 Quoted in Emil Ludwig, *Roosevelt: A Study in Fortune and Power* 53 (1941).
34 Arthur Schlesinger, Jr., *The Crisis of the Old Order* 407 (1957).
35 Arthur Schlesinger, Jr., *The Coming of the New Deal* 21 (1959).
36 Quoted in Frances Perkins, *The Roosevelt I Knew* 330 (1946).
37 Quoted in James MacGregor Burns, *Roosevelt: The Lion and the Fox* 143 (1956).
38 See Ibid., pp. 139–57; Schlesinger, *The Crisis of the Old Order,* pp. 420–39.
39 Burns, *Lion and the Fox,* p. 348.
40 Barber, *Presidential Character,* p. 167.
41 Dwight D. Eisenhower, *Public Papers of the President* 553 (1955).
42 Quoted in Barber, *Presidential Character,* p. 163.
43 Emmet John Hughes, *The Ordeal of Power* 25 (1962).
44 Quoted in Barber, *Presidential Character,* p. 296.
45 Quoted in Richard J. Whalen, *The Founding Father: The Story of Joseph P. Kennedy* 115 (1964).
46 Arthur Schlesinger, Jr., *A Thousand Days: John F. Kennedy in the White House* 79–80 (1965).
47 Quoted in Goddard Lieberson (ed.), *John Fitzgerald Kennedy: As We Remember Him* 7 (1965).
48 Quoted in Joe McCarthy, *The Remarkable Kennedys* 17 (1960).
49 Quoted in Lieberson, *John F. Kennedy,* p. 10.
50 Quoted in ibid., 13.
51 Quoted in ibid., 15.
52 Quoted in Whalen, *The Founding Father: The Story of Joseph P. Kennedy,* p. 170.
53 Quoted in Lieberson, *John F. Kennedy,* p. 23.
54 Quoted in ibid.
55 Quoted in ibid., 35.
56 Quoted in ibid., 33.
57 John F. Kennedy, *Why England Slept* 25 (Dolphin ed. 1961).
58 Ibid., 39.
59 Ibid., 184–85.
60 Ibid., 185.
61 See Robert J. Donovan, *PT-109* (1962).
62 Quoted in David Halberstam, *The Best and the Brightest* 98 (1972).
63 Quoted in ibid., p. 44.
64 Quoted in Lieberson, *John F. Kennedy,* p. 50.
65 John Buchan, *Pilgrim's Way* 27 (1940).
66 Quoted in James MacGregor Burns, *John F. Kennedy: A Political Profile* 265 (1960).
67 See 95 *Congressional Record* 1012 (1949).
68 Ibid., 295.
69 Quoted in John P. Mallon, "Massachusetts: Liberal and Corrupt," *The New Republic,* Oct. 13, 1952, p. 10. But see Arthur Holcombe, Letter to the Editor, *The New Republic,* Nov. 3, 1952, p. 2.
70 Theodore C. Sorensen, *Kennedy* 47 (1965).
71 100 *Congressional Record* 238–40 (1954). See 99 *Congressional Record* 5066 (1953).
72 100 *Congressional Record* 4672-74 (1954).

73 Quoted in Halberstam, *Best and Brightest,* p. 94.
74 103 *Congressional Record* 10780–92 (1957).
75 *New York Times,* July 3, 1957, p. 22.
76 Quoted in Arthur Tourtellot, *The Presidents and the Presidency* 433 (1964).
77 John F. Kennedy, *Profiles in Courage* 5 (1955).
78 Ibid., 216.
79 *The Speeches, Remarks, Press Conferences and Statements of John F. Kennedy,* Committee on Commerce, United States Senate, 87th Cong., 1st Sess., Report No. 994, Vol. I, p. 688 (1961).
80 Ibid., 714.
81 Ibid., 560–61.
82 Ibid., 893.
83 See e.g. 93 *Congressional Record* 3420–21 (1947); 94 *Congressional Record* 2887–88, 2976 (1948).
84 95 *Congressional Record* 5147 (1949).
85 See 97 *Congressional Record* 6113 (1951); 103 *Congressional Record* 5073 (1957); 99 *Congressional Record* 604 (1953).
86 99 *Congressional Record* 10439 (1953).
87 See e.g. ibid., 5066–70.
88 98 *Congressional Record* 8493–94 (1952).
89 99 *Congressional Record* 1474 (1953).
90 Ibid., 1082.
91 *Lowell Sun,* Dec. 9, 1951.
92 102 *Congressional Record* 9614–15 (1956).
93 Kennedy, *The Strategy of Peace* 84 (1960).
94 Quoted in *New York Times,* Nov. 1, 1960, p. 29.
95 94 *Congressional Record* 2414 (1948).
96 95 *Congressional Record* 5148 (1949).
97 97 *Congressional Record* 5154 (1951).
98 Kennedy, *The Strategy of Peace,* p. 63.
99 Quoted in *New York Times,* Jan. 15, 1960, p. 14.
100 See e.g. ibid., Sept. 7, 1960, p. 40; ibid., Sept. 9, 1960 p. 28; ibid., Sept. 10, 1960, p. 20.
101 Quoted in ibid., Jan. 15, 1960, p. 14.
102 Quoted in ibid., Nov. 6, 1960, p. 67.
103 Arthur Krock, *In the Nation: 1932–1966* 327 (1966) (from an article dated January 14, 1961).
104 Quoted in Sorensen, *Kennedy,* p. 640.
105 Schlesinger, *A Thousand Days,* p. 904.
106 John F. Kennedy, *Public Papers of the President* 16 (1961).
107 Quoted in Halberstam, *Best and Brightest,* p. 90.
108 John F. Kennedy, *Public Papers of the President* 108 (1961).
109 Quoted in Interview with Winthrop Brown, Oral History Project, John F. Kennedy Library, p. 17.
110 Interview with Theodore C. Sorensen, Oral History Project, John F. Kennedy Library, p. 161.
111 Quoted in Benjamin Bradlee, *Conversations with Kennedy* 76 (1975).
112 John F. Kennedy, *Public Papers of the President* 316–17 (1962).
113 Staff memorandum, "Steel Prices," April 12, 1962, Files of Theodore C. Sorensen, Box 39, John F. Kennedy Library.
114 Reich, "Another Such Victory . . . The President's Short War Against Steel," *The New Republic,* April 30, 1962, p. 10.
115 Benjamin Bradlee, "Conversations With Kennedy," *Washington Post,* Nov. 18, 1973, p. C3.
116 John F. Kennedy, *Public Papers of the President* 422 (1962).
117 Ibid., 471.
118 *The Speeches, Remarks, Press Conferences and Statements of John F. Kennedy,*

Committee on Commerce, United States Senate, 87th Cong., 1st Sess., Report No. 994, Vol. I, pp. 68–69 (1961).

119 Ibid., 191–92.
120 Ibid., 576.
121 See Memorandum from Fred Dutton to President Kennedy, May 26, 1961, President's Office Files, John F. Kennedy Library; Interview with Harris Wofford, Oral History Project, John F. Kennedy Library, p. 58.
122 Interview with Harris Wofford, p. 61.
123 Memorandum from Frederick G. Dutton to Dick Goodwin, Feb. 9, 1961, p. 3, President's Office Files, John F. Kennedy Library.
124 Memorandum from President Kennedy to Theodore C. Sorensen, Feb. 8, 1961, President's Office Files, John F. Kennedy Library.
125 John F. Kennedy, *Public Papers of the President* 150 (1961).
126 Quoted in Victor Navasky, *Kennedy Justice* 99 (1971).
127 John F. Kennedy, *Public Papers of the President* 259 (1962).
128 Letter from Myer Feldman, Oct. 9, 1974.
129 John F. Kennedy, *Public Papers of the President* 139 (1961).
130 Ibid., 172, 212; John F. Kennedy, *Public Papers of the President* 16 (1963).
131 Quoted in James Tracy Crown, *Kennedy in Power* 23 (1961).
132 Schlesinger, *A Thousand Days*, p. 391.
133 John F. Kennedy, *Public Papers of the President* 304 (1961).
134 Ibid., 304–6.
135 *New York Times*, April 20, 1961, p. 32.
136 Quoted in Halberstam, *Best and Brightest*, p. 174.
137 Interview with Congressman Frank Thompson, Jr., Washington, D.C., April 10, 1975.
138 *The Joint Appearances of John F. Kennedy and Richard M. Nixon*, Committee on Commerce, United States Senate, 87th Cong., 1st Sess., Report No. 994, Vol. III, p. 205 (1961).
139 John F. Kennedy, *Public Papers of the President* 476 (1961).
140 Ibid., 534.
141 *New York Times*, July 26, 1961, p. 30.
142 Quoted in Roger Hilsman, *To Move a Nation: The Politics of Foreign Policy in the Administration of John F. Kennedy* 195 (1967).
143 Robert F. Kennedy, *Thirteen Days* 67 (1969).
144 Ibid., 62–63.
145 *Newsweek*,, January 21, 1963, p. 29.
146 John F. Kennedy, *Public Papers of the President* 462 (1963).
147 John F. Kennedy, *Public Papers of the President* 903 (1962).

Chapter 2: John F. Kennedy's Methods of Decision-Making

1 John F. Kennedy, Foreword, in Sorensen, *Decision-Making in the White House* xi (1963).
2 George Reedy, *Twilight of the Presidency* 30–31 (1970).
3 Memoranda from Frederick G. Dutton to President Kennedy, January 27, 1961, January 31, 1961, President's Office Files, John F. Kennedy Library.
4 Theodore Roosevelt, *The Letters of Theodore Roosevelt* (ed. Morison, E.), Vol. VI, p. 1329 (1951–54).

5 Erwin C. Hargrove, *Presidential Leadership: Personality and Political Style* 16 (1966).
6 Pendleton Herring, *Presidential Leadership* 50 (1940).
7 Quoted in Louis W. Koenig, *The Chief Executive* 299 (rev. ed. 1968).
8 Thurman Arnold, *The Folklore of Capitalism* 217 (1937).
9 Roosevelt, *Letters,* V, p. 589.
10 Quoted in Arthur S. Link, *Wilson, The New Freedom* 5 (1956).
11 Ibid., 154.
12 Quoted in David Barber, *Predicting Performance in the White House* 60–61 (1972).
13 Diary of Edward House, June 10, 1916, quoted in George & George, *Woodrow Wilson and Colonel House* 188 (Dover ed. 1964).
14 Quoted in Frances Perkins, *The Roosevelt I Knew* 21 (1946).
15 Arthur Schlesinger, Jr., *The Crisis of the Old Order* 407 (1957).
16 Quoted in ibid., 406.
17 Quoted in Barber, *Presidential Character,* p. 233.
18 Quoted in Arthur Schlesinger, Jr., *The Coming of the New Deal* 1 (1958).
19 Quoted in Barber, *Presidential Character,* p. 233.
20 Quoted in James MacGregor Burns, *Roosevelt: The Lion and the Fox* 174 (1956).
21 Quoted in Barber, *Presidential Character,* p. 234.
22 Schlesinger, *The Coming of the New Deal,* pp. 522–23.
23 Quoted in ibid., 193.
24 See Koenig, *Chief Executive,* 338 (1964).
25 See the analysis of the court-packing plan in Chapter 1.
26 Burns, *Lion and the Fox,* p. 314.
27 Alexander Hamilton, Paper 70, *The Federalist Papers* 423 (Bantam ed. 1961).
28 Quoted in Barber, *Presidential Character,* p. 52.
29 Quoted in Rather & Gates, *The Palace Guard* 29–30 (1974).
30 Quoted in Alfred Steinberg, *Sam Johnson's Boy* 724 (1968).
31 Quoted in Hugh Sidey, *A Very Personal Presidency* 283 (1968).
32 Quoted in Barber, *Presidential Character,* p. 32.
33 Chester Cooper, *The Lost Crusade* 273–74 (1972).
34 George Reedy, in "The Powers of the Presidency: Report on a Conference," *The Center Magazine,* Jan.-Feb. 1971, pp. 12–13.
35 Reprinted in the *New York Times,* Sept. 20, 1968.
36 *The Presidential Transcripts* 77 (Dell ed. 1974).
37 Quoted in Seymour Hersch, "Colson Reports Nixon Urging; Gets 1–3 Years," *New York Times,* June 22, 1974, p. 15.
38 Quoted in Rather & Gates, *Palace Guard,* p. 236.
39 Ibid., 172–73.
40 Reprinted in *New York Times,* July 18, 1974, p. 20.
41 Rose Kennedy, *Times to Remember* 99 (1974).
42 Quoted in ibid., 170–71.
43 *Boston Globe,* Nov. 12, 1951.
44 John F. Kennedy, *The Strategy of Peace* 128 (1960).
45 John F. Kennedy, "A Democrat Looks at Foreign Policy," 36 *Foreign Affairs* 44, 59 (Oct. 1957).
46 *Boston Globe,* Nov. 19, 1951 (emphasis added).
47 E. G. Kennedy, "If India Fails," *The Progressive,* Jan. 1958, p. 8; 104 *Congressional Record* 5246–55 (1958); 103 *Congressional Record* 15446–54 (1957).
48 Quoted in *Time* magazine, Dec. 2, 1957, p. 20.
49 John F. Kennedy, *The Strategy of Peace,* p. 209.
50 Quoted in *New York Times,* January 15, 1960, p. 14.
51 Quoted in ibid. November 6, 1960, p. 67.
52 Interview with Myer Feldman, Oral History Project. John F. Kennedy Library, pp. 606–7.
53 John F. Kennedy, "America's Stake in Vietnam," *A Symposium on America's Stake in Vietnam* 10 (1956).
54 Quoted in Richard J. Barnet, *Roots of War* 276 (1972).

55 Quoted in ibid., 275.
56 Quoted in Kenneth O'Donnell & Dave Powers, *Johnny, We Hardly Knew Ye* 15–18 (1973).
57 Interview with Robert Lovett, Oral History Project, John F. Kennedy Library, p. 56.
58 Quoted in William Manchester, *Portrait of a President: John F. Kennedy in Profile* 20 (1962).
59 Interview with Benjamin Bradlee, Washington, D. C., July 28, 1967.
60 Memorandum from President Kennedy to McGeorge Bundy, Feb. 15, 1961, President's Office Files, John F. Kennedy Library.
61 Hugh Sidey, *John F. Kennedy, President,* 119 (1964).
62 Interview with Robert Lovett, p. 57.
63 Interview with Roy Wilkins, Oral History Project, John F. Kennedy Library, p. 14.
64 Interview with Joseph Rauh, Oral History Project, John F. Kennedy Library, p. 101.
65 Quoted in Manchester, *Portrait,* p. 44.
66 Quoted in Lieberson (ed.), *John Fitzgerald Kennedy: As We Remember Him* 115 (1965).
67 For a good explanation of the concept here, see Keynes, *General Theory of Employment, Interest and Money* (1936).
68 Memorandum from President Kennedy to McGeorge Bundy, May 15, 1963, President's Office Files, John F. Kennedy Library.
69 John F. Kennedy, *Public Papers of the President* 890 (1962).
70 Quoted in Arthur Schlesinger, Jr., *A Thousand Days: John F. Kennedy in the White House* 941 (1965).
71 Transcript of Telephone Conversation between the Attorney General and Governor Barnett, Sept. 25, 1962, 12:20 P.M., pp. 5–6, from Papers of Burke Marshall, Box #20, John F. Kennedy Library.
72 Transcript of Telephone Conversation between the Attorney General and Governor Barnett, Sept. 25, 1962, 7:25 P.M., p. 3, from Papers of Burke Marshall, Box #20, John F. Kennedy Library.
73 Transcript of Telephone Conversation between the President and Governor Barnett, Sept. 29, 1962, 2:30 P.M., pp. 1–2, from Papers of Burke Marshall, Box #20, John F. Kennedy Library.
74 Transcript of Telephone Conversation between the President and Governor Barnett, Sept. 29, 1962, 3:16 P.M., pp. 5–6, from Papers of Burke Marshall, Box #20, John F. Kennedy Library.
75 John F. Kennedy, *Public Papers of the President* 889 (1962).
76 Kennedy, *A Strategy of Peace,* p. 200.
77 Machiavelli, *The Prince* 124 (Penguin ed. 1967).
78 Reedy, *The Twilight of the Presidency,* p. 98.
79 Interview with Myer Feldman (Sept. 21, 1968), p. 35.
80 Memorandum from President Kennedy to McGeorge Bundy, Aug. 14, 1961, President's Office Files, John F. Kennedy Library.
81 Quoted in Benjamin Bradlee, "Conversations with Kennedy," *Washington Post,* Nov. 18, 1973, p. C1.
82 See the description of the steel price controversy in Chapter 1.
83 Quoted in Theodore C. Sorensen, *Kennedy* 462 (1965).
84 Sorensen, "The Kennedy Administration and Business," 2 (June 20, 1962), from Papers of Theodore C. Sorensen, Box #29, John F. Kennedy Library.
85 Ibid., 5.
86 Interview with Frederick G. Dutton, Washington, D. C., Sept. 18, 1974.
87 Quoted in Schlesinger, *A Thousand Days,* p. 426.
88 Quoted in ibid., 258.
89 Quoted in ibid., 240.
90 Quoted in Emmet John Hughes, *The Living Presidency* 133 (1973).
91 Quoted in Schlesinger, *A Thousand Days,* p. 633.
92 John F. Kennedy, *Public Papers of the President* 774 (1961).

93 Memorandum from Anthony Celebrezze, W. Willard Wirtz, and J. S. Gleason, Jr., to President Kennedy, November 30, 1962, Papers of Myer Feldman, Box #12, John F. Kennedy Library.
94 Quoted in Victor Navasky, *Kennedy Justice* 97 (1971).
95 Quoted in ibid.
96 Robert F. Kennedy Draft, June 1963, from Papers of Theodore C. Sorensen, Box #73, John F. Kennedy Library.
97 John F. Kennedy, *Public Papers of the President* 469 (1963).
98 Quoted in Sidey, *John F. Kennedy, President,* p. 52.
99 Interview with Winthrop Brown, Oral History Project, John F. Kennedy Library, p. 14.
100 Morton H. Halperin, "The President and the Military," 50 *Foreign Affairs* 310, 322 (1972).
101 See Interview with Robert Hurwitch, Oral History Project, John F. Kennedy Library, pp. 12, 33.
102 John F. Kennedy, *Public Papers of the President* 891 (1962).
103 Graham Allison, *Essence of Decision: Explaining the Cuban Missile Crisis* 176 (1971).
104 Quoted in James Tracy Crown, *Kennedy in Power* 162 (1961).
105 Quoted in Patrick Anderson, *The President's Men* 321 (1969).
106 Interview with Frederick G. Dutton, Oral History Project, John F. Kennedy Library, pp. 56–57.
107 Quoted in Pierre Salinger, "JFK's White House: I'm the President," *Washington Post,* May 31, 1974, p. A26.
108 Interview with Everett Dirksen, Washington, D.C., July 31, 1967.
109 See Arthur Waskow, *The Limits of Defense* (1961).
110 Letter from McGeorge Bundy, Oct. 11, 1974.
111 Quoted in Navasky, *Kennedy Justice,* p. 253.
112 Interview with Gaylord Nelson, Oral History Project, John F. Kennedy Library, pp. 12–13.
113 Interview with Wilbur Mills, Oral History Project, John F. Kennedy Library, p. 10.
114 Memorandum from President Kennedy to Richard N. Goodwin, Aug. 28, 1961, President's Office Files, John F. Kennedy Library.
115 Arthur Krock, *In the Nation: 1932–1966* 361 (1966) (from an article dated May 27, 1961).
116 120 *Congressional Record* S22288 (daily ed. December 10, 1973).
117 *Myers* v. *United States,* 272 U.S. 52, 293 (1926).
118 John F. Kennedy, *Public Papers of the President* 397–98 (1961).
119 Interview with Francisco Orlich, Oral History Project, John F. Kennedy Library, p. 2.
120 Quoted in Schlesinger, *A Thousand Days,* p. 863.
121 John F. Kennedy, *Public Papers of the President* 896 (1962).
122 Schlesinger, *A Thousand Days,* p. 864.
123 De Gaulle, "De Gaulle's Warning to Kennedy: An 'Endless Entanglement in Vietnam,'" *New York Times,* March 15, 1972, p. 43.
124 Interview with Sukarno, Oral History Project, John F. Kennedy Library, p. 2.
125 Interview with William Attwood, Oral History Project, John F. Kennedy Library.
126 Interview with Tom Mboya, Oral History Project, John F. Kennedy Library, p. 7.
127 Interview with Myer Feldman, pp. 460–62.
128 John Badeau, *The American Approach to the Arab World* 135–36 (1968).
129 See Schlesinger, *A Thousand Days,* p. 299.
130 John F. Kennedy, *Public Papers of the President* 443 (1961).
131 Letter from President Kennedy to Premier Khrushchev, Oct. 23, 1962, President's Office Files, John F. Kennedy Library.
132 Robert F. Kennedy, *Thirteen Days,* 124–45 (1969).
133 James Reston, *Sketches in the Sand* 244–45 (1967) (from an article dated December 22, 1961).

Chapter 3: John F. Kennedy As A Public Leader

1 Greenstein, "What the President Means to Americans: Presidential 'Choice' Between Elections" in James David Barber (ed.), *Choosing the President* 146 (1974).
2 James Reston, "Nibbling the Bullet," *New York Times,* Oct. 9, 1974, p. 43.
3 U.S. Constitution, Article I, section 8, clause 18.
4 U.S. Constitution, Article II, section 3.
5 See *The Federalist Papers,* Nos. 69–72.
6 Quoted in Louis Fisher, *President and Congress: Power and Policy* 21 (1972).
7 James Madison, #50, *The Federalist Papers* 317 (Bantam ed. 1961).
8 Woodrow Wilson, *Constitutional Government in the United States* 79 (1908).
9 Herbert Hoover, *The Memoirs of Herbert Hoover,* Vol. II, p. 217 (1952).
10 Quoted in James David Barber, *The Presidential Character: Predicting Performance in the White House* 25 (1972).
11 Walter Lippmann, "The Peculiar Weakness of Mr. Hoover," *Harper's* magazine, June 1930, p. 3.
12 Quoted in Louis Koenig, *The Chief Executive* 358 (1964).
13 Quoted in ibid.
14 Harris Gaylord Warren, *Herbert Hoover and the Great Depression* 208 (1959).
15 *Selected Letters of William Allen White* 329 (1947).
16 Quoted in Leila A. Sussman, "FDR and the White House Mail," *Public Opinion Quarterly* 16 (Spring, 1956).
17 *Youngstown Sheet & Tube Co.* v. *Sawyer,* 343 U.S. 579, 653–54 (1952) (Jackson, J., concurring opinion).
18 116 *Congressional Record* S8161 (daily ed. June 2, 1970).
19 Richard M. Nixon, *Public Papers of the President* 909 (1969).
20 Quoted by FCC Commissioner Nicholas Johnson in remarks before the International Association of Political Consultants, London, England, Dec. 14, 1970.
21 Newton N. Minow, John Bartlow Martin, Lee M. Mitchell, *Presidential Television* 59 (1973).
22 Ibid., 10.
23 James MacGregor Burns, *Presidential Government* 351 (1966).
24 Grant McConnell, *The Modern Presidency* 17 (1967).
25 Robert Lane, *Political Ideology: Why the Common Man Believes What He Does* 475 (1962).
26 Richard Neustadt, *Presidential Power* 106 (1964).
27 See Barber, *Choosing the President,* pp. 141, 190.
28 Erwin C. Hargrove, *Presidential Leadership: Personality and Political Style* 22 (1966).
29 Quoted in W. H. Harbaugh, *Power and Responsibility: The Life and Times of Theodore Roosevelt* 235 (1961).
30 *Selections from the Correspondence of Theodore Roosevelt and Henry Cabot Lodge,* Vol. II, p. 304 (1925).
31 Quoted in George & George, *Woodrow Wilson and Colonel House* 181 (Dover ed. 1964).
32 Quoted in ibid.
33 Quoted in Thomas Bailey, *Woodrow Wilson and the Great Betrayal* 10 (1945).
34 Quoted in George & George, *Woodrow Wilson,* p. 294.
35 Quoted in Bailey, *Great Betrayal,* p. 121.
36 Ibid., 174–75.
37 Arthur Schlesinger, Jr., *The Coming of the New Deal* 558 (1959).
38 Quoted in ibid., 13.

39 Quoted in James MacGregor Burns, *Roosevelt: The Lion and the Fox* 318 (1956).
40 Quoted in ibid., 318–19.
41 Quoted in James MacGregor Burns, *Roosevelt: The Soldier of Freedom* 26 (1970).
42 Harold Laski, *The American Presidency: An Interpretation* 267, 270 (1940).
43 Walter Lippmann, *The Public Philosophy* 23–24 (Mentor ed. 1955).
44 Quoted in Emmet John Hughes, *The Living Presidency* 113 (1973).
45 Theodore C. Sorensen, *Decision-Making in the White House* 87 (1963).
46 Quoted in Cabell Phillips, *The Truman Presidency* 109 (1966).
47 Ibid., 109–10.
48 John F. Kennedy, *Why England Slept* 180–81 (Dolphin ed. 1961).
49 See discussion in Chapter 1.
50 See discussion in Chapter 1.
51 Quoted in William Manchester, *Portrait of a President: John F. Kennedy in Profile* 88 (1962).
52 John F. Kennedy, *The Strategy of Peace* 105 (1960).
53 Ibid., 13–14.
54 Ibid., 226–27.
55 Quoted in ibid., Jan. 15, 1960, p. 14.
56 Quoted in ibid.
57 Ibid.
58 David Broder, "Kennedy's Presidential Style," *Washington Post,* Nov. 21, 1973, p. A18.
59 John F. Kennedy, "A New Approach on Foreign Policy," in *The Strategy of Peace.*
60 Quoted in *New York Times,* July 15, 1960, p. 8.
61 Quoted in ibid., Nov. 6, 1960, p. 67.
62 Ibid., Nov. 9, 1960, p. 46.
63 John Gardner (ed.), *To Turn the Tide* 5 (1962).
64 John F. Kennedy, *Public Papers of the President* 1 (1961).
65 Ibid., 3.
66 These polls were conducted by Benton & Bowles and were shown to President Kennedy in the spring of 1963 along with follow-up polls. See Memorandum from McGeorge Bundy to President Kennedy, May 16, 1963, President's Office Files, John F. Kennedy Library.
67 James Reston, *Sketches in the Sand* 439 (1967) (from an article dated January 22, 1961).
68 Theodore White, *The Making of the President 1960* 452 (Pocket Books ed. 1961).
69 Quoted in Arthur Schlesinger, Jr., *A Thousand Days: John F. Kennedy in the White House* 720 (1965).
70 William Manchester, *Portrait,* p. 19.
71 James Reston, *Sketches in the Sand,* p. 13 (from an article dated June 20, 1960).
72 Arthur Schlesinger, Jr., *A Thousand Days,* p. 722.
73 Memorandum from Walter Heller to President Kennedy, March 17, 1961, President's Office Files, John F. Kennedy Library.
74 John F. Kennedy, *Public Papers of the President* 471, 472 (1962).
75 *The Outlook for Consumer Demand, Report on Consumer Attitudes and Inclinations to Buy,* Survey Research Center, Institute for Social Research, The University of Michigan, Sept. 1962, p. 19, attached to Memorandum from Walter Heller to President Kennedy, Oct. 3, 1962, Papers of Theodore C. Sorensen, Box #46, John F. Kennedy Library.
76 John F. Kennedy, *Public Papers of the President* 662, 667 (1963).
77 John F. Kennedy, *Public Papers of the President* 2 (1961).
78 John F. Kennedy, *Public Papers of the President* 462 (1963).
79 Ibid., 737.
80 Quoted in David Halberstam, *The Best and the Brightest* 296 (1972).
81 John F. Kennedy, *Public Papers of the President* 420 (1962).
82 Ibid., 432.
83 See *Gray* v. *Sanders,* 372 U.S. 368 (1963) (establishing one man–one vote principle).

84 Quoted in Letter to the Editor from Harry Golden, *New York Times Book Review*, May 20, 1973.
85 Quoted in Arthur Krock, *In the Nation: 1932–1966* 333 (1966).
86 Interview with Burke Marshall, Oral History Project, John F. Kennedy Library, pp. 60–61.
87 Interview with Theodore C. Sorensen, Oral History Project, John F. Kennedy Library, p. 123.
88 Martin Luther King, Jr., "Fumbling on the New Frontier," *The Nation*, March 3, 1962, p. 190.
89 Memorandum from President Kennedy to Walt Rostow & Gen. Maxwell Taylor, August 7, 1961, President's Office Files, John F. Kennedy Library.
90 John F. Kennedy, *Public Papers of the President* 12–13 (1962).
91 Memorandum from Chester Bowles to President Kennedy, January 17, 1962, President's Office Files, John F. Kennedy Library.
92 John F. Kennedy, *Public Papers of the President* 870 (1962).
93 John F. Kennedy, *Public Papers of the President* 11, 16 (1963).
94 Ibid., 652.
95 Ibid., 659.
96 *New York Times*, April 14, 1961, p. 28.
97 Ibid., Sept. 6, 1963, p. 28.
98 Richard Harwood, "Few 'Revelations' for Those Who Had Been Listening," *Washington Post*, June 24, 1971, p. A18.
99 Arthur Schlesinger, Jr., *A Thousand Days*, p. 997.
100 *New York Times*, April 14, 1962, p. 24.
101 Memorandum from Arthur Schlesinger, Jr., to President Kennedy, March 16, 1961, President's Office Files, John F. Kennedy Library.
102 Quoted in Press Panel Interview, Oral History Project, John F. Kennedy Library, pp. 30–31.
103 Arthur Krock, *In the Nation*, p. 370 (from an article dated November 22, 1961).
104 Quoted in William Rivers, *The Opinion Makers* 146 (1967).
105 Interview with Gilbert Harrison, Oral History Project, John F. Kennedy Library, p. 4.
106 Hugh Sidey, *John F. Kennedy, President* 339 (1964).
107 Quoted in Press Panel Interview, p. 59. The occurrence of this incident was subsequently confirmed by George Herman, then the CBS News White House correspondent, in a telephone conversation. While they could find no records indicating that the interviews had been broadcast, CBS officials in New York City could not remember the incident and therefore could not provide any additional details.
108 John F. Kennedy, *Public Papers of the President* 336–37 (1961).
109 Kenneth O'Donnell & Dave Powers, *Johnny, We Hardly Knew Ye* 313 (1972).
110 Richard Neustadt, "Kennedy in the Presidency: A Premature Appraisal," *Political Science Quarterly* 330 (Sept. 1964).
111 John F. Kennedy, *Public Papers of the President* 19 (1961).
112 Quoted in Arthur Schlesinger, Jr., *A Thousand Days*, p. 708.
113 Arthur Krock, *In the Nation*, p. 313 (from an article dated November 9, 1960).
114 Ralph Dungan, "The Presidency As I Have Seen It," in Hughes, *The Living Presidency*, p. 328.
115 Quoted in William Manchester, *Portrait*, p 135.
116 Quoted in Arthur Schlesinger, Jr., *A Thousand Days*, p. 709.
117 Lawrence F. O'Brien, *No Final Victories: A Life in Politics From John F. Kennedy to Watergate* 112 (1974).
118 Interview with Allen Ellender, Oral History Project, John F. Kennedy Library, p. 48.
119 Interview with Mike Mansfield, Oral History Project, John F. Kennedy Library, p. 3.
120 Memorandum from President Kennedy to Mike Feldman, Feb. 16, 1961, President's Office Files, John F. Kennedy Library.

121 347 U.S. 483 (1954).
122 Interview with Burke Marshall, Oral History Project, John F. Kennedy Library, p. 69.
123 John F. Kennedy, *Public Papers of the President* 592–93 (1962).
124 John F. Kennedy, *Public Papers of the President* 333 (1963).
125 Ibid., 347.
126 Quoted in Interview with Mike Mansfield, p. 41.
127 Handwritten note from Mike Mansfield to President Kennedy on Memorandum from Robert Baker to Mike Mansfield, June 12, 1963, p. 3, attached to memorandum from Mike Mansfield to President Kennedy, June 18, 1963, from Papers of Theodore C. Sorensen, Box #30, John F. Kennedy Library.
128 Interview with Burke Marshall, pp. 62–63; Tom Wicker, *JFK and LBJ: The Influence of Personality on Politics* 174–75 (1968).
129 Interview with Theodore C. Sorensen, pp. 134, 139. See Interview with Burke Marshall, pp. 111–12; Sorensen, *Kennedy* 496–97 (1965).
130 Memorandum from President Kennedy to Secretary Celebrezze and Secretary Wirtz, June 4, 1963, President's Office Files, John F. Kennedy Library. See Memorandum from Secretary Celebrezze to President Kennedy, June 10, 1963, President's Office Files, John F. Kennedy Library.
131 Interview with Burke Marshall, p. 111.
132 John F. Kennedy, *Public Papers of the President* 77 (1962).
133 Interview with Theodore C. Sorensen, p. 112.
134 Interview with Charles Daly, Oral History Project, John F. Kennedy Library, p. 13.
135 John F. Kennedy, *Public Papers of the President* 531 (1961).
136 Memorandum from Deputy Attorney General Nicholas deB. Katzenbach to Theodore C. Sorensen, July 19, 1962, from Papers of Theodore C. Sorensen, Box #29, John F. Kennedy Library.
137 Interview with Mike Mansfield, p. 29.
138 *Speeches, Remarks, Press Conferences and Statements of John F. Kennedy,* Committee on Commerce, United States Senate, 87th Cong., 1st Sess., Report No. 994, Vol. I, p. 397 (1961).
139 John F. Kennedy, *Public Papers of the President* 142 (1961).
140 Quoted in Hellen Fuller, *Year of Trial: Kennedy's Crucial Decisions* 257 (1962).
141 Memorandum from Walter Heller to President Kennedy, May 1, 1963, from Papers of Theodore C. Sorensen, Box #31. See Memorandum from Walter Heller to Theodore C. Sorensen, November 20, 1963, from Papers of Theodore C. Sorensen, Box #31, John F. Kennedy Library.
142 William Manchester, *Portrait,* p. 23.
143 John F. Kennedy, *Public Papers of the President* 763 (1962).
144 James Reston, *Sketches in the Sand,* pp. 133–34 (from an article dated November 17, 1963).
145 Quoted in Richard J. Barnet, *Roots of War* 308 (1972).
146 Quoted in L. D. White, *The Federalists* 65 (1948).
147 John F. Kennedy, *Public Papers of the President* 725–26 (1961).
148 *The Speeches, Remarks, Press Conferences and Statements of John F. Kennedy,* Committee on Commerce, United States Senate, 87th Cong., 1st Sess., Report No. 994, Vol. I, p. 297.
149 *New York Times,* Oct. 31, 1960, p. 10.
150 John F. Kennedy, *Public Papers of the President* 2 (1961).
151 John F. Kennedy, Book Review of Liddell Hart's *Deterrent or Defense,* in *Saturday Review of Literature,* Sept 3, 1960, p. 17.
152 John F. Kennedy, *Public Papers of the President* 725 (1961).
153 John F. Kennedy, *Public Papers of the President* 891, 894 (1963).
154 John F. Kennedy, *Public Papers of the President* 230 (1961).
155 Quoted in Arthur Schelsinger, Jr., *A Thousand Days,* p. 547.
156 John F. Kennedy, *The Strategy of Peace,* p. 45.
157 Theodore C. Sorensen, *Kennedy,* p. 618.

158 Quoted in Arthur Schlesinger, Jr., *A Thousand Days*, pp. 482–83.
159 Memorandum from Theodore C. Sorensen to President Kennedy, January 25, 1962, p. 3, from Papers of Theodore C. Sorensen, Box #36, John F. Kennedy Library.
160 Quoted in Arthur Schlesinger, Jr., *A Thousand Days*, p. 496.
161 Chester Bowles, *Promises to Keep: My Years in Public Life, 1941–1969* 526 (1971).
162 Interview with Theodore C. Sorensen, pp. 85–86.
163 Interview with Mike Mansfield, pp. 31–32.
164 James Reston, *Sketches in the Sand*, p. 160 (from an article dated March 7, 1962).
165 John F. Kennedy, *Public Papers of the President* 23 (1961).
166 John F. Kennedy, *Public Papers of the President* 540–41 (1962).
167 Charles E. Bohlen, *Witness to History: 1929 to 1969* 530–31 (1973).
168 Jean Daniel, "Unofficial Envoy: An Historic Report from Two Capitals," *The New Republic*, Dec. 14, 1963, p. 15.
169 John F. Kennedy, *Public Papers of the President* 1 (1961).
170 Ibid., 205.
171 Ibid., 91–92.
172 Ibid., 174–75.
173 Memorandum from Richard N. Goodwin to President Kennedy, September 10, 1963, President's Office Files, John F. Kennedy Library.
174 Michael Harrington, "A View from the Left," *Washington Post*, Nov. 18, 1963, p. C4.
175 Jean Daniel, "Unofficial Envoy," p. 16.
176 John F. Kennedy, *Public Papers of the President* 399 (1961).
177 John F. Kennedy, *Public Papers of the President* 652 (1963).

Chapter 4: The Presidential Images of John F. Kennedy

1 Robert D. Hess & David Easton, "The Child's Changing Image of the President," 24 *Public Opinion Quarterly* 632–44 (1960).
2 Quoted in Fred Greenstein, "What the President Means to Americans: Presidential 'Choice' Between Elections," in James David Barber (ed.), *Choosing the President* 121 (1974).
3 Robert Lane, *Political Ideology: Why the Common Man Believes What He Does* 148–49, 152 (1962).
4 Jay Weitzner, "Handling the Candidate on Television," in Hiebert (ed.), *The Political Image Merchants: Strategies in the New Politics* 102 (1972).
5 Quoted in Greenstein, "What the President Means," p. 137.
6 Quoted in Patrick Anderson, *The President's Men* 220 (1969).
7 Doris Graber, "Personal Qualities in Presidential Images: The Contribution of the Press," 16 *Midwest Journal of Political Science* 46 (1972).
8 Richard M. Nixon, *Six Crises* 384 (Pyramid Bks. ed. 1968).
9 Quoted in Erik Barnouw, *The Image Empire* 169 (1972).
10 Richard M. Nixon, *Six Crises*, p. 366.
11 Quoted in *Washington Post*, Feb. 20, 1972, p. B7.
12 *Chicago Sun Times*, March 5, 1972, section 2, p. 7.
13 *The Presidential Transcripts* 455 (Dell ed. 1974).
14 Cabell Phillips, *The Truman Presidency* 429 (1966).
15 Quoted in Emmet John Hughes, *The Ordeal of Power* 131 (1962).
16 Ibid., 176.
17 Lyndon B. Johnson, *Public Papers of the President* 461 (1965).

18 Ibid., 471–73.
19 *The New Republic,* May 15, 1965, p. 5.
20 Lyndon B. Johnson, *Public Papers of the President* 1128 (1964).
21 Ibid., 1164.
22 Ibid., 1391.
23 Quoted in Eric Goldman, *The Tragedy of Lyndon Johnson* 409 (1969).
24 Richard M. Nixon, *Public Papers of the President* 526 (1971).
25 *New York Times,* Sept. 24, 1972, SIV, p. 13.
26 Ibid., Sept. 25, 1972, p. 43.
27 Graber, "Personal Qualities," pp. 54–55.
28 Arthur Schlesinger, Jr., *The Coming of the New Deal* 573 (1959).
29 John Gunther, *Roosevelt in Retrospect* 4 (1950).
30 Norman Mailer, *The Presidential Papers of Norman Mailer* 41–42 (1964).
31 Quoted in Hugh Sidey, *John F. Kennedy, President* 20 (1964).
32 Interview with Hale Boggs, Oral History Project, John F. Kennedy Library, p. 12.
33 Interview with U. Alexis Johnson, Oral History Project, John F. Kennedy Library, pp. 28, 42.
34 Benjamin Bradlee, "Conversations with Kennedy," *Washington Post,* Nov. 18, 1973, p. C3.
35 Quoted in Arthur Schlesinger, Jr., *A Thousand Days: John F. Kennedy in the White House* 674 (1965).
36 John F. Kennedy, *Public Papers of the President* 40–41 (1962).
37 Quoted in Theodore C. Sorensen, *Kennedy* 363 (1965).
38 John F. Kennedy, *Public Papers of the President* 7 (1961).
39 Interview with Myer Feldman, Oral History Project, John F. Kennedy Library, p. 36.
40 Memorandum from Theodore C. Sorensen to President Kennedy, Ausust 9, 1961, from Papers of Theodore C. Sorensen, Box #36, John F. Kennedy Library.
41 TRB, *The New Republic,* March 27, 1961, p. 2.
42 Quoted in James MacGregor Burns, "John Kennedy and His Spectators," *The New Republic,* April 3, 1961, p. 7.
43 *Newsweek,* May 8, 1961, p. 23.
44 Quoted in William Manchester, *Portrait of a President: John F. Kennedy in Profile* 22 (1962).
45 John F. Kennedy, *Public Papers of the President* 27 (1961).
46 John F. Kennedy, *Public Papers of the President* 162 (1962).
47 John F. Kennedy, *Public Papers of the President* 816–17 (1963).
48 Roger Hilsman, *To Move a Nation: The Politics of Foreign Policy in the Administration of John F. Kennedy* 568 (1967).
49 See the discussion of the bureaucracy in Chapter 2.
50 Mailer, *The Presidential Papers,* p. vi.
51 Jack Newfield, *A Prophetic Minority* 27–28 (1967).
52 Interview with Theodore C. Sorensen, Oral History Project, John F. Kennedy Library, p. 141.
53 John F. Kennedy, *Public Papers of the President* 423 (1963).
54 Ibid., 572–73.
55 See Interview with Joseph Rauh, Jr., Oral History Project, John F. Kennedy Library, p. 112.
56 Interview with Roy Wilkins, Oral History Project, John F. Kennedy Library, p. 27.
57 Interview with Simeon Booker, Oral History Project, John F. Kennedy Library, p. 38.
58 See Anthony Lewis, "Winter of Discontent," *New York Times,* April 15, 1974, p. 31.
59 Michael Harrington, "A View From the Left," *Washington Post,* Nov. 18, 1973, p. C4.
60 Theodore White, *The Making of the President 1960* 405 (Pocket Bks. ed. 1961).
61 Laura Bergquist & Stanley Tretick, *A Very Special President* 68 (1965).

62 Interview with William Lawrence, Oral History Project, John F. Kennedy Library, p. 23.
63 Interview with Henry Brandon, Oral History Project, John F. Kennedy Library, p. 5.
64 Press Panel Interview, Oral History Project, John F. Kennedy Library, p. 53.
65 Arthur Krock, *Memoirs: Sixty Years on the Firing Line* 375–76 (1968).
66 Quoted in William Rivers, *The Opinion Makers* 160 (1967).
67 Quoted in David Wise, *The Politics of Lying: Government Deception, Secrecy and Power* 269 (1973).
68 Interview with William Lawrence, p. 19.
69 Quoted in David Wise, *Politics of Lying,* p. 270.
70 Quoted in ibid.
71 Quoted in ibid., 349.
72 Memorandum from President Kennedy to Fred Dutton, Sept. 5, 1961, President's Office Files, John F. Kennedy Library.
73 Interview with Gilbert Harrison, Oral History Project, John F. Kennedy Library, p. 3.
74 *Newsweek*, April 8, 1963, p. 59.
75 Fletcher Knebel, "Kennedy and the Press," *Look,* August 28, 1962, p. 20.
76 John F. Kennedy, *Public Papers of the President* 376 (1962).
77 Ibid., 470.
78 James Reston, *Sketches in the Sand* 188 (1967).
79 Press Panel Interview, Oral History Project, John F. Kennedy Library, p. 67.
80 John F. Kennedy, *Public Papers of the President* 19 (1961).
81 Quoted in Tom Wicker, *JFK and LBJ ; The Influence of Personality on Politics* 91 (1968).
82 Interview with Paul Douglas, Oral History Project, John F. Kennedy Library, p. 26.
83 Ibid., 27.
84 Interview with Carl Albert, Oral History Project, John F. Kennedy Library, p. 23.
85 Interview with Charles Daly, Oral History Project, John F. Kennedy Library, pp. 16–18.
86 Interview with Allen Ellender, Oral History Project, John F. Kennedy Library, p. 46.
87 Quoted in Arthur Schlesinger, Jr., *A Thousand Days,* p. 276.
88 Interview with Juan Bosch, Oral History Project, John F. Kennedy Library, p. 4.
89 Interview with Roberto Campos, Oral History Project, John F. Kennedy Library, p. 33.
90 Interview with Francisco Orlich, Oral History Project, John F. Kennedy Library, pp. 1–2.
91 Herbert Matthews, "Four Continents—IV: Latin America," *New York Times,* Aug. 31, 1967, p. 35.
92 Quoted in William Manchester, *Portrait,* p. 90 (1962).
93 Quoted in ibid., 91.
94 Interview with Maurice Couve de Murville, Oral History Project, John F. Kennedy Library, p. 10.
95 Interview with David Bruce, Oral History Project, John F. Kennedy Library, p. 2.
96 Sorensen, *Kennedy,* p. 297.
97 Haynes Johnson & Bernard Gwertzman, *Fulbright: The Dissenter* 178 (1968).
98 Interview with George Kennan, Oral History Project, John F. Kennedy Library.
99 John F. Kennedy, *Public Papers of the President* 898 (1962).
100 Letter from Norodom Sihanouk to Robert F. Kennedy, April 25, 1964, Oral History Project, John F. Kennedy Library, pp. 1–2.
101 Interview with Tom Mboya, Oral History Project, John F. Kennedy Library, p. 6.
102 Quoted in Arthur Schlesinger, Jr., *A Thousand Days,* pp. 559–60.
103 Quoted in ibid., 569–70.
104 Roger Hilsman, *To Move a Nation,* p. 363.

105 Arthur Krock, *In the Nation: 1932–1966* 372 (1966) (from an article dated August 16, 1962).
106 Interview with Roberto Campos, p. 53.

Chapter 5: The Aftermath

1 See Patrick Anderson, *The President's Men* 258 (1969).
2 John F. Kennedy, *The Strategy of Peace* 199 (1960).
3 *Speeches, Remarks, Press Conferences and Statements of John F. Kennedy,* Committee on Commerce, United States Senate, 87th Cong., 1st Sess., Report No. 994, Vol. I, p. 347 (1961).
4 Ibid., 608.
5 John F. Kennedy, *Public Papers of the President* 35 (1961).
6 Interview with Carl Albert, Oral History Project, John F. Kennedy Library, p. 21.
7 Richard M. Nixon, *Public Papers of the President* 405–10 (1970).
8 Quoted in B. & M. Kalb, *Kissinger* 494 (1974).
9 Quoted in ibid., 498.
10 John F. Kennedy, *Public Papers of the President* 407 (1963).
11 Quoted in Arthur Schlesinger, Jr., *A Thousand Days: John F. Kennedy in the White House* 904 (1965).
12 John F. Kennedy, *Public Papers of the President* 462 (1963).
13 See especially Kennedy's interview with Walter Cronkite, reprinted in ibid., 650.
14 See Robert C. Tucker, "The Theory of Charismatic Leadership," *Daedulus,* Summer, 1968, p 731.
15 *Newsweek,* January 21, 1963, p. 25.
16 John F. Kennedy, *Public Papers of the President* 8 (1962).
17 Quoted in Richard Harris, "Annals of Legislation III," *The New Yorker,* March 28, 1964, p. 59.
18 Quoted in ibid., 78.
19 Quoted in ibid., 80.
20 Quoted in Hugh Sidey, *John F. Kennedy, President* 231 (1964).
21 Quoted in Chester Bowles, *Promises to Keep: My Years in Public Life 1941–1969* 523 (1971).
22 John F. Kennedy, *Public Papers of the President* 403–4 (1961).
23 James Reston, *Sketches in the Sand* 33 (1967) (from an article dated April 2, 1963).
24 Chester Bowles, *Promises to Keep,* p. 404.
25 *Katz* v. *United States,* 389 U.S. 347 (1967), overruling *Olmstead* v. *United States,* 277 U.S. 438 (1928).
26 *Olmstead* v. *United States,* 277 U.S. 438, 477 (1928) (dissenting opinion).
27 See Benjamin Bradlee, *Conversations with Kennedy* 228 (1975); Claiborne, "Ex-Official Warns of FBI Power," *Washington Post,* Nov. 25, 1974, p. 1; Safire, "The Thrill Is Gone," *New York Times,* Jan. 30, 1975, p. 35; Transcript of Conversation between President Nixon and John Dean, February 28, 1973, quoted in *Hearings before the Comm. on the Judiciary, House of Representatives, Pursuant to H. Res. 803,* 93rd Cong. 2nd Sess., p. 37 (May-June 1974).
28 Any detailed discussion of the founding fathers' intentions is beyond the scope of this book. However, some indication of those intentions—especially with respect to the Fourth Amendment and the other amendments in the Bill of Rights—is contained in James Madison's speech proposing the first ten amendments to the Constitution. 1 *Annals of Congress* 432–42 (1789).
29 Quoted in V. Navasky & N. Lewin, "Investigating the FBI—A Tough, Fair Look At the Powerful Bureau; Its Present and Future," reprinted in *Hearings before the Subcomm. on Ad. Prac. & Proc., Comm. on the Judiciary,* U.S. Senate, 92nd Cong., 2d Sess., p. 172 (June 29, 1972).

30 Memorandum from President Roosevelt to Attorney General Jackson, May 21, 1940, reprinted in ibid., 174–75.

31 See sources cited in note 27 of this chapter. For a catalog of wiretap abuses conducted under the cloak of "national security," see 120 *Congressional Record* S1138–42 (daily ed. February 4, 1974). For a good discussion of the wiretaps and "bugs" on Martin Luther King, Jr., see Navasky, *Kennedy Justice* 135–55 (1971).

32 95 *Congressional Record* 4184 (1949).

33 The only available statistics show that Eisenhower had authorized 115 national security electronic surveillances in 1960. In 1961, Kennedy authorized 140, in 1962 he authorized 198, and in 1963 he authorized as many as 244. In fairness to Kennedy, it should be pointed out that Eisenhower had authorized as many as 322 such surveillances (1954) and that Roosevelt had authorized 519 in 1945. 119 *Congressional Record* H4343 (June 5, 1973) (remarks of Gerald Ford). These figures were released by the Nixon White House and may not be entirely accurate. But there seems little doubt that Kennedy permitted extensive use of national security electronic surveillances. See Robinson, "FBI's Wiretaps Ranged Up to 100 in D.C. Area," *Washington Post,* April 22, 1975, p. 1.

34 See generally Emmet John Hughes, *The Living Presidency* Chapter 7 (1973); Arthur Schlesinger, Jr., *The Imperial Presidency* (1973); and Note, "Congress, the President and the Power to Commit Forces to Combat," 81 *Harvard Law Review* 1771 (1968).

35 John Jay, Paper #64, *The Federalist Papers* 393 (Bantam ed. 1961).

36 *In re Neagle,* 135 U.S. 1, 64, 69 (1890).

37 *United States* v. *Curtiss-Wright Export Corporation,* 299 U.S. 304, 320 (1936). But see Charles A. Lofgren, "*United States* v. *Curtiss-Wright Export Corporation:* An Historical Reassessment," 83 *Yale Law Journal* 1 (1973).

38 Edward S. Corwin,*The President: Office and Powers 1787–1957* 236 (1957).

39 Robert F. Kennedy, *Thirteen Days* 31 (1969).

40 Public Law 93–148 (November 7, 1973).

41 Norman Mailer, *The Presidential Papers of Norman Mailer* vii (1964).

INDEX